D1205942

PRINCELY BROTHERS AND SISTERS

PRINCELY BROTHERS AND SISTERS

THE SIBLING BOND IN GERMAN POLITICS, 1100–1250

JONATHAN R. LYON

CORNELL UNIVERSITY PRESS
Ithaca and London

Copyright © 2013 by Cornell University

All rights reserved. Except for brief quotations in a review, this book, or parts thereof, must not be reproduced in any form without permission in writing from the publisher. For information, address Cornell University Press, Sage House, 512 East State Street, Ithaca, New York 14850.

First published 2013 by Cornell University Press

Printed in the United States of America

Library of Congress Cataloging-in-Publication Data

Lyon, Jonathan Reed.
  Princely brothers and sisters : the sibling bond in German politics, 1100–1250 / Jonathan R. Lyon.
    p. cm.
  Includes bibliographical references and index.
  ISBN 978-0-8014-5130-0 (alk. paper)
  1. Brothers and sisters—Germany—History—To 1500.
2. Nobility—Germany—History—To 1500.
3. Germany—Politics and government—843–1273.
I. Title.
  HQ759.96.L96 2013
  306.875'3094309021—dc23   2012028364

Cornell University Press strives to use environmentally responsible suppliers and materials to the fullest extent possible in the publishing of its books. Such materials include vegetable-based, low-VOC inks and acid-free papers that are recycled, totally chlorine-free, or partly composed of nonwood fibers. For further information, visit our website at www.cornellpress.cornell.edu.

Cloth printing   10 9 8 7 6 5 4 3 2 1

In memoriam sororis meae

✑ Contents

✇ ILLUSTRATIONS

✒ ABBREVIATIONS

BUB	*Urkundenbuch zur Geschichte der Babenberger in Österreich*
CDA	*Codex diplomaticus Anhaltinus*
CDS 1 A	*Codex diplomaticus Saxoniae Regiae*, part 1, series A
CDS 2	*Codex diplomaticus Saxoniae Regiae*, part 2
Mainzer UB 2	*Mainzer Urkundenbuch*, vol. 2
MB	*Monumenta Boica*
MGH	*Monumenta Germaniae historica*
MGH Const.	*Monumenta Germaniae historica, Constitutiones et acta publica imperatorum et regum*
MGH DD F I	*Die Urkunden Friedrichs I.*
MGH DD F II	*Die Urkunden Friedrichs II.*
MGH DD K III	*Die Urkunden Konrads III. und seines Sohnes Heinrich*
MGH DD L III	*Die Urkunden Lothars III. und der Kaiserin Richenza*
MGH SS	*Monumenta Germaniae historica, Scriptores*
MGH SSrG	*Monumenta Germaniae historica, Scriptores rerum germanicarum in usum scholarum separatim editi*
MGH SSrG, NS	*Monumenta Germaniae historica, Scriptores rerum germanicarum in usum scholarum separatim editi, nova series*
MHDC	*Monumenta historica ducatus Carinthiae*
QE NF	*Quellen und Erörterungen zur bayerischen Geschichte, neue Folge*
Reg. Imp. 4	J. F. Böhmer, *Regesta imperii*, part 4
Reg. Imp. 5	J. F. Böhmer, *Regesta imperii*, part 5
UB Enns	*Urkundenbuch des Landes ob der Enns*
UB Steiermark	*Urkundenbuch des Herzogthums Steiermark*

❧ ACKNOWLEDGMENTS

In the five years spent researching and writing this book, I was consistently amazed by the support I received from friends, colleagues, librarians, and archivists in both the United States and Europe. I am therefore pleased to acknowledge the people who helped make this book possible.

To begin at the end, I would especially like to thank John Van Engen and Lisa Wolverton for reading the manuscript in the late stages and for pushing me, as they always have, to make my arguments stronger and clearer. For reading parts of the manuscript at earlier stages, I am also grateful to Rachel Fulton Brown, Constantin Fasolt, David Nirenberg, John Freed, Amy Livingstone, Constance Bouchard, and a second, anonymous reader for Cornell University Press. Along the way, I also presented parts of this book as talks in many places and benefited from countless conversations. Members of the Arbeitskreis geistliche Frauen im europäischen Mittelalter and participants in the Symposium on New Directions in Gender Studies and Medieval German Studies at Princeton University were especially helpful interlocutors. At the University of Chicago, I have been grateful for conversations with many of my colleagues in the History Department as well as with Daisy Delogu, Ryan Giles, Aden Kumler, John Padgett, and Lucy Pick. For their hospitality, support, and advice during my stays in Germany, I thank Bernd Schneidmüller, Stefan Weinfurter, Klaus Oschema, Jörg Peltzer, Andrea Briechle, and Carla Meyer in Heidelberg; Bernhard Jussen in Frankfurt; and Klaus van Eickels and Stefan Biessenecker in Bamberg.

Research for this book was made possible by a variety of grants. Much of the material on the Andechs lineage was gathered during my first extended research trip to Europe, with support from the University of Notre Dame, the J. William Fulbright Program, and the Dolores Zohrab Liebmann Fund. Later archival research was funded by a grant from the Deutscher Akademischer Austausch Dienst (DAAD) and two summer grants from the University of Chicago's Division of the Social Sciences. The staff at the archives I consulted in Germany, Austria, France, and Hungary were all extraordinarily helpful. On many of my short research trips in particular, I was immensely grateful for archivists who had charters ready for me in advance.

At Cornell University Press, Peter Potter, Susan Specter, and my copy editor, Marie Flaherty-Jones, did a wonderful job preparing the final manuscript and were always quick to answer my questions. I am also grateful to Chieko Maene, a GIS specialist at the University of Chicago, for all her work making the maps.

Finally, I would like to thank my parents and especially my wife, Brooke, for her unwavering support. Whether reading drafts or entertaining our son so I could research and write, she has always done whatever she could to help me in this endeavor. Words cannot possibly express my gratitude for all the ways in which she has made this book possible.

FIGURE 1. The German kingdom and the empire. Adapted from *Staufisches Kaisertum im 12. Jahrhundert: Konzepte—Netzwerke—Politische Praxis*, edited by Stefan Burkhardt, Thomas Metz, Bernd Schneidmüller, and Stefan Weinfurter (Regensburg: Schnell & Steiner, 2010), 19.

FIGURE 2. Saxony and its environs

Legend:
- Rivers
- Archbishopric
- Bishopric
1. Kalbe
2. Quedlinburg
3. Gernrode
4. Ballenstedt
5. Aschersleben
6. Gerbstedt
7. Lauterberg
8. Brehna
9. Delitzsch
10. Eilenburg
11. Weissenfels

1:4,000,000

Lübeck
Artlenburg
Lüneburg
Bremen
Werben
Arneburg
Gardelegen   Stendal   Köpenick
Haldensleben Rögatz Brandenburg
Brunswick   Mittenwalde
Supplinburg   Wolmirstedt
Hildesheim   Magdeburg
              Halberstadt
Drübeck   •1
          2
          3   •4 •5
Cappenberg   •6   7 8 9
Lippoldsberg   Wettin   10
         Nordhausen
                 Bonnrode   Merseburg   Groitzsch
Fritzlar   •11 Pegau   Meissen
      Ziegenhain Wartburg Erfurt Naumburg   Dresden
Cologne   Weimar   Zschillen
         Marburg   Reinhardsbrunn Orlamünde
Coblenz   Henneberg   Neumark
        Frankfurt Gelnhausen
   Mainz   Prague

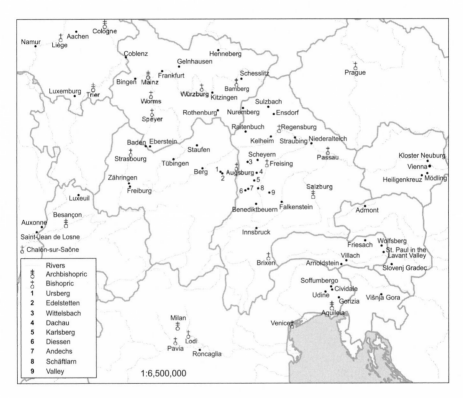

FIGURE 3. The south of the German kingdom and the empire

Introduction

According to the anonymous author of the late thirteenth-century *Chronicle of the Princes of Saxony*, the brothers and co-margraves John I (d. 1266) and Otto III (d. 1267) of Brandenburg "began [to exercise lordship] in the year of the Lord 1220. . . . After they had reached the age of majority, with one deferring to the other, they lived together harmoniously as was proper for brothers; and on account of this harmony, they trampled their enemies underfoot, exalted their friends, increased their lands and revenues, and expanded their fame, glory, and power."[1] Although chroniclers writing the histories of medieval noble lineages were frequently prone to hyperbole, sources from these two brothers' own lifetimes confirm many of the details of this dramatic description of sibling collaboration. John and Otto issued dozens of charters together.[2] They intervened in the most important political crisis of their day, jointly attempting to broker peace between Emperor Frederick II and Pope Gregory IX.[3] And even sources written on behalf of their territorial rivals acknowledged their many military successes.[4] During the middle decades of

---

1. *Chronica principum Saxoniae*, 478.
2. Fey, *Reise und Herrschaft*, 54–55.
3. MGH Const., 2:317, no. 232.
4. *Gesta archiepiscoporum Magdeburgensium*, 422.

the thirteenth century, the brothers were seemingly inseparable as they built a strong lordship for themselves and their heirs in the northeast corner of the German kingdom.

Modern scholarship on the medieval family has rarely engaged with examples such as this one for the political efficacy of sibling relationships. During the second half of the twentieth century, historians writing about medieval families—especially noble ones—debated the origins and diffusion of the lineal model of the family across Europe. Scholars have defined the prototypical noble lineage in a variety of ways over the years, but most have stressed its role in the descent of property from father to (eldest) son across multiple generations. As a result, debates about this family structure have tended to marginalize the relationships between brothers and sisters. Since the 1990s, a chorus of critics has argued that twentieth-century historiography overemphasized the explanatory power of the lineal model. Scholars increasingly highlight the centrality of the conjugal household within noble families. In the process, they are shifting their focus to the spousal bond and to the relationships parents had with all their children—not only with those sons who succeeded to their father's most important properties.[5] Because of this changing perspective, siblings are also beginning to attract the attention of medieval family historians.[6]

Paradoxically, much of this newer work has unfolded against the backdrop of the general decline of family history. There are many reasons for the field's stagnation, but one of the most important has been the steadily increasing interest in other types of social networks, most notably those based on ties of lordship and friendship.[7] Some historians have even suggested in the early twenty-first century that scholars of previous generations grossly overestimated the historical significance of the family and kinship group in the first place.[8] While the field of family history is certainly not dead, it is no longer at the forefront of theoretical and methodological developments in the historical discipline as it was during the 1970s and '80s. As one historian observed, in 2007, "Today more than ever, family history has become a ghettoized area of study disengaged from broader spheres of historical inquiry."[9] This trend is reflected in developments within the medieval field, where the shrinking

---

5. See chapter 1 for a more detailed discussion of this scholarship.

6. Lett, "Brothers and Sisters"; Cassagnes-Brouquet and Yvernault, *Frères et soeurs*.

7. See, for example, Althoff, *Family, Friends and Followers*; Oexle, "Soziale Gruppen"; Bray, *Friend*, 307–323.

8. As noted by Jussen in "Famille et parenté," 456–457. See also Lubich, *Verwandtsein*, 7, 135.

9. Milanich, "Whither Family History?" 444.

circle of family historians has yet to provide a viable alternative to the rigid model of the lineage that worked its way into grand narratives of medieval history during the late twentieth century.[10]

Family history's slow decline is further evidenced by the fact that scholars of the European Middle Ages currently employ the terms "brother" and "sister" far more frequently to refer to monks, nuns, and other religious than to actual siblings. A variety of metaphorical usages of "fraternity," "brotherhood," and "sisterhood" have come to overshadow the original meanings of this sibling terminology.[11] Nevertheless, though figurative brothers and sisters may outnumber real ones in most modern scholarship, in this book I contend that the relationships between blood siblings need to take center stage. Notions of fraternity, brotherhood, and sisterhood were invoked so frequently as metaphors for other types of social ties precisely because the sibling bond connoted a form of social equality scarcely discernible anywhere else in society.[12] Medieval people thus recognized that the relationships between actual brothers and sisters had unique qualities, and they sought to replicate those qualities in relationships outside the confines of the family with the help of metaphors of siblinghood. As modern scholars, we cannot hope to comprehend the sibling bond's powerful connotations during the Middle Ages unless we first examine the interactions between blood siblings in much more detail than historians have previously attempted.

The starting point for this analysis of medieval brothers and sisters is the simple, but nonetheless essential, fact that siblings are the contemporaries whose lives normally overlap the longest. More so than parents and children, husbands and wives, friends and lovers, or lords and vassals, brothers and sisters have the potential to develop relationships that span entire lifetimes.[13] Margraves John I and Otto III of Brandenburg, for instance, can be observed in extant documents interacting with one another for forty-six years, and they are not exceptional.[14] Moreover, the *Chronicle of the Princes of Saxony*

---

10. A point also made by Crouch in *Birth of Nobility*, 121–123. For examples of the lineal model's effect on grand narratives, see Bartlett, *Making of Europe*, 24–59; Moore, *First European Revolution,* 65–75.

11. See, for example, Van Engen, *Sisters and Brothers*; van Eickels, "Der Bruder als Freund und Gefährte"; Oschema, "Blood-Brothers"; Blamires, "'Sisterhood.'"

12. Reynolds, *Kingdoms and Communities*, 4; Dilcher, "An den Ursprüngen der Normbildung," 55. Already in late antiquity, *frater* and *soror* had become such common terms outside the family setting that writers increasingly began employing *germanus* and *germana* to distinguish clearly those people who were brothers and sisters by blood. See Mitterauer, "Mittelalter," 196.

13. Lett, "Brothers and Sisters," 15; Barthélemy, *La société dans le comté de Vendôme*, 527.

14. For more on these brothers, see chapter 7.

describes their decades-long relationship as a cooperative one that led to a series of political successes and territorial gains. This suggests that the longevity of some sibling bonds created opportunities for noble brothers and sisters to collaborate in especially potent ways. Analyzing intragenerational relationships from this perspective can therefore shine new light on how the medieval nobility exercised its power and lordship—while simultaneously interweaving two traditionally disparate fields, namely family history and political history.[15]

In this book I use the German upper aristocracy of the Staufen period (1138–1250) as a case study for examining medieval sibling relationships. Because the families belonging to this aristocracy practiced partible inheritance, not primogeniture, the interactions between brothers and sisters are an essential feature of this elite's history. I argue that noblemen—and to a lesser extent noblewomen—routinely relied on the cooperation and support of their siblings as they sought to maintain or expand their power and influence within the competitive political environment of the German kingdom. At key moments during the twelfth and early thirteenth centuries, sibling relationships played crucial roles in shaping the political and territorial interests of many of the lords who belonged to nine leading aristocratic lineages in the realm.[16] As will become clear in the pages that follow, an inescapable corollary to this argument is the significance of generational size for the composition of medieval political communities. How many men and women survived to adulthood in any given generation directly impacted the political efficacy of sibling relationships for the individual lords of that generation. Analyzing all nine of these upper aristocratic lineages together across the entire span of the Staufen period reveals shifts in generational size that help explain why some brothers and sisters had greater influence than others over German politics. The detailed analysis of sibling relationships thus provides an opportunity not only to reconceptualize the field of family history but also to rewrite the narrative of German political history during the twelfth and thirteenth centuries.

Historicizing the Sibling Bond

Not surprisingly, authors living in different times and places have expressed a wide range of opinions about the nature of the bonds between brothers and

---

15. For a similar point about the divide between political history and family history, see Auge, *Handlungsspielräume fürstlicher Politik im Mittelalter,* 5. For some exceptions to this general pattern, see Searle, *Predatory Kinship,* and n. 20, below.

16. For my use of the term *lineage* here, see chapter 1.

sisters. Writing in the early twelfth century, the chronicler Cosmas of Prague stressed the inevitably aggressive character of sibling relationships in the dramatic deathbed speech he ascribed to Duke Břetislav I of Bohemia (d. 1055):

> "God has given me five sons. It does not seem to me useful to divide the realm of Bohemia among them because every kingdom divided against itself will be brought to desolation. From the creation of the world and the beginning of the Roman Empire until today, affection among brothers has been rare, as clear examples bear witness to us: Cain and Abel, Romulus and Remus. . . . If you look at what two brothers have done, what will five do? So much more capable and more powerful do I consider them, that I predict much worse with a prophetic mind. Alas, the minds of fathers are always terrified about the uncertain fates of their sons."[17]

Břetislav's prophecy was actually Cosmas's hindsight, for the chronicler knew when he put ink to parchment many decades after the duke's death that the brothers had been bitter rivals throughout their adult lives.[18] Nevertheless, Břetislav's speech shows a medieval chronicler drawing on Old Testament and ancient Roman examples to argue that intragenerational strife is something universal, a constant in Western civilization. Cosmas thus offers a clear contrast to the anonymous author of the *Chronicle of the Princes of Saxony*, who describes the margraves John and Otto of Brandenburg living together in harmony, "as is proper for brothers."

The divergent viewpoints evident in these two sources find echoes in the scattered references to the sibling bond in modern scholarship on medieval noble families. Some historians have argued that the structure of the noble lineage, which favored elder sons over younger ones, created inequities that easily generated discord and rivalry among siblings. According to these scholars, fraternal disputes over issues of inheritance and succession were virtually unavoidable.[19] Other historians, meanwhile, have preferred to emphasize the strength of the sibling bond, especially in comparison to other types of social bonds, and have argued against conflict as a frequent

---

17. Cosmas of Prague, *Chronicle of the Czechs*, 130.
18. Wolverton, *Hastening toward Prague*, 101–103, 196–200.
19. Georges Duby has made this argument most forcefully. See especially his original article on the topic, translated as "Northwestern France." See also Aurell, "Rompre la concorde familiale," 23–28; Beitscher, "'As the Twig Is Bent,'" 189–190; Martindale, "Succession and Politics," 29–30; Leyser, "German Aristocracy," 36–37; Howard, "'We are broderen,'" 139–141.

occurrence. For these scholars, brothers were some of the best allies a nobleman could have in the complex and dangerous world of medieval politics.[20] The contrasting opinions about siblings found in both medieval and
modern works suggest that variety was the norm—that every sibling relationship was different, with some noble brothers and sisters having closer
ties than others.[21] While there is undoubtedly some truth to this claim, it
lacks nuance. As historians of the early modern and modern family have
demonstrated since the 1990s, analyzing the interactions between brothers
and sisters systematically—rather than selectively highlighting a few well-
known incidents of conflict or cooperation—opens the door to developing more complex perspectives on the character of sibling relationships.[22]
Variety may be the norm, but patterns unquestionably emerge from close
scrutiny of the sources.

To find such patterns, the interactions between brothers and sisters must
be understood within their proper historical contexts. Different societies at
different moments in time have different expectations of the sibling bond. In
a sense, brotherhood and sisterhood are therefore performative, and a person
must behave like a sibling to be recognized as one within his or her culture.[23]
This perspective on the sibling bond de-emphasizes the significance of the
bond's strictly biological definition and stresses that brothers and sisters had
to participate actively in the construction and maintenance of their relationships. Viewed in this way, the sibling bond is not something that can be rei-
fied or deemed universal across all of human history. Instead, developments
specific to individual societies play critical roles in determining whether
brothers and sisters tend to form cooperative relationships, antagonistic relationships, or no relationships at all. Medieval historians are already comfort-
able framing other familial interactions in these terms. Various scholars have
convincingly shown that both the spousal bond and the parent-child bond

20. See, for example, Crouch, *Beaumont Twins*, 96–98; Bernard Bachrach, "Henry II," 126; Holt,
"Feudal Society and the Family," 18–19; Tanner, *Families, Friends and Allies*, 130; Zečević, "Brotherly
Love."

21. For a similar observation, see Spieß, *Familie und Verwandtschaft*, 483; and more generally, Nye,
"Kinship, Male Bonds, and Masculinity," 1660; Cicirelli, "Sibling Relationships," 17.

22. See, for example, Johnson and Sabean, *Sibling Relations*; Pollock, "Rethinking Patriarchy";
Glover, *All Our Relations*, 59–86; Miller and Yavneh, "Thicker than Water"; Bastress-Dukehart, "Sibling Conflict"; Nolte, *Familie, Hof und Herrschaft*; Ruppel, *Verbündete Rivalen*. This increased interest
in the close analysis of sibling relationships is not confined to historians: see Davidoff, *Thicker than
Water*, 29–35; Ramu, *Brothers and Sisters in India*, 3–12.

23. Van Eickels, "Der Bruder als Freund und Gefährte," 222; and more generally, Carsten,
"Cultures of Relatedness."

looked quite different in the Middle Ages than they do today.[24] Recognizing the dangers of generalizations across time and space is equally vital for the study of brothers and sisters.

Thus the argument of this book is consciously grounded in developments specific to the German kingdom of the twelfth and thirteenth centuries. Sibling relationships played a prominent role in German politics during this period, as a consequence of certain distinctive features of the upper aristocracy under the Staufen kings and emperors. Despite the apparently narrow contours of my thesis, I address a series of much broader issues—succession, inheritance, lordship, and court politics, to name only a few—that provide a framework for examining brothers and sisters in the Middle Ages more generally. In the process, I will hopefully prompt others to pursue comparable studies in order to nuance still further our understanding of the medieval sibling bond.

Politics and Family Bonds

One of the first steps to historicizing sibling relationships—and to appreciating their potential political efficacy—is embracing the central role that family bonds played within medieval politics. Today, citizens of Western nation-states have grown accustomed to governmental structures that draw clear distinctions between the public and private spheres. From the perspective of modern bureaucratic institutions, familial influence over political office holding is a form of corruption, nepotism an affront to our meritocratic ideals.[25] As a result, few people in the West currently argue that family bonds should hold significant sway within the sphere of politics, that they can be a stabilizing force because of the traditions and expectations associated with kinship.[26]

The nineteenth- and twentieth-century predilection for the bureaucratic state led generations of medieval historians to trumpet the breakdown of family-dominated political systems rather than their flourishing. Joseph Strayer, for example, argued in 1970 that the thirteenth century was when

---

24. For example, Brundage, *Law, Sex, and Christian Society*; Elliott, *Spiritual Marriage*; Shahar, *Childhood in the Middle Ages*; Alexandre-Bidon and Lett, *Children in the Middle Ages*.

25. Vowinckel, *Verwandtschaft, Freundschaft*, 166; Fox, *Kinship and Marriage*, 14. The Bush and Kennedy dynasties are clear evidence that politics and family remain interconnected in the United States today, despite the popular rhetoric that calls for them to be kept separate.

26. Exceptions to this general trend include Bellow, *In Praise of Nepotism*, esp. 1–25; Reinhard, "Nepotismus."

the state replaced the family as the principal loyalty for politically active Englishmen.[27] Since then, some medievalists have drawn attention to the appearance during the twelfth century of a cadre of university-educated men who owed their positions in the church and at secular courts to knowledge and training—not family connections. These scholars have emphasized the efforts of English and French kings to cast off the influence of powerful aristocratic families and to rely on this new group of bureaucrats of lesser origins to govern their realms more effectively.[28]

In the German historiography of the nineteenth and early twentieth centuries, disdain for the family's role in medieval politics manifested itself in debates about the German *Sonderweg*.[29] For some historians, Germany's failure to emerge from the Middle Ages as a unified nation-state was the result of the increased power and influence of princely families after the Investiture Controversy. These families, as they expanded their lordship, promoted regional diversity and particularism rather than centralized government institutions—at a time when France and England were supposedly beginning to see the emergence of more effective forms of kingship. The practice within princely families of permitting multiple children to inherit allegedly exacerbated the problems for the failed German state. According to many scholars, primogeniture was the only form of inheritance able to foster the maintenance of strong polities that could, over time, develop statelike institutions. By repeatedly dividing their patrimonies, aristocratic families instead became a destabilizing force in Germany, with little interest in promoting the structures of centralized authority.[30]

Thus, the modern West's disdain for familial domination of political life has cast a long shadow over scholarship on the interrelationship between politics and family. Since the late twentieth century, however, medieval historians have demonstrated a growing appreciation for the complexities of this subject. Increasingly, scholars are arguing that the role of the family within the political sphere must be analyzed on its own terms, rather than through the clouded lens of modern political expectations.[31] There was a practical

---

27. Strayer, *Medieval Origins of the Modern State*, 45–46.

28. See, for example, Bisson, *Crisis of the Twelfth Century*; Baldwin, *Government of Philip Augustus*; Moore, *First European Revolution*; Turner, *Men Raised from the Dust*.

29. On this strand of German historiography, see Reuter, "Medieval German *Sonderweg*?"

30. See, for example, Lamprecht, *Deutsche Geschichte*, 3:78–83; Thompson, *Feudal Germany*, 287–289, 303–321; Dungern, "Constitutional Reorganisation and Reform," 208–209, 218–227.

31. Spieß, "Lordship, Kinship, and Inheritance," 58.

logic to people's reliance on close relatives at all levels of medieval politics, and it is the task of historians to understand that logic—not critique it.[32] Viewed from this perspective, research into the family's significance for politics fits within a broader framework of scholarship that argues the political structures common to past centuries can be examined effectively only if our contemporary preconceptions are set aside.[33] Studies focusing on such topics as medieval political rituals, nonjudicial forms of dispute resolution, and informal patronage networks consciously shun the public-private dichotomy and other state-based interpretive categories.[34] Detailed studies of the sibling bond's role in medieval politics likewise have the potential to offer a corrective to older models of political order.

Siblings, Politics, and German History

In the earliest years of the Staufen dynasty of kings and emperors, the relationship between two siblings stood at the center of political life in the German kingdom.[35] When the last Salian emperor, Henry V, died without a male heir in 1125, several members of the German aristocracy surfaced as contenders for the throne. One was the Staufen duke Frederick II of Swabia (d. 1147), who was related to Henry V through his mother. Frederick's familial ties to the Salians failed to swing the royal election in his favor, however, and a majority of the German princes chose the duke of Saxony,

32. Althoff, *Family, Friends and Followers*, 60.

33. This argument was made most famously by Brunner in *Land and Lordship*. See also Chittolini, "'Private,' 'Public,' State," S39.

34. For rituals, see, for example, Althoff, *Die Macht der Rituale*, and the critique of this field by Buc in *Dangers of Ritual*. For dispute resolution, see the excellent overview of the field provided by Brown and Górecki, "What Conflict Means." For informal patronage networks, see Watts, *Making of Polities*, 153–154; Huffman, *Social Politics*, 1–6.

35. Although the phrase *sacrum Romanum imperium* first appears in sources during the twelfth century, the term "Holy Roman Empire" is typically avoided by historians of the Staufen period because it brings to mind structures more common to later centuries. As a result, I will employ the (admittedly bland) term "the empire" when referring to the whole of that sprawling political entity that, during the 1100s and early 1200s, included the northern Italian and Burgundian kingdoms as well as the German realm. Labeling this third kingdom, which is the setting for much of this work, is also problematic, because its rulers titled themselves "king of the Romans" (*rex Romanorum*) prior to their imperial coronations at the hands of the pope. Since many modern readers may find this title distracting and misleading, I will follow other Anglophone historians and use "German kingdom" for this polity, which was the successor to the East Frankish kingdom of the late Carolingian period. Although some scholars prefer the term "medieval Germany," I have decided not to use it here, because several of the families I analyze were in possession of important rights and territories in regions that do not belong to the modern German state.

who became King Lothar III (1125–1137). Refusing to accept this outcome, Frederick and a small group of lords opposed to Lothar sought to elect a new king two years later, in 1127. Once again, however, the duke of Swabia was not the choice. Instead, Frederick led the way in securing the election of his younger brother, Conrad. Although this attempted coup failed, Conrad was elected again eleven years later—after Lothar III's death in 1137—and ruled the kingdom as King Conrad III until 1152.[36]

Why did Duke Frederick II of Swabia abandon his own claims to the kingship in 1127 in order to support the election of his younger brother? Why, in 1138, did the other princes again prefer Conrad as king and not his older sibling? Because there is evidence that Frederick lost an eye at an unknown moment during his career, some scholars have suggested that he may have suffered this injury between 1125 and 1127, thus rendering him physically unfit to rule as king.[37] This is merely speculation, however. No extant source explicitly states why Conrad—who is frequently identified simply as "the brother of Duke Frederick" (*frater Friderici ducis*) in texts written prior to 1138—surpassed his elder sibling and acquired the highest position in the German kingdom.[38]

Although the surviving evidence leaves much in doubt concerning the events of 1127 and 1138, the brothers' shifting claims to the German royal title nevertheless hint at the potential of sibling relationships to shape the course of political events during the Staufen period. As will become clear in the pages that follow, the Staufens shared much in common with the other lineages that are the focus of this book, and the significance of sibling interactions for their early history is representative of a much broader trend. Within many generations of those lineages that composed the German aristocratic elite during the 1100s and early 1200s, the eldest brother was not the only sibling who attained a position of power and authority. Nor was he the unquestioned head of his lineage, or someone who managed all his younger brothers' and sisters' political affairs.[39] Understanding Conrad's election as king in 1138—and Frederick's subsequent support for his younger brother's

36. For more detailed summaries of these events, see Keller, *Zwischen regionaler Begrenzung und universalem Horizont*, 199–205; Haverkamp, *Medieval Germany*, 137–144; Fuhrmann, *Germany in the High Middle Ages*, 116–122.

37. See, for example, Engels, *Die Staufer*, 27–28; Arnold, "Western Empire, 1125–1197," 413; and esp. Schwarzmaier, "*Pater imperatoris*."

38. See, for example, *Annales Palidenses*, 78; *Annalista Saxo*, 765; *Annales Ratisbonenses*, 585. More generally, see Lubich, "Beobachtungen zur Wahl Konrads III.," 312–323.

39. For more on this point, see Hechberger, "Konrad III.," 323–333.

fragile kingship—requires a more dynamic approach to the study of sibling relationships, one that recognizes the prominent roles that *all* the members of a generation could play in German politics during the twelfth and thirteenth centuries.[40]

The relationship between Duke Frederick II of Swabia and King Conrad III is certainly not the first case in medieval German history of a fraternal bond taking center stage in the kingdom's politics. For example, two centuries earlier, in the mid-900s, Emperor Otto I's younger brothers played leading roles in the political life of the realm.[41] Nevertheless, the opening decades of the twelfth century witnessed fundamental changes—in both the nature of German political life and in the organization of many prominent noble lineages—that led to a significant increase in the number of politically influential siblings within the upper aristocracy. Central to this transformation of the early twelfth century was a dramatic shift in the relationship between the rulers and the imperial princes (*principes imperii*). These magnates, who composed the uppermost stratum of the secular and ecclesiastical elite, held their principal fiefs directly from the German rulers and were therefore expected to provide counsel and support to the kings and emperors. During the decades around 1100, however, the Investiture Controversy and a series of civil wars within the kingdom made it increasingly difficult for the Salian rulers to exercise effective authority over these magnates. As a result, by the close of the Salian period, the imperial princes had come to see themselves as partners, not subordinates, of the kings and emperors in the governance of the realm.[42]

Previous generations of scholars sought the origins of the closed, narrowly defined Estate of Imperial Princes (*Reichsfürstenstand*) in this period when the leading secular and ecclesiastical magnates became the entrenched political elite of the kingdom.[43] Today, however, German historians tend to avoid such rigid models for understanding the leading magnates as a group, preferring instead to emphasize the fluidity of this elite and the fluctuating number of *principes imperii* throughout the Staufen period.[44] According to

---

40. The relationship between Frederick and Conrad will be discussed at much greater length in chapter 4.

41. Laudage, *Otto der Grosse*, 246–252.

42. Weinfurter, *Salian Century*, 173–174.

43. The foundational work on this subject remains Ficker, *Vom Reichsfuerstenstande*, 1:58–128. See also Mitteis, *Der Staat des hohen Mittelalters*, 291; Barraclough, *Origins of Modern Germany*, 194.

44. Hechberger, *Adel im fränkisch-deutschen Mittelalter*, 273–287; Moraw, "Fürstentum, Königtum und 'Reichsreform'"; Arnold, *Princes and Territories*, 26–39; and more recently, Laudage, *Friedrich Barbarossa*, 184–187.

this newer perspective, the princes did not act collectively as the members of a distinct social class with a common set of interests. Instead, personal ambition and familial interests motivated many of the actions taken by secular and ecclesiastical magnates, leading them to compete frequently with one another for rights and properties.[45] One of the places where this princely competition was most evident was the royal court, where the magnates vied with one another for *Königsnähe* (proximity to the king) in order to benefit from royal largesse.[46] The shifting group of secular and ecclesiastical princes who attended court had an influential role to play in politics for another reason as well, because the German rulers depended on consultation with this group of magnates when making key decisions that affected the kingdom and empire. This consensual form of lordship was an essential component of political life during the Staufen period and a clear manifestation of the idea that the ruler and the princes governed the kingdom jointly.[47]

Absent from these arguments emphasizing princely competition and the dynamic relationship between ruler and magnates are siblings. Throughout the late twelfth and early thirteenth centuries, the practice of partible inheritance meant that leading magnate lineages frequently included multiple brothers and sisters who held prominent positions within the German kingdom. In some cases, sibling groups consisting of two, three, or even four *principes imperii* sought to exert influence at the imperial court—while simultaneously working to expand their lordship at the expense of their rivals at the regional level. As a result, siblings often appear together in the sources from this period, and their interactions and relationships reveal much about the practice of politics under the Staufen kings and emperors.

Methodology and Sources

The evidence for this study of sibling relationships is drawn from sources for nine of the most prominent lineages belonging to the upper aristocracy of the Staufen period. All these lineages included members who belonged to the uppermost stratum of the German political elite, to the group of *principes imperii*. While the archbishops and bishops of the kingdom, as well as the abbots of imperial monasteries, were—with very few exceptions—all members

---

45. Leyser, "Frederick Barbarossa and the Hohenstaufen Polity"; Hechberger, *Staufer und Welfen*.
46. Althoff, *Spielregeln der Politik*, 126–153.
47. Schneidmüller, "Konsensuale Herrschaft"; Patzold, "Konsens und Konkurrenz"; and more generally, Reuter, "Medieval Nobility," 183–184.

of this elite, the number of secular princes was much more restricted, less than half that of the ecclesiastical princes. The exclusivity of this group means that there existed a very small group of noble lineages—approximately fifteen around the year 1200—who stood above all others and played a dispropor- tionately influential role in the political life of the kingdom.[48]

Each of the nine lineages I have chosen to analyze here was one of the preeminent noble lineages in Swabia, Bavaria, or Saxony at the start of the Staufen period. These three duchies, all of which lay east of the Rhine River and north of the Alps, had been of critical importance to the development of the German kingdom since the tenth century.[49] Focusing on lineages from these regions makes it possible to examine how and why sibling relationships could create widely divergent political and territorial strategies among nobles exercising princely lordship in key parts of the realm. Moreover, concentrat- ing on lineages from all three of these duchies helps provide a much fuller picture of noble family politics in the German kingdom than most scholars have so far attempted. Studies of German noble lineages are typically written through the lens of regional history, in the German tradition of *Landesge- schichte*, and therefore do not seek points of comparison and contrast among Swabian, Bavarian, and Saxon families.[50]

Two of the nine lineages I have chosen are the *Staufens* and *Welfs*. While the former is often equated with the line of kings and emperors—Conrad III (1138–1152), Frederick I Barbarossa (1152–1190), Henry VI (1190–1197), Philip of Swabia (1198–1208), and Frederick II (1212–1250)—these rulers were not the only influential figures in their generations of the lineage. Most had siblings who played active roles alongside their crowned brothers in shaping the political dynamics of the twelfth and early thirteenth centuries. The Welfs, the lineage that produced the other king and emperor to rule during this period—Otto IV of Brunswick (1198–1218)—included many of the leading noble lords in the German kingdom during the years under examination here. One of these was Duke Henry the Lion of Bavaria and Saxony (d. 1195), possibly the most famous German nobleman of the entire Middle Ages. His life as an only child is central to my analysis of the signifi- cance of sibling relationships within the aristocracy of the Staufen period. The other magnate lineages are the *Wettins* and *Ascanians* from the duchy of

---

48. Weller, *Die Heiratspolitik des deutschen Hochadels*, 4; Wolf, "Königswähler und königliche Tochterstämme."

49. For a good general overview, see Arnold, *Medieval Germany*.

50. Freed, "Medieval German Social History," 9–10.

Saxony along the northeastern frontiers of the empire; the lineage known to modern scholarship as the *Ludowings* of Thuringia; the *Zähringens*, who controlled extensive territories in the duchy of Swabia along what is today the German-Swiss border; the *Wittelsbach* lineage of the duchy of Bavaria; the *Babenbergs* of Austria; and the lineage known as the *Andechs*, which is difficult to designate with a regional label, since its members came to possess properties and rights that stretched from Burgundy in the west to Carniola (modern day Slovenia) in the southeast.

The richest source base for these nine lineages are the thousands of charters—issued by kings and emperors, bishops and other churchmen, and secular noblemen—that survive in German archives. The property confirmations, agreements, and settlements described in these documents frequently provide valuable evidence for brothers' and sisters' interconnected territorial rights and interests. Moreover, the witness lists written into many charters make it possible to reconstruct the itineraries of noble siblings and to determine where and when they came into contact with one another. Extrapolating about sibling *relationships* on the basis of this dry archival evidence is difficult, however, which is why I also rely heavily on other types of source material from the twelfth and early thirteenth centuries. Otto of Freising's *Gesta Friderici*, the most famous narrative source of the Staufen period, is referenced frequently in the pages that follow, as are numerous other chronicles that offer insights into the interactions between particular noble brothers and sisters. Saints' lives, necrologies, and letter collections make occasional appearances as well, since many of them contain scattered clues about the nature of specific sibling relationships. By employing such a diverse array of source material for so many different lineages from across the German kingdom, I aim to highlight the centrality of the sibling bond in the political life of the realm.

One of the advantages of focusing on the highest levels of the German political elite of the twelfth and early thirteenth centuries is the abundance of evidence that survives in these various types of sources. In many cases, sibling interactions and relationships within this elite can be examined using a combination of texts drawn from several different source genres. In this respect, the nine lineages under investigation here are unquestionably atypical; it would be impossible to reconstruct sibling bonds lower down the social ladder in similar detail. Rather than lamenting the paucity of extant sources for the family life of the medieval everyman, however, I embrace the rich material available for examining the significance of sibling relationships for the history of this one political elite. My analysis here is based on the lives of one hundred or so individuals who belonged to these nine lineages of the German upper aristocracy of the twelfth and early thirteenth centuries. Although these individuals represent a tiny fraction of the German population of the period, they played a disproportionately large role in shaping the course of political events within the kingdom. In this book I therefore seek to interweave family history and political history to tell the story of how and why siblings within this elite routinely cooperated with one another in the violent pursuit of political power under the Staufen kings and emperors.

⚘ CHAPTER 1

The Origins of Twelfth-Century Princely Lineages

For generations of medieval historians, the late eleventh and early twelfth centuries have been viewed as a critical period in the history of German noble families. According to a model first proposed by Karl Schmid in the 1950s, these years witnessed a shift from the horizontally oriented extended kinship group (*Sippe*) of the early Middle Ages to the vertically focused lineage (*Geschlecht*) of the central Middle Ages.[1] In other words, direct descent in the male line—especially from father to eldest son—became increasingly important inside noble families at the same time that other types of kin relationships were losing their significance. One reason for this shift from cognatic to agnatic family structures was the gradual decline of Carolingian political institutions between the late 800s and the early 1000s. As more and more rights and properties ceased to be under royal control and instead became heritable, noble lords reorganized their families in response to the changing dynamics of power and authority. No longer dependent on the royal court as the principal locus for the distribution of lands and rights, noblemen began establishing their own lordships at the local level and sought to bequeath those lordships to their sons. In the process,

---

1. Schmid, "Zur Problematik von Familie."

16

they constructed castles that became the focal points of these new territorial bases and founded and endowed monasteries to serve as sites of family commemoration. Thus, as Schmid argues, from the eleventh century onward "the history of the family is reflected most concretely in the history of the control of property."[2]

This theory of the rise of the noble lineage has been debated by medieval historians since it was first proposed more than a half century ago. Arguments about its plausibility and its applicability to regions beyond the duchy of Swabia, the source of Schmid's evidence, have filled the pages of countless books and journals.[3] The synthesis that has been slowly coalescing since the 1990s argues that the key to appreciating the lineal model is contextualizing it properly and carefully circumscribing its significance.[4] Although an increasing number of European noble families began to adopt the structure of the lineage during the eleventh and twelfth centuries, it never replaced preexisting structures. Instead, it was gradually superimposed on them.[5] In other words, the theory of lineage formation explains the descent of a noble family's most important offices and lordships but does not elucidate other aspects of noble family life. The development of lineages does not mean, for example, that the nuclear family of husband, wife, and children ceased to be the basic unit at the center of the noble household.[6] Nor did this agnatic inheritance structure lead to the complete devaluation of cognatic and affinal bonds. These other types of family relations continued to play essential roles within social and political settings that did not concern the direct descent of family-controlled offices and lordships. As a result, the lineage never became

---

2. Ibid., 27.

3. Overviews of this vast scholarship include Borgolte, *Sozialgeschichte des Mittelalters*, 190–218; Hechberger, *Adel im fränkisch-deutschen Mittelalter*, 303–328; and Crouch, *Birth of Nobility*, 99–123.

4. In taking this as my starting point, I am trying to move beyond a historiographical tradition that emerged in the United States soon after the French historian Georges Duby first incorporated Schmid's theories into his own arguments. What is now sometimes referred to in North American scholarship as the "Schmid-Duby thesis" is a much more all-encompassing model of noble society than Schmid's work ever proposed, and work in the late twentieth and early twenty-first century has definitively proven this thesis and model to be inaccurate. Compare Duby, "Lineage, Nobility and Knighthood," with Bouchard, *"Those of My Blood,"* 15–16; Evergates, "Feudal Imaginary of Georges Duby," 648–650; Drell, *Kinship and Conquest*, 116–117; and Livingstone, *Out of Love for My Kin*, 3–4.

5. A point stressed by Herlihy, "Making of the Medieval Family," 143; and Guerreau-Jalabert, Le Jan, and Morsel, "De l'histoire de la famille," 438–440.

6. Evergates, *Aristocracy in the County of Champagne*, 88–89; Livingstone, *Out of Love for My Kin*, 27; White, *Custom, Kinship, and Gifts*, 114; and more generally, Mitterauer, *Sozialgeschichte der Familie*, 13–19.

a framework for organizing *all* intrafamilial interactions.[7] It was a structure that pertained solely to the transmission of political authority across the generations of a noble family.[8] Thus, throughout the centuries on either side of the year 1000, noble families were much more mutable and dynamic than the model of a sharp transition from *Sippe* to *Geschlecht* implies.

Although historians now recognize the descent of power and lordship from one generation to the next to be just one dimension of noble family history, it is nevertheless a crucial dimension for understanding why some sibling relationships came to play prominent roles in the politics of the Staufen period. As a result, Schmid's theory of lineage formation—when used cautiously—can still provide a useful framework for examining many of the families that composed the upper aristocracy of the late twelfth and early thirteenth centuries. Nine lords who rose to political prominence in the decades between 1050 and 1150 emerge from the sources as the founders of the nine lineages that are the focus of this book:

- Duke Welf IV of Bavaria (d. 1101) of the Welf lineage
- Duke Frederick I of Swabia (d. 1105) of the Staufen lineage
- Duke Berthold II of Zähringen (d. 1111) of the Zähringen lineage
- Count Ludwig the Leaper of Thuringia (d. 1123) of the Ludowing lineage
- Margrave Leopold III of Austria (d. 1136) of the Babenberg lineage
- Count Berthold I of Andechs (d. 1151) of the Andechs lineage
- Count-Palatine Otto I of Bavaria (d. 1156) of the Wittelsbach lineage
- Margrave Conrad of Meissen (d. 1157) of the Wettin lineage
- Margrave Albert the Bear of Brandenburg (d. 1170) of the Ascanian lineage

Political success and territorial gains made it possible for these nine noblemen to disentangle themselves from a variety of complex intra- and intergenerational family networks over the course of their lives. In the process, they reoriented the focus of their families toward newly created lineages—

---

7. Reuter, "Medieval Nobility," 190–191.

8. Morsel, *L'aristocratie médiévale*, 250; Le Jan, *Famille et pouvoir*, 387–427. Admittedly, this is only one of several different definitions put forward in the scholarship on noble lineages. Compare Goody, *Development of the Family*, 227–232; Evergates, *Aristocracy in the County of Champagne*, 85–87; Lansing, *Florentine Magnates*, 29–31. These different definitions reflect broader divisions in the field: see Mitterauer, "Mittelalter," 160–164; Jussen, "Perspektiven der Verwandtschaftsforschung," 307–309.

paradoxically setting the stage for the sibling bond to play a more central role in their children's and grandchildren's lives than it did in their own.

New Lords, New Opportunities in the Age of the Investiture Controversy

The history of the German kingdom during the late eleventh and early twelfth centuries is dominated by the so-called Investiture Controversy, the moment when the papacy first challenged the claims of the Salian emperors to leadership of the church inside imperial lands. Pope Gregory VII's dramatic excommunication of King Henry IV in 1076, and Henry's ensuing appearance barefoot in the snow outside the Alpine castle of Canossa as a penitent, are justly famous incidents casting long shadows across narratives of this period. Nevertheless, the decades-long conflict over the limits of secular and spiritual authority set in motion by the events of the mid-1070s was more than just a clash between popes and emperors. From its beginning, the dispute was also shaped by the interests of the German aristocracy. Discontent with what they considered to be arrogant and autocratic behavior by the young Henry IV had already driven some noble lords to rebel against him even prior to his excommunication, and papal critiques of imperial power quickly helped intensify opposition to the German ruler after 1076. As a result, throughout the reigns of Henry IV (d. 1106) and his son Henry V (d. 1125), nobles and their followers were active participants in the civil wars that accompanied the Investiture Controversy.[9]

Countless nobles saw their fortunes altered during these years. Some lost their political influence, as well as their rights and properties, while others rose to new heights of power and authority. Eleventh-century sources are virtually silent about the ancestors of the later Staufen dynasty of kings and emperors until Henry IV rewarded the obscure count Frederick "of Staufen" with the duchy of Swabia in 1079.[10] It was this Count Frederick's unwavering loyalty to Henry IV, not an illustrious set of forefathers from the days of the Carolingians or Ottonians, that first laid the groundwork for his descendants' later success.[11] Other nobles also obtained important new lordships during this period when the Salian rulers and their rivals vied to win

---

9. Fenske, *Adelsopposition und kirchliche Reformbewegung*; Zotz, "Der südwestdeutsche Adel"; Arnold, *Medieval Germany*, 62–68.

10. Weller, "Auf dem Weg zum 'staufischen Haus'"; Robinson, *Henry IV of Germany*, 189.

11. Weinfurter, "Der Mut des Herzogs Friedrich I." See also Hauck, "Haus- und sippengebundene Literatur," 173.

the support of noblemen who had proved themselves politically and militarily capable.[12] With the exception of the Babenbergs, for whom the march of Austria remained the principal lordship from 976 all the way through the period of the Investiture Controversy, every other lineage examined in this book included a lord who acquired at least one new, eminent noble title during the decades on either side of the year 1100.

For the aristocracy as a whole, the inability of Henry IV and later his son Henry V to exert effective authority over most regions of the German kingdom created opportunities at the local level to seize and dominate territories. Improved techniques for constructing stone fortifications helped lords better secure control over these newly gained lands, and the period around 1100 therefore saw a rapid proliferation of noble castles throughout the kingdom.[13] As a result, the territorial foundations of the lordship exercised by many prominent noblemen of the Staufen period can be traced back to ancestors active during these years when there was no emperor capable of limiting their claims to power at the local level.[14] Count-Palatine Otto I of Bavaria, for example, spent the early part of his career strengthening his lordship in western Bavaria around his new castle of Wittelsbach, which has lent its name to his lineage. One of his neighbors, the bishop and chronicler Otto of Freising, vividly describes his own reaction to Otto's territorial ambitions, labeling the count-palatine and his relatives as tyrants, thieves, and brigands because of their efforts to seize church properties in the region.[15] Other ecclesiastical sources written during the early 1100s tell similar stories of upstart lords from across the German kingdom using any means possible to acquire their own landed fortunes, frequently at the expense of local bishoprics and monasteries.[16] Even in those families whose genealogies can be reconstructed for the period before 1050, it was these ambitious nobles from the late eleventh and early twelfth centuries who often laid the groundwork for their descendants' power and authority under the Staufen rulers.[17]

---

12. Weinfurter, *Salian Century*, 161–162; Schneidmüller, "Welf IV.," 16–17; Pätzold, *Die frühen Wettiner*, 31–33.

13. Arnold, *Power and Property*, 152–153; and more generally, Rösener, "Adel und Burg im Mittelalter," 94–98; Hechberger, *Adel im fränkisch-deutschen Mittelalter*, 331–346.

14. Keller, *Zwischen regionaler Begrenzung und universalem Horizont*, 344; Althoff, *Family, Friends and Followers*, 47–50; Fuhrmann, *Germany in the High Middle Ages*, 99–102.

15. Otto of Freising, *Chronica*, 6.20, 282–284. See also Holzfurtner, *Die Wittelsbacher*, 15–21; Flohrschütz, "Machtgrundlagen und Herrschaftspolitik," 42–46.

16. See, for example, Weissensteiner, "Tegernsee, die Bayern und Österreich," 100–141; and more generally, Bisson, *Crisis of the Twelfth Century*, 278–287.

17. On this point, compare Wolf, "Königswähler und königliche Tochterstämme"; Kannowski, "Impact of Lineage."

The history of the Welf family exemplifies this trend. The Welfs are traceable back to ninth-century Carolingian Francia, yet despite their long history, the career of Duke Welf IV of Bavaria marks a crucial break for the family.[18] The only son of Margrave Albert Azzo II of Este and his wife, Kuniza, Welf IV traveled across the Alps from his birthplace in Italy in order to claim the German inheritance of his childless maternal uncle, Welf III (d. 1055). According to the late twelfth-century text known today as the *Historia Welforum*, Welf III had wanted to give his entire inheritance to a monastery, but on his death, his mother sent messengers to Italy to summon her young grandson, Welf IV, to come claim the Welf patrimony for himself.[19] He thus acquired lands in the Alpine regions along the Bavarian-Swabian border, and there pursued a castle-building strategy designed to intensify his lordship. In 1070, King Henry IV enfeoffed him with the duchy of Bavaria, further elevating his standing within the empire.[20] The new duke soon rebelled against the king, joining the aristocratic faction that opposed the ruler during the Investiture Controversy. When the pair made peace in 1098, Welf IV succeeded in winning from Henry the concession that one of his sons would succeed him as duke. In this way, he secured his lineage's position within the uppermost ranks of the aristocracy.[21]

On the opposite end of the German kingdom from Welf IV's centers of lordship, in the frontier regions of northeastern Saxony, the Ascanian Albert the Bear's rise to prominence also shows how new opportunities could lead to dramatic shifts in the political trajectories of noble families.[22] During the early 1120s, both Emperor Henry V and his rival Duke Lothar of Saxony sought to install their own allies in the marches of Meissen and Lower Lusatia along the Elbe River. Count Albert the Bear of Ballenstedt, who first appears in an extant source in 1120, received Lower Lusatia from the Saxon duke in 1123. By 1131, he had abandoned his claim to the march for unknown reasons, but his short career as margrave helped him acquire other positions in subsequent years. Eventually, he obtained the embryonic march of Brandenburg, which became the focal point of his power and influence during the 1160s. In the process, the old county of Ballenstedt, which he

---

18. Schneidmüller, *Die Welfen*, 127–129; Baaken, "Welf IV."

19. *Historia Welforum*, 46–47, chap. 12. Margrave Leopold III of Austria was similarly the only surviving male of the Babenberg family when he succeeded his father, Leopold II.

20. Seibert, "Vom königlichen dux zum Herzog von Bayern," 230–237; Schneidmüller, *Die Welfen*, 130–149.

21. Schneidmüller, *Die Welfen*, 145–146.

22. Partenheimer, *Albrecht der Bär*; Arnold, *Princes and Territories*, 123.

had inherited from his father, lost much of its significance as a centerpiece for his lordship.[23]

Albert the Bear, Welf IV, Otto of Wittelsbach, and Frederick of Staufen all illustrate how a small number of leading lords benefited from the uncertainty and turmoil surrounding the Investiture Controversy and the concomitant civil wars. The upheaval of the late eleventh and early twelfth centuries offered numerous opportunities for these young and ambitious noblemen to acquire new positions that elevated their standing within the German aristocracy. As a result, these lords emerge from the sources as the founders of new lineages shaped by new political and territorial interests. However, the disorder accompanying the Investiture Controversy is only one reason why these four noblemen—and several of their contemporaries—played such pivotal roles in shaping the sibling relationships evident within subsequent generations of these nine lineages. Three additional features of these lords' biographies must also be taken into account: changes during their lifetimes in the nature of German noble lordships; their success in distancing themselves from the territorial interests of other members of their extended kinship networks; and their fortuitous marriages, many of which produced abundant heirs.

The Transformation of Noble Lordships in the German Kingdom

The titles of duke, margrave, and count that many lords acquired during the decades around 1100 were an essential component of the legacy they left for their descendants in the Staufen period. Under the Carolingians, such *honores*—the offices and benefices that brought prestige and political influence to the nobles who possessed them—were objects of patronage that kings could grant and revoke as the circumstances warranted.[24] A nobleman could expect an office, such as that of count (*comes*), to pass to a son only if that son had proved himself worthy and loyal to the king. Charlemagne's grandson Louis the German, who ruled the eastern portions of the Frankish Empire in the mid-800s, firmly believed that *honores* were public offices he could distribute and redistribute by royal prerogative.[25] Within a half century of Louis's death in 876, however, this feature of Carolingian kingship had

---

23. For more on Albert's actions during this period, see chapter 4.
24. Airlie, "Aristocracy," 443; more generally, Costambeys, Innes, and MacLean, *Carolingian World*, 312–323.
25. Goldberg, *Struggle for Empire*, 208.

all but disappeared from those regions that would coalesce into the German kingdom. The early Ottonian rulers, because their territorial power base was initially limited to Saxony, had little choice but to recognize the authority of the dukes and regional nobilities in other parts of the kingdom. Outside areas of immediate family influence in the northeast of the kingdom, these rulers found it difficult to maintain firm control over *honores*.[26] Titles such as count, margrave, and duke therefore began to lose some of their public character as their heritability from father to son became customary.[27]

The later Ottonian and early Salian rulers had some success reasserting their authority over the most important offices in the kingdom.[28] Under Henry IV and Henry V, however, the nature of *honores* would be transformed further. The meaning of the title of count changed significantly over the course of the late eleventh and early twelfth centuries as Carolingian forms of the county and comital office lost their relevance. A *comes* ceased to be a royal official in charge of a clearly defined *comitatus*, and very few counts of the Staufen period possessed the title because they or their ancestors had received it from a king or emperor. Instead, by the early 1100s, comital titles were more reflective of a family's wealth and preeminent standing in the empire than of a defined set of duties and obligations vis-à-vis the ruler.[29] In numerous cases, nobles adopted the title because one of their relatives, frequently someone in the maternal line, had used it—not because their own lordships had ever been counties in the past. "Count" thus became a common designation for many of the noblemen who had succeeded in building their own stone castles and establishing their own lordships in the midst of the turmoil that accompanied the Investiture Controversy.[30]

In Thuringia, for example, the nobleman Ludwig the Leaper emerged from obscure family origins during the 1070s and 1080s to create a new comital lordship that made him one of the leading figures in the region by the early twelfth century. The Wartburg, the castle where Martin Luther would later find shelter, was one of the first centers of this Count Ludwig's power and influence.[31] To the south in Bavaria, the first nobleman to be identified by the title "count of Andechs" was a Berthold who began appearing in

---

26. Leyser, "Ottonian Government," 734; Althoff, *Die Ottonen*, 45–47. For a different viewpoint, see David Bachrach, "Exercise of Royal Power."

27. Reuter, *Germany*, 191–195; Althoff, *Die Ottonen*, 239.

28. Weinfurter, *Salian Century*, 51–52; Wolfram, *Conrad II*, 6–7.

29. Arnold, *Princes and Territories*, 112; Tellenbach, "Carolingian Imperial Nobility," 219.

30. Hechberger, *Adel im fränkisch-deutschen Mittelalter*, 254–259.

31. Assing, "Der Aufstieg der Ludowinger," 266–274.

sources in the years around 1100. He presumably played a role in the construction of the castle of Andechs, yet the nature of the comital authority he exercised in the region around this fortification remains unclear.[32] Indeed, many of these new comital lordships had no territorial cohesiveness because they consisted of scattered familial estates and advocacies over monastic or episcopal properties. From region to region and family to family, the comital title seems to have meant something different.[33] Providing simple definitions for the terms "count" and "county" during the twelfth and thirteenth centuries is therefore impossible.

Duchies and marches maintained some of their public character longer than counties did, but during the Investiture Controversy, they too started to change in significant ways. By the opening decades of the 1100s, the nobles who held these titles were no longer officeholders with formal responsibilities in judicial, military, and administrative affairs. Instead, the Salian rulers and their successors increasingly treated the titles of duke, margrave, and the like as rewards meant to win or maintain the support of prominent lords inside the German kingdom. The number of dukes in the realm more than doubled in the century after the outbreak of the Investiture Controversy as the creation of new ducal titles became a way for rulers to display their largesse.[34] In 1098, for example, Henry IV recognized the ducal title of Berthold II of Zähringen—despite the fact that the title "duke of Zähringen" was not associated with a clearly defined territorial duchy. Writing a half century later, Otto of Freising scathingly refers to these dukes as possessors of "the empty name of duke (*vacuum nomen ducis*) . . . for all of them, up to the present day, are called dukes but hold no duchy."[35] The newly created title of landgrave (*lantgravius*), which does not appear in an extant source until the later eleventh century, is further evidence for this inflationary tendency in the granting of titles.[36] King Lothar III gave the eldest son of Count Ludwig the Leaper of Thuringia the title of landgrave in 1131 in order to recognize his prominent position inside Thuringia and to bind him more closely to Lothar's insecure kingship. It was only gradually over the ensuing decades, however, that this

32. Lyon, "Cooperation, Compromise and Conflict Avoidance," 297–301.

33. Compare, for example, Holzfurtner, *Die Grafschaft der Andechser*; Brüsch, *Die Brunonen*; Willoweit, "Fürst und Fürstentum," 19–20.

34. Arnold, *Princes and Territories*, 88–95; Hechberger, *Adel im fränkisch-deutschen Mittelalter*, 260–263.

35. Otto of Freising and Rahewin, *Gesta Friderici*, 1.9, 25–26. See also Althoff, "Die Zähringer," 82–86; Zotz, "Dux de Zaringen," 42–43.

36. Arnold, *Princes and Territories*, 130–132.

Landgrave Ludwig I (d. 1140) and his successors in the Ludowing lineage were able to imbue this title with any political or juridical meaning.[37]

The creation of so many new secular lordships is an indication of the waning of effective royal control over the leading nobles of the kingdom during and immediately after the Investiture Controversy. Increasingly, the kings and emperors were forced to acknowledge the independent power and influence of ambitious new lords by offering them illustrious titles—or by recognizing ex post facto their claims to lordships they had acquired without royal consent. By the mid-twelfth century, moreover, the heritability of duchies, marches, and counties from father to son was a well-established principle. According to the *Sachsenspiegel* of the early thirteenth century, it was only after a son succeeded his father that he was required to do homage to his lord. And even this was not an act of formal investiture, since the son had automatically come into possession of the lordship at the time of his father's death.[38] Kings and emperors could typically intervene in the disposition of duchies and other prestigious lordships only when a lord died without a direct male heir, and in many of those cases, rulers still had to take into account the interests of the dead lord's other relatives.[39]

Despite these developments, duchies and marches—and to a lesser extent counties as well—were not the private possessions of powerful nobles during the Staufen period. The most prestigious lordships all maintained faint traces of their character as public offices. At court gatherings in Roncaglia in Italy in 1154 and 1158, Frederick Barbarossa sought to strengthen his hold over these *honores* by issuing laws that stressed the feudo-vassalic nature of the bonds between ruler and magnates. He proclaimed, for example, that the secular and ecclesiastical princes owed him military service on his Italian campaigns in return for the fiefs they held from him. And most significantly for this study, Barbarossa decreed in 1158 that duchies, marches, and counties could not be divided since they were imperial offices and fiefs.[40] Although scholars disagree about whether this pronouncement was meant to apply to the empire as a whole or only the Italian kingdom, there is little evidence from north of the Alps for the division of such prestigious lordships until after the collapse of

37. Patze, *Die Entstehung der Landesherrschaft*, 1:208–209; Assing, "Der Aufstieg der Ludowinger," 289–292.

38. Eike von Repgow, *Sachsenspiegel: Lehnrecht*, 21–22, pp. 38–40; Reynolds, *Fiefs and Vassals*, 453–454.

39. Schieffer, "Das Lehnswesen in den deutschen Königsurkunden"; more generally, Goez, *Der Leihezwang*, 95. For more on this point, see chapter 2.

40. MGH DD F I, 2:36, no. 242. See also Struve, "Die Rolle des römischen Rechts," 91–93.

Staufen rule in the 1250s.[41] That a nobleman could not split a duchy or other imperial fief into two, three, or four parts as a means of satisfying multiple sons' claims to the patrimony is an indication that the upper aristocracy could not treat these lordships like they were family property.[42]

The founders of the lineages under investigation here were not passive observers of the changes affecting noble lordships during the late eleventh and early twelfth centuries. As the holders of some of the most illustrious titles and valuable *honores* in the German kingdom, these lords and their descendants played prominent roles in determining the character of princely lordships under the Staufen kings and emperors. Barbarossa's efforts at reform at Roncaglia in 1154 and 1158 reveal that the German rulers had their own ideas about the nature of the offices of duke, margrave, and count. In the wake of the Investiture Controversy, however, the leading magnates of the realm had gained sufficient power and influence to be able to enjoy the fruits of their lordship as they saw fit—at least in most circumstances. Moreover, by acquiring princely titles, the founders of the lineages under investigation here had assured themselves a consultative role at the imperial court as members of the group of *principes imperii*. The German rulers of the twelfth and thirteenth centuries could not make decisions affecting the princes without their approval and support. Gaining access to the circle of imperial princes therefore gave the members of these lineages the opportunity to cultivate *Königsnähe* and influence politics at the highest levels.[43] The transformation of noble lordships that occurred in the decades around 1100 thus opened new doors for these nine founders and their successors.

New Lords, Old Kinship Networks: Changing Family Dynamics

Throughout the central Middle Ages, the acquisition of new lordships created opportunities for noblemen to move in new directions and to pursue new interests. For many lords, the *honores* obtained during the period of the Investiture Controversy proved to be the catalyst for a reorientation of their

---

41. Dendorfer, "Roncaglia"; Krieger, *Die Lehnshoheit*, 74–75; Reynolds, *Fiefs and Vassals*, 447–448.

42. Spieß, "Lordship, Kinship, and Inheritance," 60–62. For more on this point, see chapters 2 and 7.

43. For more on this point, see the introduction.

territorial and political foci. As they shifted their attention to new lands and rights and to newly built castles, these nobles frequently distanced themselves from the territorial and political interests of other members of their extended kinship networks. Over the course of their lives, they became less and less reliant for their standing in noble society on older familial lands and rights in regions where other relatives also had claims. The lordships that many nobles acquired and developed during the late eleventh and early twelfth centuries thus made it possible for them to establish independent positions for themselves and to found new lineages.

In medieval German noble society, the nuclear family served as the main avenue for the descent of property.[44] Nevertheless, there was a tendency for inheritance patterns to become increasingly complex over the course of multiple generations.[45] Where a single lord was initially in possession of a large territory, eventually a diverse array of his descendants could find themselves all sharing property or holding small pieces of land in close proximity to one another. In a well-known example from the mid-1070s, a group of nobles that included the Swabian duke Rudolf of Rheinfelden, the Bavarian count of Diessen and his son, and the Saxon margrave of Meissen jointly donated a piece of property to a Swabian monastery. How this eclectic collection of lords from across the German kingdom came into joint possession of this land remains the subject of debate.[46] Regardless, this donation highlights the potential intricacies of inheritance rights inside an extended kinship network that traced its origins back to a common ancestor from the distant past. Not surprisingly, nobles oftentimes seized the opportunity to free themselves from such complicated landholding situations.[47]

Count-Palatine Otto I of Bavaria, the founder of the Wittelsbach lineage, illustrates this trend. According to the early thirteenth-century chronicler Conrad of Scheyern, in the years around 1100 "the mountain and castle of Scheyern were not inhabited by one or two princes (*principes*) but by many in common."[48] Conrad then explains how, in subsequent decades, some of these lords constructed a new castle at Dachau and began naming themselves after this fortification, while others built and took the name of the castle

---

44. See chapter 2 for more on this point.

45. Schmid, "Zur Problematik von Familie," 29, 38.

46. See, for example, Parlow, *Die Zähringer*, 53–54, no. 82; Hlawitschka, *Untersuchungen zu den Thronwechseln*, 111–115; and Schmid, "Zur Problematik von Familie," 28–29.

47. Arnold, *Princes and Territories*, 144–145.

48. Conrad of Scheyern, *Chronicon*, 620. See also Fried, "Die Herkunft der Wittelsbacher," 38; Arnold, *Power and Property*, 166–169.

of Valley. Count-Palatine Otto I of Bavaria also had a claim to Scheyern but shifted his focus westward toward his castle at Wittelsbach. Eventually, the old family residence at Scheyern was converted into a monastery, and the newly separated branches of the family pursued their own, independent territorial strategies.[49] During the same period, Count Berthold I of Andechs also belonged to an extended family network whose members had overlapping lands and rights. The conversion of the old familial castle of Diessen in western Bavaria into a house of Augustinian canons and the construction of a series of new castles—including Andechs—enabled Berthold and his numerous brothers, nephews, and cousins to disentangle many of their territorial interests. As a result, fewer and fewer distant relatives are named alongside the count of Andechs in charters and chronicles from the years after 1130.[50]

A similar situation is evident in the early generations of the Zähringen family. Following his father's death in 1078, the future duke Berthold II of Zähringen inherited family lands that lay in close proximity to properties acquired by his nephew Margrave Herman II of Baden. But in the 1090s, after the unexpected deaths of Berthold's father-in-law and brother-in-law, he came into possession of his wife's valuable Rheinfelden inheritance.[51] Soon thereafter, he secured a ducal title, further elevating his standing in the empire. Berthold and his nephew Herman then seem to have reached an agreement that created two distinct spheres of familial interest inside Swabia: one along the upper Rhine River for the duke and the other along the Neckar River for the margrave. In subsequent years and later generations, these separate spheres helped spur the creation of two separate branches inside the family, and there is little evidence for close contacts between these Zähringen and Baden lines during the 1100s.[52]

For other noblemen, the unexpected deaths of other members of their extended kinship group also played a role in their ability to found new lineages. In these cases, ancestral lands and valuable lordships that had been divided among multiple close and distant relatives were consolidated in the hands of a single lord who could then distribute those lordships freely among his sons. Conrad of Wettin, for example, emerged as the leading figure in his kin group because of the childless deaths of two relatives. After his twenty-year-old cousin Henry II of Eilenburg died in 1123, he received Henry's

---

49. Genzinger, "Grafschaft und Vogtei," 116–117. For the phenomenon of nobles converting castles into monasteries during this period, see Arnold, *Power and Property*, 151–166.

50. Lyon, "Cooperation, Compromise and Conflict Avoidance," 297–310.

51. Keller, "Die Zähringer," 22.

52. Lamke, "Die frühen Markgrafen von Baden," 40–42; Zettler, "Zähringerburgen," 98–101.

THE ORIGINS OF TWELFTH-CENTURY PRINCELY LINEAGES 29

march of Meissen from Duke Lothar of Saxony, the future king. One year later, Conrad's older brother, Dedo, failed to return from a pilgrimage to the Holy Land, and Conrad therefore acquired his sibling's share of their father's patrimony.[53] Before he turned thirty, Conrad was the only surviving adult male within his extended agnatic family. As a result, when he died in 1157, his children had exclusive claims to the impressive collection of rights and properties he controlled.[54]

While the unexpected deaths of family members and the untangling of family property rights affected different nobles in diverse and unpredictable ways, there is a common thread running through all nine of these lords' biographies. At some point in his life, each came to control a network of valuable lordships and territories that was not intertwined in any significant manner with the lands and rights of other relatives, whether siblings, uncles, or cousins. This does not necessarily mean that these noblemen had rid themselves entirely of ancestral properties in regions where other family members once had claims. Rather, it means that these ancestral properties were no longer the cornerstone of their power and influence inside the German kingdom.[55] In terms of the composition and organization of their patrimonies, they had acquired independent positions for themselves within their broader kin groups.

Marriage, Children, and the Formation of New Lineages

By distancing themselves from the territorial interests of other members of their extended kinship networks, the leading lords of the late eleventh and early twelfth centuries secured the place of their descendants within the upper echelons of the German aristocracy. Their own children did not have to concern themselves with rival claims from distant relatives as they sought to capitalize on their fathers' success in accumulating properties, rights, and lordships during the tumultuous years of the Investiture Controversy. This shift away from the extended kinship network would not have mattered for subsequent generations, however, if the nine lords I am discussing here had failed to produce heirs. None of them could have become the founder of a lineage, obviously, if he had not fathered legitimate sons who survived to adulthood—and who, in turn, sired sons of their own.

---

53. Rogge, *Die Wettiner*, 29–33; Pätzold, *Die frühen Wettiner*, 27–33; Groß, *Die Wettiner*, 34–36.

54. Albert the Bear's acquisition of his childless cousin's lands and rights around Weimar and Orlamünde is a similar example; see Partenheimer, *Albrecht der Bär*, 81–82. Count Ludwig the Leaper of Thuringia also benefited territorially from the early death of his younger brother, Berenger; Patze, *Die Entstehung der Landesherrschaft*, 1:175–176.

55. For an excellent example of this scenario, see Freed, *Counts of Falkenstein*, 36–40.

Because these nine lords all became prominent figures in the German kingdom as young men, they had few difficulties finding wives who could strengthen their positions within the upper aristocracy.[56] Some married high-ranking heiresses whose lands and rights helped lay the foundation for the new lordships these noblemen were establishing. Count Berthold I of Andechs, for example, married one of the margrave of Istria's daughters, the heiress Sophia, who brought into their union lands and rights in the far southeast of the empire in what is today Slovenia.[57] Others married into the imperial family. When the Salian ruler Henry IV rewarded the obscure count Frederick of Staufen with the duchy of Swabia in 1079, he also gave the new duke his daughter, Agnes, in marriage. Following Frederick's death in 1105, Agnes was married again—this time by her brother Henry V—to Margrave Leopold III of Austria, who would emerge as one of the contenders for the throne in 1125 precisely because of his wife's blood connections to the last Salian rulers.[58]

The political and territorial gains achieved through these marriages would have been fleeting if the unions had failed to produce children. Examples abound of powerful nobles from the late eleventh and early twelfth centuries who saw their lordships dissolved and their legacies lost to obscurity because they lacked heirs.[59] Along the northeastern frontier of Saxony, one of Conrad of Wettin's and Albert the Bear's strongest rivals was the lord Wiprecht of Groitzsch, who was poised in the 1110s and early 1120s to be the founder of a powerful new princely lineage. When he died in 1123, however, he was survived by only one son, who died childless in 1135. Wiprecht's lineage thus came to a sudden end, despite the fact that he had been just as successful as the nine lords under investigation here at establishing a new lordship amid the upheaval of the early twelfth century.[60] In contrast, Henry IV's daughter Agnes bore her first husband, Duke Frederick I of Swabia, three children who all outlived him by more than forty years. Agnes and her second husband, Margrave Leopold III of Austria, then had *eighteen* sons and daughters—though seven died young.[61] Indeed, all nine of these noblemen

---

56. These marriages are all discussed in Weller, *Die Heiratspolitik des deutschen Hochadels.*

57. Štih, "Krain in der Zeit der Grafen von Andechs," 11–12.

58. For the significance of this marriage for Leopold III, see Dienst, "Werden und Entwicklung," 94–95; Lechner, *Die Babenberger,* 118–121; Brunner, *Österreichische Geschichte,* 356–361.

59. For example, the lineage of the anti-king Rudolf of Rheinfelden (d. 1080) and his only son, Berthold, who died childless in 1090.

60. Vogtherr, "Wiprecht von Groitzsch"; Groß, *Die Wettiner,* 33–34; Fenske, *Adelsopposition und kirchliche Reformbewegung,* 255–272.

61. *Annales Austriae,* 610; Weller, *Die Heiratspolitik des deutschen Hochadels,* 197–211.

had at least two sons reach adulthood. Most impressively, Albert the Bear was survived by seven grown sons when he died in 1170 after a fifty-year career.

Obviously, good luck played a role in these successful marriages. The founders of these nine lineages were fortunate to be virile enough to father so many heirs—and to marry women who proved capable of safely bearing such an abundance of children. Luck alone was likely not the only factor, however. As members of the uppermost elite of aristocratic society, they were some of the best-fed people in the German kingdom. As a result, they were in a better position nutritionally than most of the population to have large families and to raise children who could survive to adulthood.[62] Nevertheless, even this seems insufficient to explain the numerous offspring born to these nine lords, because their descendants tended not to have as many children as they did. For reasons that remain unclear, this generation produced an unusually large number of sons and daughters who reached adulthood.[63] Regardless of the explanation, this abundance of children is crucial for understanding the history of the German upper aristocracy during the Staufen period, since it ensured the survival of these nine lords' lineages into the next generation.

Toward the Princely Lineages of the Staufen Period

The founding of new lineages by the nine noblemen examined here forms the necessary backdrop for examining the sibling relationships that came to play such a prominent role in subsequent generations of these families. The lords who had weathered the storms of the Investiture Controversy most successfully had greatly enriched themselves by accumulating titles, lands, monastic advocacies, and various other rights. In addition, many had been able to build not one but several castles on their territories as a means of strengthening their authority within their lordships. How did these noblemen and their wives envision this multifaceted patrimony passing to the next generation of their own nuclear families, given that they had few if any distant relatives with claims to their titles and rights?

The annalist Lampert of Hersfeld, in his entry for the year 1071, describes how succession operated inside one prominent noble lineage of the later eleventh century:

> In the comital office of Baldwin [V of Flanders] and in his family, it was preserved for many centuries as if sanctioned by eternal law that one

---

62. Reuter, "Nobles and Others," 116–117.
63. See chapters 5 and 7 for more on this point, as well as some possible explanations for this trend.

son, who was especially pleasing to his father, would receive his father's name and would alone obtain the rule of all of Flanders by hereditary succession. His other brothers either would lead an inglorious life subordinated to and obeying him; or having traveled abroad, they would strive to flourish more by their own deeds; or having devoted themselves to idleness and indolence, they would console their extreme poverty with the empty fame of their ancestors. This was done lest, with the province having been divided into many pieces, the reputation of that family be sullied on account of a lack of family property. Therefore, after Baldwin [V] had fathered two sons, Baldwin [VI] and Robert, he designated Baldwin the heir to everything he possessed. As soon as Robert first reached mature age and was having to be assigned some means of support, his father prepared for him ships and offered him sufficient gold, silver, and other outlays for a long journey. Then the father ordered that the son go among foreign peoples and, if he were man enough, that he obtain for himself by his own virtue a kingdom and riches.[64]

Although the county of Flanders straddled the western frontier of the empire, the succession strategy that Lambert describes is strikingly different from those used east of the Rhine by the nine princely lineages under investigation here. The aristocracy of the German kingdom had never practiced primogeniture, or unigeniture of any sort. Indeed, the eldest son's exclusive right to family property would not be recognized in German-speaking lands until the early modern period.[65] Partible inheritance was the norm throughout the Middle Ages.[66] The lords who had acquired large collections of rights, properties, and lordships during the late eleventh and early twelfth centuries therefore made no effort to preserve the territorial integrity of these patrimonies for later generations. Instead, they immediately began the process of dividing their lands and rights among their children. Although they were prevented from splitting their duchies, marches, and comital lordships into smaller pieces, they nevertheless arranged the succession and inheritance in ways that ensured multiple sons and daughters would have close ties to their father's patrimony. In this way, they laid the foundation for the sibling relationships that would develop in the next generation of their lineages.

---

64. Lampert of Hersfeld, *Annales*, 121.

65. Spieß, *Familie und Verwandtschaft*, 272–289; Rogge, *Herrschaftsweitergabe*, 48; Freed, *Noble Bondsmen*, 113–116; Leyser, "German Aristocracy," 38.

66. Le Jan, *Famille et pouvoir*, 238–239; Leyser, *Rule and Conflict*, 61; Pischke, *Die Landesteilungen der Welfen*, 1.

❧ CHAPTER 2

Forging the Bonds between Siblings
Succession, Inheritance, and Church Careers

Modern assumptions about the prevalence of primogeniture during the central Middle Ages have long obscured scholarly visions of noble lineages. For the German upper aristocracy of the Staufen period, lineages were not based on narrow lines of descent from father to eldest son. Instead, they embraced multiple children with equal claims to rights and properties. During the late eleventh and early twelfth centuries, lords who had succeeded in establishing independent positions for themselves distributed their patrimonies in ways that ensured the interconnectedness of their offspring's interests. When members of this next generation married and had children of their own, they followed in their parents' footsteps, maintaining the tradition of partible inheritance within their own nuclear families. As a result, the generations of the German upper aristocracy that came of age in the late twelfth and early thirteenth centuries frequently included groups of siblings with overlapping political and territorial concerns.

In subsequent chapters, I will examine how many of the brothers and sisters who belonged to these generations worked together to influence the course of politics within the German kingdom. First, however, it is necessary to understand the types of relationships that siblings could develop with one another in this society. Within the upper aristocracy, parents' decisions— about which sons to designate as heirs and which to place in the church, and about which daughters to marry off and which to send to religious communities—played pivotal roles in determining how their children were able to interact with each other as adults.[1]

Succession and Inheritance in the Twelfth Century: The Tradition of Partibility

For much of the central Middle Ages, the German aristocracy did not rely on the written word when arranging intrafamilial matters like inheritance and succession. Extant charters drawn up in the name of secular lords are rare from the eleventh and twelfth centuries, and most of the documents that do survive record nobles' agreements with religious communities, not with other family members. As a result, historians frequently know more about the entrance gifts given to religious communities when sons and daughters joined these houses than they do about daughters' dowries or the precise division of a patrimony among heirs.[2] Family archives for the preservation of such records as marriage contracts and testaments are not extant—and probably never existed.[3] Not until the mid-thirteenth century do intrafamilial records, such as dynastic treaties detailing the arrangement of the succession inside individual families (*Hausverträge*), become commonplace.[4] Charters and other documents generated by the imperial court are also silent about most issues relating to the descent of noble patrimonies, because the German kings and emperors were only occasionally able to exert some influence from the periphery over the internal affairs of noble families, even when imperial fiefs were involved.[5]

This lack of source material complicates the study of succession and inheritance arrangements, because German nobles were not expected to follow a fixed set of rules when dividing their patrimonies. Beyond an imprecisely defined tradition of partibility, there was no body of inheritance law or property law that strictly governed the descent of rights and lands for the king-

---

1. Stepchildren and illegitimate children will be discussed on a case-by-case basis in subsequent chapters because it is much more difficult to generalize about their interactions with their siblings.

2. See, for example, UB Steiermark, 1:148, no. 139, and *Salzburger Urkundenbuch*, 2:274, no. 188. For the earliest known example from any of these nine lineages of siblings drawing up a written agreement to divide family property, see chapter 5.

3. For more on this point, see Freed, "*Codex Falkensteinensis*," 209–210. Intrafamilial documents from this period survive in more abundance in other parts of Europe: Kosto, *Making Agreements*, 113–118; Drell, *Kinship and Conquest*, 90–112; Martindale, "Succession and Politics," 25–26.

4. See chapter 7 for more on this point.

5. See chapter 1.

dom's aristocracy.[6] The nuclear family, with its predominantly oral culture, was the site where most decisions about the division of the family's lands and rights were made. The personal choices of individual lords—presumably in consultation with their immediate family members and their households—were crucial for shaping succession and inheritance within lineages.[7] A father, in his role as head of the family, sought to use his patriarchal authority to plan and enforce a division of the patrimony that all his children would respect and follow.[8] Constructing a comprehensive model that can effectively explain the distribution of property and lordships within all the lineages of the upper aristocracy is therefore an impossible task. Differences in the sizes of sibling groups, combined with disparities in the composition of nobles' patrimonies, ensured that succession and inheritance would follow a different course in each generation of each princely lineage.

Even a narrow focus on the nine lords who were the founders of the lineages examined here does not make generalizing any easier. These lords had acquired abundant rights and properties in the decades around 1100, and they could consider a broad range of options when dividing their patrimonies among their multiple children. Some of the nine, for example, were in possession of more than one eminent title and could therefore bestow prominent lordships on more than one heir. Albert the Bear of the Ascanian lineage placed only two of his seven sons in the church; the other five each received a march or a county. In one of Albert's own charters from 1160—a decade before his death—his intentions for his sons are already apparent. The document records a gift to the Hospital of Saint John in Jerusalem made by Albert "with the consent of my legitimate heirs Margrave Otto, Count Herman, Henry canon of the church of Saint Maurice at Magdeburg, and Counts Adalbert, Dietrich, and Bernhard."[9] Siegfried, who pursued an ecclesiastical career, is the only son absent from the charter. The six others are all identified by the titles they would use after their father died in 1170.[10]

6. Arnold, *Princes and Territories*, 239–240; Tellenbach, "Carolingian Imperial Nobility," 224–225; Spieß, *Familie und Verwandtschaft*, 199–201; and more broadly, Martindale, "Succession and Politics," 20–21.

7. Althoff, *Family, Friends and Followers*, 62. For similar observations about other regions of Europe, see Crouch and de Trafford, "Forgotten Family," 45; Hajdu, "Family and Feudal Ties," 131; Drell, *Kinship and Conquest*, 116–117.

8. Spieß, *Familie und Verwandtschaft*, 454–455.

9. CDA, 1, pt. 2:333, no. 456.

10. For more on these brothers, see chapter 4.

Conrad of Wettin also possessed five discrete lordships, which he distributed among all five of his sons, but the founders of most other lineages did not control such vast patrimonies.[11] As a result, they distributed rights and properties differently. Count Ludwig the Leaper of Thuringia arranged for two of his three surviving sons to succeed him in his two lordships, granting his Thuringian county to his eldest heir and his Hessian comital rights to his second son.[12] Count Berthold I of Andechs also intended to grant comital lordships to two of his three sons. However, when the eldest heir predeceased his father while participating in the Second Crusade, the second son, Berthold II, acquired all of Berthold I's lordships, significantly narrowing the descent of the patrimony within this lineage.[13]

Other lords did not have the luxury of giving multiple prestigious lordships to multiple heirs, because they possessed only a single duchy, march, or county to pass along to the next generation. Nevertheless, even in these lineages, the tradition of partible inheritance is evident. Second sons in these families routinely acquired valuable pieces of the patrimony—in the form of alodial property—from their fathers.[14] The heirs of Duke Berthold II of Zähringen and his wife, Agnes of Rheinfelden, are an especially well-documented example. The elder son, Berthold III, succeeded as duke of Zähringen on their father's death in 1111. The younger son, Conrad, did not receive a lordship of his own. He is identified simply as Duke Berthold III's brother (*frater eius Conradus*) or as *dominus* in sources from the 1110s and early 1120s.[15] Despite his lack of a title, he was in possession of his own rights and properties in the upper Rhine region, the heartland of the Zähringen lineage's power and influence. Most significantly, Conrad founded a market in Freiburg im Breisgau—"in a place of my own jurisdiction" (*in loco mei proprii iuris*)—while his older brother Berthold was still duke.[16]

---

11. For Conrad's sons, see chapter 3.

12. Patze, *Die Entstehung der Landesherrschaft*, 1:192–193, 198.

13. Lyon, "Cooperation, Compromise and Conflict Avoidance," 186–194.

14. For the importance of the alod for German noble patrimonies, see Reynolds, *Fiefs and Vassals*, 415–416, 457.

15. Parlow, *Die Zähringer*, 127–129, no. 186; 145–146, no. 209; 147–148, no. 211. For *dominus*: ibid., 129–130, no. 187; 131–133, nos. 190–191. Kienast (*Der Herzogstitel*, 339–340) notes that some of Henry V's charters label Conrad *dux* prior to his older brother's death; however, because they are all dated to the months just before Berthold died, I am not inclined to read as much into them as Kienast does.

16. Parlow, *Die Zähringer*, 141–142, no. 204; Keller, "Die Zähringer." For more on Conrad's activities during his brother's lifetime, see Parlow, *Die Zähringer*, 139–141, no. 202; Büttner, "Allerheiligen in Schaffhausen," 196–197.

All of these succession and inheritance arrangements complicate the model traditionally put forth by medieval historians about younger sons and their positions within their lineages. Many scholars have argued that noblemen who permitted more than one son to remain in the secular sphere tended to view the younger ones mainly as an insurance policy against the early death of the eldest. As a result, according to this model, younger brothers played carefully circumscribed roles in their families.[17] However, while keeping sons "in reserve" was almost certainly one aspect of some lords' succession plans, the evidence from the German upper aristocracy indicates that younger brothers were not marginalized members of their families. The custom of partible inheritance ensured them a more prominent position in their lineages than historians have typically acknowledged. Indeed, one need look no further than the first Staufen king, Conrad III, to see the opportunities that younger sons could have. When Duke Frederick I of Swabia died in 1105, his eldest son, Frederick II, succeeded him as Swabian duke. Conrad, the second son, inherited family lands in northern Swabia as well as Franconia that provided him the chance to exercise his own authority as an independent lord. During subsequent years, he acquired comital rights in the same region and even seems to have held briefly the title of duke of Franconia (*dux Francorum orientalium*) before his eventual election as king.[18]

Because partible inheritance was a long-standing tradition within the German upper aristocracy, the leading lords of the late eleventh and early twelfth centuries were not introducing any new ideas when they involved younger sons in the division of their patrimonies. This may help explain why the founders of these nine lineages were generally quite successful in ensuring a smooth transition of power and authority to their heirs. In eight of the nine lineages, there is no evidence for succession or inheritance disputes erupting in the next generation in the wake of a father's death. In the ninth lineage, the Babenbergs, the outbreak of conflict is revealing, because a father seems to have quite consciously ignored the norms of succession within German noble society. Margrave Leopold III of Austria (d. 1136), who was survived by six sons, kept four of these heirs in the secular sphere. One son, Adalbert, is named alongside his parents in 1128, and since no other

---

17. Althoff, *Family, Friends and Followers*, 45–46; Schneidmüller, *Die Welfen*, 150; Freed, *Noble Bondsmen*, 116–117; and most famously, Duby, *Knight, Lady and Priest*, 105–106, 248–249, 269. For a critique of this model, see Evergates, *Aristocracy in the County of Champagne*, 83–85.

18. Lubich, *Auf dem Weg zur "Güldenen Freiheit,"* 151–178.

son appears in a source for another eight years, he was almost certainly the eldest.[19] Following Leopold III's death, however, this Adalbert did not succeed as margrave of Austria. Instead, Leopold IV, who was the third-born son, became the next margrave.

Why the succession unfolded in this manner is difficult to determine. One chronicle reports that Margrave Leopold III loved his second son, Henry Jasomirgott, less than the others, but it offers no explanation for why the first son, Adalbert, was bypassed.[20] What is clear is that this plan for the succession led to problems. Pope Innocent II's condolence letter to Leopold III's widow and children hints that there were tensions inside the family, for the pope urges mother and sons "to live in peace and concord."[21] A charter from several years later also references these tensions when it describes an earlier reconciliation between the two brothers Adalbert and Leopold.[22] None of this evidence, unfortunately, explains whether this succession dispute became violent. Since Margrave Leopold IV made a property donation in 1137 "through the hand of his brother A[dalbert]," the two brothers may have reconciled quite quickly.[23] And with Adalbert dying in 1138/1139 and Leopold IV in 1141, any lingering tensions came to an abrupt end. Five years after the death of Margrave Leopold III, Henry Jasomirgott was the only one of his sons who remained in the secular sphere. This succession dispute therefore seems to have had no long-lasting repercussions. Nevertheless, Margrave Leopold III—by choosing to arrange the succession in a way that left his eldest son without a clearly defined role within the lineage—helped initiate the conflict that erupted after his death.[24]

Serious fraternal disputes were rare within the families of the German upper aristocracy, especially in the period immediately following a father's death. Nonetheless, this conflict among the Babenberg brothers suggests that a lord's plans for the division of his patrimony among his children were not etched in stone. Once he died, disputes or unexpected circumstances could emerge, prompting the members of the next generation to alter their father's

19. BUB, 1:3–4, no. 3. Some scholars have argued that Adalbert must have been born to a different mother than his younger siblings, but this is impossible to prove on the basis of the surviving evidence. Compare Weller, *Die Heiratspolitik des deutschen Hochadels*, 340–343; Brunner, *Österreichische Geschichte*, 354; Lechner, *Die Babenberger*, 120.

20. *Annales Austriae*, 610. Henry Jasomirgott may also have been bypassed because he had received his mother's inheritance: Dopsch, *Österreichische Geschichte*, 124–125.

21. BUB, 4, pt. 1:96, no. 703. See also Brunner, *Österreichische Geschichte*, 371–372.

22. BUB, 1:34–35, no. 25.

23. Ibid., 1:14–16, no. 11.

24. For a similar situation, see chapter 5.

succession and inheritance arrangements. When that happened, none of the siblings could exert any kind of patriarchal authority over the others; not even the eldest brother was in a position to control his younger siblings. In other regions of western Europe during the central Middle Ages, younger heirs held their pieces of the patrimony from their eldest brother, making them subordinate to him.[25] Otto of Freising, in his *Gesta Friderici*, calls attention to this practice when he observes of the kingdom of Burgundy, "The custom in that region, which is preserved in nearly all the provinces of Gaul, has remained that the authority over the paternal inheritance always passes to the elder brother and his children, whether male or female, the others looking to him as if to their lord."[26] In the German kingdom, however, the practice of permitting multiple sons to succeed to lordships created an independent position for each brother.

Two letters preserved in a collection from the monastery of Reinhardsbrunn and composed in the name of Landgrave Ludwig II of Thuringia (d. 1172) offer a glimpse into some of the frustrations that could result from this situation.[27] Both pieces of correspondence show Ludwig II, who was the eldest of the three sons of Landgrave Ludwig I, attempting to intervene in his younger brothers' affairs. In the first, the landgrave complains to the abbot of Reinhardsbrunn, "My brother L[udwig *minor*], whom I offered to God . . . , abstains from the monastic garb and tonsure by your counsel."[28] The younger Ludwig's apparent act of defiance highlights the difficulties that one brother could have forcing another brother to obey his commands. Indeed, Ludwig II seems to have failed in his plans, for his younger sibling Ludwig *minor* later received a small comital lordship belonging to the Ludowing family and remained in the secular sphere until his death in 1189.[29]

Landgrave Ludwig II addressed the second letter to his brother Henry II Raspe, who had acquired their father's comital rights in Hesse in 1140. It reads, "How I wish, brother most dear to my soul (*frater animo meo carissime*),

---

25. Macé, "Les frères"; Evergates, *Aristocracy in the County of Champagne*, 34–35; Duby, *Knight, Lady and Priest*, 277; Holt, "Politics and Property," 44. For the German kingdom, see Freed, *Noble Bondsmen*, 116.

26. Otto of Freising and Rahewin, *Gesta Friderici*, 2.48, 155.

27. For the close ties between the Ludowing lineage and the monastery of Reinhardsbrunn, see *Die Reinhardsbrunner Briefsammlung*, xvi–xvii. For some of the challenges of using twelfth-century letter collections in general, see Constable, *Letters and Letter-Collections*, 56–62.

28. *Die Reinhardsbrunner Briefsammlung*, 21–22, no. 22.

29. *Cronica Reinhardsbrunnensis*, 544.

that you would stay away from useless knightly games of arms during times of peace. Seduced by such games on numerous occasions, in the manner of a youth, you have met with danger to your life. You should preferably make your virtue and industry shine forth for the public affairs of the kingdom, as is fitting for a prince."[30] Although this is rather generic advice for a twelfth-century nobleman to give, it points to Ludwig II's concern that another of his brothers was not properly fulfilling his role as one of the preeminent lords in the kingdom.[31] As with the first letter, there is no evidence to suggest that this piece of correspondence resulted from—or led to—a serious dispute between the siblings. Nevertheless, both texts indicate that there were limits placed on a lord's ability to control the actions and behavior of his younger brothers.

The inability of any one brother to act as the head of the lineage, over and above his other brothers, manifested itself most clearly in cases of fraternal succession. Regardless of how well a nobleman had arranged for the distribution of his rights and properties among his sons, his plans could easily be thrown into disarray once the members of the next generation began to succumb to death. If any of a magnate's sons died without legitimate children of his own, his siblings became his heirs, and this reshuffling of the lineage's rights and properties could have a profound effect on the relationships among the surviving brothers. For the leading lineages of the Staufen period, such situations were further complicated by the fact that fraternal succession was viewed differently by German noble society than succession from father to son. When one of the *principes imperii* died without a son, his imperial fiefs reverted to the emperor rather than passing automatically to a surviving brother.[32] Because there was a strong tradition of familial domination of office holding by the mid-twelfth century, most of the Staufen rulers were not in a position to ignore entirely a brother's claim to a lordship.[33] Regardless, the lack of firm intrafamilial control over fraternal succession could occasionally test brothers' relationships.[34]

---

30. *Die Reinhardsbrunner Briefsammlung*, 57–58, no. 63. On the question of whether this letter is a forgery, I follow the lead of Patze, *Die Entstehung der Landesherrschaft*, 1:219.

31. Other letter collections preserve similar evidence for one brother's concern over another's behavior, but it is difficult to argue on the basis of any of this material that serious intragenerational strife was commonplace. See, for example, *Das Baumgartenberger Formelbuch*, 317–318, no. 18.

32. See chapter 1, and Hauser, *Staufische Lehnspolitik*, 288–291.

33. Hauser, *Staufische Lehnspolitik*, 304–311.

34. I will analyze several cases of fraternal succession in later chapters.

For sons born into the German upper aristocracy during the Staufen period, the tradition of partible inheritance laid the groundwork for many of the fraternal interactions they would have as adults. Fathers, as the ones who typically arranged the succession and inheritance for their children, divided their lands and rights in ways that saw multiple brothers succeed to lordships—or, at the very least, inherit large pieces of the patrimony. In most generations of the nine lineages under investigation here, there is little if any evidence for disputes erupting among these heirs. Instead, as I will demonstrate in subsequent chapters, brothers who remained in the secular sphere tended to cooperate effectively with each other both before and after their father's death. Overlapping territorial interests helped bind these siblings closely to one another when they were adults, giving many of them opportunities to work together to influence politics at the regional level and at the imperial court.

Sons, Brothers, and Church Careers

Succession and inheritance arrangements designed to give secular authority to more than one heir demonstrate that most magnates of the Staufen period preferred to keep several sons active in the world. As a result, very few members of the lineages examined here experienced long ecclesiastical careers. Within the generations of the upper aristocracy that form the foundation for this book, fewer than twenty-five churchmen can be identified in the extant sources.[35] Three lineages—the Staufens, Welfs, and Zähringens—each included only one churchman during the twelfth and early thirteenth centuries. There were greater numbers of ecclesiastics in some other princely lineages, but the ratio of churchmen to secular lords was low throughout the upper aristocracy. In the Ascanian lineage, for example, sixteen men exercised secular lordship during the Staufen period, while only three pursued careers in the church.[36] Many prominent noblemen of the kingdom therefore had

---

35. This is the number I have reached through my own research. It is probably too low. No scholarly consensus has emerged on the question of how frequently nobles used monasteries as places to hide sickly or disabled children. Religious communities with close affiliations to German princely lineages may have housed unwanted children who are never named in surviving documents. On this point, compare Bouchard, *Sword, Miter, and Cloister*, 62–63, and Reuter, "Nobles and Others," 116–117.

36. One of these three churchmen, the cathedral provost Johann of Halberstadt, is mentioned in Ascanian historiography but does not appear in the secondary literature on the chapter of Halberstadt. Compare Marcus, *Herzog Bernhard von Anhalt*, 170, with Meier, *Die Domkapitel*.

no brothers in the church. Moreover, while some generations of princely lineages had as many as five brothers all exercising secular lordship simultaneously, no generation contained more than two brothers who became ecclesiastics.

A century ago, the German historian Aloys Schulte observed on the basis of similar findings that the leading lineages of the kingdom included far fewer churchmen than the families of the middle and lower aristocracy.[37] In the late twentieth century, scholars drew comparable conclusions for other regions of western Europe, further strengthening the impression that the most prominent noble families tended not to dominate the hierarchy of the Latin church during the central Middle Ages.[38] Nobles with sufficient resources to support several heirs did not consider ecclesiastical careers to be attractive options for their sons. The small number of churchmen drawn from the German upper aristocracy of the Staufen period thus provides further evidence that the model of the noble lineage that emerged during the 1950s and 1960s—which presumes large numbers of unwanted and disinherited younger sons forced to join religious communities—is flawed.[39] Further complicating the traditional picture of the noble lineage, it is not clear in many cases whether those sons who were placed in the church were the youngest members of their generation.[40] There are instances in which elder sons joined the church while younger heirs remained in the secular sphere and succeeded to their father's lordships.

Because the German upper aristocracy lacked a tradition of placing large numbers of younger sons in the church, the uneven distribution of churchmen across lineages and generations suggests that most secular lords directed sons toward the ecclesiastical sphere for specific reasons. To understand why a nobleman might decide to begin a male child along an ecclesiastical path, it is necessary to take a closer look at the relationship between the German aristocracy and the German church. The century preceding the election of

37. Schulte, *Der Adel und die deutsche Kirche*, 279. See also Duggan, *Bishop and Chapter*, 46–50. As an example of a family just below the level of princely status, the lineage of the Swabian counts of Berg included one generation during the Staufen period in which four brothers became churchmen. See Eberl, "Die Grafen von Berg," 37–40.

38. Bouchard, *Sword, Miter, and Cloister*, 67–76; Crouch and de Trafford, "Forgotten Family," 47.

39. See, for example, Althoff, *Family, Friends and Followers*, 42–43; Freed, *Noble Bondsmen*, 124–126; and most famously, Duby, *Knight, Lady and Priest*, 104–105.

40. For more on this point, see below. This trend is not unique to German magnate families; see, for example, Lambert of Ardres, *Counts of Guines and Lords of Ardres*, 154–155.

the first Staufen king in 1138 was an era of rapid and intense change for the church throughout western Europe. As the papacy sought to free the ecclesiastical hierarchy from secular control, and as a wave of new religious orders appeared on the scene, many of the institutions of the Latin church entered a phase of reorganization and renewal.[41] The European aristocracy played a crucial role in promoting reform agendas during this period, founding and endowing monastic communities while also providing political and military support for the new generations of church leaders.[42]

Occasionally, the atmosphere of spiritual rejuvenation inspired members of German noble families to take more dramatic action as well. The brothers and counts Godfrey and Otto of Cappenberg laid down their arms in the early 1120s while they were still young men and joined the house of Premonstratensian canons they had founded on the site of their lineage's castle.[43] The story of a similar religious conversion is preserved in the Welf family chronicle known today as the *Historia Welforum*. According to this text, the youngest of the three sons of Duke Henry the Black of Bavaria, Conrad (d. 1126),

> after he was instructed at home during his childhood years in the study of letters, was ordained into clerical orders. He was entrusted at the age of maturity to the archbishop of Cologne to be educated in higher studies and monastic discipline. There, he progressed so much in both [fields]—while at the same time avoiding vices and greatly embellishing himself with other virtues—that he was loved by everyone, clergy and laity alike, and was judged worthy by all of the highest esteem. But he fled honors, wealth, and human praise and associated himself with certain monks, with whom he entered the monastery of Clairvaux without anyone else's knowledge. There, he became a monk. Later, after some time had passed, he went to Jerusalem, where he remained. He attached himself to a certain servant of God in a hermitage and administered all necessities to him in all humility.[44]

By the middle of the twelfth century, the sudden burst of religious zeal accompanying the reform movements of the late 1000s and early 1100s seems to have lost much of its energy within the German aristocracy. The bishop

41. Constable, *Reformation of the Twelfth Century*, 4–5.
42. Howe, "Reform of the Medieval Church."
43. Grundmann, *Der Cappenberger Barbarossakopf*, 17–26; Arnold, *Power and Property*, 163.
44. *Historia Welforum*, 54–57, chap. 15.

and chronicler Otto of Freising, who will be discussed in subsequent chapters, was one of the last males of a princely lineage to experience a dramatic
religious conversion during the period explored here—and he died in 1158.
Throughout the late twelfth and early thirteenth centuries, neither lay nor
clerical members of the noble elite were attracted to the most austere forms
of the religious life. Instead, churchmen who had been born into the leading
lineages of the German kingdom tended to pursue ecclesiastical careers that
kept them in close contact with their secular relatives. In this respect, these
ecclesiastics were following in the footsteps of the many nobles who had
joined the German church during the Ottonian and early Salian periods—
before the reform movements had inspired some sons to distance themselves
from their families.[45]

During their earliest years in the church, most of the ecclesiastics examined here maintained various connections to their siblings. Only one legitimate male from these nine lineages was placed in a monastery as a child
oblate, never to be seen again in familial settings.[46] Instead, many continued
to be tied to their fathers' households during their youths. According to
the *Historia Welforum,* the aforementioned Conrad was initially educated
at home, and this story may be indicative of a broader trend. The surviving
charter evidence frequently fails to distinguish between young sons who
would succeed to lordships and those who would become churchmen. For
example, on September 13, 1155, Margrave Albert the Bear of Brandenburg,
his wife, and six of his sons were present when the archbishop of Magdeburg consecrated a church.[47] The listing of Albert's sons—"Otto, Herman,
Siegfried, Henry, Adalbert, Dietrich"—suggests that Siegfried and Henry,
who would later have long careers in the church, remained fully integrated
members of their nuclear family. The order in which the sons are named may
also be an indication that they were not the youngest and were not destined
from birth to become ecclesiastics. A charter concerning the Wettin lineage
provides similar evidence for sons before they entered the church.[48] On
September 13, 1159, Count Dedo of Groitzsch sold a piece of property to a
monastery in Magdeburg with the consent of his sons Dietrich and Philip.
Both of these brothers would later become churchmen, yet they were almost

---

45. Reuter, "'Imperial Church System,'" 330–333.
46. MHDC, 3:330–331, no. 847; Deuer, "Abt Heinrich."
47. CDA, 1, pt. 2:301–302, no. 412. Henry would be named again in a charter in 1157 without
any indication he was an ecclesiastic: CDA, 1, pt. 2:322–323, no. 441.
48. CDS 1 A, 2:198, no. 290.

certainly Dedo's eldest heirs; none of their other brothers would be named in a charter for another fifteen years.[49]

The *Historia Welforum* reports that the young Conrad from the Welf lineage, after his initial education at home, began his formal ecclesiastical training once he attained the age of majority. Only then did he travel to Cologne to receive a rigorous education under the direction of the archbishop. This career trajectory seems to have been typical for churchmen from the upper aristocracy more generally. In the German kingdom, cathedral schools—including the one at Cologne—remained the main centers of clerical education throughout the twelfth and early thirteenth centuries.[50] Overall, only fifteen German bishops are known to have studied at Paris during the 1100s.[51] Among the churchmen being considered here, fewer than five traveled abroad for their educations. One was Conrad of Wittelsbach (d. 1200), a son of Count-Palatine Otto I of Bavaria. His university training is briefly described in a letter Peter of Blois wrote to him during the early 1190s, in which Peter recalls fondly their time studying together under the same teacher.[52] However, another letter suggests that Conrad spent most of his early life much closer to the Wittelsbachs' Bavarian lordships: when Frederick Barbarossa's chancery announced Conrad's elevation to the archbishopric of Salzburg in 1177, it described him as being raised (*enutritus*) in the church at Salzburg.[53] Long periods spent studying abroad—thoroughly disconnected from their close relatives—seem to have been very rare for churchmen from the upper aristocracy.

Most ecclesiastics from princely lineages used their educations in cathedral schools as a first step toward attaining positions as cathedral canons, frequently in the same diocese where they were schooled.[54] The office of cathedral canon was therefore crucial in shaping the careers of many of the ecclesiastics investigated here. The term "canon" (*canonicus*) had a broad range of meanings in the central Middle Ages and encompassed a wide variety of different roles within the church. In general, however, canons can be contrasted with monks, for most types of canons were neither cloistered nor

---

49. CDS 1 A, 2:280–281, no. 404. Dedo's son Philip maintained few if any contacts with his siblings during his brief career as provost of Xanten: see Pätzold, *Die frühen Wettiner*, 291–292. For Dietrich, see below.

50. Barrow, "Education and Recruitment of Canons," 120.

51. Ehlers, "Deutsche Scholaren in Frankreich," 114.

52. Mainzer UB 2, pt. 2:945, no. 573.

53. MGH DD F I, 3:214–216, no. 693. See also Burkhardt, *Mit Stab und Schwert*, 39–40.

54. Barrow, "Education and Recruitment of Canons," 123.

bound by strict rules.[55] Moreover, canons typically played a much more direct and active role ministering to the laity than monks ever did.[56] Originally, cathedral canons had been tasked with fulfilling many of the day-to-day roles that other priests also fulfilled within the diocese, including the celebration of the liturgy. By the twelfth century, however, the administration of the chapter's economic interests came to eclipse this earlier function.[57] The cathedral provost, as the head of the chapter, emerged as the most important figure in overseeing the community's lands and wealth, but other cathedral canons also came to exercise significant influence over diocesan affairs—including the election of new bishops.[58]

Three aspects of the office of cathedral canon are important to highlight here, because they shaped the types of roles churchmen could play within their sibling groups. First, most canons from princely lineages tended to belong to cathedral chapters that had close connections to their lineage's secular lordships.[59] For example, Dietrich, the son of the Wettin count Dedo of Groitzsch, initially joined the cathedral chapter at Naumburg—for which his father was the advocate—and later became a canon at Magdeburg, where his lineage had long been interested in establishing a stronger presence.[60] Margrave Albert the Bear's two sons Henry and Siegfried also became canons at nearby Magdeburg. Henry appears with the title "canon of the church of Saint Maurice at Magdeburg" alongside his five secular brothers in one of his father's charters from 1160—evidence for ongoing ties to his lineage after he entered the chapter.[61] Otto of Andechs is first identified as a canon in the cathedral chapter of Bamberg in the year 1164, in a charter that also lists his brother, Count Berthold II of Andechs, as a witness. Since Berthold was the most prominent landholder in the eastern part of the diocese of Bamberg, his appearance in this document may be an indication that he helped Otto obtain this office.[62] Regardless, males of the upper aristocracy who joined cathedral chapters typically did not travel far from familial centers of lordship.

---

55. Lynch, *Medieval Church*, 209–210; Constable, *Reformation of the Twelfth Century*, 11, 233–234; Moraw, "Typologie, Chronologie und Geographie der Stiftskirche."

56. Southern, *Western Society and the Church*, 248.

57. Duggan, *Bishop and Chapter*, 44–46.

58. Barrow, "Cathedrals, Provosts and Prebends," 538–552.

59. For similar points, see Barrow, "Education and Recruitment of Canons," 120–122; Bouchard, *Sword, Miter, and Cloister*, 50.

60. CDS 1 A, 2:249–250, no. 360. See also Pätzold, *Die frühen Wettiner*, 111–113.

61. CDA, 1, pt. 2:333, no. 456.

62. *Die Traditionen des Klosters Asbach*, 87–89, no. 4. See also Frenken, "Hausmachtpolitik und Bischofsstuhl," 725–726.

Second, cathedral canons in the German kingdom could inherit property.[63] As a result, these ecclesiastics frequently remained linked to their siblings through overlapping rights and neighboring territorial interests. They
appear as consenters in close relatives' property arrangements, and they also
had property of their own that they could sell or donate with the approval
of their nearest kin. Otto of Andechs, for example, remained an heir to his
father's patrimony even after becoming bishop of Bamberg. In 1182, he
made a series of gifts to his parents' religious foundation at Diessen, including
a church he possessed "by hereditary right" (*hereditario iure*).[64] His nephew
Poppo of Andechs (d. 1245), a cathedral canon at Bamberg who later became cathedral provost and bishop-elect, also appears in a variety of sources
in his role as an heir to his father, Margrave Berthold II of Istria. Soon after
Berthold II's death in 1188, Poppo and his older half brother, Berthold III,
made a joint property donation to a local monastery for the salvation of their
father's soul.[65] In an 1192 treaty concerning marriages between Andechs
ministerials and the ministerials of the cathedral church of Bamberg, Poppo
is named alongside Berthold III as one of the parties to the treaty—in his role
as an Andechs heir, not as a Bamberg cathedral canon.[66] And in 1231, more
than forty years after he joined the cathedral chapter, he made a property
donation to the church at Bamberg "for the salvation of my soul and also
the soul of my father, who with paternal affection made me a beloved heir
to his patrimony."[67] Poppo's career thus provides some of the best surviving
evidence for just how deeply enmeshed a cathedral canon could be in his
lineage's territorial interests throughout his lifetime.

Third, cathedral canons could leave the church with relative ease and rejoin the laity. Emperor Frederick I Barbarossa's son Philip, who was a canon
and bishop-elect before eventually becoming German king in 1198, is one
of the best-known examples.[68] The aforementioned Dietrich, son of Count
Dedo of Groitzsch, abandoned his position as a canon under especially dramatic circumstances. According to the *Chronicon Montis Sereni*, "[Dietrich],
at the time when he was a canon in the church of Magdeburg, had been

---

63. Barrow, "Cathedrals, Provosts and Prebends," 549.

64. *Die Traditionen des Stiftes Diessen*, 36–38, no. 27.

65. MB, 25:108, no. 6.

66. *Die Traditionen des Stiftes Diessen*, 109–112, no. 6.

67. Bamberg, Staatsarchiv, Bamberger Urkunden no. 551; Herrmann, "Zur Stadtentwicklung
in Nordbayern," 76.

68. See chapter 5.

promoted to the rank of subdeacon. However, it so happened while he was in school in Paris that a dispute arose between the townspeople and the clerics. His servants, whom he sent to help the clerics, committed a murder. It is said (*dicitur*) that on account of this, despairing over his further advancement, he cast aside his clerical status."[69] These events must have occurred during the 1180s, because after his father died in 1190, Dietrich immediately began to appear in sources as a layman—and as the holder of one of his father's lordships. Viewed from this perspective, the author's inclusion of *dicitur* is interesting; he may be suggesting that he knew an alternative version to this story, one in which Dietrich set aside his clerical status because he *wanted* to succeed his father.[70] Even if the chronicler, himself a churchman, thought he needed to give Dietrich a better justification for leaving the church, rejoining the secular sphere for reasons of succession and inheritance was nonetheless a commonplace practice. Another canon who left the church and later became an important secular lord within his family was the Ludowing Frederick (d. after 1209), the younger brother of Landgrave Ludwig III of Thuringia. He is identified in an 1171 document as the provost of a house of canons at Mainz, but by 1186 at the latest, he had married the heiress to the county of Ziegenhain in Hesse.[71]

These three features of the office of cathedral canon help explain why noblemen who joined cathedral chapters were able to maintain close connections to their relatives who controlled their lineages' secular lordships. Interactions with parents and siblings continued uninterrupted in many cases because canons never isolated themselves from the lay world in any significant way. For churchmen from princely lineages, the position of cathedral canon could be important for another reason as well. The office was frequently a stepping stone for ecclesiastics of high noble birth to a position as bishop somewhere in the German kingdom—oftentimes the same cathedral. Since the canonical age for attaining the episcopal office was thirty, ecclesiastics typically became bishops after their fathers had died and their brothers had succeeded as the lineage's secular lords. As a result, I will argue in subsequent chapters that many of these bishops were able to play prominent

---

69. *Chronicon Montis Sereni*, 204–205.

70. For more on this point, see chapter 3.

71. Mainzer UB 2, pt. 1:573–574, no. 338; Weller, *Die Heiratspolitik des deutschen Hochadels*, 615–616. In one of his brother Ludwig III's charters from 1178, he is named in the witness list without any title, an indication that he may have already relinquished his position as canon by this time: see CDS 1 A, 2:296–297, no. 428.

roles in shaping the political and territorial interests of the other members of their sibling groups.

Daughters and Sisters

Because the leading lords of the German upper aristocracy did not seek to separate any of their legitimate sons from their birth families, almost all the males of the lineages under investigation here maintained connections to at least some of their siblings throughout their adult lives. The same cannot be said for the women born into these lineages, whose ties to the other members of their generation tended to be much more sporadic. Indeed, significantly less evidence survives for sororal interactions than fraternal ones within the princely lineages of the Staufen period. Nineteenth-century historians of the medieval German aristocracy explained this discrepancy by assuming that women were excluded from their birth families once they married or joined a religious community.[72] In the second half of the twentieth century, scholarship started to nuance this view, but the study of noblewomen's sibling relationships remains in its initial stages.[73] Historical approaches to the sororal bond have only begun to garner sustained interest during the last two decades.[74] New research is just starting to demonstrate that analyzing the category of sister can provide a different perspective on women's roles in their families than the categories of wife, mother, and daughter—all of which have been examined in greater detail by historians.

Although scholars no longer accept the idea that women were excluded from their birth families once they married or entered a convent, any attempt to study noblewomen's sibling relationships during the Staufen period must nevertheless contend with the problem of a lack of sources. A comparison with the men born into the nine lineages examined here is revealing. As noted above, the twelfth-century aristocracy did not produce sources that clearly outlined the division of a patrimony. Nevertheless, succession and inheritance in the male line can frequently be reconstructed on the basis of a wide variety of sources, and in most generations of these lineages, it

---

72. For an especially blunt statement of this position, see Oefele, *Geschichte der Grafen von Andechs*, foreword. More generally, see Weinhold, *Die deutschen Frauen*, 1:297–298.

73. See, for example, Griffiths, "Siblings and the Sexes." Discussions of sororal relationships are more common for the later Middle Ages: Spieß, *Familie und Verwandtschaft*, 483–485; Bastress-Dukehart, "Sibling Conflict"; Nolte, *Familie, Hof und Herrschaft*, 276–290.

74. Davidoff, "Kinship as a Categorical Concept"; Pollock, "Rethinking Patriarchy"; Glover, *All Our Relations*; Miller and Yavneh, "Thicker than Water."

is possible to reconstruct—at least partially—the distribution of property among sons. For daughters, on the other hand, comparable evidence is much harder to find.

A text concerning Count Berthold I of Andechs's daughter Mechthild (d. 1160) provides an unusually detailed discussion of women's property rights in the German kingdom during the Staufen period. According to a section of Mechthild's vita that was most likely written in the early thirteenth century, she had a conversation with her parents about their failure to provide an entrance gift when she joined the community of Augustinian canonesses at Diessen:

> Turning to her parents, her father Berthold and her mother Sophia, the blessed Mechthild said in a calm voice before everyone, "O father, remember that you sent me as a young girl into this church. . . . Now, my father, if you had betrothed me to a mortal man, you would have given to him a part of your property as my dowry, would you not? And thereafter, he would have considered himself to be more than just a son-in-law; he would have assumed himself to be an heir to all your property, would he not? But in truth, because the King of Kings and Lord of Lords Jesus Christ chose me, your daughter, to be his wife, you resolved never to give any marriage gifts to my sweet Husband— your Creator, Redeemer, and Savior—for me and for your soul. . . . Therefore, most beloved father, give to my immortal Husband—not from what is yours but from what is His—that which He chose for Himself at the creation of the world. I say, I beseech, give as a marriage gift to me and thus justly and fitly to my Husband who is making the request, a tenth of the revenue from the property that you are recognized as possessing in the region near the Isar River, within the limits of Oberding [in Bavaria]." Her father, having understood the petition of his beloved daughter and bride of Christ, consulted with his relatives. Joyfully and affectionately fulfilling the petition, he then said, "O daughter, compared to every other kin connection, yours is the most dear to me. Because of my love for you, I confer to this church of Saint Mary in Diessen a tenth of the revenue from my property in the region near the Isar River, within the limits of Oberding."[75]

Although this passage reflects the interests of the religious community at Diessen more than the interests of Mechthild's family—indeed, there is no

---

75. Engelhard of Langheim, *Vita Mechtildis*, 445–446, chap. 21.

reason to think this conversation ever actually took place—it nevertheless points to the strong tradition of partible inheritance in German noble society. All daughters ought to receive a share of the patrimony, whether in the form of a dowry or an entrance gift.[76]

Finding evidence in other sources to support this passage, which is buried in the vita of an obscure canoness and abbess who was never canonized, is surprisingly difficult. Charters, an essential body of evidence for reconstructing which pieces of the patrimony the males of a lineage acquired, rarely reference women in their roles as daughters or sisters. One reason for the silence of these archival sources is that German noblewomen typically did not serve as witnesses during the central Middle Ages.[77] Their legal status was more akin to that of underage children than that of their adult brothers, limiting their opportunities to be named alongside their male siblings in witness lists, even when family property was concerned.[78] Historians who have analyzed extant charters from medieval France have frequently noted that sisters make appearances with their brothers in these documents in other roles, as cograntors or as consenters in family property arrangements.[79] Among German princely families, however, this was clearly not standard practice.

For example, only two authentic archival sources dating to the twelfth century name women born into the Babenberg family with any of their siblings. In the late 1120s or early 1130s, Margrave Leopold III of Austria, his son Leopold IV, and his daughter Bertha made a joint donation to a religious community for the salvation of their souls.[80] Three decades later, on April 22, 1161, Duke Henry Jasomirgott of Austria drew up a charter of privileges for one of his monastic foundations, and all three of his children—his two sons and his daughter, Agnes—consented.[81] In both cases, these noblewomen acted together with their brothers while they were all still young and unmarried.[82] Bertha and Agnes remained linked to their fathers' households during their earliest years but then apparently severed ties after they married and their fathers died.

---

76. For a similar point, see Spieß, *Familie und Verwandtschaft*, 327–337.

77. Freed, *Noble Bondsmen*, 115. The situation in England during the same period was noticeably different; see Johns, *Noblewomen, Aristocracy and Power*, 81–98.

78. See more generally van Houts, "Gender and Authority."

79. See, for example, White, *Custom, Kinship, and Gifts*, 96–97; Livingstone, "Aristocratic Women in the Chartrain," 52; Gold, *Lady and Virgin*, 123–124.

80. BUB, 4, pt. 1:66, no. 642.

81. Ibid., 1:42–44, no. 29.

82. For their marriages, see Weller, *Die Heiratspolitik des deutschen Hochadels*, 363–364, 380.

A later text concerning the Andechs lineage does hint at an adult woman's claims to a piece of her father's patrimony, but the source is unfortunately too vague to be the basis for broader conclusions about sisters' roles in inheritance arrangements. On February 6, 1202, Duke Berthold III of Merania and his two oldest sons were at Udine in northeastern Italy in the residence of the patriarch of Aquileia. There, an imperial notary drew up a charter recording a loan of one thousand marks that the patriarch agreed to give to the duke. As collateral, Berthold III and his two sons offered a series of properties in nearby Carniola. However, according to the charter, "because there was an inheritance dispute between the duke and his sister concerning a quarter part of those possessions," Berthold III and his heirs also agreed to provide other properties instead should the unnamed sister's claims prove to be legitimate.[83] While the language of the text is striking, little is known about the sibling relationship at the heart of this passage. The duke of Merania had four sisters—all of whom may still have been alive in 1202—and the loan agreement is the only surviving reference to this dispute over the inheritance.

Archival sources for other lineages typically reveal even less about female members' stakes in the division of a family's property.[84] Noblewomen begin to appear more frequently in charters only after they are married—and then only as cograntors or consenters alongside their husbands, not as members of their birth families.[85] This lack of archival evidence for sororal ties is problematic, because charters are the most quotidian of the extant sources for the upper aristocracy. As the texts that offer the clearest glimpses of family members coming together in different settings to protect and promote their own interests, charters tend to provide the best evidence for those moments when brothers met to discuss many different kinds of family business. Without comparable source material for sisters, it is difficult to determine whether noblewomen ever joined any of their siblings at the imperial court, at regional meetings of magnates, or even at family gatherings.

Yet the silence of the charters cannot by itself be read as evidence that sororal interactions were so very different from fraternal interactions. Another

83. *Urkunden- und Regestenbuch des Herzogtums Krain*, 2:5–6, no. 7. The reference to a "quarter part" is noteworthy: compare Rady, "Filial Quarter and Female Inheritance."
84. For some exceptions to this general pattern, see MB, 2:189–190, no. 9; Bamberg, Staatsarchiv, Bamberger Urkunden no. 515; CDS 1 A, 3:181–182, no. 249; *Die Urkunden und Urbare des Klosters Schäftlarn*, 14–15, no. 9; *Die Traditionen des Klosters Neustift*, 90–92, no. 16.
85. For women's property rights more generally, see White, *Custom, Kinship, and Gifts*, 105–106; Herlihy, "Land, Family and Women," 101–102; Bumke, *Courtly Culture*, 348.

consideration is geography. Most upper aristocratic women married and became separated from their birth families by long distances.[86] German magnates typically needed to look outside the regions where they exercised lordship to find marital partners of equal or higher social standing for daughters and sisters—and to avoid the church's prohibitions against consanguineous marriages.[87] In some cases, these noblewomen were even matched with prominent lords from beyond the borders of the German kingdom. Hungary, France, Denmark, and Poland are only a few of the places where the daughters and sisters of German princes were sent during the Staufen period. Inside the kingdom, it was not unusual for families at opposite ends of the kingdom to arrange marriages with one another. There are numerous examples of members of the Wittelsbach, Babenberg, and Andechs lineages of the south marrying members of the Ludowing, Wettin, and Ascanian lineages of the north during the late twelfth and early thirteenth centuries.

Most noblewomen who married distant lords vanish from the extant sources for their birth families. Indeed, within the nine lineages under investigation here, fewer than a dozen married women can be closely tied to any of their siblings during their adult lives. This is a small number, approximately twenty percent of the total number of women from these lineages who married during the Staufen period. Geographical distance clearly had a role to play in this figure. Moreover, while sons intended for the church seem to have been raised at or near home and sent to cathedral schools close to family lordships, noble girls were sometimes separated from their birth families at a young age in order to be raised at the court of their betrothed's parents.[88] In such cases, noblewomen may not have had the opportunity to establish close connections to any of their siblings—even as children.

A source from west of the Rhine, concerning a princely lineage not examined here, indicates that there were occasional exceptions to this general pattern. According to the chronicler Gilbert of Mons, Count Baldwin IV of Hainaut (d. 1171), whose lands lay in the frontier region between the German and French kingdoms, was willing to travel well beyond his lands to support one of his sisters. Gilbert writes, "Count Baldwin of Hainaut, hearing

---

86. Schulte (*Der Adel und die deutsche Kirche*, 274–280) concluded that 73.8% of upper aristocratic women married, though he admitted that the sources allowed no definitive conclusions.

87. Bouchard, *"Those of My Blood,"* 39–58.

88. For some examples of this, see chapter 6. In most cases, it is difficult to determine how old a noblewoman was when she left home for her betrothal or marriage.

that his sister who was married at Tosny had been oppressed gravely by certain powerful men who were her neighbors, did not fear to hasten to assist her with three hundred knights. Having sought neither permission nor an escort, he safely crossed through France and exacted very severe vengeance on his sister's enemies. Having left her in a good peace and a good state, he returned to his own lands."[89] Since Gilbert worked at the court of Baldwin IV's son, he may well have embellished elements of this story.[90] Nevertheless, this account suggests that Count Baldwin IV had some knowledge of what was occurring at his sister's new home far from Hainaut—and that he was willing to intercede on her behalf.

By contrast, within the nine lineages investigated here, noblewomen who married closer to home appear with their brothers in the extant sources much more frequently. When a prominent lord arranged to marry a daughter or sister into a neighboring noble lineage, he was—intentionally or unintentionally—creating more opportunities for this noblewoman to collaborate with her brothers at different moments during their lives.[91] In 1177, for example, the provost of Raitenbuch in Bavaria wrote a letter to Countess Matilda of Sulzbach (d. 1183) concerning her brother Welf VI (d. 1191). The provost writes,

> You know, most loving lady, how strenuously and how faithfully I have exerted myself in the service of your brother for these many years, how I have endured the most severe threats from the emperor in return for serving him. . . . Now that favor [I have shown by] my labors and my service is rewarded in such a way that he has not only risen up against me in grave anger but has also encouraged my servants to oppose me. . . . We have said all of these things, which had to be set forth to your reverence starkly and openly for this reason, in order that you might send letters or messengers and restrain his spirit. Because you draw your descent from that house and derive from the blood of the Welfs (*sanguine Catulorum*), you ought to censure and rebuke your brother with much boldness if he departs from paternal virtue and if he inflicts abuse on me or any of his followers for faithful service. . . . How great the harmony of fraternal affection (*fraterne*

---

89. Gilbert of Mons, *La chronique de Gislebert de Mons*, 71–72, chap. 38.

90. See the translator's note: Gilbert of Mons, *Chronicle of Hainaut*, 42, n. 186.

91. For some of the factors that could influence aristocratic marriage arrangements, see Spieß, *Familie und Verwandtschaft*, 36–82.

dilectionis concordia) has always been between you and him, and how constant and devoted he has always been to you, I have on the best authority.[92]

The provost's request that Matilda intervene on his behalf with Welf VI is not unusual, considering that queens and noblewomen frequently acted as intercessors at the courts of kings and noble lords in the medieval German kingdom.[93] Nevertheless, the language of this letter is striking. Was a sister really in a position to "censure and rebuke" one of the leading princes in the kingdom? In Matilda's case, this seems plausible. She had not traveled far from family centers of lordship during her lifetime. Both her marriages were to prominent Bavarian lords, and her brother Welf VI spent much of his later career on his own Bavarian lands.[94] The provost of Raitenbuch, himself deeply enmeshed in Bavarian affairs, suggests in his letter to Matilda that he knew the siblings had a close relationship, and there is no reason to doubt that he expected his letter to find a willing audience.

Noblewomen who married closer to home also had more occasions to interact with their siblings after their husbands died. Indeed, some of the best evidence for sisters playing active roles in their sibling groups concerns widows. For medieval historians, this will come as no surprise; recent research has consistently demonstrated that women frequently had the most influence and independence in society after their husbands died.[95] The chronicle known today as the *Historia Welforum* includes a story about two of Welf VI and Countess Matilda's siblings, the widow Sophia and her brother Duke Henry the Proud of Bavaria (d. 1139). According to this text, the duke began to besiege one of the castles of the bishop of Regensburg in or around the year 1130: "While these things were happening in Bavaria, the emperor [Lothar III] was besieging Speyer, a city on the Rhine, to the injury of Duke Frederick [II of Swabia]. The emperor sent a messenger to Duke Henry [the Proud] and asked him to come as quickly as possible to his aid. Without any hesitation, [Henry] entrusted the siege and all other matters to his widowed sister Margravine Sophia, who had arrived at that time with eight hundred armored warriors, and hastened to the emperor with more than six hundred

---

92. *Die Tegernseer Briefsammlung*, 106–108, no. 80.
93. Fichtenau, *Living in the Tenth Century*, 176.
94. Schneidmüller, *Die Welfen*, 159, 201–203.
95. See, for example, Rogge, "Nur verkaufte Töchter?" 242; Freed, *Noble Bondsmen*, 157; Evergates, *Aristocracy in the County of Champagne*, 96–99; Drell, *Kinship and Conquest*, 103–106.

knights."[96] Where did Sophia find eight hundred warriors who were willing to support her brother's military pursuits? This campaign occurred soon
after the death of her husband, Margrave Leopold of Styria (d. 1129), when
she was serving as regent for their underage son. She was therefore in a position of power and authority in Styria and was able to use this position for
the benefit of her nearby sibling, the Bavarian duke. Thus, for at least a few
married women and widows, the sibling bond could occasionally emerge as
a meaningful connection in their lives.

For women who joined religious communities, evidence for close sibling
relationships is also difficult to find. However, the reasons for this lack of
sources are different from those for their married sisters. Most significantly,
far fewer women from the upper aristocracy joined religious communities than married. Indeed, in four of the nine lineages under investigation
here, there is no evidence for any legitimate daughters or sisters entering the
church during the Staufen period.[97] Those women who did join religious
communities tended to do so as young children and never appear in the
extant sources in any other context but that of the spiritual life.[98] None of
this means, however, that these female members of the upper aristocracy
completely severed ties to their siblings. Recent work on aristocratic nuns
suggests that some of these women maintained connections to at least some
of their brothers and sisters.[99]

Abbess Hildegard of Bingen (d. 1179), in one of her many letters, made
it clear that noble status remained operative behind the closed doors of the
convent. When the head of a community of canonesses criticized Hildegard for accepting only noblewomen into the convent at Bingen, Hildegard
was quick to defend herself, noting that people of higher and lower status
should not mix since God is the one who created separate ranks on earth.[100]
Because this view was a common one during the Staufen period, noblewomen born into the princely lineages of the German kingdom tended to
be placed in a limited number of prestigious convents. In some cases, these
female religious communities had been founded and endowed by a secular

96. *Historia Welforum*, 58–59, chap. 17. See also Leyser, "German Aristocracy," 51; Elpers, "*Während sie die Markgrafschaft leitete*," 162–164.

97. The small number may also reflect a lack of source material for these women since many simply vanish from family sources: Schlütter-Schindler, "Wittelsbacherinnen," 371–373.

98. Compare ibid., 403; Spieß, *Familie und Verwandtschaft*, 372; Thomson, "Place of Germany," 28–32; and Venarde, *Women's Monasticism*, 100–101.

99. Griffiths, "Siblings and the Sexes"; Kleinjung, "Geistliche Töchter."

100. Hildegard of Bingen, *Epistolarium*, 127–130, no. 52r.

lord and his heirs specifically to house daughters, sisters, and other close female relatives.[101] The convent at Gerbstedt in Saxony, for example, was a foundation with longstanding ties to the Wettin lineage, and several women from the lineage joined the community during the twelfth and early thirteenth centuries.[102]

This tendency to place daughters and sisters into family foundations or other especially illustrious convents had two significant effects on these women's sibling relationships. First, many female members of the upper aristocracy entered religious communities located close to their lineage's centers of lordship.[103] Unlike some of their sisters who married distant noblemen, women destined for the church were typically not sent hundreds of miles away from all their siblings when they were young children or teenagers. As a result, they had more opportunities to interact with those brothers and sisters who also remained linked to the family's homeland. Second, these women frequently joined religious communities where one or more of their sisters were also residents. A source from the convent of Lippoldsberg in Hesse provides some of the best archival evidence for this kind of sibling relationship. According to a short charter written in the year 1198,

> Let it be known to everyone reading this both in the present and in a future age that in the convent of Lippoldsberg, whose church is dedicated to Saint George, there are two sisters in the flesh (*sorores carnales*), Mechthild and Gisela. With the permission of their provost F., they procured so much from their mother and their brother and their friends and relatives that a mill was built in Eilwardshausen. [This was done] in such a way and by such agreement that any profit coming from that place . . . may belong to them while they are living, for the purpose of supplementing their clothing. [This was done] because our place is situated in such a way that we are not wanting in anything. When they die, the profits are to remain with the community in perpetuity.[104]

This charter provides clear evidence for a pair of sisters living in the same convent and having overlapping interests, in this case in the profits from a

---

101. Griffiths, "Siblings and the Sexes," 39, 45.
102. Pätzold, *Die frühen Wettiner*, 186.
103. Ibid., 181–187.
104. Marburg, Hessisches Staatsarchiv, Urk. A II Kl. Lippoldsberg 1198. For this convent, see Hotchin, "Women's Reading and Monastic Reform," 143–149.

mill. It also shows that these sisters were able to maintain contacts with family members and friends who wanted them to enjoy a privileged status inside the convent.

During the Staufen period, noblewomen who joined religious communities also had other kinds of links to siblings outside the walls of their convent. Brothers and sisters sometimes played a role in nuns and canonesses moving from one house to another—when, for example, a new community was founded and needed to be populated by experienced religious.[105] Thus, in the early 1140s, Landgrave Ludwig II of Thuringia sent a letter to the abbess of Drübeck, writing, "I beg, ask, and pray that you be willing to send my sister [Adelheid] to me. We are looking to house her among other women at our manor, which is called Bonnrode, on account of the protective nature of that place."[106] Soon thereafter, a convent was established at Bonnrode, and in the later twelfth century, Adelheid became the abbess of another female community with close ties to her Ludowing family.[107] Countess Gisela of Berg, daughter of Count Berthold I of Andechs, may have played a similar role in arranging for her sister Mechthild, the aforementioned Diessen canoness, to become abbess of the Swabian convent of Edelstetten in the mid-1150s.[108]

Both these cases of religious women transferring from one community to another culminated in their becoming abbesses of new houses. Within the magnate families of the Staufen period, however, sisters who rose to become abbesses are rare, in part because so few female members of these families were ever placed in religious communities. The number of abbesses from the nine families I am examining here is roughly equivalent to the number of bishops from these families.[109] This comparison is deceptive, however, because the evidence for most abbesses' sibling relationships is significantly thinner than the evidence for bishops' intragenerational bonds. As a result, much less is known about these abbesses' interactions with their brothers and sisters. Abbess Sophia of Gernrode from the Ascanians is one of the best-documented religious women from any of these nine lineages. In 1221, she was present alongside her mother and her brother, Count Henry of

---

105. For a detailed example of this phenomenon, see chapter 6.

106. *Die Reinhardsbrunner Briefsammlung,* 24–25, no. 25.

107. Patze, *Die Entstehung der Landesherrschaft,* 1:381.

108. Seitz, "Zur Person der Gisela." For an additional example, see Wiethaus, "Medieval Women's Friendships," 105–110.

109. For an excellent discussion of an abbess from a slightly lower level of the aristocracy, see Zunker, "Familie, Herrschaft, Reich."

Anhalt, in the castle of Quedlinburg for a gathering of regional notables.[110] Two years later, Count Henry confirmed a property agreement between his sister Sophia and one of his ministerials. According to this charter, the count, "valuing highly the favorable condition and honor of the church [at Gernrode] and desiring to extend fraternal affection to our sister (*nostre sorori fraternum affectum impendere cupientes*), renounced every claim on these properties."[111] For the German upper aristocracy of the Staufen period, this is one of the few surviving charters that points to a close connection between a leading magnate and his sister in the church.[112]

Within the princely lineages examined here, lords made no effort to give their undivided patrimonies to a single heir.[113] Instead, succession and inheritance arrangements were designed to provide support for all sons and daughters. As a result, multiple children were bound throughout their lifetimes to their parents' political and territorial legacies. Even sons who entered the church as cathedral canons, and daughters who married local lords or joined local convents, had numerous reasons to maintain ties to their siblings. Thus, while partible inheritance may have had the effect of fragmenting the patrimony in the long term, it nevertheless ensured that brothers—and occasionally some of their sisters as well—would possess overlapping interests in the short term. Sibling interactions therefore remained a central feature of noble family life throughout the twelfth and thirteenth centuries. As I will show in the next chapter, these overlapping interests became the basis for especially durable—and politically efficacious—relationships in the first generation of the upper aristocracy of the Staufen period.

---

110. CDA, 2:47, no. 56.

111. CDA, 2:53–54, no. 65.

112. Here, we see a clear contrast with the earlier situation inside the German kingdom, particularly the duchy of Saxony, during the Ottonian period, when abbesses were oftentimes significant figures from either the royal family or from upper aristocratic families. See Leyser, *Rule and Conflict*, 63–73.

113. Compare the somewhat more negative assessments of the effects of partible inheritance in Spieß, *Familie und Verwandtschaft*, 272–273, and Arnold, *Princes and Territories*, 245.

✍ CHAPTER 3

Baby Boomers

The First Generation of the Staufen Upper Aristocracy

The generation of young nobles who first began to appear in the surviving sources during the 1130s and 1140s included many lords who would dominate the political scene in the German kingdom throughout the later twelfth century. Because their fathers or grandfathers had been the noblemen who had most benefited from the upheaval that accompanied the Investiture Controversy, one of the defining characteristics of this generation was abundance—not only of lands and rights but also of siblings. Numerous brothers in the nine lineages under investigation here were able to succeed to lordships and to receive substantial pieces of their father's patrimony. This generation also saw more of its members become cathedral canons and bishops than any other generation of the Staufen upper aristocracy. As a result, siblings were seemingly ubiquitous during the middle decades of the twelfth century.

In this chapter, I will focus on the sets of brothers active within five lineages and will examine the diverse array of sources that provide insights into their fraternal interactions. From the five Wettin brothers who succeeded to secular lordships, to the three Wittelsbach brothers who all used the same title, to the Babenberg bishop Otto of Freising and his brothers, the members of these lineages demonstrate some of the ways that fraternal relationships shaped the political and territorial interests of the German upper aristocracy. At the regional level, many of these siblings collaborated to support the same monastic foundations and to expand their lordships at the expense of rival nobles and prelates. Meanwhile, at the imperial court, princely brothers routinely cooperated with one another to gain rights and privileges from the emperor's hand—and to demonstrate their lineage's loyalty to the ruler by supporting his military campaigns north and south of the Alps.

The Five Sons of Conrad of Wettin

Conrad of Wettin (d. 1157), one of the founders of the nine lineages examined here, was born in 1098–1099. By the late 1110s, he was already active in imperial politics, and he soon came to control an impressive network of rights and properties across eastern Saxony. These included alodial lands from the inheritances of his father, brother, and childless cousin; comital rights in the region around the castle of Wettin; the advocacy over the cathedral church of Naumburg; and multiple monastic advocacies.[1] In 1123, he also received the march of Meissen from Duke Lothar of Saxony, and thirteen years later Lothar, now emperor, granted him the march of Lower Lusatia as well. Over the course of the late 1130s and early 1140s, Conrad continued to acquire additional lands and rights, including the properties of the neighboring lineage of the counts of Groitzsch, which had become extinct in the male line.[2]

It was also during the early 1140s that his five sons began to be listed alongside him in extant sources. They were all named together with Conrad for the first time in the year 1145.[3] During the next decade, these young men continued to appear with him—some more frequently than others—in various charters.[4] As they reached the age of majority, they were frequently permitted to exercise aspects of Conrad's territorial lordship, a practice that gave a nobleman the opportunity to train his heirs for their future careers as independent lords.[5] Then, on November 30, 1156, Conrad made his final preparations for his withdrawal from the secular world and entrance into a house of Augustinian canons he had helped found, Saint Peter's on the Lauterberg to the east of Wettin.[6] A charter from that day lists the extensive

---

1. Pätzold, *Die frühen Wettiner*, 31–32.
2. Ibid., 34–35.
3. CDS 1 A, 2:127–128, no. 181; 2:132, no. 188.
4. See, for example, ibid., 2:154–155, no. 224; 2:159–160, no. 233; and 2:167, no. 249.
5. Lyon, "Fathers and Sons"; Lewis, "Anticipatory Association," 915–916.
6. For more on Conrad's decision to become a canon, see Lyon, "Withdrawal of Aged Noblemen," 154–163.

collection of properties he was donating to the community. According to this text, he gave these lands through his own hand and "through the hands of my sons, Margrave Otto, Margrave Dietrich, Count Henry, Count Dedo, and Frederick."[7] That four of his five sons are identified in the charter with titles is a clear indication that Conrad had sought to arrange the succession prior to his becoming a canon. By establishing his sons in their lordships, Conrad limited the number of decisions that had to be made about the disposition of the patrimony and lessened the potential for any kind of succession crisis after his death.

Later sources confirm that Conrad's children followed through with the distribution of titles as it appears in the 1156 document. Otto and Dietrich, the two oldest, received the Saxon marches of Meissen and Lower Lusatia respectively. Henry became count of Wettin and thus succeeded to the comital lordship after which his father had first been named in 1116.[8] Dedo acquired, among other properties, the lands and rights his father had received after the death of the last count of Groitzsch.[9] Frederick, the only son to be listed without a title in his father's charter, was almost certainly still a minor at the time. He first appears with the title *comes* in 1165 and is identified one year later as the count of Brehna.[10]

During the next quarter century after Conrad's withdrawal from the secular world in 1156, his five sons shared the political stage in eastern Saxony. Death did not begin to thin their ranks until the 1180s, with the final two—Otto and Dedo—dying in 1190, forty-eight years after they were first named together in one of their father's charters.[11] Throughout much of the second half of the twelfth century, the members of this generation appear alongside one another in a broad range of sources. While documents from this period occasionally describe one of the five acting independently from his siblings without their active support or involvement, they are much rarer than ones showing collaboration among various groupings of these brothers.[12] Indeed, none of these Wettin siblings passed more than four years of

---

7. CDS 1 A, 2:176–179, no. 262.

8. Ibid., 2:43, no. 50.

9. Pätzold, *Die frühen Wettiner*, 242.

10. Ibid., 41, 241–242; MGH DD F I, 2:454, no. 516. Though Frederick is the first member of his family to use this title, his ancestors had possessed comital rights in the region around Brehna since the eleventh century.

11. CDS 1 A, 2:110–111, no. 154.

12. For examples of charters that name only one brother, see (among other documents) CDS 1 A, 2:208, no. 305; 2:249–250, no. 360; and 2:252, no. 364.

his adult life without appearing together with at least one of his brothers in a surviving document.[13]

Not surprisingly, many of the extant charters describe the brothers as witnessing or consenting to one another's property arrangements with local religious communities. This was a common practice throughout much of medieval Europe, since most land could not be alienated without the agreement of close relatives.[14] Thus, a charter from 1161 records an exchange of properties between Margrave Dietrich of Lower Lusatia and the canons of Saint Peter's on the Lauterberg; according to the text, all four of the margrave's brothers are listed as having been present for the arrangement.[15] Thirteen years later, in 1174, Count Dedo of Groitzsch founded and endowed a new community of Augustinian canons at Zschillen, and his four brothers are all named in the charter as witnesses.[16] While such documents typically do not provide evidence concerning the strength or intensity of these siblings' relationships, they do indicate that—at a minimum—the brothers came together at various moments throughout their lifetimes to confer about family property.

The numerous contacts that the Wettin brothers had with one another were facilitated by the close proximity of their lordships in eastern Saxony.[17] Because they were neighbors, they frequently had opportunities to gather together and to exert significant influence as a group in support of their common interests. A story preserved in the *Chronicon Montis Sereni* vividly illustrates the efficacy of this group dynamic. Written in the 1220s by one of the canons of Saint Peter's on the Lauterberg, this chronicle is our richest narrative source for the Wettin lineage in the twelfth century. According to the text, the only legitimate son of Margrave Dietrich of Lower Lusatia, Count Conrad, was killed in November of 1175 from a lance wound suffered during a tournament. Because the archbishop of Magdeburg had previously sought to eliminate the "pernicious sport" (*pestifer ludus*) of the tournament inside his archdiocese by excommunicating anyone who participated,

---

13. The longest gap I have been able to locate in the sources concerns Count Henry of Wettin, who is not named alongside any of his brothers in any source between the years 1161 and 1165. One explanation for this gap is that Henry does not seem to have participated in Barbarossa's second or third Italian campaigns, a point to which I will return below.

14. Freed, *Counts of Falkenstein*, 14; White, *Custom, Kinship, and Gifts*, 1–2; Rosenwein, *Neighbor of Saint Peter*, 47–48.

15. CDS 1 A, 2:203–204, no. 298.

16. Ibid., 2:280–281, no. 404.

17. For examples of these close links, see ibid., 2:252–254, no. 365, and 2:308–310, no. 446.

he declared that Conrad's body could not receive a proper Christian burial. A short time later, when the archbishop and his suffragans were gathered for a provincial council, "the dead count's father and his brothers—namely Margrave Otto of Meissen, Count Dedo of Groitzsch, Count Henry of Wettin, and Count Frederick of Brehna—arrived with many nobles and ministerials and fell down with great wailing and tears at the feet of the archbishop and all the clergy. They asked that he [the archbishop] grant to the dead man, through a proper burial, the community of the faithful, and they firmly assured him that the dead man, penitent and absolved from sin before he died, had received holy communion."[18] The five brothers' petition must have been successful, for according to the *Chronicon*, Conrad was buried in the church at Saint Peter's on the Lauterberg in January of 1176. A charter that records Margrave Dietrich's confirmation of a gift made by his brother Count Frederick to Gottesgnaden describes the scene; the confirmation occurred "in the presence of our venerable lord Archbishop Wichmann of Magdeburg at Saint Peter's on the Lauterberg after the funeral ceremony of Count Conrad had been celebrated; it was given before me, with our other brothers standing nearby and offering their willing assent."[19] Conrad's death thus provided the five Wettin brothers the opportunity to demonstrate their collective influence through an impressive display of sibling solidarity.

Imperial charters offer a different perspective on the brothers' activities than the Saxon sources. Since the late twentieth century, medieval historians have increasingly used the witness lists of these documents to analyze the composition of the imperial court and to identify nobles with especially strong ties to the Staufen kings and emperors.[20] According to these scholars, a nobleman had a close connection to the king (*Königsnähe*) if he was routinely named as a witness in charters that did not concern his own territorial interests and if he was frequently present for charters written outside the regions where he exercised lordship.[21] In other words, the more often a magnate traveled outside his own homeland to attend the imperial court and the more often he was involved in affairs that did not directly concern him,

---

18. *Chronicon Montis Sereni*, 155–156. For the language of tears and prostration in sources written during the Staufen period, see Garnier, *Die Kultur der Bitte*, 188–201.

19. CDS 1 A, 2:295, no. 426. See also ibid., 2:296, no. 427, and *Regesta Archiepiscopatus Magdeburgensis*, 1:645, no. 1554.

20. Petke, *Kanzlei, Kapelle und Kurie*, 106–117; Plassmann, *Die Struktur des Hofes*, 1–19; Hillen, *Curia Regis*, 16–29.

21. Dendorfer, *Adelige Gruppenbildung und Königsherrschaft*, 320–321.

the stronger his bond to the ruler must have been. From this perspective, it is striking that already in March of 1144, more than a decade before their father died, the two eldest Wettin brothers, Otto and Dietrich, were present in Würzburg to witness a charter of King Conrad III for a Thuringian monastery.[22] The text is an early piece of evidence for the close ties they would develop to the Staufen rulers. Alongside their younger brother Count Dedo of Groitzsch, both Otto and Dietrich would become regular visitors to the court of Emperor Frederick I Barbarossa in later years.

A series of imperial charters from the early 1160s details the participation of this trio of Wettin siblings in Barbarossa's second Italian expedition. On December 4, 1161, they are first named with one another south of the Alps at Lodi, and since none of the three is named in an earlier source from northern Italy, they presumably made the long journey from Saxony together.[23] Throughout the winter and spring months of 1162, Otto, Dietrich, and Dedo continue to appear as witnesses in various imperial charters while Barbarossa and his court resided in the regions around Lodi and later Pavia.[24] For their participation in this Italian expedition, the emperor rewarded the two eldest Wettin brothers. In January of 1162, he agreed to Dietrich's request to donate properties that the margrave had been holding in fief from the emperor to the episcopal church of Merseburg: "On account of the love and petition of our most faithful Margrave Dietrich, who has never shrunk back from sweating with us in our constant labors and from sharing in daily dangers for the state of the imperial crown, we handed over seven *mansi*."[25] One month later, Barbarossa agreed to a similar arrangement between Margrave Otto of Meissen and a Saxon monastery.[26] Since the arrival of all three brothers coincided with Frederick's ongoing efforts to force Milan to capitulate during the winter months of 1161–1162, these grants suggest the Wettin siblings brought much-needed support to the emperor's army at a crucial moment.[27]

Otto, Dietrich, and Dedo's active roles in the Italian campaign of the early 1160s highlight an important divide within this generation of the Wettin

22. MGH DD K III, 174–176, no. 98.

23. MGH DD F I, 2:182–183, no. 344.

24. See, for example, ibid., 2:193–195, no. 353; 2:198–203, no. 356; and 2:206–207, no. 359.

25. Ibid., 2:186–187, no. 348. Dietrich's brothers Otto and Dedo are both named in the witness list.

26. Ibid., 2:189–190, no. 350.

27. Berwinkel, *Verwüsten und Belagern*, 195–201.

lineage. They appear much more frequently in the emperor's charters than their siblings Henry and Frederick.[28] While this is not necessarily surprising in the cases of Otto and Dietrich, who held imperial marches rather than only comital lordships, it is more noteworthy in the case of Count Dedo of Groitzsch. Throughout his adult life, Dedo emerges from the extant charter evidence as a figure of comparable regional influence to his two older brothers and as a nobleman able to achieve *Königsnähe*. Alongside Dietrich, he joined Emperor Frederick I in Italy again during the summer of 1177. While in Venice to celebrate the end of Barbarossa's long-standing rift with Pope Alexander III, the brothers were two of the ten nobles and churchmen who swore to uphold the emperor's treaty with the king of Sicily.[29] Count Dedo of Groitzsch's activities therefore demonstrate how a younger son could emerge as a prominent figure in imperial politics during the lifetimes of his older siblings—even if he was not in possession of a prestigious imperial fief.

Despite all the evidence for close contacts between the brothers in eastern Saxony and at the imperial court, each one's control over his own, independent lordship gave him the opportunity to pursue his own family plans. All five of them married, either before their father died or soon thereafter.[30] In this, one of the leading lineages of the German upper aristocracy again fails to conform to the traditional scholarly model of the noble lineage, which contends that fathers typically prevented younger sons from marrying and creating branches off the main line of descent.[31] All five Wettin brothers sired legitimate sons, and as a result, an abundance of first cousins would flourish within the extended Wettin kin group of the next generation. The numerous sons born to these five Wettin brothers also led to the brothers' generation experiencing only one case of fraternal succession. Margrave Dietrich of Lower Lusatia died in 1185 without a legitimate heir, because of the untimely death of his aforementioned son, Conrad, a decade earlier while jousting. Dietrich's last two surviving brothers, Margrave Otto of Meissen and Count Dedo of Groitzsch, divided his alodial lands, but they could not

---

28. Plassmann, *Die Struktur des Hofes*, 54. Plassmann incorrectly states that Count Frederick of Brehna participated in Barbarossa's Italian campaign of 1166–1167 with two of his older brothers. There is no evidence to support this contention.

29. MGH DD F I, 3:216–218, no. 694.

30. Weller, *Die Heiratspolitik des deutschen Hochadels*, 645–658.

31. Althoff, *Family, Friends and Followers*, 44–45; and most famously, Duby, *Knight, Lady and Priest*, 267–268.

do the same with his march.[32] Instead, Dedo purchased it from Emperor Frederick I Barbarossa for four thousand marks.[33]

Why Otto, who was the eldest of the brothers, did not buy the march is unclear, especially considering that in 1185 he had two sons but only a single prestigious lordship to give them.[34] Dedo's acquisition of Lower Lusatia thus strengthens the impression that he was one of the most influential and politically skilled members of his generation, despite being a younger son. Moreover, no evidence suggests that Dedo's purchase of the march led to conflict or tension with his older brother. In 1186, Dedo witnessed one of Margrave Otto's charters settling a local dispute, and on two occasions in 1187–1188, they were together at the imperial court.[35] But according to the *Chronicon Montis Sereni*, Dedo was a coconspirator with his nephew Albert when the latter captured and imprisoned his own father, Margrave Otto, in 1188–1189.[36] Since there is no evidence for conflict between Otto and Dedo during the previous four decades, the sudden change in their relationship is difficult to explain. Nevertheless, the incident highlights the brothers' different career trajectories in their final years, after their father's original succession plan had undergone significant transformations. While Otto's branch of the Wettin lineage suffered through a succession crisis, Dedo's branch experienced a peaceful transition from one generation to the next, with Dedo distributing his two lordships—his county of Groitzsch and the recently purchased march of Lower Lusatia—to his two sons.[37]

This split between Otto and Dedo—during the final year of this generation's existence—is the only evidence for conflict among any of the five Wettin brothers during the more than forty years they appear together in the surviving sources. Although each one married and had children, none of the five sought to distance himself from the others or to focus solely on the interests of his own household. All five appear together consistently throughout their lifetimes, suggesting a strong sense of sibling solidarity. From northern Italy to the Saxon frontier, their interactions highlight some of the many ways brothers could support each other's territorial interests—and some of

---

32. *Chronicon Montis Sereni*, 160, 163.
33. *Genealogia Wettinensis*, 230; Rogge, *Die Wettiner*, 43.
34. For more on these two sons, see chapter 5.
35. CDS 1 A, 2:361–362, no. 523; MGH DD F I, 4:228–230, no. 956; 4:263–268, nos. 981–982.
36. *Chronicon Montis Sereni*, 161
37. Pätzold, *Die frühen Wettiner*, 56. For more on this next generation, see chapter 5.

the many ways they could work together as a fraternal bloc to influence politics both regionally and at the imperial court.[38]

The Four Wittelsbach Brothers

Another of the founders of a leading lineage, Count-Palatine Otto I of Bavaria (d. 1156), fathered four sons who reached adulthood. One became a churchman, while the other three remained in the secular sphere.[39] Otto and Frederick, the two eldest heirs, were frequently with their father prior to his death in 1156. They were already witnesses with him in the late 1130s to a property donation made to a Bavarian monastery, and they are recorded together at the court of King Conrad III in Salzburg in 1149.[40] It is presumably these same two sons who are referenced by the chronicler Otto of Freising when he reports that the king, while in Regensburg a short time later, "outlawed Count-Palatine Otto on account of his sons' crimes. [The king] laid siege to his nearby castle called Kelheim . . . and, at this place, forced him to give one of his sons as a hostage."[41] Though nothing else is known about this incident, including the precise nature of the crimes or the identity of the hostage, the background is almost certainly the long-standing dispute between the bishop of Freising and the Wittelsbachs over control of episcopal properties and rights, especially the advocacy for the church of Freising.[42] This conflict would continue in later years, and whichever son is meant by the chronicler seems not to have been a hostage for very long. Both appear in sources during the early years of Frederick Barbarossa's reign, and after Count-Palatine Otto I died, a third son—who rather confusingly was named Otto (*minor*) like his eldest brother—also began to play an active role in Bavarian and imperial affairs.[43] For a quarter century until the death of the firstborn Otto (*maior*) in 1183, these brothers

---

38. For more on this point, see chapter 4.

39. Some earlier historians have identified a fifth son, a provost, but on the basis of very limited sources: Dungern, *Genealogisches Handbuch*, 31, 35; Tyroller, *Genealogie des altbayerischen Adels*, 254.

40. *Die Traditionen des Klosters Scheyern*, 27–28, no. 20; MGH DD K III, 363–365, no. 201. Both brothers had appeared separately at the imperial court in earlier years, and they may be the "Otto et Fridericus comites" in the witness list of a charter dated February 13, 1147, at Regensburg: MGH DD K III, 311–312, no. 172.

41. Otto of Freising and Rahewin, *Gesta Friderici*, 1.69, 97–98.

42. *Die Tegernseer Briefsammlung*, 122–123, no. 92 and 155–156, no. 124.

43. It was not uncommon for parents to give the same name to two children within medieval noble families: see Mayer, "Gleichnamige Geschwister im Mittelalter."

appear together and separately in a broad range of sources from inside and outside Bavaria.

In an imperial charter from the year 1162, the brothers are identified in the witness list as "Count-Palatine Otto of Wittelsbach and his brothers Frederick and Otto" (*Otto palatinus comes de Withelinsbach et fratres eius Fridericus et Otto*).[44] But a few years later, in another of Barbarossa's charters, they are "the counts-palatine of Wittelsbach, namely the elder Otto and his brothers" (*palatini comites de Witelinesbac Otto videlicet senior et fratres eius*).[45] The plural construction "counts-palatine" is noteworthy, and there is ample evidence in the Bavarian source material that all three siblings made use of the title.[46] However, the two younger Wittelsbach brothers are identified only intermittently by the title *comes palatinus* in the surviving sources, while Otto *maior* appears consistently with this label.[47] This perhaps suggests that the county-palatine of Bavaria was in the process of losing its status as an imperial *honor* during this period and was instead becoming a familial designation.[48] And yet Frederick's only extant seal, which dates to the period before 1166, is an equestrian seal with a knight holding a banner decorated with an imperial eagle—an image that implies Frederick had a legitimate claim to the formal authority exercised by the counts-palatine of Bavaria and was not simply using the title as a family honorific.[49] Different types of source material thus provide inconsistent, and sometimes even contradictory, information about the brothers' use of this title, making it difficult to determine with any clarity how the siblings and their contemporaries understood their roles as *comites palatini*.

While the brothers seem to have shared the title of count-palatine of Bavaria, each of them otherwise possessed his own independent set of family rights and properties. In the mid-1170s, for example, Otto *maior* granted half the profits of a *curtis* to the religious community of Neustift near Freising—without the consent of either of his brothers.[50] There are separate entries

---

44. MGH DD F I, 2:257–259, no. 388.

45. Ibid., 3:26–27, no. 561.

46. See, for example, *Die Traditionen des Hochstifts Freising*, 2:380, no. 1550b; 2:385, no. 1554; and 2:388, no. 1557e; *Die Traditionen des Klosters Weihenstephan*, 193, no. 237 and 242–243, no. 298.

47. Throughout the 1150s and 1160s, imperial charters (including those known to have been produced in the imperial chancery) are inconsistent in their treatment of the two younger brothers, sometimes using the title for both, sometimes for only one, and sometimes for neither of them.

48. Even the fourth brother in this generation, the churchman Conrad, appears with the title in one of Frederick Barbarossa's charters from 1177: MGH DD F I, 3:214–216, no. 693. See also Paulus, *Das Pfalzgrafenamt in Bayern*, 53–54.

49. Kahsnitz, "Siegel des Pfalzgrafen Friedrich"; Paulus, *Das Pfalzgrafenamt in Bayern*, 61–63; Schöntag, "Das Reitersiegel als Rechtssymbol," 99–101.

50. *Die Traditionen des Klosters Neustift bei Freising*, 88–89, no. 12.

for fiefs held from "Count-Palatine Frederick" and "Count-Palatine Otto, namely the younger one" in the *Codex Falkensteinensis*, compiled for the heirs of Count Sigiboto IV of Falkenstein as he prepared to depart on Barbarossa's Italian expedition of 1166.[51] And Frederick's lengthy testament, which he prepared on the eve of his departure for a pilgrimage to the Holy Land in the early 1170s, shows more clearly than any other source the extensive rights and properties held by one of the siblings. It lists dozens of alods as well as vineyards, cow pastures, and castles.[52]

Like their contemporaries in the Wettin lineage, all three of these brothers married and begat legitimate children.[53] Unlike the five Wettin brothers, however, abundant sources show these brothers acting independently from one another. This is a surprising point of contrast, because like the Wettins, the Wittelsbach lineage's rights and properties were concentrated territorially (within the old Bavarian heartland, between the Danube and the Alps), meaning the brothers' spheres of interest overlapped to a large extent.[54] Nevertheless, they frequently acted as independent lords. Although Frederick Barbarossa would enfeoff Otto *maior* with the duchy of Bavaria in 1180, thus establishing the Wittelsbach line of dukes, contemporary sources from the 1150s through the 1170s do not single him out as the only influential figure in this generation. As one historian has suggested, the second son, Frederick, may have been more important than his older brother for the development of the lineage's territorial position in Bavaria.[55] Even after he decided to join a religious community in the mid-1170s, Frederick continued to be named in a wide range of Bavarian sources. He was not cloistered, and although he begins to appear with the title *dominus* instead of *comes palatinus* in some documents, the latter title persists in other texts even after he laid down his sword.[56] Otto *minor* is likewise named without his brothers in a variety of sources, suggesting that he too had carved out his own position within the lineage's territorial power base in Bavaria.[57]

51. *Codex Falkensteinensis*, 4–7, no. 2. See also *Die Traditionen des Klosters Schäftlarn*, 204–206, no. 208; and 207–209, no. 211.

52. *Die Urkunden des Klosters Indersdorf*, 10–13, no. 18.

53. Weller, *Die Heiratspolitik des deutschen Hochadels*, 764–768.

54. For a discussion of the Wittelsbach family's most important centers of lordship, see Seibert, "Die entstehende 'territoriale Ordnung.'"

55. Paulus, "Zwischen König, Herzog und Bruder," 251.

56. Paulus, *Das Pfalzgrafenamt in Bayern*, 305–310.

57. See, for example, *Die Traditionen und das älteste Urbar des Klosters St. Ulrich und Afra*, 174–175, no. 210; *Die Traditionen des Klosters Schäftlarn*, 213, no. 215.

None of this means that the brothers did not collaborate with one another. They appear together at the court of Duke Henry the Lion in the late 1150s and early 1160s.[58] And later, we catch a brief glimpse of a familial scene in a text recording a property donation to Schäftlarn that was finalized "in the castle Karlsberg, when Count-Palatine Otto *maior* was staying for Pentecost, gathered there with his younger brother Otto, their wives, and many knights."[59] The brothers also attended the imperial court together during the late 1150s and 1160s. For these court visits, the *Gesta Friderici* of Otto of Freising and his continuator, Rahewin, is an invaluable source. The two chroniclers focus especially on Otto *maior*, describing him as a successful military commander during Frederick Barbarossa's first Italian expedition and as a trusted ambassador for the emperor on his second journey south of the Alps.[60] Despite the impressive image of Otto *maior* that emerges from these passages, Rahewin reveals that the eldest brother was not the only member of his generation to play a role in imperial affairs. At the siege of Milan, during Barbarossa's second Italian expedition,

> Count-Palatine Otto of Bavaria, . . . along with his two brothers Frederick and Otto *iunior* and the other knights joined with them at the gate they had surrounded, were observing the efforts of the enemy very attentively. Consequently, one day when they saw that their enemies were conducting themselves in a relaxed fashion and that there were few guards around the gate, it seemed to them that they had to put fortune to the test. . . . The counts [the three brothers], who were the battle commanders in this fight, just as they were in many others, exposed themselves to every danger, and like the best warriors, they made the strength of their bodies and the greatness of their spirits shine forth for all to see.[61]

Documentary evidence supports this description of Frederick and Otto *minor* as prominent figures at court alongside their older brother. During the Italian expedition of 1158–1162, Otto *maior* is the sibling who is named most

58. For Henry's court, see *Die Urkunden Heinrichs des Löwen*, 53–54, no. 38 and 78–79, no. 54.

59. *Die Traditionen des Klosters Schäftlarn*, 169–170, no. 169.

60. Otto of Freising and Rahewin, *Gesta Friderici*, 2.20, 122; 2.22, 126; 2.40, 148; 3.52, 227–228; and 4.23, 266. See also Berwinkel, *Verwüsten und Belagern*, 62–112. Otto *maior* also famously drew his sword during a gathering of the imperial court in Besançon, threatening a papal legate who had the temerity to suggest that Frederick held the empire from the pope: Otto of Freising and Rahewin, *Gesta Friderici*, 3.10, 177.

61. Otto of Freising and Rahewin, *Gesta Friderici*, 3.39, 212–213.

frequently as a witness in Barbarossa's charters, appearing a total of twenty-five times. But Frederick is included in the witness lists of ten charters and Otto *minor* of six. The three brothers are named together in five of these charters.[62] All three continue to be listed as witnesses in subsequent years, sometimes individually and sometimes as a group, suggesting that each possessed *Königsnähe* at various times during his career.[63]

On September 7, 1162, the three brothers were together for a grand gathering of the imperial court in Burgundy as the emperor returned from Italy.[64] There they were joined by their fourth brother, the churchman Conrad. One year earlier, Frederick Barbarossa had chosen Conrad for the position of archbishop of Mainz, and it clearly helped Conrad's case that he came from a lineage traditionally among the most loyal to the Staufen rulers.[65] Indeed, all three of his lay brothers were traveling with Barbarossa south of the Alps in June of 1161, when Conrad was named archbishop.[66] A short time after his consecration, Conrad himself crossed the mountains to join the emperor's ongoing second Italian campaign. He was present alongside his brother Count-Palatine Otto *maior* at the imperial court in June of 1162, and these two brothers accompanied Barbarossa in Italy for the remainder of the summer before returning with him north of the Alps, where they met their other brothers for the Burgundian court meeting.[67]

In the years after his election, Archbishop Conrad became a pivotal figure in his fraternal group, as documents from the archdiocese of Mainz reveal. One of the first charters drawn up in Conrad of Wittelsbach's name after his election to the archiepiscopal office is dated to the opening months of 1162 and provides an early indication of the close ties Conrad would maintain with his brothers throughout the following decades.[68] The document, which involves Conrad's grant of several fiefs of the church of Mainz to a local monastery, does not appear to concern the Wittelsbach lineage or its territorial interests in any manner. Nevertheless, Conrad's brother Frederick is named as a witness, in the first position among laymen. A short time later, "Count-Palatine Frederick, brother of the bishop" (*Fredericus palatinus frater*

---

62. MGH DD F I, 2:13–15, no. 228; 2:85–86, no. 275; 2:90–91, no. 279; 2:136–138, no. 315; 2:152–153, no. 326.

63. Plassmann, *Die Struktur des Hofes*, 76–78.

64. MGH DD F I, 2:257–259, no. 388; Opll, *Friedrich Barbarossa*, 81–84.

65. Burkhardt, *Mit Stab und Schwert*, 70–72.

66. For Conrad's predecessor as archbishop, Rudolf of Zähringen, see below.

67. MGH DD F I, 2:233–236, no. 372; 2:237–239, no. 374; 2:248–251, no. 382.

68. Mainzer UB 2, pt. 1:473–475, no. 266.

episcopi) appeared again in the witness list of one of Conrad's charters.[69] The following year, one of the archbishop-elect's brothers named Otto—it is not clear whether *maior* or *minor*—witnessed an agreement between Conrad and the cathedral chapter at Mainz.[70] And a charter drawn up in 1169 by Conrad's successor as archbishop suggests that Conrad had granted church lands in fief to one of these Ottos.[71]

Conrad's decision to involve his brothers in his episcopacy from its earliest years suggests that his Wittelsbach siblings, although they had no territorial interests in the archdiocese of Mainz, saw the advantages of having their brother exercise archiepiscopal office. However, any long-term plans the brothers may have had for Mainz ended abruptly when the papal schism engulfed Conrad's career. Since 1160, Barbarossa had refused to acknowledge Alexander III as the rightful pope and had instead favored another claimant to the papal throne, Victor IV. When Victor died in 1164, the emperor's allies again put forward their own pope. The following year, at a gathering of the imperial court in Würzburg, Barbarossa demanded that the German princes take an oath never to recognize Alexander III. This heavy-handed move, which met with considerable resistance, cost the emperor the support of many leading ecclesiastics—including Conrad of Wittelsbach.[72] Soon thereafter, Conrad fled the German kingdom for Rome. For the next twelve years, he was an important figure in the Alexandrine party and was named cardinal-priest, then cardinal-bishop, and ultimately papal legate for the German realm.[73]

Nevertheless, the emperor did not retaliate. During the late 1160s and early 1170s, Conrad was able to serve as papal legate within his lineage's homeland of Bavaria. Barbarossa, apparently unwilling to risk losing the support of any of his siblings, allowed Conrad to travel freely.[74] His brother Frederick's testament, drawn up at some point in the early 1170s as Frederick made preparations to go on pilgrimage to the Holy Land, even names Conrad as one of his principal heirs. Conrad would receive a series of

---

69. Ibid., pt. 1:478–479, no. 269.

70. Ibid., pt. 1:488–489, no. 276.

71. Ibid., pt. 1:543–545, no. 318. The text does not explicitly state that Conrad was the one who enfeoffed his brother with these properties, but this seems likely, considering that Otto returned the fiefs to the archbishopric soon after Conrad left office in the mid-1160s.

72. For an overview of this papal schism, see Fuhrmann, *Germany in the High Middle Ages,* 157–162.

73. Oehring, *Erzbischof Konrad I. von Mainz,* 56–68.

74. Dopsch, "Die Wittelsbacher," 270.

properties in Bavaria, including a castle, if Frederick should die on the journey.[75]

Conrad returned to Barbarossa's good graces only in 1177, following the end of the emperor's conflict with Alexander III. The interactions among the Wittelsbach brothers in these later years will be discussed in the next chapter, where I will argue that their relationships had a significant effect on imperial politics during the period around 1180. As the first twenty-five years of their adult lives demonstrate, all four siblings were prominent figures in Bavaria and the German kingdom more widely. The three brothers who succeeded their father as count-palatine had inherited separate sets of rights and properties that led them to act independently at times, but they also worked together on numerous occasions in Bavaria and at the imperial court. Conrad, the fourth brother, also maintained connections to all three of his male siblings throughout his early church career, though he never used his archiepiscopal office as a significant source of patronage for these close relatives. His granting of fiefs to one of his brothers during his early years in Mainz is the only evidence from his career for this type of familial strategy, which suggests that his ties to his siblings did not center on Wittelsbach territorial expansion. In contrast, prelates born into some of the other lineages under investigation here were much more willing to view their episcopal office through the lens of their brothers' lordship.

Prelates and Secular Princes: The Zähringen and Andechs Brothers

Duke Conrad of Zähringen (d. 1152) had four sons, three of whom remained in the secular sphere. Two of the younger siblings, Hugo and Adalbert, are difficult to trace in the surviving sources and appear only occasionally during the lifetime of their eldest brother, Duke Berthold IV (d. 1186).[76] In contrast, there is abundant evidence for the relationship between Berthold and his brother in the church, Rudolf (d. 1191). The ties between these two siblings first manifested themselves on the political scene in the autumn of the year 1162, when the duke sent a letter to King Louis VII of France.[77] The text, a lengthy diatribe directed against Frederick Barbarossa, was designed to gain

---

75. *Die Urkunden des Klosters Indersdorf*, 10–13, no. 18. Another of their brothers, Otto *minor*, was tasked with carrying out the transfer of these estates.

76. See the list of sources for the pair in Parlow, *Die Zähringer*, 157–158.

77. Ibid., 276, no. 435.

the French king's support against the emperor. It was hand delivered by Berthold's younger brother Rudolf, who had been elected archbishop of Mainz in 1160—only to be deposed by Barbarossa and his pope a short time later in favor of the Wittelsbach Conrad.[78] In the letter, Berthold complains that "our most dear brother Rudolf" (*dilectissimus frater noster Radulfus*), though canonically elected, was forced out of the archiepiscopal office by the emperor "on account of his hatred of our lineage." The letter closes by emphasizing the close connection between the siblings: "In truth, concerning anything else whatsoever, our brother [Rudolf] will reply to you with his living voice as if from our person, since you ought to know without any ambiguity what is true and acceptable to us."[79]

The chronicler Gilbert of Mons, writing three decades later, is not as quick to criticize Barbarossa in his account of these events. He does, however, lend credence to the idea that the emperor's actions were directed against the duke of Zähringen. According to Gilbert, Frederick feared the power of the duke of Zähringen and therefore "removed from his spiritual office Rudolf, who had been elected to the seat of Mainz."[80] The connection between Rudolf's deposition and his brother Berthold's political interests suggests that people both inside and outside the Zähringen lineage recognized the potentially potent bond between ecclesiastical office holding and a lineage's territorial expansion. In the case of Rudolf and Berthold, this link seems justified.

Seven years after being deposed as archbishop of Mainz in 1160, Rudolf was elected bishop of Liège.[81] This diocese, which was located in the northwest of the kingdom, lay a significant distance from the Zähringen lands in the southern parts of the duchy of Swabia. Rudolf therefore acquired a bishopric where his older brother did not control any rights and properties. This does not mean, however, that Berthold was a disinterested bystander to his brother's election—or that he and Rudolf ceased to have contact with one another after 1167. Because their maternal uncle Count Henry of Namur-Luxemburg had no children, questions regarding potential heirs to his extensive patrimony interested a broad array of his relatives—as well as the emperor. With much of the Namur-Luxemburg properties located in the region between Liège and the Zähringen lands, the issue of the inheritance

---

78. Burkhardt, *Mit Stab und Schwert*, 76–78.

79. Parlow, *Die Zähringer*, 276, no. 435. For the significance of this type of language in diplomatic correspondence, see Leyser, "Frederick Barbarossa, Henry II and the Hand of St. James," 486–487.

80. Gilbert of Mons, *La chronique de Gislebert de Mons*, 65, chap. 33.

81. For Rudolf's career in Liège, see Schoolmeesters, *Les regesta de Raoul de Zaehringen*.

helped forge an enduring connection between the new bishop and his older brother.

A document from the year 1171 provides an early glimpse into the siblings' ties during Rudolf's years in Liège.[82] The text is a treaty drawn up between Duke Berthold IV and his young son Berthold V on the one hand and the archbishop of Trier on the other. It concerns Count Henry of Namur-Luxemburg's inheritance, specifically lands the count held in fief from the archbishop. These were to be granted to the duke of Zähringen and his son on the count's death. In return for these fiefs, Berthold IV and Berthold V promised to pay the archbishop 350 marks of silver. Bishop Rudolf of Liège was given a prominent role in ensuring that his brother and nephew would fulfill their side of the agreement. If Duke Berthold IV died before his son, Berthold V, reached the age of majority, Rudolf would act as his young nephew's legal guardian and make certain the treaty's terms were followed. Moreover, Rudolf agreed to act as one of the guarantors for the treaty by offering a piece of his church's property as security.

Because Count Henry of Namur-Luxemburg's wife gave birth to a daughter in 1186, the terms of this treaty were never enacted. Regardless, questions about the division of the count's patrimony continued to swirl throughout the late 1170s and early 1180s, providing the opportunity for additional contacts between Rudolf and his brother. In 1182, Duke Berthold IV of Zähringen appeared alongside Count Henry as a witness in one of Bishop Rudolf's charters. This document, drawn up at Liège, shows that the significant distance between the siblings' power bases did not prevent them from meeting when mutual interests required it.[83] Two years later, in 1184, the brothers were once more together, this time at a gathering of the imperial court in Mainz, where the question of possible divisions of the Namur-Luxemburg patrimony was again addressed.[84]

In 1187, the year after Duke Berthold IV of Zähringen died, his brother Bishop Rudolf of Liège arranged for the payment of forty schillings to a local religious community.[85] The money was to be used to help preserve the memories of the bishop's parents and sibling. Since Rudolf's father had died in 1152 and his mother in 1158, the death of his brother Berthold was the immediate impulse for the bishop's decision to arrange this family memorial.

---

82. Parlow, *Die Zähringer*, 292–293, no. 463. See also Büttner, "Zähringerpolitik im Trierer Raum."

83. Parlow, *Die Zähringer*, 314, no. 496.

84. Gilbert of Mons, *La chronique de Gislebert de Mons*, 160–161, chap. 109.

85. Parlow, *Die Zähringer*, 342, no. 530.

Documents preserving donations by one brother for the soul of another are rare from the Staufen period, and this text therefore points to an especially strong sibling relationship. Rudolf and Berthold spent more than a quarter century in contact with one another, and not even the great distances between Liège and Zähringen lands could sever this fraternal bond. Nevertheless, as the case of these two siblings demonstrates, the relationship between a prominent secular lord and his brother in the church did not always generate tangible political and territorial benefits—for either one.

In contrast, two brothers from the Andechs lineage provide evidence for the real advantages that could result from close cooperation between siblings who were ecclesiastical and secular lords. Otto of Andechs—who served as bishop-elect of Brixen (1165–1170) and later bishop of Bamberg (1177–1196)—acquired episcopal offices in two regions where his own brother, Margrave Berthold II of Istria, exercised secular lordship. Otto's ties to his older sibling are already apparent in the earliest sources for their lives. Twice during the mid-1140s, while their father, Count Berthold I of Andechs, was still alive, Otto witnessed property donations to a Bavarian monastery that had close connections to the lineage; on one of these occasions, Berthold II was also present.[86] Several years later, in 1151, shortly after Berthold II succeeded their father, Otto was named for the first time in a document as a *clericus*.[87] Precisely when he entered the church is unclear, but there is no indication in the surviving sources that his becoming an ecclesiastic led him to sever ties with his brother. In 1153, he traveled together with Berthold II to a gathering of regional magnates in the town of Villach in Carinthia in order to confirm a property donation.[88]

Otto appeared alongside his brother again in 1164 when they both witnessed a charter of the bishop of Bamberg.[89] Otto, who is labeled a cathedral canon in this document, spent only a short time in Bamberg, however, for one year later he was designated bishop-elect of Brixen with the support of the emperor. For Frederick Barbarossa, it was essential to have an ally in Brixen because this diocese in Tyrol lay along one of the best routes between the German kingdom and Italy. The emperor therefore chose a churchman from a lineage long loyal to the Staufen.[90] Otto's brother Berthold II had

---

86. Baumann, "Das Benediktbeurer Traditionsbuch," 25, no. 50, and 18, no. 30.

87. UB Steiermark, 1:329–330, no. 342.

88. *Salzburger Urkundenbuch*, 2:425, no. 304.

89. See chapter 2.

90. Schütz, "Das Geschlecht der Andechs-Meranier," 63–64. For Andechs interests in the Tyrol region, see also Bitschnau, "Gries-Morit."

been a strong supporter of Frederick Barbarossa from the earliest years of
his reign, and Otto himself had close ties to the emperor as well. Otto is
even identified in one imperial charter from the mid-1160s as Frederick's
"*nepos*"—though their kin connection was not a close one—and as "provost
of Aachen," an office with particularly close ties to the German kings.[91]

Despite holding the position of bishop-elect for only five years before
the politics of the papal schism forced him from office, Otto was able to
significantly increase his brother Berthold II's influence within the diocese
of Brixen. With Otto's assistance, Berthold acquired the advocacies for the
church of Brixen and for Neustift, a nearby house of Augustinian canons.[92]
Otto also enfeoffed his brother with two counties that the bishops of Brixen
possessed, including one that lay in the Inn River valley and provided access
to the Brenner Pass into Italy.[93] These were not the first rights Berthold II
had acquired in this diocese, but he seems to have shown little interest in
the region until Otto's election.[94] Only after 1165 did Berthold II become
a regular visitor to the area around Brixen.[95] His establishment of a market
at Innsbruck in 1180 demonstrates with particular clarity how his brother's
episcopacy transformed Tyrol into a region at the center of the Andechs
lineage's long-term political and territorial strategies.[96]

Following the end of his short stay at Brixen, Otto disappears from the
surviving sources for only a brief period before being identified again as
provost of Aachen in an imperial charter dated to March of 1174.[97] Later
that same year, Otto is named for the first time as cathedral provost of Bamberg.[98] Significantly, this was another diocese where his brother Berthold
had strong interests and where the emperor liked to have close allies, owing
to the bishopric's extensive landholdings in Franconia and along important

---

91. MGH DD F I, 2:429–430, no. 501. See also Göldel, *Servitium Regis und Tafelgüterverzeichnis*,
162–165; Müssel, "Bischof Otto II. von Bamberg," 12–13.

92. Schütz, "Das Geschlecht der Andechs-Meranier," 64. See also *Die Traditionsbücher des Hochstifts Brixen*, 174, nos. 496a–b.

93. Oefele, *Geschichte der Grafen von Andechs*, 61–65; Hye, "Die Grafen von Andechs und Tirol,"
48–49.

94. For his earlier acquisitions in Tyrol, see Schütz, "Das Geschlecht der Andechs-Meranier,"
44, 63.

95. *Die Traditionsbücher des Hochstifts Brixen*, 174, nos. 496a–b; 175, no. 498; 176, no. 501; 178,
no. 507b; 179, no. 508a.

96. For a similar argument, see Ertl, "Die Geschichte Innsbrucks," 37–38.

97. MGH DD F I, 3:103–104, no. 614. He appears with the same title again on May 23: ibid.,
3:113–114, no. 621. For more on Otto as provost of Aachen, see Arnold, *Power and Property*, 90–97.

98. MGH DD F I, 3:119–120, no. 625.

roads through the eastern Alps.[99] In the summer of 1177, Otto was elected bishop by the cathedral chapter, and while no source directly connects either Barbarossa or Berthold II to this event, they presumably exerted some influence over the process.[100]

The diocese of Bamberg, more than any other region where the Andechs lineage possessed lordships, had already witnessed the almost complete entanglement of the family's territorial interests with those of the bishopric—long before Otto had first joined the cathedral chapter in 1164. After 1177, therefore, Otto was in a position to exploit this situation to his brother Berthold's advantage. The region around Bamberg became the centerpiece of Andechs lordship during the closing decades of the twelfth century.[101] However, some of the best evidence for the sibling relationship between Otto and Berthold concerns the bishopric's extensive rights and properties outside the diocese, especially in Carinthia. This region, which bordered the Andechs lordship in Carniola in modern Slovenia, has attracted little attention from scholars working on the Andechs-Bamberg connection.[102]

It is clear, however, that the two brothers recognized its significance for their lineage. Soon after Otto's election, as he was returning northward from the imperial court in Italy, he stopped at Wolfsberg in the duchy of Carinthia, where the bishops of Bamberg possessed a castle. There, in early 1178, he drew up a charter to settle a dispute between an episcopal ministerial and the nearby monastery of Saint Paul in the Lavant Valley. The lead witness to the document was Berthold II.[103] Soon thereafter, in a charter from 1180, Bishop Otto II exchanged lands with the Bamberg-owned monastery of Arnoldstein in Carinthia, which lay along roads that led south across the Alps into both Italy and Carniola. In return for granting the monastery various lands near Arnoldstein, the bishopric received among other territories "the mountain that in the vernacular is called Krainegg," which lay to the southeast of Arnoldstein near the Würzen Pass into Carniola.[104] Berthold is identified in the witness list of this document as "advocate," presumably for

99. Pflefka, *Das Bistum Bamberg*, 16–18; van Eickels and Kunde, "Die Herrschaft Friedburg," 199–210.

100. Van Eickels, "Die Andechs-Meranier," 146.

101. For their relationship's impact on Franconia, see Frenken, "Hausmachtpolitik und Bischofsstuhl."

102. For more on this point, see Lyon, "Cooperation, Compromise and Conflict Avoidance," 227–245.

103. MHDC, 3:470–471, no. 1242.

104. Ibid., 3:479, no. 1271.

the monastery of Arnoldstein.[105] With this advocacy in Berthold's hands and the bishop in control of Krainegg, the brothers had significantly expanded their influence in the southeast of the empire along the Carinthia-Carniola border. In later years, they would both emerge as prominent figures in imperial politics as well.[106]

The careers of the three bishops Conrad of Wittelsbach, Rudolf of Zähringen, and Otto of Andechs demonstrate how brothers in the church could play a diverse set of roles within their sibling groups during the opening decades of the Staufen period. Like their brothers who remained in the secular sphere and succeeded to their father's lordships, these men maintained close ties to the other members of their generation. All showed at least some interest in advancing the territorial interests of their brothers by helping them acquire rights and properties, but some were in better positions to do this than others. But in this first generation of the Staufen upper aristocracy, not every bishop remained so closely linked to his siblings who were secular lords. The Babenberg lineage offers a very different perspective on the fraternal relationships of churchmen during these years when siblings were so abundant in the upper aristocracy.

The Babenberg Brothers

Margrave Leopold III of Austria (d. 1136) and his wife, Agnes, the daughter of the Salian ruler Henry IV, had six sons who survived to adulthood. The youngest two of the six were named Otto and Conrad, and as the last-born heirs of a father who possessed only one prominent lordship, both appear to have been intended for church careers from a young age.[107] For Otto, the future chronicler and bishop of Freising, we are fortunate to have a source that provides a detailed description of his early years: a chronicle written inside the community of canons at Neuburg, one of his father's religious foundations. According to this work, Otto was named provost of Neuburg while he was still a young student (*scholaris*). During the late 1120s, however, Leopold made the decision to send his son outside the empire to pursue an education in Paris. There, Otto received extensive training in theology. Returning to his homeland in 1132/1133, his education complete, Otto stopped to spend a night in the Cistercian monastery of Morimond. The next day, he and

---

105. For this advocacy, see Klebel, "Die Grafen von Görz," 68–70.
106. See chapter 4.
107. For their four older brothers, see chapter 2.

fifteen of his fellow travelers decided to take the monastic vow—apparently without the knowledge of any of his close relatives.[108]

Although Margrave Leopold III of Austria was expecting his young son to return to his position as provost of Neuburg after finishing in Paris, he appears to have done nothing to hinder Otto's sudden change in careers. Otto remained a monk in Morimond for the next several years and was even elected abbot of the community in 1138. Within a few months of this election, however, his stay in the monastery ended abruptly. One of the first actions taken by the newly crowned German king Conrad III, who was Otto's half brother on his mother's side, was to install Otto as bishop of Freising.[109] The new prelate had spent most of the preceding decade separated from his family. But with his elevation to a Bavarian bishopric with properties scattered across the southeastern part of the kingdom, Otto was thrust into the middle of Babenberg and Staufen politics.[110] His reintegration into this familial dynamic is already apparent in 1139, when King Conrad III made a grant to the religious community at Neuburg "through the intervention of our most beloved mother, Agnes, and our brother Otto, the venerable bishop of the church of Freising, and our brother Duke Leopold [IV] of Bavaria."[111] The grant was witnessed by another sibling, Otto's younger full brother Conrad, who had become a member of the king's royal chapel earlier the same year.

Throughout the 1140s, Bishop Otto of Freising's fraternal relationships made him a central figure in both regional politics and the affairs of the kingdom as a whole. During these years, the duchy of Bavaria was one of the places where supporters and opponents of King Conrad III struggled for supremacy, and Otto inevitably became entangled in these conflicts. Two of his full brothers—Leopold IV (d. 1141) and Henry Jasomirgott (d. 1177)—claimed the title of duke during Otto's episcopacy, while also continuing to exercise lordship in the march of Austria, where the church of Freising had various rights and properties.[112] Moreover, as a regular visitor to the royal court, Otto also maintained frequent contacts with his two Staufen half

---

108. This is the story of his monastic conversion that has come down to us: *Annales Austriae*, 610–611. For a more plausible account of what probably occurred, see Kirchner-Feyerabend, *Otto von Freising*, 24–30.

109. For a more detailed consideration of Conrad III's motives, see chapter 4.

110. For an overview of this diocese, see Weinfurter, "Die kirchliche Ordnung," 279–283.

111. MGH DD K III, 60–61, no. 37.

112. See, for example, BUB, 1:17–19, no. 13.

brothers—King Conrad and Duke Frederick II of Swabia.[113] One of the most impressive sibling gatherings of this period dates from the summer of 1141 at Regensburg, when Otto, Leopold, and Henry were three of the fourteen people named in the witness list of Conrad III's charter for a Bavarian monastery.[114] Later in the decade, the bishop of Freising accompanied his half brother Conrad III on the Second Crusade, where they were joined by Henry Jasomirgott.[115]

In 1146, shortly before his departure on crusade, Otto finished writing the first of his two major chronicles, the *Historia de duabus civitatibus*. For the study of his sibling relationships, this is an invaluable text. Throughout the work, which spans the years from biblical times to the reign of King Conrad III, he offers few kind words for nobles who threatened the church's properties. The Wittelsbach counts-palatine of Bavaria, who possessed the advocacy for the see of Freising, were some of the most frequent targets of his wrath.[116] But he was also quick to criticize many of the rival magnates who claimed the title of duke of Bavaria during the opening years of his prelacy—including his own brothers. Early in the text, in the midst of his account of ancient history, Otto paused to interject a lament about one of these siblings: "A clamor is heard in all lands, but especially in our province, which the nobleman Welf [VI] recently invaded in a hostile manner, laying waste to the fields and plundering the goods of God's churches. . . . Indeed, because there is a dispute over the duchy between him and Duke Henry [Jasomirgott] of Bavaria, both of whom are exemplary youths of impetuous courage, what can be expected from either of them . . . other than the ruin of the poor and the devastation of churches?"[117] Later in the same work, in the chapter dedicated to the career of his brother Leopold IV, Otto complained that Leopold "advanced all the way to the Lech River with an armed force and, after destroying the fortifications of certain of his enemies there and laying waste to everything on all sides, returned through our territories to the great detriment of our church."[118]

In neither of these passages does the bishop acknowledge that Henry and Leopold are his own brothers. Indeed, Otto avoids identifying anyone as his

---

113. See, for example, MGH DD K III, 127–129, no. 72; 174–176, no. 98; and 189–192, no. 106.

114. Ibid., 106–108, no. 61.

115. Extant sources reveal very little about the three siblings' interactions during this expedition. See Kirchner-Feyerabend, *Otto von Freising*, 231–236.

116. See chapter 1 for more on this point.

117. Otto of Freising, *Chronica*, 2, prologue, 68.

118. Ibid., 7.25, 350.

kinsman in this chronicle.[119] Twelfth-century readers would undoubtedly have known of his close blood ties to the Staufen and Babenberg lineages, but it is nevertheless striking how he distances himself from his own relatives in the text. His negative attitude toward his brother Henry seems to have only intensified in subsequent years. Throughout the early part of the reign of Frederick Barbarossa, the new king sought to settle the dispute between Henry Jasomirgott and the Welf Henry the Lion over their competing claims to the duchy of Bavaria. Otto provides one of the best surviving accounts of this dispute in his *Gesta Friderici*, yet he gives no indication that he supported his brother's cause. In his description of the events of the year 1155, he depicts himself only as a mediator between the two rivals.[120] His presence at the imperial court at Regensburg in 1156, when the dispute was finally settled, is also difficult to interpret through the lens of fraternal bonds, since Otto himself is careful not to describe the gathering from this perspective.[121] Rahewin, the Freising canon who continued the *Gesta* after Otto's death, offers one possible explanation for the bishop's persistent antipathy toward his sibling. He reports that two years later, in 1158, during an imperial diet, the emperor "restored to pristine peace and brotherly concord (*fraternam concordiam*) his paternal uncles Bishop Otto of Freising and Duke Henry of Austria, who were in opposition because the aforesaid bishop was completely against his brother, who wanted to usurp church property illicitly for himself."[122]

Otto's death came later in the year 1158. A committed monk throughout his years as bishop, he died while visiting the monastery of Morimond on a journey to attend the general chapter of the Cistercian order.[123] This dedication to his monastic vow suggests that Otto's conflicts with his secular brothers, as well as his critiques of their behavior, were products of the antiworldly outlook that was central to Cistercian monasticism. The bishop's early university education may have been a factor as well; debates about the legitimacy of secular lordship were commonplace within northern French academic circles during the early twelfth century, and Otto's time in Paris may have introduced him to contemporary critiques of lay power over the church.[124] Regardless of the reason, the bishop of Freising emerges from the

---

119. Goetz, *Das Geschichtsbild Ottos von Freising*, 25.
120. Otto of Freising and Rahewin, *Gesta Friderici*, 2.42, 150–151.
121. Appelt, *Privilegium minus*, 38–44.
122. Otto of Freising and Rahewin, *Gesta Friderici*, 3.14, 183.
123. *Annales Austriae*, 611.
124. For Paris in this period, see Buc, "*Principes gentium dominantur eorum.*"

extant sources as a prelate who was more supportive of his church than he was of his brothers and their political interests.[125] Although Conrad III appointed Otto to Freising because the new king wanted a relative and ally as bishop there, fraternal bonds seem—unexpectedly—to have meant little to Otto.

By contrast, Otto's younger full brother Conrad appears in the sources as someone more willing to seek common ground with his siblings. Nothing is known about Conrad of Babenberg's life prior to his first appearance as a royal chaplain (*capellanus regis*) in the year 1139.[126] Unlike his older brother Otto, who rose through the ranks of the Cistercian order without significant support from his family, Conrad owed all his early positions in the church to his half brother Conrad III. Sources from the early and mid-1140s indicate that Conrad of Babenberg was chosen on several occasions to play important roles in the king's diplomacy. As a cathedral canon in Cologne, then the cathedral provost of Utrecht and later Hildesheim, he served as one of Conrad III's most trusted allies in the north of the kingdom, where the Staufens had traditionally possessed little influence.[127] These offices kept the young churchman Conrad separated from his family for much of the decade between 1139 and his election as bishop of Passau in 1148. He attended King Conrad III's court less frequently than Bishop Otto of Freising did; during the 1140s, the two brothers are named together in the witness lists of royal charters only twice.[128] Similarly, Conrad apparently had little contact with his secular brothers from the Babenberg lineage during the same period.[129] This would change only after he became bishop of Passau, a promotion that was almost certainly influenced by King Conrad III.[130]

The bishopric of Passau, like Freising, belonged to the archdiocese of Salzburg. Moreover, much of the duchy of Austria lay within its diocesan borders. Not surprisingly, therefore, Conrad was immediately drawn into close contact with his Babenberg brothers once his episcopacy began. In 1150, Conrad joined his brother Otto in Salzburg for a provincial synod.[131]

---

125. Kirchner-Feyerabend, *Otto von Freising*, 247–254.

126. *Annales Austriae*, 611, has much less to say about Conrad than Otto.

127. Zurstraßen, *Die Passauer Bischöfe*, 106–107.

128. MGH DD K III, 184–186, no. 104 and 312–314, no. 173, the latter of which has been identified as a possible forgery.

129. One example of contact is ibid., 60–61, no. 37, discussed above. See also ibid., 58–60, no. 36 and 312–314, no. 173.

130. Zurstraßen, *Die Passauer Bischöfe*, 108–109.

131. *Die Regesten der Bischöfe von Passau*, 1:212, no. 691; Weissthanner, "Regesten des Freisinger Bischofs Otto I.," 188, no. 101.

Two years later, he was present with Otto and their brother Henry Jasomir-gott when the newly elected king Frederick I was staying in Regensburg.[132] All three were together again with Barbarossa in Bamberg in 1154.[133] While the royal court seems to be the only place where Bishop Otto of Freising and his brother Henry came into contact with one another in this period, there is evidence from a much broader range of settings for interactions between Bishop Conrad and Henry Jasomirgott. At some point between 1149 and 1156, Henry and Conrad made a joint property donation to the monastery of Heiligenkreuz near Vienna for the salvation of their souls and the souls of their parents.[134] During the same period, the two also supported the foundation of a community of Premonstratensians at Pernegg northwest of Vienna.[135] And between 1156 and 1164, Conrad drew up a charter while residing in Vienna, concerning the punishment of an excommunicate; the witness list is led by "my brother the lord Henry, duke of Austria."[136]

Bishop Conrad of Passau's ties to Henry Jasomirgott during these years suggest that he played a role in the 1158 settlement that finally ended the territorial disputes between Henry and their brother Otto of Freising. Al-though Rahewin, the continuator of the *Gesta Friderici*, makes no mention of Conrad in his description of the settlement, other sources indicate that the bishop of Passau was in close contact with his siblings in this period. All three were at Barbarossa's court in Regensburg in January of 1158.[137] And a short time later, Conrad played an intermediary role in an exchange of lands that involved both Otto and Henry.[138] This is the earliest piece of surviving evidence to indicate that the bishop of Freising and the duke of Austria had begun to interact peaceably, and Conrad's presence is therefore noteworthy. He emerges from the sources as someone who was able to work well with both of his siblings.

Conrad's own relationship with Henry Jasomirgott did not worsen until the 1160s, in the period after the death of Bishop Otto of Freising. While the reason for the conflict is unknown, their relationship had grown sufficiently tense by 1164 to attract the attention of their nephew, Emperor Frederick, who asked the archbishop of Salzburg and other magnates from the southeast

---

132. MGH DD F I, 1:26–27, no. 14.
133. Ibid., 1:116–117, no. 70.
134. BUB, 1:23–25, no. 17.
135. *Die Regesten der Bischöfe von Passau*, 1:239, no. 768. See also 1:235–236, no. 759.
136. Ibid., 1:248–249, no. 797. See also 1:249–250, no. 801.
137. MGH DD F I, 1:335–337, no. 201.
138. *Codex Diplomaticus Austriaco-Frisingensis*, 102–103, no. 105. See also ibid., 104–105, no. 106.

of the kingdom to intervene and end the dispute.[139] Whether peace was restored between Conrad and Henry on this occasion is uncertain, for only a
few months later the political landscape changed dramatically. Conrad was
elected archbishop by the cathedral chapter of Salzburg, a community that
strongly supported Pope Alexander III. Soon thereafter, Conrad chose to
side openly with Alexander's party. According to one contemporary chronicle, Duke Henry Jasomirgott of Austria sought to convince his brother to
make peace with the emperor, but he was unsuccessful.[140] A short time later,
Barbarossa responded to Conrad's intransigence by urging Duke Henry to
attack his brother's interests in Salzburg.[141] There is no indication that Henry
ever took such dramatic action. Nevertheless, between early 1166 and Conrad's death in 1168, we know of no further contact between the brothers.[142]

The decision by Conrad of Babenberg—and Conrad of Wittelsbach as
well—to side with Pope Alexander III during the papal schism of the 1160s
highlights one of the most important differences between ecclesiastical and
secular lords. The latter were never forced to choose between their lineage's
political and territorial interests on the one hand and their official duties on
the other. During the Staufen period, dukes, margraves, and counts were not
officeholders with responsibilities that could potentially interfere with their
siblings' exercise of lordship.[143] Moreover, secular lords were not surrounded
by a rhetoric that sought to create for them, in effect, new families. The language of spiritual kinship within the Christian tradition and the theory that
a bishop was wedded to his church both sought to minimize the significance
of a churchman's birth family in ways that lay magnates would not have
encountered as holders of secular titles.[144] The careers of both Archbishop
Conrad of Salzburg and his older brother Bishop Otto of Freising thus illustrate some of the ways in which the church could create dividing lines
inside sibling groups.

On the other hand, Otto of Andechs's willingness to use his episcopal
offices to increase his brother's territorial holdings and to strengthen his

---

139. *Die Admonter Briefsammlung*, 177–178, no. 19. See also *Gesta archiepiscoporum Salisburgensium*,
82. For the argument that this conflict began several years earlier, see Lechner, *Die Babenberger*, 165.

140. *Annales Reicherspergenses*, 473.

141. *Die Admonter Briefsammlung*, 165, no. 10.

142. For Conrad's brief career as archbishop of Salzburg, see Dopsch, "Salzburg im Hochmittelalter," 284–288. The only reference to the brothers I have found dating to 1167–1168 is in a letter, but
it does not suggest interactions between the two. See *Die Admonter Briefsammlung*, 174–175, no. 16.

143. See chapter 1.

144. Griffiths, "Siblings and the Sexes," 29; d'Avray, *Medieval Marriage*, 87.

brother's lordship suggests that the ecclesiastical-secular line could also be quite blurry. That Otto twice became bishop in a diocese where the Andechs lineage already held rights and properties certainly contributed to his extraordinary largesse. But as the career of the Babenberg Bishop Otto of Freising demonstrates, geographical proximity did not guarantee a strong bond between a prelate and his lay brothers who were secular lords. In many ways, therefore, these two bishops named Otto represent the opposite ends of the spectrum of possible relationships that ecclesiastical princes could share with their siblings in the secular sphere. One was committed to helping his brother build power and influence, while the other was committed to protecting his church's rights—even against his family's interests.

As this chapter has shown, even the most prominent secular lords of the Staufen period did not have the power to influence every facet of their sons' and brothers' ecclesiastical careers. They could not install relatives in specific bishoprics whenever they chose, and they could not ensure that churchmen would give precedence to familial interests over ecclesiastical politics and diocesan territorial rights. As a result, the odds of churchmen emerging to play pivotal roles in a lineage's politics were low—perhaps too low to justify removing sons and brothers from the lineage's succession arrangements, where they could be more valuable. This may help explain why this generation of the Staufen upper aristocracy was the last to attempt to advance its political and territorial interests by securing ecclesiastical appointments for so many younger sons and brothers. Far fewer males of princely lineages became ecclesiastics during the early thirteenth century—and some of these were bastard children rather than legitimate heirs.[145]

During the middle decades of the twelfth century, the leading figures inside most of the princely lineages of the German kingdom were sets of brothers. Fathers in possession of substantial collections of rights and properties allowed multiple sons to remain in the secular sphere and to succeed to lordships—setting the stage for these heirs' frequent collaborations throughout their careers. At the same time, many of these fathers also placed at least one of their many sons in the church, typically in a cathedral chapter, where they too could potentially have a role to play in extending their lineage's influence. Examples of younger sons who disappear from the sources after their father's death are rare within the German upper aristocracy as a whole,

---

145. See chapters 6 and 7.

but this trend is especially striking in this first generation of the Staufen period. Charters and other sources make it possible to see how, from gatherings at family castles and monasteries to meetings of the imperial court in Italy, groups of brothers regularly played central roles in one another's lives. The significance of these fraternal relationships is evident in a variety of settings within the spheres of politics and princely lordship. Brothers in this generation of the upper aristocracy cofounded monastic houses, acted as ambassadors and peace negotiators for one another, helped each other acquire fiefs and imperial privileges, and fought together on the emperor's Italian campaigns. In short, sibling relationships permeated much of the fabric of German upper aristocratic society during the mid-twelfth century.

However, alongside all the large fraternal groups active in this period, two lords who lacked comparable numbers of brothers also rose to prominence. One was Henry the Lion (d. 1195) of the Welf lineage, whose acquisition of the duchies of Saxony and Bavaria early in his career made him one of the most powerful princes in the realm. The other was Duke Frederick III of Swabia (d. 1190), who was elected German king in 1152 and crowned emperor in 1155; he is better known today as Frederick Barbarossa. Frederick was probably born in 1122 and Henry in 1133/1135, meaning they had shared the political stage for decades prior to their dramatic clash in the years around 1180 that ended in Henry the Lion's ouster. This dispute has helped make Frederick and Henry the two most famous members of the twelfth-century German aristocracy, but the pair is noteworthy for another reason as well. Within the nine lineages investigated here, they had fewer brothers than any of their contemporaries who rose to prominence during the early Staufen period. Henry the Lion was an only child, while Frederick Barbarossa had just one male sibling, a half brother who was significantly younger than he was. Understanding what these family situations meant for imperial politics during an age dominated by prominent fraternal groups is the aim of the next chapter.

CHAPTER 4

Frederick Barbarossa and Henry the Lion

Cousins in an Age of Brothers

For a quarter century from the mid–1150s to the late 1170s, Duke Henry the Lion of Saxony and Bavaria was the most powerful magnate in the German kingdom. Then, in the years around 1180, he fell precipitously from his perch atop the princely hierarchy. Emperor Frederick I Barbarossa, acting in conjunction with many of the *principes imperii*, stripped him of his duchies and other imperial fiefs. Soon thereafter, Henry left the German kingdom for exile in the Angevin lands ruled by his father-in-law, King Henry II of England. He would eventually return, but his position as the preeminent magnate within the German upper aristocracy was forever lost. During the final years before his death in 1195, he let his sons play an increasingly active role in imperial politics as he withdrew to his family lands in and around Brunswick in Saxony.

While numerous aspects of Duke Henry the Lion's long career have been thoroughly researched and analyzed by modern scholars, the events surrounding the loss of his duchies have consistently been the focus of the most intense scrutiny. At the center of many debates has been the question of whether the emperor or a faction of magnates was the driving force behind the actions taken against the duke in the late 1170s and early 1180s. To phrase this more dramatically: Was Frederick Barbarossa the aggressor—the "Lion hunter"—or was he forced to accede to the demands of influential princes?[1] In this chapter, I aim to provide a fresh perspective on the magnates' involvement in Henry the Lion's fall by analyzing sibling relationships—and family relationships more generally—within the German upper aristocracy of the early Staufen period. The cooperative bonds, I argue, operating within several leading fraternal groups played a pivotal role in Barbarossa's decision to strip Henry of his fiefs.

This family-oriented approach to the events of the late 1170s and early 1180s takes as its starting point the kin connection between Emperor Frederick I and Duke Henry the Lion. The two were first cousins, and for both Frederick and Henry, this relationship proved to be essential in developing their political and territorial interests throughout the 1150s and 1160s.[2] Their close ties of cooperation and support did not begin to unravel until the 1170s, when their extended kinship group underwent significant changes. As we saw in the previous chapter, it was during this same period that influential sibling groups were emerging in other princely lineages. Thus, to understand why Frederick and Henry's bond as cousins ultimately proved to be an unreliable foundation for both of their positions in the German kingdom, it is necessary to place their relationship within the broader context of the twelfth-century histories of all nine of the lineages under investigation here. This means examining first the role of princely brothers in imperial politics during the reign of King Conrad III (1138–1152) and the early years of Barbarossa's rule. In this way, the nature of the family groups operating inside the German upper aristocracy during the years around 1180 will come into clearer focus. Viewing the interactions between Frederick Barbarossa and Henry the Lion through the lens of these shifting family dynamics across multiple decades can reveal much about their own complicated relationship—and about the significance of the sibling bond for the practice of politics during the early Staufen period.

Sibling Relationships in the Aftermath of the 1138 Royal Election

The generation of Frederick and Henry's fathers dominated the political landscape of the German kingdom during the second quarter of the twelfth century. When Emperor Lothar III died without sons on December 4, 1137, Duke Henry the Proud of Saxony and Bavaria was the most prominent

---

1. For this phrasing, see Schneidmüller, *Die Welfen,* 226, and Görich, "Jäger des Löwen?"

2. See the genealogical charts for the Staufen and Welf lineages in the appendix. Duke Henry the Black of Bavaria and his wife, Wulfhild, were the grandparents of both Henry and Frederick.

member of the German upper aristocracy. This duke had married Lothar's only daughter, Gertrude, a decade earlier, and the aging emperor had lived long enough to see the couple provide him with a grandson, Henry the Lion.[3] The boy Henry was too young to be considered a possible successor to Lothar in 1137, however. Instead, his father, Henry the Proud, was the nobleman expected to become the next king when the German magnates gathered in the spring of 1138 at Mainz for the royal election. But before this meeting of the princes ever occurred, a small group of secular and ecclesiastical lords elected Conrad from the Staufen lineage on March 7, 1138, at Coblenz.[4] Although this election followed few if any of the accepted conventions for choosing a German king, Conrad nevertheless soon succeeded in gaining the support of many of the leading magnates of the realm. According to Otto of Freising, Henry the Proud's arrogance was the main reason why the other princes blocked his path to the kingship, but this was not the only reason for Conrad's election.[5] Like Henry, Conrad had family connections that bolstered his candidacy. He was the grandson of the Salian ruler Henry IV and the nephew of Henry V.[6] Moreover, Conrad had supported Lothar III in the closing years of the emperor's life and seems to have been well respected in court circles during the years 1135–1137.[7]

Although it was a small group of churchmen that orchestrated Conrad's election at Coblenz, the new king's older brother, Duke Frederick II of Swabia, quickly established himself as one of the leading figures at the royal court. Within six weeks of Conrad becoming king, both Frederick II and his young son Frederick Barbarossa had joined the new ruler in Mainz.[8] During subsequent years, Duke Frederick II was frequently at his younger brother's side.[9] Conrad's election thus marked the beginning of a new phase in what was already a complicated sibling relationship. Thirteen years earlier, in 1125, Frederick II had been the magnate expected to succeed Emperor Henry V, only to have the electors unexpectedly choose Lothar of Supplinburg instead. When the duke formed a conspiracy against Lothar a short time later, he abandoned his own claim to the kingship and supported his younger brother.

---

3. For Henry's birth in the early or mid-1130s, see Jordan, "Heinrich der Löwe," 112–117, and Ehlers, *Heinrich der Löwe*, 47–48.

4. For this election, see Schlick, *König, Fürsten und Reich*, 131–142.

5. Otto of Freising and Rahewin, *Gesta Friderici*, 1.23, 36.

6. For more on kinship ties and the 1138 election, see Weiler, "Suitability and Right," 74.

7. Lubich, "Beobachtungen zur Wahl Konrads III.," 320–321.

8. MGH DD K III, 15–16, no. 8. Barbarossa was probably fifteen years of age at the time: Opll, *Friedrich Barbarossa*, 29; Görich, *Friedrich Barbarossa*, 59.

9. See various charters in MGH DD K III, 18–69, nos. 10–42.

The siblings had little success in their efforts to orchestrate a coup, however, and they eventually reconciled with Lothar in 1135. Three years later, Conrad's election finally brought them the kingship they had spent more than a decade trying to obtain.[10]

How did the relationship between Frederick and Conrad affect imperial politics during the 1130s and 1140s? According to the model of German history that pervaded most twentieth-century scholarship on this period, Conrad and Henry the Proud were the candidates put forward in 1138 by the two greatest noble lineages of their day, the Staufens and Welfs.[11] Historians working within this narrative of Staufen-Welf rivalry assumed that Conrad and his older brother, Frederick—because they belonged to the same noble "house" (*Haus*)—cooperated with one another in a single-minded commitment to promote the political interests of their lineage.[12] In other words, they were thought to possess a mutual sense of "Staufen" self-understanding (*Selbstverständnis*) and self-awareness (*Selbstbewußtsein*) that shaped all their decisions and actions.[13] In the late twentieth and early twenty-first centuries, however, German scholars have increasingly sought to complicate this traditional model of the Staufen-Welf conflict. The theory of the rigid noble "house" has been revised in order to take into account the fluidity of kinship structures during the central Middle Ages. Historians now recognize that every lord labeled a "Welf" or a "Staufen" in the modern scholarship did not automatically share a common identity with every other member of his lineage, however that lineage may be defined.[14]

A much more nuanced understanding of the relationship between Frederick II and Conrad emerges from the sources when they are read from this newer perspective. On the one hand, there is no evidence to suggest that the two brothers were ever on opposite sides of a dispute or conflict. Indeed, various sources indicate that the pair frequently supported each other militarily from the 1120s onward.[15] On the other hand, both charters and chronicles demonstrate that their political and territorial interests did not always overlap. The earliest sources for their actions as lords, which date from the time

10. See the introduction for more on this point.

11. For a classic account of the "Guelf-Ghibelline feud" in English, see Thompson, *Feudal Germany*, 266–291, esp. 272.

12. See, for example, Heuermann, *Die Hausmachtpolitik der Staufer*, 83–111.

13. Even Werner Hechberger, the strongest critic of the Staufen-Welf model, argues this about the brothers: Hechberger, *Staufer und Welfen*, 160, 225.

14. Ibid., 160–171; Schneidmüller, *Die Welfen*, 15–40.

15. On this point, compare Lubich, "Beobachtungen zur Wahl Konrads III.," 329–338, and Hechberger, "Konrad III.," 334–335.

of Emperor Henry V, indicate that they had inherited rights and properties in different parts of the German kingdom following their father's death. As a result, Frederick II focused on exercising lordship in his duchy of Swabia while Conrad spent much of his early career on his lands in Franconia.[16] Then, in the late 1120s and early 1130s, Conrad lived for at least three years in Italy—without his brother—while trying to gain support for his fragile antikingship and his efforts to overthrow Lothar III.[17] And after the two siblings reconciled with Lothar, Conrad became a more regular visitor to the imperial court than his older brother did.[18]

Thus, during the early decades of the brothers' lives, Frederick II and Conrad sometimes worked closely together, but just as often followed separate paths. This same pattern is evident after Conrad's election as king. Although the duke witnessed more than sixty of his brother's royal charters between the years 1138 and 1147, he did not follow Conrad everywhere the king went in the realm. The vast majority of Frederick II's appearances at court occurred when Conrad was in Swabia and the upper Rhine River valley.[19] This is the same region where the duke had been exercising lordship and exerting his authority for a quarter century.[20] Many of the brothers' joint military operations against rival lords, especially those from the Welf and Zähringen lineages, also occurred in this southwest corner of the kingdom.[21] Frederick and Conrad thus maintained a close relationship after 1138, but the duke of Swabia was most willing to work alongside his younger brother when Conrad's itinerant court was residing in the neighborhood of his own lordships.

Outside of Swabia and the upper Rhine valley, Conrad III relied on other members of his sibling group for support. The king benefited from having numerous younger half siblings who had been born to his mother, Agnes, and her second husband, Margrave Leopold III of Austria (d. 1136) from the Babenberg lineage. Unlike Conrad's older brother, Frederick II, who was in his late forties and had already been duke of Swabia for more than three

---

16. Lubich, *Auf dem Weg zur "Güldenen Freiheit,"* 151–204.

17. Engels, *Die Staufer*, 28; Niederkorn, "Konrad III. als Gegenkönig," 596–597; Lubich, "Beobachtungen zur Wahl Konrads III.," 331.

18. MGH DD L III, 155, no. 97; 163, no. 101; 187, no. 117; 202, no. 120.

19. Schwarzmaier, "*Pater imperatoris*," 279; Ziegler, *König Konrad III.*, 345–355.

20. Otto of Freising stresses the duke's long-standing interest in dominating the area between Basel and Mainz: Otto of Freising and Rahewin, *Gesta Friderici*, 1.12, 27–28.

21. See, for example, the sources for the siege of Weinberg in 1140, especially *Chronica regia Coloniensis*, 77, and MGH DD K III, 89–90, no. 53. Their military cooperation in this region extends back to the earlier years of their careers: see *Historia Welforum*, 62–63, chap. 20.

decades when Conrad was elected, most of these half siblings were only beginning to emerge as active political figures in the late 1130s. As a result, the new king could integrate them more easily into his practice of kingship. Soon after his election, he convinced his half brother Otto, the Cistercian abbot of Morimond, to accept the vacant position of bishop of Freising. A short time later, Otto's younger brother, Conrad, became a royal chaplain— and eventually bishop of Passau.[22] After the new king stripped his rival, Henry the Proud, of the duchies of Saxony and Bavaria in the year 1138, he also relied on his Babenberg siblings for help establishing a new political order inside the kingdom.[23] His half brother Leopold IV, who had succeeded to the march of Austria in 1136, received Henry the Proud's former duchy of Bavaria from Conrad III in early 1139.

One of the closest relationships the king developed with any of his siblings was with his half brother Henry Jasomirgott.[24] In 1140, the king enfeoffed him with the county-palatine of the Rhine, and three years later, this Henry succeeded his brother Leopold IV as duke of Bavaria. Conrad III also arranged a prestigious marriage alliance for Henry Jasomirgott during this same period. Gertrude, the only daughter of Emperor Lothar III, was widowed when Henry the Proud died in late 1139 a few months after losing his duchies. Since her son, Henry the Lion, was still a minor at the time, Gertrude emerged as an influential figure in Saxon politics during the early 1140s. The king therefore orchestrated the union between Henry Jasomirgott and Gertrude in 1142 in an attempt to establish a position of power and authority for his half sibling within the duchy of Saxony.[25] The move proved ineffective because most Saxon nobles supported the young Henry the Lion instead, but this marriage is nevertheless additional evidence for the king's reliance on his siblings as he sought to expand the reach of his kingship. Indeed, four of Conrad's half brothers from the Babenberg lineage owed their positions to his efforts to bring stability to the turbulent Saxon and Bavarian duchies during the opening years of his reign.

Otto of Freising, in his *Historia de duabus civitatibus*, identifies Duke Leopold IV of Bavaria at one point as "[Conrad III's] brother on his mother's

---

22. For the churchmen Otto and Conrad, see chapter 3.

23. For the stripping of Henry the Proud's duchies, see Schneidmüller, *Die Welfen*, 174–177, and Patzold, "Konflikte im Stauferreich," 150–155.

24. Ziegler, *König Konrad III.*, 392–405. For Henry Jasomirgott, see also chapters 2 and 3.

25. Weller, *Die Heiratspolitik des deutschen Hochadels*, 355–357. Henry's next marriage was also orchestrated by Conrad III (ibid., 357–360), as were the marriages of some of Conrad's half sisters (ibid., 363–378).

side" (*frater suus ex parte matris*).[26] Other contemporary sources, however, are rarely so precise in their descriptions of the blood connection linking the king to his Babenberg half brothers. More typical is a royal charter from the year 1139 that records a grant Conrad made "through the intervention of our most beloved mother, Agnes, and our brother (*fratris*) Otto, the venerable bishop of the church of Freising, and our brother (*fratris*) Duke Leopold [IV] of Bavaria."[27] The witness list of the same charter includes "our brother (*frater*) Duke Frederick . . . [and] our brother (*frater*) Conrad." At the royal court, the distinction between full siblings and half siblings seems not to have been a significant one as Conrad III sought to stabilize his kingship and exert effective authority inside the German kingdom. The combined Staufen-Babenberg sibling group with which he surrounded himself thus emerges from the sources as an essential component of the imperial politics of the late 1130s and 1140s.[28]

Conrad's decision to place his brothers in key positions throughout the kingdom was certainly not innovative. Other German kings and emperors had pursued similar strategies for their siblings and more distant relatives in previous centuries.[29] Nevertheless, the size and composition of the sibling group supporting Conrad's kingship is significant for three reasons. First, because he was not the eldest sibling, Conrad was not the only member of his generation to have acquired a strong position in the kingdom prior to his election. His older brother, Frederick II, was firmly entrenched in the duchy of Swabia by 1138 and had already been a prominent figure in the German upper aristocracy for decades. As a result, the new ruler already had a key foundation stone for his kingship in place even before he was elected. Second, Conrad benefited from having four half brothers who were much newer to the political scene in 1138—and were therefore ready to fill vacant positions as they became available. These Babenbergs provided the king with a pool of brothers who could expand considerably the reach of his political influence in the critical months and years immediately after his election.

The third reason for the distinctiveness of King Conrad III's sibling group is a product of the broader contemporary context. The Staufen-Babenberg

---

26. Otto of Freising, *Chronica*, 7.23, 347.

27. MGH DD K III, 60–61, no. 37.

28. Weller, "Auf dem Weg zum 'staufischen Haus,'" 54–55; Schlick, *König, Fürsten und Reich*, 146–147; Engels, *Die Staufer*, 44–45.

29. The emperors Otto I (936–973) and Henry II (1002–1024) are two of the best examples of earlier German rulers who placed brothers in key positions in the kingdom.

fraternal group was significantly larger than any other sibling group active within the German upper aristocracy during the late 1130s and early 1140s. Conrad's chief rival for the throne in 1138, Duke Henry the Proud of Saxony and Bavaria, had only two brothers. One of these was a Cistercian monk who had died in 1126.[30] The other was Welf VI, with whom Henry developed a close relationship during the early and mid-1130s. Extant sources indicate that these siblings supported each other militarily in this period, and Henry the Proud even arranged his younger brother's marriage to a prominent heiress.[31] However, Henry's death only eighteen months after Conrad's election promptly severed this sibling bond, and the connection between Welf VI and his young nephew Henry the Lion seems not to have been close during the 1140s.[32] Of the nine princely lineages examined here, the Ludowings were the only other one with adult brothers who were politically active when Conrad became king. The siblings Landgrave Ludwig I of Thuringia and Bishop Udo of Naumburg (1125–1148) are named together in various sources from the 1130s, and both supported Conrad III after his election.[33] With Ludwig's death in 1140, however, this sibling group also came to an abrupt end very early in Conrad's reign.[34]

At the time of the 1138 royal election, four other princely lineages were headed by the lords I have identified as the founders of these lineages: Count Berthold I of Andechs, the Ascanian margrave Albert the Bear of Brandenburg, the Wettin margrave Conrad of Meissen, and the Wittelsbach count-palatine Otto I of Bavaria.[35] These nobles had sought to distance themselves from the other members of their extended kinship groups, and like the head of another lineage—Duke Conrad of Zähringen (d. 1152)—they had no living brothers.[36] Moreover, in each of these cases, the next generation of these lineages—the baby-boom generation discussed in the previous chapter—was just beginning to appear regularly in the surviving sources during the late 1130s and early 1140s. The sibling group that surrounded King Conrad III was therefore unrivaled in size and influence during the opening years of

---

30. See chapter 2.

31. *Historia Welforum*, 60–63, chaps. 19–20.

32. Hechberger, *Staufer und Welfen*, 201–216.

33. MGH DD K III, 21–22, no. 13, and 53–55, no. 33, and various entries in *Regesta diplomatica necnon epistolaria*, 1:262–290, nos. 1251–1387.

34. Unfortunately, the sibling relationships in the next generation of the Ludowing lineage are not well documented (see chapter 2).

35. See chapter 1.

36. Duke Conrad's older brother, Berthold III, had died several years earlier: see Parlow, *Die Zähringer*, 157–158.

the Staufen period. Four decades later, when the conflict between Emperor Frederick I Barbarossa and Duke Henry the Lion began, the situation inside the German upper aristocracy would look quite different. The Andechses, Ascanians, Wettins, Wittelsbachs and Zähringens would all be led by sets of brothers that included at least two *principes imperii*.

Although King Conrad III's sibling group helped him stabilize his kingship in the months and years immediately following his election, its political efficacy was ultimately short-lived. As noted in previous chapters, the sons of Margrave Leopold III of Austria were one of the least cooperative groups of brothers active in the German upper aristocracy during the Staufen period. They did not support one another as well as they supported their half brother the king, and the duchy of Bavaria remained a focal point of political upheaval throughout the years after 1139, despite the presence of multiple Babenberg brothers there.[37] Conrad's fraternal group further unraveled during the mid-1140s when his nephew Frederick Barbarossa began to play an increasingly active role in the politics and lordship of the aging duke Frederick II of Swabia. Uncle and nephew did not have as close a relationship in this period as the two brothers had, and they were even on opposite sides of a dispute in the year 1143 over the succession to the duchy of Bavaria.[38] Thus, despite surrounding himself with a group of brothers that included five secular and ecclesiastical magnates, Conrad was unable to rely consistently on these siblings during the final years of his reign.[39] I will return to this point in the next chapter, for Conrad's experience with his brothers has important parallels with the experiences that later German kings and emperors had with their brothers.

A Generational Shift

One of the last significant gatherings of King Conrad III's sibling group occurred in 1147–1148, when his half brothers Duke Henry Jasomirgott and Bishop Otto of Freising joined him on the Second Crusade. His older brother, Duke Frederick II of Swabia, had died in the months leading up to the king's departure for the Holy Land, but the crusade nevertheless seems to have been the cause of a rift between the pair in the duke's final days. According to Otto of Freising, when the young Frederick Barbarossa made

37. See chapters 2 and 3, and more generally, Dopsch, *Österreichische Geschichte*, 126–132.
38. Hechberger, *Staufer und Welfen*, 32–35, 216–217.
39. Ibid., 257–258; Ziegler, *König Konrad III.*, 227–229.

the decision to join the expedition, "[his father,] the most noble Duke Frederick [II,] was staying in Gaul, delayed by a grave illness. He bore in his mind fierce indignation against his lord and brother King Conrad because Conrad had permitted his son Frederick to take the cross. The duke had made Frederick—who, as the first-born and only son of his most noble first wife, had been entrusted by the duke's grace with his second wife and their little son—the heir to all his lands. . . . The duke, after living not many more days, could no longer endure the force of his sorrow and died."[40] Barbarossa returned unscathed from his journey to the Holy Land, but Otto's account of Duke Frederick II's death nevertheless highlights a key issue in the long career of Emperor Frederick I. He had only one brother, a half sibling named Conrad who was significantly younger than he was.[41] As a result, when his father died, in 1147, he not only succeeded as duke of Swabia but also received all of Frederick II's rights and properties. No group of adult brothers existed to divide the patrimony—or to offer the new duke support.

Five years later when Barbarossa became king, the kinship network surrounding him reflected his unusual family situation. The royal election of 1152 had been made necessary by the unexpected death of King Conrad III's eldest son two years earlier; Conrad's only other son was a minor who was quickly overlooked in the events that followed the king's own death.[42] Unfortunately, the precise details of the negotiations that led to Frederick being elected by the princes are obscured by the biases of the extant sources.[43] Nevertheless, the evidence does indicate that two of the new king's strongest supporters in the days and weeks after his election were his maternal uncle Welf VI and his first cousin Duke Henry the Lion of Saxony.[44] Like Frederick, both of these noblemen belonged to very small nuclear families during the early 1150s. Welf VI was the last surviving male member of his generation of the Welf lineage and had only one son, who was probably still a minor in this period.[45] Henry the Lion, meanwhile, was an only child. He had married in 1147 while still a teenager, but the one son born to this first wife had died as an infant a short time later.[46] The family group on which Frederick Barbarossa relied immediately after his

---

40. Otto of Freising and Rahewin, *Gesta Friderici*, 1.41, 59–60.

41. For his sisters, see Weller, *Die Heiratspolitik des deutschen Hochadels*, 38–43.

42. Althoff, "Friedrich von Rothenburg," 308–311.

43. Engels, "Geschichte der Staufer," 58–91.

44. Ehlers, *Heinrich der Löwe*, 80–83; Hechberger, *Staufer und Welfen*, 258.

45. Feldmann, "Welf VI. und sein Sohn," 23 (with n. 77).

46. Jordan, "Heinrich der Löwe," 118–119.

election thus looked very different from the family group that surrounded King Conrad III in 1138.[47]

During the early 1150s, King Frederick I's family group also looked very different from the family groups in some of the other leading princely lineages. Only two months after his election, he was joined by many prominent members of the Saxon aristocracy at a gathering of the royal court in Merseburg. There, on May 18, 1152, the witnesses to one of his charters included "Duke Henry [the Lion] of Saxony, his uncle the lord Welf [VI], Margrave Conrad of Meissen and his sons, and Margrave Albert [the Bear] and his sons."[48] Since Margrave Conrad and Margrave Albert both had at least three or four adult sons in the year 1152, it is impossible to know just how large the Wettin and Ascanian family groups were who attended this meeting of the court. Regardless, they must have rivaled in size the group of Staufen–Welf relatives present in Merseburg.[49] A similar situation is also evident in July of the same year when Frederick Barbarossa held court at Regensburg in Bavaria. Included in the witness list of one royal charter are his maternal uncle Welf VI and two of his paternal uncles from the Babenberg lineage, Duke Henry Jasomirgott of Bavaria and Bishop Conrad of Passau. Also named as witnesses are "Count-Palatine Otto [I of Bavaria] and his two sons Otto and Frederick."[50] Thus, while Frederick was surrounded by uncles from an older generation of his extended family, the Wittelsbach lineage of the count-palatine consisted of a father and his sons.[51] In the coming years, the siblings belonging to this younger generation of the Wittelsbachs—as well as the Ascanians and Wettins—would begin to acquire increasingly influential positions on the political stage of the kingdom.

Viewing the early careers of both Frederick Barbarossa and Henry the Lion through the lens of their smaller-than-average sibling groups—at least in comparison to other princely lineages of the day—sheds new light on two key issues in the imperial politics of this period. First, it explains why Duke Henry the Lion of Saxony and Bavaria was such a loyal supporter of the king and emperor throughout the 1150s and 1160s. Some historians have suggested that Frederick bought his cousin's vote in the election of 1152 by promising to enfeoff him with the duchy of Bavaria, which had formerly

---

47. Görich, "Jäger des Löwen?" 106.

48. MGH DD F I, 1:19–22, no. 11. See also Lindner, "Friedrich Barbarossa, Heinrich der Löwe," 202–203.

49. See chapters 2 and 3 for more on the Wettins and Ascanians in this period.

50. MGH DD F I, 1:24–25, no. 13.

51. See chapter 3 for more on this point.

been held by Henry's father, Henry the Proud.[52] While this is certainly plausible, Henry the Lion stood to gain much more than just a ducal title by supporting Barbarossa's kingship. He needed Frederick as an ally, because the duke had no other close relatives in this period except his paternal uncle Welf VI, who showed little interest in working cooperatively with his nephew.[53] Moreover, Henry the Lion lacked strong networks of friends and allies in either Bavaria or his duchy of Saxony, and as a result, he depended first and foremost on his cousin Frederick for the maintenance of his position in the upper aristocracy.[54]

Second, this perspective on the opening years of Barbarossa's reign explains why the king and emperor relied on such a diverse array of relatives in pursuing his own political and territorial interests. Numerous leading secular and ecclesiastical lords in the German kingdom are referred to as Frederick's *consanguinei* in his charters, evidence for his efforts to bind as many distant kinsmen to his rule as possible.[55] The group of his closest relatives who regularly attended his court in the 1150s and 1160s included several magnates who have already been mentioned: his first cousin Henry the Lion; his maternal uncle Welf VI; and his paternal uncles from the Babenberg lineage, namely Duke Henry Jasomirgott of Bavaria, Bishop Conrad of Passau, and Bishop Otto of Freising.[56] Another frequent court attendee was another of the emperor's first cousins: Frederick of Rothenburg (d. 1167), the younger son of King Conrad III. This Frederick received the duchy of Swabia from Barbarossa in the early 1150s and traveled across the Alps with the emperor on two of his Italian expeditions.[57] The ruler's two brothers-in-law, Duke Matthew of Upper Lotharingia and Landgrave Ludwig II of Thuringia, also provided him with political and military support on various occasions.[58]

The final member of this group of closest kin was Barbarossa's younger half brother, Conrad (d. 1195). In the autumn of 1156, the emperor enfeoffed him with the county-palatine of the Rhine, thus elevating him into

---

52. Engels, "Geschichte der Staufer," 80–82; Töpfer, "Kaiser Friedrich Barbarossa," 13–14; Ehlers, *Heinrich der Löwe*, 82.

53. Hechberger, *Staufer und Welfen*, 288–289.

54. Ehlers, *Heinrich der Löwe*, 136–139, 162–165, 399.

55. See, for example, MGH DD F I, 3:34–35, no. 565; 3:133–135, no. 636; 3:214–216, no. 693; 3:341–343, no. 782; 3:360–363, no. 795.

56. For an example of this kin network's involvement in imperial politics, see Görich, *Friedrich Barbarossa*, 292–294.

57. Althoff, "Friedrich von Rothenburg," 311–313; Plassmann, *Die Struktur des Hofes*, 215–216.

58. Plassmann, *Die Struktur des Hofes*, 55–56, 126; Parisse, "Les ducs et le duché de Lorraine," 90, 93; Patze, *Die Entstehung der Landesherrschaft*, 1:214–218.

the ranks of the *principes imperii*.[59] Conrad became a frequent visitor to the imperial court and is identified as the emperor's *"frater"* in many of Frederick's charters.[60] During the mid-1160s, however, the gulf between the half brothers' political interests grew wider. When Conrad attempted to expand his authority and influence as count-palatine by involving himself in the politics of the archdioceses of Mainz, Trier, and Cologne, the emperor refused to support his expansionary tactics in the Rhine River valley. Barbarossa was unwilling to promote his half brother's interests at the expense of his relationships with three of the archbishops of the kingdom.[61] Nevertheless, Conrad continued to appear occasionally at the imperial court throughout the 1170s and 1180s. Though he rarely attached himself to his half brother for extended periods of time—presumably because he was determined to build his own lordship inside his county-palatine—the relationship between the brothers seems to have been a strong one in later years.[62] Much like Duke Frederick II of Swabia in the previous generation, therefore, Count-Palatine Conrad showed himself to be a supporter of his brother, but one who was more interested in advancing his own lordship than that of his ruling sibling.[63]

The somewhat cool relationship between the half brothers Frederick Barbarossa and Conrad during the mid-1160s fits into a broader pattern visible inside the emperor's close family. As impressive as this collection of secular and ecclesiastical princes was, it was not as consistently reliable as the sibling groups discussed in the previous chapter. Most of the members of this kin group distanced themselves from Barbarossa at one point or another during his reign. Henry the Lion, the clearest example of this trend, will be considered below, but there are several other noteworthy cases as well. Duke Henry Jasomirgott of Bavaria was not a strong supporter of Frederick during the early 1150s, because Barbarossa was backing Henry the Lion's claim to his duchy.[64] Only after the emperor issued the charter known as the *Privilegium minus* on September 17, 1156, thus transforming the march of Austria into an independent duchy, did Henry Jasomirgott become a

---

59. Opll, *Friedrich Barbarossa*, 54–55.

60. See, for example, MGH DD F I, 1:110–111, no. 65; 2:79–80, no. 271; 3:103–104, no. 614.

61. Brinken, *Die Politik Konrads von Staufen*, 188–195, 231–232.

62. Plassmann, *Die Struktur des Hofes*, 217–218. See especially MGH DD F I, 3:243–244, no. 709.

63. For more on the brothers of kings and emperors, see chapter 5.

64. Ehlers, *Heinrich der Löwe*, 82; Görich, "'. . . damit die Ehre unseres Onkels'"; Lechner, *Die Babenberger*, 151–152.

more consistent ally.[65] Soon thereafter, however, another of Frederick's paternal uncles—Bishop Conrad of Passau, who later became archbishop of Salzburg—clashed with his nephew as a result of the papal schism of the 1160s.[66] Barbarossa's maternal uncle Welf VI also sided with Pope Alexander III against the emperor during the schism and was absent from the imperial court for more than a decade after his only son died on Frederick's Italian campaign of 1167.[67] The emperor's cousin Frederick of Rothenburg, the duke of Swabia, similarly refused to back Barbarossa's papal politics in the mid-1160s. During the same period, his active support for Welf VI's enemies in the so-called Tübingen feud is further evidence for the lack of solidarity inside the emperor's kin group.[68]

While Frederick Barbarossa was surrounding himself with this unpredictable collection of uncles and cousins—and one half brother—drawn from his extended Staufen-Welf-Babenberg kinship group, other magnate lineages were seeing the emergence of much more cohesive family groups based predominantly on the sibling bond. As discussed in the previous chapter, the Andechs, Wettin, Wittelsbach, and Zähringen lineages all had generations consisting of multiple brothers come to power in the late 1150s and early 1160s. By 1172, two other magnate lineages—the Ascanians and Ludowings—were also being led by groups of brothers. Significantly, the arrival on the political scene of so many new sibling groups inside the German upper aristocracy coincided with the most intense phase of the relationship between Frederick Barbarossa and Henry the Lion. In 1162, at the behest of the emperor, the duke of Saxony and Bavaria divorced his wife, Clementia, the sister of the emperor's chief rivals in the Zähringen lineage: Duke Berthold IV and Rudolf. Three years later, Barbarossa rewarded his cousin's loyalty by helping to arrange an illustrious marriage for Henry with Matilda, a daughter of King Henry II of England.[69] The duke, meanwhile, continued to show his support for the emperor by siding closely with Frederick in the papal schism.[70] And during the late 1160s, Barbarossa consistently backed Henry the Lion in the latter's efforts to suppress an uprising within the Saxon aristocracy.[71]

---

65. MGH DD F I, 1:255–260, no. 151; Appelt, *Privilegium minus*.

66. See chapter 3.

67. Schneidmüller, *Die Welfen*, 200–203; Plassmann, *Die Struktur des Hofes*, 136–137.

68. Althoff, "Friedrich von Rothenburg," 313–315; Görich, *Friedrich Barbarossa*, 137–141.

69. Ehlers, *Heinrich der Löwe*, 183–185. The marriage between Henry and Matilda took place in 1168.

70. Ibid., 187–188.

71. See below.

The cousinly bond between emperor and duke was thus at its strongest in these years when the sibling bond was rapidly growing in significance within other princely lineages. Lacking other reliable family relationships, Frederick and Henry depended heavily on one another as they sought to navigate the complex politics surrounding the papal schism, marriage alliances among the princely elite, and aristocratic discontent in the sprawling duchy of Saxony. Only a decade later, however, their close relationship had begun to fray. And as their bond of cooperation and support weakened, the siblings active inside several other lineages took advantage of the changing political situation.

Siblings and the Fall of Henry the Lion

In 1174, Frederick Barbarossa crossed the Alps for the fifth time during his reign and resumed his decades-long struggle to exercise effective authority in northern Italy. The army he brought with him on this occasion was a relatively small one consisting mostly of mercenaries and contingents provided by ecclesiastical princes.[72] After failing to make any significant military gains in the opening months of the expedition, he arranged a truce with the northern Italian towns of the Lombard League in April of 1175 and then disbanded much of his army. When fighting flared again in autumn of the same year, the emperor found himself lacking sufficient troops to continue campaigning. He therefore appealed to Henry the Lion for help at a meeting in January of 1176 at Chiavenna north of Lake Como.[73] However, the duke of Saxony and Bavaria refused to provide any military support. Other German magnates led by Archbishop Philip of Cologne did agree to provide additional troops, but on May 29, 1176, these reinforcements failed to give Barbarossa a victory at the Battle of Legnano. A year later in the summer of 1177, the emperor finally made peace at Venice with his Italian rivals, including the Lombard League and Pope Alexander III.[74]

When Barbarossa returned to the German kingdom in the autumn of 1178, war was raging in the duchy of Saxony. Archbishop Philip of Cologne, who had departed Italy prior to the emperor, had invaded Henry the Lion's lands during the summer and had destroyed several of the duke's castles. On November 11, 1178, Frederick held court at Speyer in an attempt to

---

72. Opll, *Friedrich Barbarossa*, 115; Stöckel, "Reichsbischöfe und Reichsheerfahrt," 74.

73. For Chiavenna, see Garnier, *Die Kultur der Bitte*, 188–201; Ehlers, *Heinrich der Löwe*, 220–227; and Stöckel, "Die Weigerung Heinrichs des Löwen."

74. For the Peace of Venice, see Weinfurter, "Venedig 1177," 9–12, and Raccagni, *Lombard League*, 92–102.

restore peace. Henry the Lion and Philip were both present. In the aftermath of the events at Chiavenna, Barbarossa was no longer inclined to offer his unwavering support to his first cousin as he had done in earlier years. Instead, he called for a meeting at Worms in January of 1179 and summoned both sides in the conflict to have their complaints heard there by him and the *principes imperii*. Henry the Lion chose not to attend this meeting, however, and when Barbarossa held court six months later in June at Magdeburg, the duke of Saxony and Bavaria again failed to appear. A short time later, Frederick and Henry the Lion met privately. Barbarossa reportedly offered to mediate the duke's dispute with his enemies in exchange for five thousand silver marks, but Henry the Lion refused, further straining their relationship. On January 13, 1180, at Würzburg, after the duke once more failed to appear at the imperial court, the emperor and the princes deprived him of the duchies of Saxony and Bavaria and all his other imperial fiefs.

In a charter issued on April 13, 1180, at Gelnhausen, Frederick formally enfeoffed Archbishop Philip of Cologne with a new duchy, consisting of the western portions of Henry the Lion's old duchy of Saxony. The eastern sections of the Saxon duchy were granted to a member of the Ascanian lineage, Count Bernhard of Aschersleben. A few months later, the emperor enfeoffed Count-Palatine Otto *maior* of the Wittelsbach lineage with the duchy of Bavaria. Like Saxony, the Bavarian duchy was divided as part of this process, with the march of Styria becoming a separate duchy independent from the Bavarian dukes. Throughout this period when the emperor was carving up and distributing Henry the Lion's fiefs among various German magnates, the former duke fought desperately to maintain his power and authority, waging a vicious war against his rivals in Saxony. Despite a few initial military successes, however, he was unable to regain his ducal titles. At a meeting of the imperial court at Erfurt in November of 1181, the princes confirmed the loss of his duchies—in his presence. A few months later, he departed the kingdom and went into exile in the lands of his father-in-law, King Henry II of England.[75]

The list of secular and ecclesiastical lords who were involved in Henry the Lion's fall—and benefited from his disgrace—is long. Some of these lords, including most notably Archbishop Philip of Cologne, were not members

---

75. Jordan, *Henry the Lion*, 160–182, is one of the best accounts of these events in English, though it is now somewhat dated. Recent works that complicate the straightforward narrative I provide here include Görich, "Jäger des Löwen?" 109–116; Ehlers, *Heinrich der Löwe*, 317–344; Patzold, "Konflikte im Stauferreich," 158–160; Hechberger, *Staufer und Welfen*, 310–332; Althoff, "Konfliktverhalten und Rechtsbewußtsein"; and Heinemeyer, "Der Prozeß Heinrichs des Löwen."

of the nine lineages investigated here.[76] As a result, my aim here is not to reconstruct *all* the political networks that influenced the events of the late 1170s and early 1180s but to examine the roles played by several prominent sibling groups at the imperial court during this period. In five princely lineages, multiple brothers worked closely with the emperor in these years and formed fraternal groups of impressive durability and strength during the conflict with Henry the Lion. Many of the brothers in these sibling groups received new lordships in the late 1170s and early 1180s, and the influence that these siblings exerted over the emperor was crucial to the successful rise of several of them into the ranks of the *principes imperii*.

Before shifting to these sibling groups, a final observation about Frederick Barbarossa's and Henry the Lion's familial situations is necessary. During the late 1170s, after the relationship between the first cousins grew strained, both the emperor and the duke had few other close relatives on whom they could rely. In Barbarossa's case, his family in these years bore little resemblance to the family that had surrounded him a quarter century earlier. All his paternal uncles from the Babenberg lineage were dead—as were his Staufen cousin Frederick of Rothenburg and his two brothers-in-law.[77] His maternal uncle Welf VI was still alive, but since the death of his only son in 1167, Welf VI had largely withdrawn from imperial politics.[78] Count-Palatine Conrad of the Rhine, Frederick's half brother, is therefore the only close relative whose presence at the imperial court can be traced from the 1150s through the 1180s. Conrad is named alongside his brother on various occasions during the pivotal years around 1180. As noted above, however, the count-palatine also had his own territorial interests to pursue, and as a result, he was not a constant presence at his half brother's side throughout this period.[79] Further limiting the size of the emperor's kin group during this period was the situation inside his own nuclear family. Frederick's first marriage had been childless. In 1156, he had married his second wife, Beatrice of Burgundy, but they did not begin to have children until the mid-1160s.[80] As a result, Barbarossa's two eldest sons—Henry and Frederick—were just beginning

---

76. Weinfurter, "Erzbischof Philipp von Köln."

77. Several of the children of these uncles and brothers-in-law will be discussed below. However, not all the children of these lords maintained close ties to the emperor: see, for example, Plassmann, *Die Struktur des Hofes*, 126.

78. Schneidmüller, *Die Welfen*, 201–202.

79. Conrad witnessed one of the emperor's charters in 1179, one in 1180, four in 1182, and one in 1183.

80. Assmann, "Friedrich Barbarossas Kinder," 459.

to appear regularly in imperial charters in the late 1170s and would not be knighted until 1184.[81]

Henry the Lion's children, meanwhile, were even younger. His three eldest sons were all born in the mid-1170s, and none was older than seven when he lost his duchies.[82] Two additional factors also contributed to the duke's small family in this period. First, his closest blood relative besides Frederick Barbarossa was his paternal uncle Welf VI, who offered him no support during the late 1170s and early 1180s. In 1178, Welf VI even agreed to sell his extensive landholdings along the Swabian-Bavarian border to his nephew Frederick Barbarossa, his sister's son, rather than to his nephew Henry the Lion, his brother's son.[83] Second, while the duke's marriage in 1168 to King Henry II of England's daughter Matilda brought him significant prestige, it did not expand his network of relatives and allies in the German kingdom. For Henry the Lion, the disadvantages that came with being an only child were thus on full display in the years after 1176. Fraternal groups inside five other princely lineages—the Ascanians, Wittelsbachs, Andechses, Ludowings, and Wettins—were prepared to take his place and to exert their influence at court once Frederick and Henry's relationship fractured.

The Ascanian Brothers

Margrave Albert the Bear of Brandenburg, who was one of Henry the Lion's most bitter rivals in Saxony, died in 1170 after a career that spanned almost a half century. According to some scholars, the division of his vast patrimony among his many sons marked the beginning of the end for his Ascanian lineage, because his lordships would never again be united under the control of a single family member.[84] This argument, which looks forward to the history of the lineage in the late thirteenth and early fourteenth centuries, reflects medieval historians' traditional emphasis on the multigenerational structure of the lineage. However, a narrower focus on the 1170s and 1180s and the generation of Albert's children reveals a sibling group with significant power and influence within the sphere of imperial politics. All seven of the margrave's sons—the five who succeeded to his secular lordships and the two who entered the church—had reached adulthood by the time of

---

81. For more on these sons, see chapter 5.
82. Ehlers, *Heinrich der Löwe*, 194, 227.
83. Schneidmüller, *Die Welfen*, 226–227.
84. Schwineköper, "Heinrich der Löwe," 137; Arnold, *Princes and Territories*, 245.

his death and were in a position to play an active role in their lineage. Two
of these brothers died before the conflict with Henry the Lion erupted in
1178–1179, but four other members of this fraternal group emerged as key
figures in the events surrounding the downfall of the duke of Saxony and
Bavaria.[85]

Even before their father's death, many of the Ascanian brothers had already been involved in the early clashes between Henry the Lion and the
Saxon aristocracy. In an agreement drawn up on July 12, 1167, the churches
and townspeople of Cologne and Magdeburg established a "pact of friendship" (*fedus amicicie*) directed against the duke.[86] The nobles who agreed to
join this alliance included Albert the Bear and four of his sons: Margrave
Otto I of Brandenburg, Count Herman of Orlamünde, Count Adalbert
of Ballenstedt, and Count Bernhard of Aschersleben. By the end of 1168,
another of the Ascanian brothers had also emerged as a prominent figure
in the lineage's rivalry with the duke. After the archbishop of Bremen died
on October 11, the cathedral chapter split into two rival factions, and each
elected its own archbishop. The canons opposed to Henry the Lion's harsh
lordship in Saxony chose Albert's son Siegfried, who was a cathedral canon
in Magdeburg at the time.[87] But Siegfried was unable to establish himself in
Bremen because the duke's supporters prevented him from remaining in the
town. Then, only a few months later, Frederick Barbarossa announced that
both of the cathedral canons' elections were invalid. The emperor installed
his own choice in Bremen, a local churchman who was a staunch supporter
of Henry the Lion.[88] Siegfried would have to wait another decade before he
could return to this ecclesiastical office.

Barbarossa's consistent backing of Henry the Lion during the Saxon uprising of the late 1160s strained his relationship with the Ascanians. In the
early 1170s, the sons of Albert the Bear showed little interest in cultivating
Königsnähe, and none traveled outside the duchy of Saxony and neighboring
Thuringia to attend the imperial court.[89] In 1173, some of them even came

---

85. The seventh member of this fraternal group, the Magdeburg cathedral canon Henry, may
have played an important role in these events too, since the archbishop of Magdeburg was one of
Henry the Lion's opponents. However, the sources for him are not as rich as they are for his brothers.

86. CDS 1 A, 2:234–235, no. 344. For Ascanian opposition to Henry the Lion in this period, see
also Schwineköper, "Heinrich der Löwe," 134–138, and Görich, *Friedrich Barbarossa*, 465.

87. *Annales Stadenses*, 346.

88. Partenheimer, *Albrecht der Bär*, 176–186; Ehlers, *Heinrich der Löwe*, 146–149; Jordan, *Henry
the Lion*, 99–106.

89. The only imperial charters from the years 1170–1175 to name any of the brothers as witnesses are MGH DD F I, 3:37–38, no. 567; 3:62–64, no. 585; 3:73–75, no. 594; 3:82–85, nos.
599–600; and 3:97–98, no. 610.

into conflict with the emperor as a result of an inheritance dispute.[90] According to the annals of the Saxon monastery of Pegau, "Landgrave Ludwig [III of Thuringia] attacked the sons of Margrave Albert for the sake of his uncle, the emperor. In response, they laid waste to Thuringia. After that, Weimar was destroyed by the landgrave."[91] Peace must have been restored quickly between the emperor and the brothers, however, because later the same year Barbarossa accepted Siegfried's election as bishop of Brandenburg. Some historians have seen this as an early indication of the growing distance between Frederick and Henry the Lion, for Siegfried's acquisition of a bishopric in the heartland of his secular brothers' lordships significantly strengthened the Ascanian fraternal group.[92] In the wake of Henry the Lion's refusal at Chiavenna to support Barbarossa's Italian expedition, Siegfried further helped bind his lineage to the emperor by traveling south of the Alps with his own military contingent. He first appears in Italy in July of 1176, and he was present with thirty of his knights for the Peace of Venice one year later.[93] This must have been an expensive undertaking for the bishop, and his willingness to spend such an extended period of time far from Brandenburg suggests he was anxious to strengthen his position at court at a time when tensions were growing between Barbarossa and the Ascanians' most serious rival in Saxony.[94]

After Frederick I returned from Italy, the surviving Ascanian brothers became more frequent visitors to the imperial court. Margrave Otto I of Brandenburg, Bishop Siegfried of Brandenburg, Count Bernhard of Aschersleben, and Count Dietrich of Werben were all in Magdeburg with the emperor in early July of 1179—when Henry the Lion failed to appear before Barbarossa and the princes. At this gathering of the imperial court, the emperor issued a charter in which he took the church of Brandenburg into his protection and confirmed the bishopric's possession of its rights and properties.[95] This privilege in support of Bishop Siegfried was witnessed by his three brothers and stands as evidence for the altered political landscape in Saxony. A decade earlier, the emperor had sided against the Ascanians in their

90. *Chronica regia Coloniensis*, 124; Partenheimer, *Albrecht der Bär*, 187; Marcus, *Herzog Bernhard von Anhalt*, 72–75.

91. *Annales Pegavienses*, 261.

92. Ehlers, "Heinrich der Löwe," 466–467; Marcus, *Herzog Bernhard von Anhalt*, 74–75. See also CDA, 1, pt. 3:402, no. 544 and 407, no. 550.

93. MGH DD F I, 3:157–158, no. 653; *Historia ducum Veneticorum*, 85. See also Georgi, "Wichmann, Christian, Philipp und Konrad," 72–77.

94. For a similar point, see Patzold, "Konsens und Konkurrenz," 101.

95. MGH DD F I, 3:340–341, no. 781. See also CDA, 1, pt. 3:425–426, no. 576.

efforts to expand their influence and stabilize their authority. The brothers would be rewarded even more richly the following year—after the duke of Saxony and Bavaria was stripped of his imperial fiefs. As the *Chronicon Montis Sereni* succinctly reports, "Bishop Siegfried of Brandenburg, son of Margrave Albert, was translated to the archbishopric of Bremen in the presence of the papal legates at Gelnhausen. Also, his brother Count Bernhard obtained the duchy of Saxony from the emperor."[96]

The early thirteenth-century chronicler Arnold of Lübeck, who wrote one of the most detailed surviving accounts of the events of the late 1170s and early 1180s, describes the strength of the Ascanian fraternal group during these years. Arnold had close connections to the Welf lineage throughout his career and chose to depict Henry the Lion quite positively in much of his chronicle.[97] As a result, Henry's enemies—especially Count Bernhard of Aschersleben—are frequently cast in a negative light.[98] Nevertheless, Arnold acknowledges the cooperation among the Ascanian siblings in several passages. For example, in his discussion of Siegfried's election to the archbishopric of Bremen in 1179, he suggests that the churchman and his brother Bernhard were initially allies of Henry the Lion: "Siegfried, the son of Margrave Albert, succeeded [as archbishop]. The duke stood by him most devotedly in all things, both on his account and on account of his brother Count Bernhard of [Aschersleben], for at that time they were the best of friends."[99] Later in the chronicle, he gives a backhanded compliment to Bernhard when he notes, "When he [Bernhard] was first placed in his comital lordship, he was the most vigorous of his brothers (*strennuissimus fratrum suorum*)."[100] Arnold's description of Bernhard's earliest actions as duke also indicates that Bernhard and his brother Margrave Otto I of Brandenburg jointly held court at Artlenburg in an effort to gain the support of the Saxon aristocracy.[101] And in one especially harsh passage, he writes, "Duke Bernhard, wanting to extend the power of his name, . . . began to oppress his people. Having ignored the counsel of old men, he acquiesced in the counsel of youths . . . and made his people's yoke heavier. . . . Also, his brother Archbishop Siegfried of Bremen presumed to take the county of

---

96. *Chronicon Montis Sereni*, 157. See also Marcus, *Herzog Bernhard von Anhalt*, 87–91.

97. Althoff, "Die Historiographie bewältigt," 166–167; Panzer, "Die Chronik Arnolds von Lübeck," 52–57.

98. Scior, "Zwischen *terra nostra* und *terra sancta*," 158.

99. Arnold of Lübeck, *Chronica Slavorum*, 2.9, 47. For Arnold's reasons for casting their relationship in this light, see Marcus, *Herzog Bernhard von Anhalt*, 84.

100. Arnold of Lübeck, *Chronica Slavorum*, 3.1, 68.

101. Ibid., 3.1, 69.

Ditmarschen from Count Adolf [III of Holstein] and to transfer it to his brother, the duke."[102]

Other sources support Arnold's depiction of a close-knit Ascanian fraternal group in the years around 1180. Otto, Siegfried, Bernhard, and their brother Count Dietrich are named in various combinations in several charters from this period.[103] One of the most impressive family gatherings occurred at the imperial court at Erfurt in November of 1181, when the emperor and the princes confirmed Henry the Lion's deposition. There, Barbarossa issued a privilege confirming his grant of a castle and town to Archbishop Siegfried of Bremen; Margrave Otto and Duke Bernhard were both witnesses.[104] Two weeks later at Erfurt, all three of these *principes imperii* witnessed another of the emperor's charters, this one agreeing to their childless brother Dietrich's grant to a monastery.[105] Since they were all Dietrich's heirs, the siblings Siegfried, Otto, and Bernhard each issued a charter of his own consenting to this donation as well. All three versions of the confirmation state that Dietrich made this grant "for the welfare of his soul and of our whole lineage."[106] These documents thus strengthen the impression that the brothers at the center of this generation of the Ascanian lineage cooperated especially closely with one another. Throughout the period from the late 1160s to the early 1180s, the bond among the siblings remained unbroken. In the immediate aftermath of Henry the Lion's fall from grace, three brothers in particular—a margrave, a duke, and an archbishop—combined to form one of the most impressive fraternal groups active in the German kingdom of the twelfth and thirteenth centuries.

The Wittelsbach Brothers

On September 7, 1162, all four sons of Count-Palatine Otto I of Bavaria were in attendance for a grand gathering of the imperial court at Saint-Jean-de-Losne in Burgundy.[107] In a charter issued on that day, Archbishop Conrad of Mainz leads the list of ecclesiastical witnesses, while the list of secular lords includes his three siblings "Count-Palatine Otto [*maior*] of Wittelsbach and

102. Ibid., 3.1, 70.
103. See, for example, MGH DD F I, 3:372–373, no. 801; CDS 1 A, 2:316, no. 456; and CDA, 1, pt. 3:460, no. 622. See also Freytag, "Der Nordosten des Reiches," 526–530.
104. MGH DD F I, 4:14–15, no. 814.
105. Ibid., 4:18–19, no. 817.
106. CDA, 1, pt. 3:445–447, nos. 603–605. Siegfried's version uses the term *cognatio*, while Otto and Bernhard's versions use the term *generatio*.
107. For these brothers' relationships during the 1150s and 1160s, see chapter 3.

his brothers Frederick and Otto [*minor*]."[108] In the ensuing years, this fraternal group's influence at court waned considerably. Conrad, who refused to support the emperor's side in the papal schism, fled to Rome during the mid-1160s. The archbishop's brother Frederick made his final appearance in an imperial charter in the year 1169—three decades before his death. Otto *minor* acted as a witness at the imperial court on only one occasion in the decade between 1168 and 1177. Of the four brothers, only Count-Palatine Otto *maior*, who had been one of Frederick I's strongest supporters since the earliest days of his kingship, continued to cultivate *Königsnähe* throughout these years.

The Wittelsbach brothers reemerged as an influential force in imperial politics during the summer of 1177, in the days and months following the Peace of Venice. Conrad, the former archbishop of Mainz, was quickly reconciled with the emperor once Barbarossa and Pope Alexander III settled their differences. On August 9, Frederick wrote to the clergy, ministerials, and people of the archdiocese of Salzburg to announce that he had accepted Conrad's election as their new archbishop.[109] Whether Conrad's older brother Otto *maior* helped obtain this office for him is unclear, but sources do indicate that the count-palatine was present for the peace negotiations at Venice.[110] Significantly, Otto *minor* also began to reestablish his *Königsnähe* only one year later, when he witnessed Barbarossa's privilege for his brother Conrad confirming the church of Salzburg's rights and properties.[11] Then, in September of 1179, the three brothers Otto *maior*, Otto *minor*, and Conrad all were present when the emperor made a grant to the church of Brixen while holding court at Augsburg.[112] The reemergence of this sibling bloc is also evident in another event from the year 1179. Archbishop Conrad consecrated the church and altars at Ensdorf, a monastery with close ties to the Wittelsbachs, in the presence of all three of his brothers; both he and his brother Frederick donated land to the community during this same gathering.[113]

Since the Wittelsbach lineage's secular lordships—and portions of Conrad's archdiocese of Salzburg—all lay within the duchy of Bavaria, the brothers inevitably became embroiled in the conflict with Henry the Lion. Throughout

---

108. MGH DD F I, 2:257–259, no. 388.
109. Ibid., 3:214–216, no. 693.
110. *Historia ducum Veneticorum*, 84, lists the two brothers together among the attendees.
111. MGH DD F I, 3:272–277, no. 732.
112. Ibid., 3:352–353, no. 789.
113. *Fundatio et notae monasterii Ensdorfensis*, 1083. See also *Salzburger Urkundenbuch*, 2:573–577, nos. 416–418.

his long career, however, Henry the Lion had shown much less interest in Bavaria than Saxony, and he had never asserted his ducal authority there as energetically as he had in his northern duchy.[114] As a result, Bavaria never became a battlefront in the war against the duke during the years around 1180. Henry had few supporters in the region when he was stripped of his imperial fiefs.[115] Emperor Frederick I was therefore able to establish a new political order there quite quickly. Shortly after settling Saxon affairs at Gelnhausen in April of 1180, he traveled to Bavaria and briefly held court there before returning to the north to campaign against Henry the Lion. In a charter dated July 13 at Regensburg, the Wittelsbach brothers Otto *maior*, Conrad, and Otto *minor* were three of the seven witnesses called to support the bishop of Freising's accusations in a dispute against Henry the Lion.[116] This impressive display of the fraternal group's influence highlights the lineage's leading position in Bavaria during this period. Then, in September of the same year, the emperor rewarded Otto *maior* for his longtime support and *Königsnähe* by enfeoffing him with the duchy of Bavaria. Thereafter, Otto *minor* became the only brother to be identified consistently with the title of count-palatine.[117]

In the ensuing three years, until his death in 1183, Duke Otto I of Bavaria received little support from the leading nobles of the duchy; instead, his fraternal group formed a cornerstone of his lordship.[118] The duke and the archbishop both undertook construction projects in Regensburg, the traditional capital of Bavaria, in order to establish their power and influence there.[119] His younger brother Frederick, who had distanced himself from the imperial court in the 1170s, emerged as a strong supporter of Otto *maior* in the years 1180–1183, attending the ducal court on several occasions—oftentimes alongside his sibling Otto *minor*.[120] The Wittelsbach fraternal group continued to play an active role at the emperor's side as well. The three brothers Otto *maior*, Conrad, and Otto *minor* all attended the imperial court together in March of 1181 at Nuremberg and again in September of 1182 at Regensburg.[121] Even after Duke Otto I's death, the surviving members of

---

114. Ehlers, *Heinrich der Löwe*, 100.
115. Kraus, "Heinrich der Löwe und Bayern," 212.
116. MGH DD F I, 3:366–368, no. 798.
117. Spindler, "Grundlegung und Aufbau," 16–17. For the brothers' use of this title in earlier years, see chapter 3.
118. Kraus, "Das Herzogtum der Wittelsbacher," 165.
119. Schlütter-Schindler, "Herzog Otto I. von Wittelsbach," 93–94. For these two brothers, see also Seibert, "Die entstehende 'territoriale Ordnung,'" 270.
120. See, for example, *Die Traditionen des Klosters Schäftlarn*, 247–248, no. 249, and *Die Traditionen des Klosters Scheyern*, 50–51, nos. 48–49.
121. MGH DD F I, 4:2–3, no. 804; 4:40–41, no. 831.

this fraternal group—including Conrad, who returned to the archbishopric of Mainz in 1183—worked closely together to support their young nephew Ludwig, Otto *maior*'s son and heir.[122]

One of the clearest statements of Wittelsbach fraternal solidarity in this generation comes from an early thirteenth-century chronicle. The Bavarian abbot Conrad of Scheyern, who had close ties to the Wittelsbachs, included in his history of the lineage a brief summary of the career of Archbishop Conrad:

> First [arch]bishop of Mainz, later of Salzburg, still later—because he did not agree with Emperor Frederick about Octavian [the antipope Victor IV], whom the same emperor had chosen for himself as pope instead of Alexander [III]—he went to Rome. He remained there for quite some time with [Pope] Alexander and was appointed [cardinal-] bishop of Sabina by him. After Octavian died, [Conrad] returned into the grace of the emperor through the intervention of his brothers (*interventu fratrum suorum*)—on whose counsel the royal will was then hanging—[and] was appointed in a praiseworthy manner to the [arch] bishopric of Mainz by the emperor.[123]

The chronicler offers a very confused chronology of events here. He suggests that the death of Victor IV (in 1164) was the reason why Conrad was reconciled with Barbarossa (in 1177) and restored to the archbishopric of Mainz (in 1183)—when in reality, the Peace of Venice had been the basis for Conrad's reconciliation with the emperor. Nevertheless, his claim that the Wittelsbach brothers collectively wielded a great deal of influence during this period finds support in a second thirteenth-century chronicler. Burchard of Ursberg, a Premonstratensian canon in the duchy of Swabia, wrote a chronicle of imperial history around the year 1230.[124] Throughout much of his work, he makes only passing references to various members of the Wittelsbach lineage. However, in his account of Henry the Lion's loss of his duchies, the chronicler observes, "And so it happened that he [the emperor] granted the duchy of Bavaria to Count-Palatine Otto of Wittelsbach. . . . [Otto] relied on the help of his brothers (*auxilio fratrum suorum*)—namely Archbishop Conrad of Salzburg, who afterward was archbishop of Mainz, his brother Otto, whom he made count-palatine, . . . and Frederick, who

---

122. See especially Mainzer UB 2, pt. 2:743–745; no. 458. See also ibid., 2:745–748, no. 459; 2:845–847, no. 514; 2:912–914, no. 552; and 2:917–918, no. 554.

123. Conrad of Scheyern, *Chronicon*, 621.

124. Neel, "Work of Burchard of Ursberg, III," 20.

was called the Bearded. With the help of these brothers, as I said, he bravely obtained the duchy and expelled the duke [Henry the Lion] from those parts."[125] Two chroniclers writing in the half century after the year 1180 thus recognized the pivotal role these four brothers played in shaping the history of the Wittelsbach lineage during the later twelfth century.

Magnate Brothers and Secular Lordships, 1180–1181

Members of three other fraternal groups had much to gain from Henry the Lion's fall as well. Like the Ascanians and Wittelsbachs, the Andechs, Ludowing, and Wettin lineages were all in possession of rights and properties in Saxony or Bavaria around the year 1180. As a result, the sibling groups active in these lineages also became involved in the scramble for new lordships in the wake of Henry's loss of his duchies.[126] These three fraternal groups can therefore provide points of comparison and contrast with the Ascanians and Wittelsbachs. In addition, all five of these princely lineages—when analyzed together—demonstrate the complex nature of the political realignment that took place inside the German kingdom during the early 1180s.

On the eve of Henry the Lion's fall, two brothers were the leading figures inside the Andechses, the most prominent Bavarian noble lineage after the Wittelsbachs: Berthold II, who had received the march of Istria from Emperor Frederick I in 1173, and the newly elected Bishop Otto II of Bamberg.[127] Otto's predecessor, Bishop Herman II of Bamberg, had died on July 12, 1177, while in Venice for the peace negotiations between Barbarossa and his Italian rivals.[128] Otto, who had already witnessed an imperial charter as cathedral provost of Bamberg in May of 1177, first appears as "*Otto Babimbergensis electus*" in an imperial charter in January of 1178.[129] In both cases, he was attending Barbarossa's court in Italy. Thus, during the months immediately preceding and following his election, he had—like the Ascanian bishop Siegfried of Brandenburg and the Wittelsbach archbishop Conrad of Salzburg—successfully cultivated *Königsnähe* on the emperor's Italian expedition.

In later years, Otto frequently joined his brother, Margrave Berthold II of Istria, at the imperial court. Both were present at Gelnhausen in April of

---

125. Burchard of Ursberg, *Die Chronik*, 198.
126. The Zähringen and Babenberg lineages also included prominent sets of brothers in this period, but neither of these lineages directly benefited from Henry the Lion's fall.
127. See chapter 3 and Kraus, "Heinrich der Löwe und Bayern," 203.
128. *Historia ducum Veneticorum*, 85.
129. MGH DD F I, 3:186–189, no. 672; 3:264–266, no. 727.

1180 when Barbarossa divided Henry the Lion's duchy of Saxony.[130] Also in attendance on this occasion was Berthold II's son Berthold III, who received the duchy of Merania from the emperor at some point in the year 1180.[131] According to many historians, Frederick I granted the duchy of Merania to Berthold III in order to keep the Andechses on equal footing with their chief rivals, the Wittelsbachs, after Otto *maior* received the duchy of Bavaria. Elevating Berthold III to ducal status was thus intended to free him and his lineage from the authority of the new duke of Bavaria—despite their possession of an extensive collection of Bavarian rights and properties.[132] While this argument is plausible, it fails to explain why Barbarossa enfeoffed Berthold III rather than Berthold II with Merania. This question, which has largely been ignored by historians, is critical to understanding the distribution of lordships that occurred after Henry the Lion's fall.

Extant sources give no indication that Margrave Berthold II was opposed to Berthold III receiving the duchy instead of receiving it himself. He remained active in imperial politics in the years after 1180, appearing at court alongside his brother and his son at Nuremberg in March of 1181 and again in March of 1183.[133] Berthold II and Bishop Otto also crossed the Alps together in the autumn of 1184 and spent approximately two months participating in Barbarossa's sixth and final Italian expedition.[134] If the emperor's granting of Merania to Berthold III was not motivated by a souring of his close relationship to the Andechs brothers, then Berthold III's acquisition of the duchy must be viewed from a perspective that acknowledges Andechs family solidarity. As a result, a comparison with the strong Wittelsbach family group of this same period is revealing. While historians have emphasized the fact that both of these lineages acquired ducal titles in 1180, the Wittelsbach and Andechs lineages actually each had three members who were imperial magnates in the years immediately following Henry the Lion's fall. All six of these prominent lords regularly attended the imperial court after 1180, suggesting that the emperor's granting of Merania to Berthold III rather than Berthold II was intended to keep the lineages evenly balanced in terms of total number of *principes imperii*.

The history of the Ludowing and Wettin lineages during this same period lends support to this contention. When Landgrave Ludwig II of Thuringia

---

130. MGH DD F I, 3:364–365, no. 796.
131. See chapter 6 for more on this duchy.
132. Opll, *Friedrich Barbarossa*, 237; Hauser, *Staufische Lehnspolitik*, 59–60; Schütz, "Das Geschlecht der Andechs-Meranier," 66.
133. MGH DD F I, 4:1–2, no. 803 and 4:50–51, no. 840.
134. Ibid., 4:115–135, nos. 876–887.

died in 1172, his eldest son, Ludwig III, succeeded as landgrave, while his second son, Henry III Raspe, acquired the lineage's lands and rights in Hesse to the west of Thuringia. On July 29, 1179, in the midst of the growing conflict with Henry the Lion, these two siblings—"Landgrave Ludwig and his brother Count Henry Raspe"—both witnessed an imperial charter while Barbarossa was holding court at Erfurt.[135] A short time later, Henry III Raspe died childless, and his rights and properties in Hesse passed to his older brother. Ludwig III then gained additional lands and rights in April of 1180 at Gelnhausen, when Barbarossa enfeoffed him with the county-palatine of Saxony.[136] The landgrave, in the span of only a few months, had thus significantly increased his prestige and territorial power in the kingdom.

In his efforts to maintain and expand his authority, Landgrave Ludwig III found support in the early 1180s from another of his brothers, the young Herman.[137] According to Arnold of Lübeck, "With the coming of May [1180], the duke [Henry the Lion] entered Thuringia on a military campaign and burned the royal town called Nordhausen. Landgrave Ludwig came upon him [there] with a great multitude, and there was a battle between them. The Thuringians fled, and the landgrave was captured along with his brother Herman . . . and a multitude of knights."[138] The brothers were released the following year in time to attend the meeting of the imperial court at Erfurt in November of 1181. There, according to the *Cronica S. Petri Erfordensis*, "Herman, the brother of Landgrave Ludwig, was appointed count-palatine of Saxony, his brother voluntarily removing himself from the same dignity."[139] Ludwig's renunciation of the county-palatine in favor of his brother bound the two siblings closely to each other, and Herman appeared regularly as a witness in Ludwig's charters during the 1180s.[140]

While the surviving evidence points to a strong relationship between Ludwig and Herman, the landgrave's willingness to concede his recently acquired county-palatine of Saxony to his younger sibling is nevertheless

---

135. Ibid., 3:344–346, no. 785.

136. Patze, *Die Entstehung der Landesherrschaft*, 1:234–235.

137. The two youngest brothers in this generation, Herman and Frederick, are obscure figures in the 1170s, possibly because they were still minors. They first appear in an extant source on June 9, 1178, when they witnessed one of their brother Ludwig III's charters. See CDS 1 A, 2:296–297, no. 428.

138. Arnold of Lübeck, *Chronica Slavorum*, 2.16, 55. See also *Cronica S. Petri Erfordensis moderna*, 189.

139. *Cronica S. Petri Erfordensis moderna*, 191.

140. See, for example, CDS 1 A, 2:326–327, nos. 469–470; 2:344, no. 497; 2:355–356, no. 514; and 2:360, no. 521. The brothers also attended the imperial court together in the summer of 1188: MGH DD F I, 4:252–253, no. 972 and 4:258–260, no. 978.

striking. This decision suggests that Ludwig—in the wake of Count Henry III Raspe's death—was anxious to have another brother with sufficient status and prestige to play a prominent role in regional and imperial politics. In the process, he also made the Ludowings another princely lineage headed by two secular *principes imperii* in the years after Henry the Lion's fall. Rather than hoarding titles for himself, he supported the elevation of his younger sibling into the ranks of the imperial magnates. Such a move is comparable to the Wittelsbach Otto *maior*'s apparent renunciation of the county-palatine of Bavaria, in favor of his younger brother Otto *minor*, after he became duke. It also provides context for the situation inside the Ascanian lineage, where the younger brother Bernhard received the duchy of Saxony in 1180 rather than the older Margrave Otto I of Brandenburg. One of Frederick Barbarossa's modern biographers suggests that the emperor chose Bernhard in order to prevent Otto from consolidating too much power and authority in his own hands.[141] But Bernhard's enfeoffment, when viewed alongside similar enfeoffments in the Wittelsbach, Ludowing, and Andechs lineages, fits a more general pattern within the upper aristocracy. It was not the emperor but rather the members of princely lineages who favored elevating multiple close relatives into the ranks of the *principes imperii*.

The complexity of lordship distribution among and within magnate lineages after Henry the Lion's fall is further demonstrated by the Wettins. In 1180, five brothers from this lineage were exercising lordship in the northeast of the kingdom, and all of them played active roles in Saxon and imperial politics during this period.[142] Three were present at Worms in January 1179, when Henry the Lion failed to appear at the imperial court for the first time to respond to the Saxon aristocracy's complaints.[143] Half a year later at Magdeburg, when the duke failed to appear for the second time, all five Wettin brothers were in attendance.[144] According to Arnold of Lübeck, it was on this occasion that one of these siblings, Margrave Dietrich of Lower Lusatia, challenged Henry the Lion to a duel.[145] Different groupings within this generation continued to join the emperor at other major gatherings of the imperial court called to discuss the fate of Henry the Lion: Gelnhausen in April of 1180, Altenburg in October of the same year, and Erfurt in November of 1181.[146] The brothers were also prominent figures on the

---

141. Opll, *Friedrich Barbarossa*, 128–129.
142. See chapter 3.
143. MGH DD F I, 3:325–326, no. 772.
144. Ibid., 3:340–341, no. 781.
145. Arnold of Lübeck, *Chronica Slavorum*, 2.10, 48.

military side of the conflict with the duke of Saxony and Bavaria. Margrave Otto I of Meissen is named most frequently in the extant sources that describe the campaigns of the late 1170s and early 1180s, but his siblings also fought alongside him on occasion.[147]

Despite all this evidence for the central role played by the Wettin lineage in Henry the Lion's fall, none of the five brothers was elevated into the ranks of the *principes imperii* in the years 1180–1181. Members of the Ascanian, Wittelsbach, Andechs, and Ludowing lineages all received new *honores* after Henry the Lion lost his duchies, but the Wettin fraternal group did not. Why was this lineage overlooked? In keeping with the argument I am making here, one plausible answer to this question is that two of these brothers were already *principes imperii* in 1180. The Wettins were the only lineage with a pair of secular lords in possession of princely titles in the 1170s: Margrave Otto I of Meissen and Margrave Dietrich of Lower Lusatia. Although some other lineages included combinations of secular and ecclesiastical lords, none had two brothers who were secular magnates immediately prior to Henry the Lion's fall. By the end of 1181, however, the Wettins had been joined by four other lineages—the Ascanians, Wittelsbachs, Andechses, and Ludowings—whose members included two secular *principes imperii*. Indeed, these five princely lineages with ties to Saxony and Bavaria collectively included *thirteen* imperial princes in the aftermath of Henry the Lion's loss of his duchies.

Two general trends thus emerge from the close analysis of sibling relationships and imperial politics in the years around 1180. First, five of the most successful princely lineages of this period were led by durable and stable fraternal groups with multiple members who cultivated *Königsnähe*. Adult brothers in these lineages worked together effectively to maintain—and expand—their own lineage's power and influence in the wake of Henry the Lion's fall. Most significantly, the Ascanians, Wittelsbachs, Andechses, and Ludowings all acquired new *honores* during the late 1170s and early 1180s that made it possible for family members to join the ranks of the *principes imperii*. Second, the intense competition for secular and ecclesiastical lordships among the lineages of the German upper aristocracy prompted Emperor Frederick I Barbarossa to distribute *honores* as evenly as possible during these

---

146. MGH DD F I, 3:360–363, no. 795; 3:370–371, no. 800; and 4:14–15, no. 814.
147. *Chronicon Montis Sereni*, 158. See also *Annales Pegavienses*, 262, and Arnold of Lübeck, *Chronica Slavorum*, 2.20, 62.

years in order to keep the leading princely lineages relatively balanced in terms of their influence and authority. The centrality of fraternal groups for imperial politics in this period is most evident in the way these lordships were allocated. Individual magnates did not accumulate *honores* exclusively for themselves and their own children. Instead, the younger brothers of these *principes imperii* were some of the most frequent beneficiaries of the political realignment that occurred after Henry the Lion was stripped of his duchies.

The question posed at the beginning of this chapter asked who played the leading role in Henry the Lion's fall, the emperor or the imperial princes. I have sought here to provide a new framework and methodology for answering this question by reconstructing the shifting family groups operating inside the German upper aristocracy during the reigns of Conrad III and Frederick I Barbarossa. What becomes evident from such an analysis is that the years around 1180 saw an especially large number of fraternal groups active in imperial politics. At a time when five prominent Saxon and Bavarian princely lineages were being led by groups of brothers, Emperor Frederick I and Duke Henry the Lion were both surrounded by relatively small families that provided them with little political support. The influence that these fraternal groups exerted at the imperial court—as evidenced by the success these siblings had obtaining new *honores* during this period—indicates that the emperor was not in a position to ignore the brothers who belonged to these princely lineages. Consensual lordship, the foundation of the relationship between the emperor and the princes during the Staufen period, gave these groups of brothers a powerful voice at the imperial court in the years around 1180.[148] At this moment, more so than any other in the twelfth or early thirteenth century, the political efficacy of sibling solidarity was on full display.

---

148. Compare Görich, "Versuch zur Rettung von Kontingenz," 191–196; Laudage, *Friedrich Barbarossa*, 300; and Patzold, "Konsens und Konkurrenz," 102–103.

❧ CHAPTER 5

Cooperation, Conflict, and the Rise of a New Generation, ca. 1180–1210

By the close of the year 1181, those fraternal groups who had acquired pieces of Henry the Lion's once-sprawling collection of lordships had dramatically reshaped the political landscape of the German kingdom. Several of these lineages were at the height of their authority and influence in subsequent months. However, this age of princely brothers did not last long. Most of the nobles and churchmen of the upper aristocracy who played central roles in the events of the late 1170s and early 1180s had been born decades earlier in the first years of the twelfth century. As a result, death soon thinned their ranks. Duke Otto I of Bavaria, Margrave Berthold II of Istria, Margrave Otto I of Brandenburg, Archbishop Siegfried of Bremen, Landgrave Ludwig III of Thuringia, and all five Wettin brothers were dead by the close of 1190. The baby-boom generation of the mid-twelfth century was fading from the scene, to be replaced by a new generation that bore little if any resemblance to the previous one. By the early 1190s, the two largest fraternal groups active within the German upper aristocracy belonged to the Staufens and Welfs, the two lineages so lacking in adult males a decade earlier. Meanwhile, in the seven other lineages under investigation here, the same period saw a noticeable decline in the size of fraternal groups. Generational change thus reshaped family dynamics—and imperial politics—during the late twelfth and early thirteenth centuries.

New Generations, Old Lordships: The Upper Aristocracy after 1180

The succession strategy pursued by the Wettin lineage's founder Conrad (d. 1157), who gave either a march or a county to each of his five sons, was not a typical one within the princely lineages of the Staufen period. Conrad's neighbor and contemporary in northeastern Saxony, the Ascanian Albert the Bear (d. 1170), is the only other magnate who had as many as five lordships to distribute among five sons.[1] Even within the uppermost stratum of the aristocracy, such abundance became much less commonplace as the twelfth century progressed. For the members of a princely lineage to be able to give a prestigious lordship to each of several sons in more than one generation, these noblemen needed to acquire new *honores* on a consistent basis. Yet the changing political environment inside the German kingdom made this increasingly difficult as the 1100s progressed. The turmoil that accompanied the Investiture Controversy and the reigns of Emperor Lothar III and King Conrad III subsided in the years following Frederick Barbarossa's election as king in 1152.[2] For four of the princely lineages under consideration here, Henry the Lion's downfall led directly to the acquisition of new lordships, but this was a singular moment in the history of the Staufen period. Prestigious *honores* typically did not circulate within the upper aristocracy in such abundance. As a result, for the preeminent lords of the kingdom, there were few opportunities in the later twelfth century to use newly acquired *honores* to augment their patrimonies. Many magnates had little if anything beyond the lands and rights they had acquired from their own fathers to pass to their heirs.

Thus, while Conrad of Wettin and Albert the Bear together had ten sons who received prestigious secular lordships in the 1150s and 1160s, only two of those sons were able to arrange the succession in their own families in a similar fashion. Even these two, Count Dedo of Groitzsch and Count Bernhard of Aschersleben, were not in possession of large numbers of prestigious titles; each had acquired only one new lordship during his lifetime, giving him only two to distribute among his sons.[3] Significantly, this decline in the number of magnates holding multiple lordships coincided with a decline in

---

1. See below for the sons of Frederick Barbarossa, four of whom were given secular lordships. Prior to 1250, this is the last generation of any of these nine lineages to see four sons succeed to secular lordships.

2. Keller, *Zwischen regionaler Begrenzung und universalem Horizont*, 375–379; Opll, *Friedrich Barbarossa*, 41–42.

3. See chapter 3 for Dedo's purchase of his dead brother's march of Lower Lusatia, and chapter 4 for Bernhard's enfeoffment with the duchy of Saxony.

the number of princely couples having five, six, or seven sons who reached adulthood. Although all five of Conrad of Wettin's sons married, they were survived by only ten legitimate male heirs. Each of the three Wittelsbach brothers who used the title *comes palatinus* in the 1160s and 1170s had only one son to succeed him. And while Margrave Leopold III of Austria (d. 1136) was survived by six sons, no subsequent secular lord in his lineage was survived by more than two. The abundance of heirs that was such a pronounced characteristic of the upper aristocracy during the early Staufen period very quickly ceased to be a feature of later generations.

This shift is especially striking when one considers that neither fathers nor eldest brothers within these princely lineages sought to prevent younger heirs from marrying. The only exceptions to this general pattern can be found in the Ludowing lineage, where the second son in each generation never married during the lifetime of his eldest brother.[4] In other lineages, multiple sons routinely married while their fathers were still alive, or soon thereafter, yet most of these unions produced few if any children, male or female.[5] This suggests that the lords who belonged to the upper aristocracy during the late twelfth and early thirteenth centuries may have been intentionally trying to limit the number of heirs born into their families. The shortage of available lordships to distribute among these sons is one possible reason for this trend. Because the custom of partible inheritance was a well-established feature of German noble society by the Staufen period, controlling family size was one of the only ways to maintain the integrity of smaller patrimonies that lacked significant numbers of *honores*.

Attempting to limit the number of legitimate children born into a family was a risky strategy during a time when child mortality rates were high and noble culture was awash in dangerous pursuits.[6] The numerous German noble lineages that went extinct in the male line during the first half of the thirteenth century—including the Babenbergs, Andechses, Ludowings, and the main branch of the Zähringens—attest to the hazards of pursuing such a policy.[7] Moreover, even when a magnate succeeded in controlling the size of his family, he still needed to divide his patrimony among his heirs, however

---

4. For more on this point, see chapter 7.

5. This explanation for the small size of noble lineages differs from what many other historians have proposed. For the argument that nobles tended to *restrict* the number of sons who could marry in order to limit the growth of their lineages, see Duby, *Medieval Marriage*, 10–11, and Althoff, *Family, Friends and Followers,* 42–46.

6. Alexandre-Bidon and Lett, *Children in the Middle Ages*, 32–36, 110–111.

7. For theories concerning the extinction of noble lineages in this period, see Freed, *Counts of Falkenstein*, 63–67.

small the number. If he possessed only a single prestigious lordship, the survival of just two or three sons to adulthood could complicate succession plans.
Placing younger sons in the church—a commonplace strategy among some
other European noble lineages during this period—actually became less popular within the German upper aristocracy over the course of the late twelfth
and early thirteenth centuries.[8] As a result, in the princely lineages examined
here, succession and inheritance looked quite different after 1180 than they
did in the first generation that rose to prominence during the Staufen period.

A revealing example, because of how unusual it was in the way its succession unfolded across the late 1100s and early 1200s, is the branch of the
Ascanians that possessed the comital lordship of Orlamünde to the south of
Weimar. Count Herman I of Orlamünde (d. 1176), one of the seven sons
of Margrave Albert the Bear of Brandenburg, was unable to expand significantly on the small collection of lands and rights he acquired from his
father.[9] Herman had no difficulty arranging the succession, however, because
he had only a single heir of his own, Siegfried, who received his father's undivided patrimony. This Count Siegfried of Orlamünde (d. 1206) married
a daughter of King Waldemar I of Denmark, and the new couple soon had
two sons. Although Siegfried failed to acquire any additional lordships during his lifetime, he was not forced to use his county of Orlamünde to endow
both of these heirs. Instead, his father-in-law intervened and granted to the
elder son, Albert (d. 1245), a series of rights and territories along Denmark's
contested frontier with the German kingdom. By 1204 at the latest, Albert
had begun to exercise lordship in this region.[10] As a result, after Siegfried died
in 1206, the second son, Herman II (d. 1247), was able to succeed as count
of Orlamünde. Although Albert also employed the title *comes de Orlamunde*
in some of his own charters, he rarely visited this comital lordship. He left
his younger brother, Herman, in control of their father's rights and properties, intervening only rarely to consent to Herman's grants of pieces of the
patrimony.[11] Thus, for almost eighty years after the death of Margrave Albert
the Bear of Brandenburg, the small comital lordship of Orlamünde survived
undivided in the hands of a single son (Herman I), grandson (Siegfried), and
great-grandson (Herman II).

---

8. For more on this point, see chapter 7.

9. For the acquisition of this lordship by the Ascanians, see Partenheimer, *Albrecht der Bär*, 86.

10. Lammers, *Geschichte Schleswig-Holsteins*, 4, pt. 1:387–388; Biereye, "Albrecht von Orlamünde und Holstein"; Reitzenstein, *Regesten der Grafen von Orlamuende*, 68–84.

11. See, for example, Gotha, Thüringisches Staatsarchiv, QQ I d 20a and QQ I d 21. The first of these charters is printed in *Thuringia Sacra,* 482–483.

Succession rarely followed such a straightforward course, however. Most noblemen with a single prestigious lordship and multiple heirs did not have the king of Denmark as a father-in-law. During the late twelfth and early thirteenth centuries, secular lords typically had to find other ways to provide lands and rights to second and third sons. One option that became increasingly popular among the lineages investigated here was to create new lordships by dividing the existing patrimony. Because many noble lordships were little more than scattered collections of rights and territories lacking any inherent unity, this was not necessarily a difficult task. A castle peripheral to the lineage's main centers of power and authority could be transformed with relative ease into the focal point of a new lordship. Moreover, because the titles of duke, margrave, and count were increasingly being perceived as family honorifics rather than official titles during the later Staufen period, younger sons could adopt the prestigious titles used by their older brothers.[12] Multiple brothers could thus use eminent titles and possess valuable pieces of the patrimony— even when their fathers had failed to acquire new *honores* to distribute to them.

The closing decades of the twelfth century were a period when several leading princes divided their patrimonies in this fashion, and three cases in particular highlight the range of fraternal relationships that could emerge from this type of succession plan. The first involves the Babenberg brothers Duke Leopold V of Austria (d. 1194) and Henry of Mödling (d. 1223). These two siblings were knighted together in 1174, an indication that there was little age difference between them.[13] After their father, Duke Henry II Jasomirgott of Austria, died in 1177, Leopold succeeded as duke. Henry, meanwhile, inherited an extensive collection of rights and properties, including a monastic advocacy.[14] In a charter of donation from the late 1170s or early 1180s for the monastery of Heiligenkreuz, he is identified as "Henry of Mödling" (*Heinricus de Medlich*), and it is this castle that would become the center of his lordship during later years.[15] He eventually began to use the title "duke of Mödling," but the first appearance of this designation dates from a decade after his older brother's death.[16]

---

12. One of the most detailed discussions of this issue continues to be Ficker, *Vom Reichsfuerstenstande*, 1:239–254. See more recently Hechberger, "Konrad III.," 333–334.

13. The two had already appeared together on April 22, 1161, more than fifteen years before the death of their father, as consenters in one of his charters: BUB, 1:42–44, no. 29. See also Gall, "Die 'Herzoge' von Mödling," 6–8.

14. His holdings are listed in Gall, "Die 'Herzoge' von Mödling," 14–18. See also Lechner, *Die Babenberger*, 169.

15. BUB, 1:80–81, no. 60.

16. Ibid., 1:197–198, no. 152. For a similar situation inside the Zähringens involving the younger brothers of Duke Berthold IV, see Heyck, *Geschichte der Herzoge von Zähringen*, 418–419.

Henry's charter for Heiligenkreuz records a grant he made to the monastery "for the salvation of not only our own soul but also the souls of our relatives: Margrave Leopold [III]; our father, Duke Henry; our brother, Duke Leopold; our nephew Frederick; and [our] wife, Richza."[17] This passage is noteworthy for two reasons. First, it demonstrates that Henry was already married in the years immediately after his father's death, clear evidence for his standing as a prominent heir alongside Leopold V. Second, it expresses a concern for the salvation of a living brother's soul that is uncommon in the charters of donation drawn up by the nobles of the Staufen period. The inclusion of Henry's older brother and young nephew in this text suggests that the siblings maintained especially close ties after their father's death. Other sources strengthen this impression. For example, Leopold and Henry were together at the imperial court in Augsburg in September 1179.[18] A decade later on August 25, 1190, the two were present together in Vienna.[19] From there, Leopold departed Austria to join the German contingent of the Third Crusade. Henry, meanwhile, traveled to Italy, where he was present for the imperial coronation of King Henry VI in the spring of 1191.[20] The timing of his first known appearance at a Staufen court without his older brother is surely not coincidental; Henry must have been acting as the Babenberg representative at court, tasked with recognizing Henry VI's claims to the kingship and the imperial title after news of Barbarossa's death reached the empire. Thus, these two brothers seem to have developed a successful partnership during their careers, working closely together both inside Austria and beyond its borders to promote and protect their own interests.

A second, more complicated example of this form of succession involves the heirs of Margrave Otto I of Brandenburg (d. 1184) from the Ascanian lineage. Otto had two sons by his first wife and another son by his second wife. In the years immediately following his death, the eldest of these three heirs, Otto II, began using the title of margrave of Brandenburg. Henry, the second son, appears in charters as "count of Gardelegen" and is the first person to be named in any document with such a title, indicating that it was cre-

---

17. BUB, 1:81, no. 60.

18. MGH DD F I, 3:352–353, no. 789: "*Livpoldus dux Austrie et frater suus Heinricus.*" See also BUB, 1:67–68, no. 51; 1:92–94, no. 68; and 1:98–100, no. 73.

19. BUB, 1:106–107, no. 77.

20. MGH Const., 1:471–477, nos. 332–333. The latter of these charters labels him "*Heinricus dux Austrie.*" The confusion is probably attributable to an Italian scribe who did not understand Henry's position inside his lineage, but the mistake is also evidence for his eminent standing at Henry VI's court in early 1191.

ated specifically for him.[21] However, according to one of Margrave Otto II's charters from the year 1190, these two brothers had not simply divided the patrimony. This text, which concerns a donation to the house of canons that the pair of siblings had cofounded and endowed at Stendal, explains that Otto II was making his grant "with the consent and by the petition of . . . our brother the count of Gardelegen, who together with us received the march [of Brandenburg] by feudal law from the royal hand."[22] Otto II and Henry thus shared the imperial fief but used different titles. Several charters from the late 1180s and early 1190s provide evidence for how this situation functioned in practice, and these documents show the pair working closely together to support their foundation at Stendal.[23] Thus, like the Babenberg brothers, these two siblings apparently had a strong relationship in the years after their father's death.

When Count Henry of Gardelegen died in 1192, the dynamics inside this generation quickly changed. Albert, the younger half brother of Otto II and Henry, had appeared occasionally in previous years as "count of Arneburg"—another new title within the Ascanian lineage.[24] After Count Henry's death, Albert initiated a conflict with his surviving half brother, Margrave Otto II. According to the *Chronicle of the Princes of Saxony* from the late thirteenth century, "[Otto] seized his brother Albert, who was devastating his lands, and imprisoned him. At length, Otto repented over this and freed him from prison. [Otto] then announced that [Albert] would be the heir to his lordship."[25] No other source provides any evidence for this dispute, making it difficult to assess this case of sibling conflict. Since the two began to appear together regularly in charters from 1194 onward, there is no reason to suspect that their relationship was permanently damaged.[26] Moreover, in 1196, they cooperated with one another in an extraordinary act, granting all their alodial lands and rights to the archbishopric of Magdeburg and receiving them back as fiefs.[27] At the time, both were childless, and as a result, they may have been working together to prepare for the impending extinction of their branch

21. Fey, *Reise und Herrschaft*, 42–44.

22. Magdeburg, Landeshauptarchiv Sachsen-Anhalt, Rep. U 21 IV Domstift Stendal no. 8. Summarized in *Regesten der Markgrafen von Brandenburg*, 2:94, no. 467.

23. Magdeburg, Landeshauptarchiv Sachsen-Anhalt, Rep. U 21 IV Domstift Stendal nos. 2, 15, and 16. See also Beumann, "Der altmärkische Bistumsplan."

24. Fey, *Reise und Herrschaft*, 37–38.

25. *Chronica principum Saxoniae*, 477. For the date of this conflict, *Regesten der Markgrafen von Brandenburg*, 2:97–98, no. 481.

26. See, for example, *Regesten der Markgrafen von Brandenburg*, 2:98, nos. 482, 485, and 487.

27. Magdeburg, Landeshauptarchiv Sachsen-Anhalt, Rep. U 1 XVIII no. 4b.

of the Ascanians.[28] Margrave Otto II did indeed die in 1205 without any children, but Albert, who succeeded him, eventually fathered two sons who preserved the lineage's control of Brandenburg.[29]

The third example of this form of succession involves one of the most serious cases of sibling conflict to occur during the Staufen period in any of the nine princely lineages. Conrad of Wettin's eldest son, Margrave Otto of Meissen (d. 1190), had two sons of his own. The elder, Albert, began appearing alongside his father during the early 1180s, and throughout much of the decade, he seems to have been Otto's designated successor in the march of Meissen.[30] Dietrich, the second son, was initially in line to acquire a new comital lordship centered on the castle of Weissenfels.[31] However, in 1188 or 1189, Margrave Otto of Meissen—at the behest of his wife, according to one source—changed his mind about his succession plans and named his second son, Dietrich, as the next margrave.[32] Albert soon rebelled against his father, captured him, and had him imprisoned.[33] Margrave Otto eventually regained his freedom but was forced to restore Albert to his position as successor in the march. When Otto died a few months later, Albert followed him as margrave of Meissen, and his younger brother, Dietrich, began using the title "count of Weissenfels."[34]

Margrave Otto's death did not settle the succession dispute, however. Dietrich, who had accompanied Frederick Barbarossa on the Third Crusade, was absent from the German kingdom when his father died. Soon after he returned from the Holy Land in the year 1191, Albert invaded his lands and sought to disinherit (*exhereditare*) him.[35] Dietrich turned to Landgrave Herman of Thuringia for support and agreed to marry one of the landgrave's daughters in order to cement their alliance. With Herman's help, Dietrich was able to arrange a short peace with his brother, Albert, but the conflict soon resumed. As the *Chronicon Montis Sereni* explains in its entry for the year 1194, "Count Dietrich of Weissenfels, oppressed a short time ago by the violence of his brother (*fratris sui violencia*), went to Landgrave Herman

---

28. This is only speculation, however. The brothers' decision to grant their lands to Magdeburg has perplexed scholars for decades. See Marcus, *Herzog Bernhard von Anhalt*, 171–190, and Krabbo, "Otto I., Otto II. und Albrecht II. von Brandenburg," 350–352.

29. For these two brothers, see chapter 7.

30. Lyon, "Fathers and Sons," 308–309.

31. Pätzold, *Die frühen Wettiner*, 146–147.

32. *Chronicon Montis Sereni*, 161.

33. See chapter 3 for the support Albert received from his uncle, Count Dedo of Groitzsch.

34. See, for example, CDS 1 A, 2:411–412, no. 597.

35. *Chronicon Montis Sereni*, 165–166. See also *Cronica Reinhardsbrunnensis*, 550 and 552–553.

of Thuringia in order to ask for his help."[36] Once again, the landgrave agreed to lend military assistance to Count Dietrich, and this second phase of the war was still unsettled when Margrave Albert died without sons in 1195. Dietrich eventually acquired his brother's march of Meissen, but only after the death of Emperor Henry VI, who had claimed the march for himself as an imperial fief that had reverted to the crown.[37]

The conflict between Albert and Dietrich is the longest and most violent example of a succession dispute between two brothers manifest in the sources for the upper aristocracy of the Staufen period. While one reason for this conflict was Margrave Otto of Meissen's possession of only one prestigious lordship to pass on to his sons, his decision to alter his succession plans late in his career—apparently as a result of intrafamilial disagreements—also helped lay the foundation for this dispute. When Otto abandoned his original division of the patrimony, he invited disaster. Indeed, the case of Margrave Otto and his sons, Albert and Dietrich, illustrates why most members of the upper aristocracy tried to maintain strong and close relationships among sons and brothers. Once Count Dietrich of Weissenfels sought support from Landgrave Herman of Thuringia in his dispute with Margrave Albert, the conflict between the brothers became a regional war involving significant resources—and the devastation of both of their lordships.[38] When fraternal solidarity fractured and disagreements spread beyond the confines of the sibling group, it was the lineage as a whole that paid the price.[39]

The Sons of Frederick Barbarossa

In contrast to the lineages discussed above, the Staufens and Welfs both saw large fraternal groups—in possession of abundant lordships—rise to prominence in the closing decades of the twelfth century. Only four years after Henry the Lion's loss of his duchies, in the spring of 1184, Emperor Frederick I celebrated the shifting family dynamics in the Staufen lineage by holding one of the grandest and most elaborate courts of his reign in the fields outside Mainz. At least one member of all nine lineages investigated here was present—alongside thousands of other nobles, churchmen, and ministerials.[40] The courtly festivities

---

36. *Chronicon Montis Sereni*, 165.

37. See Hauser, *Staufische Lehnspolitik*, 309–310, and the discussion of fraternal succession in chapter 1.

38. *Cronica Reinhardsbrunnensis*, 552–553.

39. For a similar point, see Seidel, *Freunde und Verwandte*, 262.

40. Gilbert of Mons, *La chronique de Gislebert de Mons*, 159–162, chap. 109. See also Mortimer, "Knights and Knighthood," 99–100.

on this occasion included the knighting ceremony for Barbarossa's two eldest sons, Henry and Frederick. Henry had been elected king as a young boy in 1169, and Frederick had begun witnessing his father's charters as duke of Swabia in the early 1170s. As a result, neither of these teenagers was new to the political scene in 1184.[41] The ceremony at Mainz nevertheless marked a new phase of greater independence in their lives. Most significantly, Henry soon began holding court separately from his father, and in 1186 he married Constance, the daughter of King Roger II of Sicily.[42] The emperor's decision to knight Henry and Frederick in front of such an impressive audience of *principes imperii* and other lords was therefore intended to send a clear message that the next generation of the Staufens was ready to become more active in imperial politics.[43]

By the close of the decade, Frederick Barbarossa's three younger sons, Otto, Conrad, and Philip, had also begun to play more substantive roles in their father's political and territorial strategies.[44] The emperor, who had only one brother of his own—Conrad, his half brother—apparently worked to build a much stronger sibling group in the next generation by arranging for all five of his heirs to acquire prestigious positions. In 1188, for example, Barbarossa and King Alfonso VIII of Castile agreed to a marriage between the emperor's son Conrad and Alfonso's daughter Berengaria, who was the king's only child at the time. The surviving marriage contract identifies Conrad as "duke of Rothenburg"—a title previously used by King Conrad III's son Frederick—and includes a list of all the properties in Franconia and Swabia that Conrad would bring with him into the marriage as a dower.[45] Although this proposed union was never consummated and had no lasting political impact, the contract nevertheless reveals that Frederick Barbarossa wanted to fully integrate his younger sons into his succession and inheritance plans. Additional evidence for the emperor's intentions survives from a year later, in 1189, when he made a joint grant with his son Otto, "whom with God's favor we placed in his maternal inheritance in the county of Burgundy with the common counsel and support of our faithful men of the same county."[46]

---

41. For their earlier appearances at the imperial court, see, for example, MGH DD F I, 3:57–58, no. 581; 3:95–96, no. 608; and 3:161–165, no. 658. See also *Annales Pegavienses*, 262, for an early reference to the emperor's succession and inheritance plans.

42. Csendes, *Heinrich VI.*, 58–61.

43. Wolter, "Der Mainzer Hoftag," 194.

44. For the early lives of these younger sons, see Assmann, "Friedrich Barbarossas Kinder," 457–472. Barbarossa's daughters were all dead by the year 1184.

45. MGH DD F I, 4:247–251, no. 970.

46. Ibid., 4:283–284, no. 994. See also Opll, *Friedrich Barbarossa*, 163, and Mariotte, *Le comté de Bourgogne*, 50–52.

One of the most impressive Staufen family gatherings to occur during Barbarossa's lifetime took place in the spring of 1189 on the eve of the emperor's departure on the Third Crusade. An imperial charter from May 1 granting protection to a house of Augustinian canons includes in the witness list "our son Philip, provost of Aachen, . . . [and] our sons Duke Frederick of Swabia, Count Otto of Burgundy, and Conrad."[47] Although King Henry VI was absent on this occasion, he had been present at his father's court only two weeks earlier, when he had witnessed a charter alongside his brothers Otto and Conrad.[48] These documents thus show all five of the emperor's sons—including Philip, the youngest—at their father's side as he worked to settle affairs in the German kingdom before he departed on crusade. The charters also call attention to the eminent positions that all five sons held in the empire by this time. As Karl Leyser has argued, "The endowment of the Hohenstaufen princes meant of course that they could mix as equals with their like, the *principes regni*, that consolidating group whose verdict had been decisive in the process against the Lion. . . . It would be an exaggeration to say that Frederick I packed the Estate of Princes with his sons, but their presence was, all the same, noticeable and weighty."[49] The emperor's reasons for pursuing such a strategy are not difficult to discern. Placing four sons in prominent secular lordships and a fifth in the church was clearly an attempt to mimic the types of patrimonial divisions used so successfully earlier in his reign within other princely lineages, especially the Wittelsbachs and Ascanians.

Duke Frederick of Swabia was the only one of the emperor's sons to accompany him on crusade when he departed the German kingdom for the Holy Land in May of 1189. By then, the fraternal group at the heart of the next generation of the Staufen lineage was sufficiently well entrenched in imperial politics that Barbarossa's unexpected death in 1190 while crossing Asia Minor did not lead to a succession crisis. More significant for the lineage's future was the childless death of Duke Frederick in January of 1191 during the siege of Acre.[50] News of the young duke's death had reached the empire by April 9 of the same year, less than a week before King Henry VI's imperial coronation in Rome. In a charter from that day, the king and his three surviving brothers—Count-Palatine Otto of Burgundy, Duke Conrad of Rothenburg, and Philip, who is identified as bishop-elect of Würzburg—made a grant for the souls

---

47. MGH DD F I, 4:288–289, no. 998. See also ibid., 4:285–286, no. 996.
48. Ibid., 4:282, no. 993; Görich, *Friedrich Barbarossa*, 547.
49. Leyser, "Frederick Barbarossa," 173.
50. For their deaths on crusade, see Opll, *Friedrich Barbarossa*, 169–170.

of their father, mother, and brother, Frederick.[51] The duke of Swabia's death meant that the succession plan that the emperor had so carefully constructed for his sons during the 1180s had to be altered to accommodate a new sibling dynamic. No extant source explains how the remaining brothers decided the succession, but by 1192, Conrad had begun to act as duke of Swabia— cementing his position as the most prominent lord in the lineage after his older sibling Henry VI.[52]

The four brothers who became the leaders of the Staufen lineage in the wake of Emperor Frederick Barbarossa's and Duke Frederick's deaths did not share the political stage for very long. Conrad died in 1196, Henry in 1197, and Otto in 1200, meaning that only one of these siblings—Philip— survived their father by more than a decade.[53] Nevertheless, as the case of King Conrad III and his Babenberg half brothers has shown, even short-lived fraternal groups could have a significant effect on imperial politics. A wide range of sources from the early and mid-1190s attests to interactions between Emperor Henry VI and his brothers. Such evidence highlights three specific ways in which the fraternal groups operating inside the imperial family differed from upper aristocratic fraternal groups more generally.

First, the court of Henry VI was the focal point of all sibling relationships within this generation. As I have argued in previous chapters, the eldest brother in princely lineages was not the only node from which a generation's political networks could originate. Younger brothers and sisters frequently supported each other without involving their oldest male sibling. In the case of Barbarossa's sons, however, no evidence suggests that Conrad, Otto, and Philip interacted closely anywhere outside Henry's court. All three younger brothers are named in various combinations in imperial charters issued between 1191 and 1196, but sources for other ties between them are lacking.[54] Henry VI's royal and imperial titles set him apart from the dukes, margraves, and counts who were the eldest sons in other princely lineages and thus created a very different dynamic inside his lineage, one that led the other members of his generation to gravitate more readily to him and his court. This impact of the royal title on sibling relationships had also been evident during the reign of King Conrad III two generations earlier: although his

---

51. Reg. Imp. 4, vol. 3:61–62, no. 144.

52. Schwarzmaier, "Konrad von Rothenburg," 29.

53. Emperor Frederick I Barbarossa's half brother, Count-Palatine Conrad, lived until 1195 and also played a role in imperial politics in this period. See Seltmann, *Heinrich VI.*, 168–171.

54. For their presence at court, see, for example, Reg. Imp. 4, vol. 3:113, no. 276; 3:129, no. 317; and 3:141, no. 347.

Babenberg half brothers had very tense relationships with one another, they nevertheless frequently gathered together at the royal court to support Conrad's kingship.[55]

Second, Henry VI's efforts to rule a sprawling empire north and south of the Alps—while simultaneously pressing his wife's claims in the kingdom of Sicily—paradoxically lessened the intensity of the sibling relationships that developed in this generation. While Conrad witnessed fifty of Henry VI's charters and Otto witnessed almost twenty during the early and mid-1190s, neither attached himself to the imperial court for more than a few weeks or months at a time.[56] Moreover, after 1191, neither joined any of Henry VI's Italian expeditions. Instead, each tended to concentrate on his own lordships north of the Alps, visiting Henry VI's court only when the emperor was passing through regions where they possessed lands and rights. In Conrad's case, the vast collection of properties he held in Swabia, Franconia, and western Bavaria occupied much of his attention, and he rarely ventured beyond the southwestern parts of the kingdom to attend his brother's court.[57] Meanwhile, the most intense period of interaction between Henry VI and his younger brother Otto came in 1196 when the emperor was in and around Otto's county-palatine of Burgundy. On July 1, near Luxeuil, "our lord and brother Henry, holy and august emperor of the Romans," witnessed one of the count-palatine's charters, a rare example of a German ruler acting as a witness for another lord's agreement.[58] Otto then remained with Henry VI for the next two weeks as the emperor held court in Besançon.[59] In general, however, their meetings were brief; Otto simply did not venture very far east of the Rhine River valley to attend his older brother's court or to enmesh himself deeply in imperial politics.[60]

Since both Otto and Conrad had received prestigious lordships and had inherited significant portions of the patrimony prior to their father's death, neither was dependent on Henry's largesse for his standing in the empire. To the contrary, Henry VI may have been the one who was reliant on his brothers—in order to maintain the lineage's position north of the Alps while he was in Italy.[61] Viewed from this perspective, the sprawling nature of Henry VI's

---

55. See chapters 2, 3, and 4.
56. These numbers are based on my analysis of Reg. Imp. 4, vol. 3.
57. Schwarzmaier, "Konrad von Rothenburg," 30–31.
58. *Cartulaire des comtes de Bourgogne*, 6, no. 4.
59. Reg. Imp. 4, vol. 3:215–217, nos. 529–533.
60. The most detailed account of Otto's career remains Woltmann, *Pfalzgraf Otto von Burgund*. For his ties to Henry VI, see Seltmann, *Heinrich VI.*, 172–174.
61. Schwarzmaier, "Konrad von Rothenburg," 31. Evidence to support this argument can be found in Burchard of Ursberg, *Die Chronik*, 230.

territories prevented him from developing close relationships with Conrad and Otto, but their much narrower political interests—tied to their own lordships—had the advantage of keeping the imperial family firmly anchored in the German kingdom. Frederick Barbarossa's interactions with his younger half brother, Count-Palatine Conrad of the Rhine, can perhaps be understood from this perspective as well.[62] In other lineages, meanwhile, brothers frequently benefited from their control of *neighboring* properties, rights, and lordships. This form of succession and inheritance made it much easier for these siblings to maintain close ties and to cooperate effectively with one another, because their territorial and political interests overlapped to a much greater extent than those of the Staufen brothers during the 1190s.

Third, the relationship between Henry VI and his youngest brother, Philip, proved to be the most durable relationship in this generation—further evidence that the Staufen rulers formed their strongest sibling bonds with brothers who lacked established positions in imperial politics. Here, it is possible to identify clear parallels with King Conrad III and his siblings. While Conrad III's older brother, Frederick II, pursued his own territorial interests because of his decades-long possession of the title of duke of Swabia, the king's Babenberg half brothers—who were significantly younger than he was—were much more reliant on Conrad's largesse. He gave several of them positions in the realm that they could use to help him stabilize and expand his kingship. Similarly, Emperor Henry VI was able to rely on the support of his youngest brother, Philip, because Philip, at the time of Barbarossa's death, held the position of provost of Aachen, from which he could easily be moved. Thus, when the bishop of Würzburg died in 1190 on the Third Crusade, Henry VI quickly sought to place his youngest brother in this key ecclesiastical post.[63] Since Philip was a teenager at the time, however, there was little hope of his election being recognized as canonical; by October of 1192, Philip was once more provost of Aachen.[64] In July of 1193, he was identified simply as "Philip, brother of the emperor" in one of Henry VI's charters—an early piece of evidence for his withdrawal from the religious life.[65] During this period when he lacked a title or lordship, he joined Henry VI's Italian expedition of 1194–1195 and crossed the whole of the peninsula

62. See chapter 4. As with Barbarossa and his half brother, Conrad, there is some evidence for minor disagreements between Henry VI and his brothers because they had disparate territorial interests: *Chronicon Ottenburanum*, 622.

63. Csendes, *Philipp von Schwaben*, 24–25.

64. Reg. Imp. 4, vol. 3:104, no. 254.

65. Ibid., 3:125–126, no. 308. For canons leaving the religious life and becoming secular lords, see chapter 2.

with his older brother, eventually joining him in Sicily.[66] Henry soon rewarded his brother's loyalty, naming Philip duke of Tuscany in early 1195.[67]
A year later, in the wake of their brother Conrad's death, Philip received
the duchy of Swabia from the emperor.[68] Philip, more so than either Otto
or Conrad, appears in the sources as a consistent supporter of Henry VI, as
someone who was frequently at the emperor's side, and as someone who had
earned his oldest brother's trust.[69] Because he was the youngest of the Staufen
siblings and did not have a prestigious lordship of his own when his father
died, Philip forged a close bond with Henry VI that worked to both of their
advantages throughout the early and mid-1190s.

Despite the short length of time that these four brothers shared the political stage, there is abundant evidence to demonstrate that the members of
this generation operated quite differently from the fraternal groups within
other princely lineages of the twelfth century. Sibling relationships among the
Staufens were unique, because the royal and imperial titles created a different
political dynamic. Such differences are most apparent during the early and
mid-1190s, when Henry VI was attempting to exert effective authority over
the empire and the kingdom of Sicily simultaneously. But the situation did not
change significantly in later years when only two members of this generation
remained. Emperor Henry VI died on September 28, 1197, leaving behind
only one son—the future Emperor Frederick II, born only three years earlier.
Henry had secured Frederick's election as German king prior to his own death,
but the boy was too young to succeed his father immediately. As a result, on
March 6, 1198, Duke Philip of Swabia—not his older brother Count-Palatine
Otto of Burgundy—was elected German king by a group of imperial princes.[70]

The election of the younger brother should come as no surprise, since
sixty years earlier, Conrad III had likewise been elected instead of his older
brother, Duke Frederick II of Swabia. Indeed, the election of 1198 has
definite analogs to the 1138 election when viewed through the lens of
Staufen family politics. Philip, like Conrad III, had been a regular visitor to the imperial court in the years immediately preceding his election,
whereas Otto—much like Duke Frederick II—had preferred to focus on
his own lordships.[71] Philip must therefore have been much better known to

66. Ibid., 3:144–179, nos. 352–438.
67. Csendes, *Philipp von Schwaben*, 29–32.
68. Otto of St. Blasien, *Chronica*, 130; Burchard of Ursberg, *Die Chronik*, 230.
69. Seltmann, *Heinrich VI.*, 180–181.
70. Csendes, *Philipp von Schwaben*, 71–72. For more on this election, see below.
71. See chapter 4.

the other *principes imperii* than Otto—and was probably in a better position to gain their support.[72] Here, however, the parallels between 1138 and 1198 end. After Conrad III's election, his older brother, Frederick II, had quickly emerged as an important figure at court, while the same cannot be said for Count-Palatine Otto of Burgundy. He and his younger brother Philip may never have been very close. During the reign of Henry VI, they witnessed only four imperial charters together: one in 1193, two in 1194, and one in 1195.[73] Their contacts did not increase after Henry VI's death. Chronicles indicate that Philip and Otto shared a mutual enemy in the years after 1198, namely the bishop of Strasbourg, but there is no evidence for the count-palatine ever attending Philip's court.[74] These two brothers, who had few overlapping political or territorial interests earlier in their lives, thus failed to develop close ties even after they became the only surviving members of their generation.

The Staufen fraternal group that, on the eve of the Third Crusade, looked to be on the verge of becoming a dominant force in imperial politics for decades to come, disappeared quietly in 1200. King Philip of Swabia spent the final years of his reign, until his assassination in 1208, without any siblings and relied on other types of networks to support his kingship.[75] When he and his brothers first rose to prominence in the mid-1180s, their father, Emperor Frederick I Barbarossa, had grand plans for them. Employing the same tactics that other princely lineages had used in earlier years, he sought to establish a fraternal group with far-reaching influence and authority. But he could not duplicate the success of his older contemporaries Margrave Conrad of Meissen, Margrave Albert the Bear of Brandenburg, and Count-Palatine Otto I of Bavaria. The vast geographical distances that frequently divided his sons—and their diverse political and territorial interests—prevented the next generation of the imperial dynasty from becoming a strong and cohesive fraternal group comparable to those at the center of the Wettin, Ascanian, and Wittelsbach lineages during preceding decades.

---

72. Shortly before his death, Henry VI also asked Philip to come to Italy in order to meet the young Frederick II and bring him to the German kingdom: Csendes, *Heinrich VI.*, 194. Philip's reputation as a trusted supporter of the emperor can be contrasted with Otto's reputation as a cruel and violent lord: Woltmann, *Pfalzgraf Otto von Burgund*, 51.

73. Reg. Imp. 4, vol. 3:117–118, no. 288; 3:141–142, nos. 347–348; and 3:191–192, no. 473.

74. For their conflicts with the bishop of Strasbourg, see *Annales Marbacenses*, 200–204, and Mariotte, *Le comté de Bourgogne sous les Hohenstaufen 1156–1208*, 52–53. The only hint of Otto's support for Philip comes in a letter written by some of the imperial princes to Pope Innocent III in 1199: MGH Const., 2:3–4, no. 3.

75. For one of these networks, see chapter 6.

Still, although Emperor Henry VI and his brothers did not cooperate as closely as some other twelfth-century siblings, they nevertheless maintained Staufen authority in the German kingdom throughout the early and mid-1190s. As noted above, this was a period of upheaval in many of the other lineages of the upper aristocracy. The fraternal groups of the late 1170s and early 1180s were disappearing, and there was much uncertainty surrounding issues of succession and inheritance in various princely lineages. Branches of the Ascanians and Wettins experienced fraternal conflict in the years around 1190. In the Ludowing lineage, the death of Landgrave Ludwig III of Thuringia in 1190 without sons led to his younger brother Herman suddenly and unexpectedly becoming the head of the lineage.[76] Meanwhile, the Andechs, Wittelsbach, and Zähringen lineages were led by generations that had only one lord active in the secular sphere.[77] Throughout the upper aristocracy, therefore, the early 1190s were a time of adjustment. The Staufens, led by a group of four brothers, were in a much more stable position than many other lineages, even if those siblings did not have especially close relationships. By the late 1190s, the situation had begun to change, and a new fraternal group emerged to challenge Staufen ascendancy—and Staufen claims to the kingship.

The Sons of Henry the Lion

On June 9, 1198, three months after the election of Philip of Swabia as king, a small group of imperial princes led by the archbishop of Cologne elected a rival candidate for the throne: Henry the Lion's son Otto.[78] Like Philip, Otto was not the eldest living member of his generation. His older brother, Count-Palatine Henry of the Rhine (d. 1227), was unquestionably the more prominent figure in imperial politics in this period and might have been elected king instead of Otto if he had not been crusading in the Holy Land during the spring and summer of 1198.[79] Henry returned to the German kingdom later the same year and began to appear at his younger brother's side in 1199, setting the stage for the emergence of a new sibling dynamic at the

76. For this critical moment in Ludowing history, see Patze, *Die Entstehung der Landesherrschaft*, 1:249–253.

77. These lords were Duke Berthold III of Merania, Duke Ludwig I of Bavaria, and Duke Berthold V of Zähringen.

78. For the double election of 1198, see Csendes, "Die Doppelwahl von 1198," and Gropper, *Die Doppelwahlen von 1198 und 1257*, 10–95.

79. For the possibility of Henry's election, see Hucker, *Kaiser Otto IV*, 22–23, and Heinemann, *Heinrich von Braunschweig*, 63–64.

heart of imperial politics. Henry's position at court during the opening years of Otto's reign comes into focus in a letter from mid-1201, in which a notary reporting on Otto's activities to Pope Innocent III mentions "his brother the count-palatine, who is always in all matters the better part of the king's council."[80] Only three years later, however, this fraternal relationship fractured. As the *Chronica regia Coloniensis* entry for the year 1204 relates, "The unfaithful count-palatine, who was at his brother's side, abandoned him and went over to Philip, corrupted by his money and the promise of the duchy of Saxony."[81]

Numerous scholars have examined the complicated relationship between Henry and Otto, and my intention here is not to reconstruct all of their interactions during Otto's two decades as king and emperor.[82] Instead, I will consider some of the reasons that may explain why Henry split from his brother and supported Philip until the latter's assassination in 1208. The relationship between Otto and Henry appears to have suffered from two weaknesses that offer important insights into the factors that could lead to fraternal conflict among the members of the German upper aristocracy. First, these brothers did not have the opportunity to develop a strong relationship during the early years of their lives. Second, unexpected events—in this case, Otto's election—forced the brothers to renegotiate their father's plans for the division of the patrimony.

When Duke Henry the Lion of Saxony and Bavaria lost his imperial fiefs in 1180–1181, he and his wife Matilda were the parents of four children: a daughter and three sons, all born in the years between 1172 and 1177. Three of these young children—the daughter Matilda and the sons Henry and Otto—accompanied Henry the Lion and Matilda when they went into exile in July of 1182 in the lands of Matilda's father, King Henry II of England. The second-born son, Lothar, remained behind in the German kingdom, possibly because the emperor was holding him as a hostage to ensure Henry's good behavior.[83] While at the Angevin court, Henry the Lion and Matilda had a fourth son, who was given the name William.[84] This was a common name in Matilda's family, but not among the Welfs, and thus provides an early piece of evidence for the extraordinary influence that Matilda's natal family would exert over her children. Indeed, when Henry the Lion made peace

---

80. *Regestum Innocentii III papae*, 141, no. 52.
81. *Chronica regia Coloniensis*, 217–218.
82. See, for example, Hucker, *Kaiser Otto IV*, 359–367; Schneidmüller, *Die Welfen*, 243–267; and Heinemann, *Heinrich von Braunschweig*, 61–168.
83. Ehlers, *Heinrich der Löwe*, 354.
84. For all these children, see Jordan, "Heinrich der Löwe," 128–140.

with the emperor and returned to Saxony from his initial exile in the year 1185, he was joined by his wife and only one of their children: the eldest son, Henry. Their youngest sons, Otto and William, both remained behind at the Angevin court. Also staying behind was their daughter, Matilda, whose various betrothals and marriages were arranged by her grandfather King Henry II and her two maternal uncles, King Richard I and King John—but never by her own father or brothers.[85]

Although Henry the Lion and the other members of his nuclear family occasionally traveled back and forth between the German kingdom and the Angevin lands during the late 1180s and early 1190s, the relationships within the younger generation of the Welf lineage were nevertheless affected in significant ways by the long distances that frequently separated the siblings.[86] The older brothers, Henry and Lothar, developed political and territorial interests centered on the German kingdom, while the younger brothers, Otto and William, spent most of this period living in the lands of their mother's family. The siblings' differing orientations are first evident in accounts of their father's and uncle's conflicts with the Staufen ruler Henry VI. In the summer of 1190, Henry VI was anxious to negotiate a new peace with Henry the Lion so he could cross the Alps and push his claims to the kingdom of Sicily. Henry the Lion, hoping this peace agreement would lay the groundwork for the restoration of his position in the empire, agreed to various concessions and offered his eldest sons, Henry and Lothar, to Henry VI as hostages to guarantee his good behavior.[87] Four years later when Emperor Henry VI agreed to release his prisoner King Richard I of England from captivity so Richard could collect his ransom, the younger sons of Henry the Lion—Otto and William—were the ones given to Henry VI as hostages to ensure the king of England's good faith.[88]

Other evidence from the early 1190s confirms the existence of separate spheres of influence for these siblings. Lothar disappears quickly from the sources, dying under mysterious circumstances as a hostage of Henry VI in 1190, while the eldest brother, Henry, emerged during this period as the key figure alongside his father in Saxony.[89] Moreover, in 1194 he married Agnes, the daughter and heiress of the Staufen count-palatine Conrad of the Rhine,

---

85. Ehlers, *Heinrich der Löwe*, 366; Bartlett, *England under the Norman and Angevin Kings*, 104–105; Weller, *Die Heiratspolitik des deutschen Hochadels*, 277–282.

86. For additional travels back and forth, see Ehlers, *Heinrich der Löwe*, 377–381.

87. Csendes, *Heinrich VI.*, 82.

88. Hucker, *Kaiser Otto IV.*, 12–13; Jordan, "Heinrich der Löwe," 139.

89. Lyon, "Fathers and Sons," 303–304.

thus assuring his position as a prominent player in imperial politics in the ensuing years.[90] Otto and William, meanwhile, remained tied to the court of their uncle King Richard. Otto was briefly enfeoffed with the county of York in 1190 and may have held the county of La Marche for a short time thereafter. When he returned to the Angevin lands in late 1194, after his time as a hostage for Richard, Otto was also considered for a lordship along the English-Scottish border before eventually receiving the county of Poitou—and possibly the duchy of Aquitaine as well—from Richard in 1196.[91] William seems not to have acquired any fiefs from his Angevin relatives, but Henry II and then Richard did pay all the expenses for his early upbringing. Moreover, it has been suggested that Richard planned a marriage for his young nephew in the early 1190s.[92] William's journey to the German kingdom in 1193 to serve as a hostage after Richard's release was quite possibly his first visit to the land of his father's birth.

When Henry the Lion died in 1195, the division of his patrimony reflected the divergent career trajectories of his three surviving sons. Henry, the eldest, inherited his father's most important rights and properties in Saxony, including the former duke's principal residence of Brunswick. With the death of his father-in-law later in 1195, Henry also became count-palatine of the Rhine—a title that elevated him into the ranks of the *principes imperii*. The Rhine region remained of secondary interest to Henry during subsequent years, however, as he spent most of his time securing his Saxon inheritance and pushing his father's old claims to the ducal title.[93] Meanwhile, the second son, Otto, received a much smaller portion of Henry the Lion's patrimony. He acquired the town of Haldensleben and all its appurtenances, but this was an insufficient basis for an independent lordship.[94] As previous chapters have shown, second sons within the German upper aristocracy typically inherited significant pieces of their fathers' patrimonies, making Otto unusual. In this case, however, the reason for the small inheritance is clear: Otto's uncle King Richard I of England had taken on the responsibility of providing him with a lordship in the Angevin lands.[95] William, the third son of Henry the Lion, seems to have received more of his father's patrimony

---

90. Weller, *Die Heiratspolitik des deutschen Hochadels*, 180–187.

91. For all these titles and lordships, see Hucker, *Kaiser Otto IV*, 9–16, and Bartlett, *England under the Norman and Angevin Kings*, 105.

92. Ehlers, *Heinrich der Löwe*, 373.

93. Schneidmüller, *Die Welfen*, 240.

94. Hucker, *Kaiser Otto IV*, 13–14; *Die Urkunden Heinrichs des Löwen*, 193–194, no. 140.

95. Hucker, *Kaiser Otto IV*, 14. The fact that Richard was childless and had few other close relatives on whom he could rely was an important factor in his favoring of the young Otto.

than his older brother Otto did. Although he had been raised at the Angevin court, William was given the town of Lüneburg and other valuable rights and properties in Saxony with which he could establish his own lordship. He maintained some ties to his Angevin relatives after 1195, but increasingly the focus of his attention shifted to the German kingdom.[96] Thus, William is the only one of the three brothers to have the locus of his political and territorial interests shift after the death of Henry the Lion.

Sources from the years 1196–1197 provide important clues into the relationships among the siblings Henry, Otto, and William after their father died. Throughout this period, Otto was separated from his brothers by significant distances. He alone resided in the Angevin lands, where he actively supported King Richard while also attempting to build his lordship in Aquitaine and Poitou.[97] The only evidence for any contacts between Otto and his brothers can be found in some of Henry's charters from these years. In a document dated September 8, 1196, for example, a ministerial made a property donation to a Saxon religious community "with our [Henry's] permission and that of our brothers, William and Otto."[98] It is not clear, however, how Otto actually gave his permission and consent, since there is no indication he was present for this agreement. Indeed, only one of Henry's charters from this period shows any of these brothers together on any occasion: at some point early in 1197, Henry confirmed a property donation made by one of his ministerials "in our presence and that of our brother William."[99] A short time after this charter was written, Henry departed for the Holy Land on crusade—unaccompanied by either of his brothers—and did not return to the German kingdom until the autumn of 1198.[100]

In Henry's absence, the princely faction opposed to the Staufens chose to elect his younger brother Otto as king. For Otto, this was a dramatic shift in the course of his political career. He had spent most of the previous two decades in the Angevin lands and had no experience exercising lordship in the German kingdom. When he first arrived in the kingdom, he seems not

---

96. Ibid., 368–369.

97. Several of his charters survive, as does a single copy of his seal (which shows no signs of having been influenced in any way by seals from the Welf side of his family). See Reg. Imp. 5, vol. 1:52–55, nos. 186–198.

98. Wolfenbüttel, Niedersächsisches Landesarchiv, Staatsarchiv, StA WO 17 Urk 12. I am most grateful to Andrea Briechle at the University of Heidelberg for sharing with me an early draft of her dissertation on Count-Palatine Henry's charters.

99. Wolfenbüttel, Niedersächsisches Landesarchiv, Staatsarchiv, StA WO 25 Urk 27.

100. Heinemann, *Heinrich von Braunschweig*, 51–72. Hucker (*Kaiser Otto IV.*, 369) argues that Henry gave his brother William the responsibility of exercising lordship in his Saxon lands while he was on crusade.

to have had strong ties with any of the leading magnates of the empire—including his older brother, Count-Palatine Henry.[101] A royal charter from January of 1199, seven months after Otto's election, is the first extant source to place these siblings together in the same place at the same time since the early years of their father's exile at the Angevin court.[102] Their contacts gradually increased in the period after 1199, but their lack of close connections during the preceding years may help explain why their fraternal relationship was not strong enough to prevent Henry from switching his support to King Philip of Swabia in 1204. The sibling bond may have had little if any inherent meaning for brothers who began to interact regularly only later in their lives.[103]

A second reason for the outbreak of the conflict between Otto and Henry concerns the new division of the patrimony that the brothers undertook in the wake of the 1198 royal election. As I have shown in earlier chapters, fraternal groups tended to be most stable when the succession and inheritance plan enacted by a father during his own lifetime did not require significant adjustments during later years. In the case of this generation of the Welfs, however, changing circumstances in the period after Henry the Lion's death forced a renegotiation of his plan. When Otto arrived in the German kingdom in 1198 to begin the fight for the crown against Philip of Swabia, he was not in possession of any imperial lordships. Moreover, Henry the Lion had given him only a small portion of the Welfs' alodial properties in Saxony, because Otto seemed destined to spend his life in France and England. As a result, Otto initially had no choice but to rely on the financial backing of his uncle King Richard I of England and on the revenues he was receiving from his fiefs in the Angevin lands.[104]

However, Richard died on April 6, 1199, less than a year after Otto's arrival in the German kingdom. Richard's younger brother John, who succeeded him as king, was not as supportive of Otto in the months immediately following his ascension to the throne of England.[105] According to the English chronicler Roger of Howden, in or around September of 1200, Otto "sent Duke Henry of Saxony and William of Winchester, his brothers, to their uncle King John of England, seeking from him the county of

---

101. Otto very quickly married the daughter and heiress of the duke of Brabant to strengthen his position: Schneidmüller, *Die Welfen*, 243–244.

102. Reg. Imp. 5, vol. 1:60, no. 211. Their younger brother, William, may also have been present.

103. For a similar point, see chapter 6.

104. Huffman, *Social Politics*, 166–169.

105. John's withdrawal of his financial support for his nephew was the result of a peace he had arranged with King Philip II Augustus of France: Csendes, "Die Doppelwahl von 1198," 168.

York and the county of Poitou, which King Richard of England had given to him."[106] Another English chronicle suggests that John owed his nephew 25,000 silver marks.[107] But the siblings Henry and William failed in their negotiations with John and returned to the German kingdom without any additional money to help fund Otto's kingship.[108] To continue his struggle against Philip of Swabia, Otto would therefore need to find a new reliable source of income.

It is in this context that a new division of the Welf patrimony among the three brothers Henry, Otto, and William is best understood. On May 1, 1202, Otto and Henry each issued a pair of charters detailing which brother would hold which rights and properties in Saxony; William sealed the two charters that directly concerned the portion he would receive.[109] Preparations for this revised inheritance plan had almost certainly been taking place since Otto's election in 1198.[110] Nevertheless, the brothers' decision to preserve the terms of the division in writing is significant. For the nine lineages examined here, these are the earliest extant documents to provide a written description of how siblings chose to partition a patrimony. The unique circumstances shaping fraternal relationships in this generation of the Welfs must have influenced the creation of these charters. While Henry was willing to accommodate Otto, the bond between them was apparently not strong enough for them to be satisfied with an oral agreement. Otto was probably most keen to preserve the fraternal agreement in writing, since he desperately needed the stable territorial foundation for his kingship that only a portion of the patrimony could provide.[111]

The details of the division outlined in the 1202 charters are not important for this book, except to emphasize one point. Count-Palatine Henry of the Rhine, who had been in possession of the largest and most valuable portion of the patrimony after Henry the Lion died in 1195, was the brother who lost the most. He essentially agreed to create a lordship for his younger brother Otto out of the collection of Saxon lands and rights he had been holding for the previous seven years. Henry even acknowledged Otto's control over the most important town in Welf hands, Henry the Lion's chief residence at Brunswick. Because Henry maintained titular authority

---

106. Roger of Howden, *Chronica*, 4:116.

107. *Annales monasterii de Wintonia*, 2:73.

108. Huffman, *Social Politics*, 179–181.

109. *Origines Guelficae*, 3:626–629, 852–854. See also *Braunschweigische Reimchronik von Gandersheim*, 530, lines 5680–5691.

110. Hucker, *Kaiser Otto IV.*, 49–50.

111. For possible motives, see Pischke, *Die Landesteilungen der Welfen*, 12–13.

over the county-palatine of the Rhine, his status as a *princeps imperii* was unaffected by the events of 1202. Nevertheless, he did not possess a single traditional center of Welf lordship in the wake of the division.[112] Not surprisingly, many historians regard Henry's loss of so many valuable pieces of the patrimony in Saxony as the reason for his defection from Otto's camp in 1204.[113]

Contemporary accounts of Henry's split from Otto clearly link his support of King Philip with his weakened position in Saxony after the 1202 partition. As noted above, the *Chronica regia Coloniensis* reports that Philip was able to bribe Henry by promising him the duchy of Saxony. Henry had been titling himself duke of Saxony since the mid-1190s, but the Staufen king and his supporters had never recognized him as the legitimate holder of the duchy.[114] Arnold of Lübeck, meanwhile, assigns a somewhat different motivation to the count-palatine in his detailed account of Henry's switching of sides. According to him, Philip warned Henry that he would lose the county-palatine of the Rhine unless he joined the Staufen camp. Henry therefore went to his brother Otto to seek compensation if that were to happen. Arnold records the meeting between the two siblings in the form of an extraordinary dialogue:

> [Henry:] "In truth, brother, I am doubly bound to serve you by the bond of blood and by the fealty owed the royal majesty. Accordingly, in order that I may be able to support you more fully, it is just that I should receive from you something of advantage. You should therefore give up to me, if it is pleasing, the town of Brunswick and the castle of Lichtenberg, in order that I, strengthened by these fortifications, will be ready to resist all your adversaries on every side." His brother the king, having heard these things, responded not without scorn, "Not so, my brother! It is more advantageous for me, as the first in the realm, to hold the government strongly. And so, everything that you want, you should hold together with me equally. I do not want, like one terrified by some fear, to seem to be doing something now that I may perhaps be forced to change in the future as if regretful." What more is there? The count-palatine, without deliberation or need, abandoned

---

112. Ibid., 33; Hucker, *Kaiser Otto IV.*, 50–51.

113. Krieb, *Vermitteln und Versöhnen*, 36–38; Pischke, *Die Landesteilungen der Welfen*, 33–34; Hucker, *Kaiser Otto IV.*, 361–362; Schneidmüller, *Die Welfen*, 251–252; Heinemann, *Heinrich von Braunschweig*, 105–107.

114. For Henry's early use of the title in his charters, see, for example, Wolfenbüttel, Niedersächsisches Landesarchiv, Staatsarchiv, StA WO 17 Urk 12 (from the year 1196).

his brother and, with many people marveling or even shedding tears, crossed over to Philip.[115]

Arnold, who is one of our best-informed sources for the Welfs during this period, suggests here that Henry's failed efforts to reacquire for himself key pieces of Henry the Lion's patrimony from his brother, including Brunswick, spurred his defection. Nine years after their father's death, the division of the inheritance apparently remained a point of contention between the siblings. This property dispute—combined with the absence of a close relationship between Henry and Otto during earlier years—explains why the count-palatine was willing to do something that few other noblemen of the Staufen period did: side with another lord against his own brother.

Although Henry never seems to have plotted actively against Otto between 1204 and 1208, he disappears from his brother's side in the sources from this period. That he ceased to be a trusted counselor to his younger sibling soon caught the attention of Pope Innocent III. At some point during the middle months of 1205, Innocent addressed a scathing letter to Henry: "It redounds upon the infamy of your name and the perpetual disgrace of your posterity that you abandoned our most dear son in Christ, the illustrious King Otto, elect emperor of the Romans, your brother, . . . and drew near to the duke of Swabia."[116] By turning away from his own brother and switching his support to Philip, the pope hinted, Henry was risking excommunication. Innocent's threats seem to have had little effect on Henry. The count-palatine did not reappear at his brother Otto's court until the summer months of 1208—after King Philip of Swabia's assassination. However, reconciliation between the siblings followed quickly thereafter. Otto wrote Pope Innocent III in July or August of that year and reported, "Our brother the count-palatine of the Rhine, thanks be to God, has returned fully to our affection."[117] In subsequent years, Henry remained a loyal supporter of his brother, and the two maintained close ties with one another.[118]

During the early years of the thirteenth century, the Welf brothers formed the most impressive fraternal group active in the German kingdom. Otto relied heavily on his brothers Henry and William as he pushed his claims to the kingship, and both of these siblings were initially willing to support him in

115. Arnold of Lübeck, *Chronica Slavorum*, 6.6, 226–227. See also *Chronicon Montis Sereni*, 171, where it is suggested that Henry was bribed with the promise of the advocacy for Goslar.

116. *Regestum Innocentii III papae*, 298, no. 121.

117. Ibid., 361, no. 160.

118. Hucker, *Kaiser Otto IV.*, 363–365.

his efforts. Questions over the division of the patrimony soon revealed cracks in the facade of sibling solidarity, however, and Henry and Otto's differing backgrounds helped intensify the rift. For four crucial years in the middle of the civil war that engulfed the German kingdom, there is no evidence for the two brothers having any contact with one another. This relationship thus emerges from the sources as one of the weakest fraternal relationships within the nine princely lineages under investigation here. But given their lineage's complicated connections to the German kingdom and the Angevin lands, which led to unusual childhoods and inheritance problems for both Henry and Otto, the tenuous bond between them is relatively easy to comprehend. Here, as elsewhere in the German upper aristocracy, a dispute between siblings was the by-product of a decidedly atypical set of family circumstances.

Civil War in an Age of Shrinking Sibling Groups

The double royal election of the year 1198 and the ensuing conflict between the supporters of King Philip of Swabia and King Otto IV of Brunswick divided the political elite of the German kingdom until Philip's assassination in 1208. Count-Palatine Henry of the Rhine, as the brother of one of the rival claimants to the throne, was the most prominent magnate to switch sides during the war, but he was not the only one. Both the bishop of Strasbourg and the duke of Brabant were also persuaded—or rather bribed—to abandon Otto and support Philip. Landgrave Herman of Thuringia from the Ludowing lineage, whose lordship lay in the heart of the kingdom and was therefore the focal point of military campaigns by both kings, changed sides on multiple occasions during the early 1200s.[119] Among the lineages examined here, however, the Welfs were the only one to experience the fragmenting of a sibling group as a result of the civil war.

One reason why other princely lineages were not fractured by the civil war was the continuing decline in the number of adult siblings in the early thirteenth century. Lords who had no living brothers led the Staufen, Babenberg, Wittelsbach, and Zähringen lineages during this period. Only one of the three surviving branches of the Ascanian lineage, that of the aforementioned counts of Orlamünde, had brothers active in this period, but long distances separated them. And in the Ludowings, Landgrave Herman of Thuringia's two older brothers had already died, while his younger brother, Count Frederick of Ziegenhain, was an obscure figure who appears only

---

119. For these three magnates, see Krieb, *Vermitteln und Versöhnen*, 35–57.

once with Herman during these years.[120] Early deaths, apparently in combination with some form of family planning in these lineages, had dramatically reduced the size of the upper aristocracy in the quarter century since 1180. Besides the Welfs, only the Wettin and Andechs lineages included adult siblings who played active roles in imperial politics during the opening decade of the thirteenth century.

Among the Wettins, two separate branches of the lineage provide evidence for sibling solidarity in the midst of the conflict between Philip and Otto. The first consisted of the sons of Count Dedo of Groitzsch. Dedo, who had purchased his dead brother's march of Lower Lusatia from Barbarossa in 1185, had been able to give prestigious secular lordships to both of his surviving sons on his death in 1190.[121] Conrad (d. 1210) received the march, while Dietrich (d. 1207) received the county of Groitzsch. These brothers therefore constitute one of the rare instances of princely brothers who were able to divide their father's patrimony easily in the later twelfth century. The *Chronicon Montis Sereni,* in its entry for the year 1205, suggests close ties between the siblings. It reports that "Margrave Albert of Brandenburg took as his wife the older daughter of Margrave Conrad of Lower Lusatia, who was named Mechthild. . . . Count Dietrich of [Groitzsch] hosted the wedding celebration in his castle of Groitzsch with great honor and an abundance of expenditures."[122] This pair of brothers thus held a grand family celebration in the midst of one of the harshest phases of the civil war. Two years later, in 1207, they demonstrated their mutual support for King Philip of Swabia by both witnessing one of his charters while he was holding court in Frankfurt.[123]

The second branch of the Wettin lineage offers a more complicated example of sibling solidarity. In or around the year 1180, Margrave Otto of Meissen's daughter, Adela, married Přemysl Otakar (d. 1232), who would succeed as Bohemian duke and be crowned king of Bohemia, both in 1198. The couple had several children during the early years of their marriage, but soon after Přemysl Otakar's royal coronation, he decided to end the union. At a church council headed by the bishop of Prague, the new king claimed consanguinity and the improper giving of consent—among other reasons— in order to secure a divorce.[124] Shortly thereafter, he married the sister of the

---

120. Weller, *Die Heiratspolitik des deutschen Hochadels,* 616.
121. See chapter 3.
122. *Chronicon Montis Sereni,* 172.
123. CDS 1 A, 3:88–89, no. 109.
124. *Codex diplomaticus et epistolarius regni Bohemiae,* 2:6–8, no. 8.

king of Hungary, a more prestigious wife for the newly crowned ruler of Bohemia. However, neither his first wife, Adela, nor her brother, Margrave Dietrich of Meissen (d. 1221), recognized the proceedings of the church council. As a result, a dispute soon erupted.[125]

Throughout the empire, the politics of the late 1190s were intricately linked to the conflict between Philip of Swabia and Otto of Brunswick for control of the German kingdom and the imperial crown. Not surprisingly, therefore, Adela's marriage and divorce quickly became entangled in these machinations. Arnold of Lübeck is explicit in describing how her brother Dietrich sought to connect his sister's situation to imperial politics: "After Otakar of Bohemia repudiated his legitimate wife, he took another from Hungary. This disturbed the brother of the repudiated wife, Margrave Dietrich of Meissen, and together with Duke Bernhard [of Saxony]—both of whom were familiars of King Philip—they obtained this from [Philip], namely that he would take the kingdom (or duchy) of Bohemia away from the adulterer Otakar and transfer it [to another]. This was done."[126] Dietrich's efforts to overthrow Přemysl Otakar led the king of Bohemia to switch his allegiance from Philip to Otto of Brunswick. As a result, Dietrich and the Bohemian ruler would remain on opposite sides of the civil war in subsequent years. Nevertheless, Dietrich continually pressed the Bohemian ruler to take Adela back. By 1206 at the latest, the dispute had attracted the interest of Pope Innocent III. In a letter sent to three German churchmen in April of that year, he asked them to investigate the situation.[127] This document supports Arnold of Lübeck's contention that Dietrich was a central figure in the dispute alongside his sister: "On behalf of my beloved son, the nobleman [Dietrich] margrave of Meissen, and his sister, Adela, it has been brought to our attention that . . ." The margrave's active involvement did not help his sister's cause, however. Because Innocent III wanted Přemysl Otakar to continue to support Otto of Brunswick's kingship, the pope made little effort to move the investigation along quickly.[128] In April of 1210, more than a decade after the dispute had begun, Innocent III finally wrote directly "to the noblewoman Adela, sister of that nobleman the margrave of Meissen"

---

125. For Dietrich, who left the church in order to succeed his father as margrave of Meissen, see also chapter 2. For this dispute, see also Pätzold, *Die frühen Wettiner*, 102–103, and Weller, *Die Heiratspolitik des deutschen Hochadels*, 678–686. For Přemysl Otakar, see Wolverton, *Hastening toward Prague*, 219–220, 254.

126. Arnold of Lübeck, *Chronica Slavorum*, 6.5, 223.

127. *Die Register Innocenz' III.*, 9:108–110, no. 60. See also *Codex diplomaticus et epistolarius regni Bohemiae*, 2:14–16, no. 20.

128. *Codex diplomaticus et epistolarius regni Bohemiae*, 2:75–76, no. 81.

and acknowledged Adela's ongoing attempts to fight her divorce.[129] Adela nonetheless died in 1211 without having been restored to her position as Přemysl Otakar's wife.

Significantly, Margrave Dietrich of Meissen continued to show interest in Bohemian affairs even after his sister's death. In a 1212 treaty, Dietrich promised to support Emperor Otto IV of Brunswick against his enemies. The emperor, in return, agreed to grant the kingdom of Bohemia to Dietrich's nephew Vratislav—Adela's son by Přemysl Otakar.[130] This text offers an important piece of evidence for Dietrich's motives in supporting his sister's case so strongly during earlier years. When Přemysl Otakar was crowned king in 1198, Adela was poised to become queen and her son to become the heir to the throne. However, the dissolution of the marriage eliminated this possibility—and robbed Dietrich of the opportunity to have family members ensconced in key positions at the Bohemian royal court for years to come. Thus, despite the evidence for solidarity between Dietrich and Adela, this brother-sister pair failed to develop a politically efficacious sibling bond in the period of the civil war. Moreover, like their cousins Count Dietrich of Groitzsch and Margrave Conrad of Lower Lusatia, Adela and Margrave Dietrich of Meissen were the last surviving members of their generation and did not belong to a larger sibling group. As a result, as in most other lineages, sibling relationships did not form a strong foundation for the lordship and politics of the Wettins during the first decade of the thirteenth century.

Besides the Welf brothers, therefore, only one other sibling group emerges from the extant sources as an influential force in imperial politics during the period of the civil war. This sibling group, the most prominent generation of the Andechs lineage, became notorious in the early 1200s for its links to the assassination of King Philip of Swabia. Philip was killed on June 21, 1208, only hours after the Andechs lord Duke Otto I of Merania had married the king's niece. Two of Otto's brothers, Bishop Ekbert of Bamberg and Margrave Henry of Istria, were implicated in the murder and fled the German kingdom. This is unquestionably the most famous incident in the history of this generation of the Andechs lineage. However, it is only one small piece to the story of this sibling group's place in imperial politics during the thirteenth century. Four brothers and four sisters belonged to this generation, and many of these siblings played influential roles on the European political stage between the late 1190s and the early 1250s.

---

129. Ibid., 2:81–85, no. 88.
130. Ibid., 2:89–91, no. 94.

For their day, these Andechs brothers and sisters were anomalous. None of the other nine lineages had so many members playing active roles in politics in this period. Indeed, this generation resembles the sibling groups of the early decades of Frederick Barbarossa's reign more than it does contemporary sibling groups in other lineages. These Andechs brothers and sisters differ from the generation of the 1160s and 1170s in one important respect, however. Thanks to the greater volume of surviving sources from the early thirteenth century, their relationships can be analyzed in much greater detail. For this reason, as we will see in the next chapter, these Andechs brothers and sisters are an ideal case study for examining the political efficacy of sibling relationships within the German upper aristocracy of the later Staufen period.

In the decades following Henry the Lion's loss of his duchies, the German upper aristocracy underwent a dramatic transformation. Within the nine lineages under investigation here, a generation dominated by large fraternal groups gave way to a generation made up of significantly fewer brothers. The abundance of children and lordships that had typified the opening years of the Staufen period was gone. Instead, shrinking families and shrinking patrimonies combined to alter sibling dynamics in a variety of ways. While fraternal relationships remained a prominent feature of upper aristocratic society throughout the late twelfth and early thirteenth centuries, there is more evidence for conflict than in earlier years—and fewer cases of collaborative bonds shaping the development of regional lordships and imperial politics. Only the Staufens and Welfs, the two smallest lineages during Emperor Frederick I Barbarossa's reign, saw numerous brothers come of age during the 1180s and early 1190s. Even within these fraternal groups, cooperative bonds were neither as prevalent nor as consistently efficacious as such bonds had been in other lineages in the previous generation. In less than half a century, the emergence of new sibling groups and new intragenerational relationships had combined to alter the character of both the German upper aristocracy and imperial politics. These changes provide the backdrop for the rise to prominence of the eight Andechs siblings who came of age in the 1190s—and for their involvement in the dramatic events of 1208.

CHAPTER 6

From Bamberg to Budapest

*Four Brothers and Four Sisters in the Early
Thirteenth Century*

The largest and most dynamic sibling group operating within the German upper aristocracy during the period of the civil war included eight brothers and sisters from the Andechs lineage. Because of the unusually rich source material that survives for this generation, these Andechs siblings offer an excellent opportunity for exploring the interactions and relationships among noble brothers and sisters. This generation's multifaceted role in imperial politics—and European politics more generally—also enables detailed analysis of the political aspects of the sibling bond. For this sibling group, King Philip of Swabia's assassination on June 21, 1208, was the darkest day in its history, and this event has cast a long shadow across the whole lineage's history. In contrast, the brightest day may have been March 26, 1267, when Duchess Hedwig of Silesia—one of these eight Andechs siblings—was canonized. Saint Hedwig lent an aura of sanctity to the whole of her lineage, even to her brothers who had been implicated in Philip's death. Somewhere between the two extremes of the violence of 1208 and the canonization of 1267, these four brothers and four sisters spent their lives interacting in ways that demonstrate the many complexities of medieval sibling relationships.

The Schlackenwerther Codex, which was commissioned in 1353 by one of Saint Hedwig's descendants in the Polish aristocracy, provides some of the best evidence for the positive depiction of this generation of the

FIGURE 4. Duke Berthold III of Merania and his wife, Agnes (center), with their eight children and their granddaughter Saint Elizabeth. J. Paul Getty Museum, Los Angeles, Ms. Ludwig XI 7, fol. 10v. Detail: *The Family of Berthold VI* [III]. Court workshop of Duke Ludwig I of Liegnitz and Brieg, 1353. Tempera colors, colored washes, and ink on parchment. Leaf: 34.1 x 24.8 cm. Courtesy of J. Paul Getty Museum.

Andechs lineage. The manuscript includes two accounts of Hedwig's life and miracles, a copy of the papal bull for her canonization, a prayer for the saint, and other texts. It contains numerous illuminations as well, including an image depicting Hedwig with ten of her Andechs relatives (figure 4).[1] At the center of the picture sit her parents, Duke Berthold III of Merania and his wife, Agnes. Seated to their left are their four sons, Hedwig's brothers, who were all prominent secular and ecclesiastical lords in the empire: Patriarch Berthold of Aquileia, Bishop Ekbert of Bamberg, Duke Otto I of Merania, and Margrave Henry of Istria. To the right of Berthold III and Agnes are three of their daughters. Hedwig is closest to her parents, followed by her sister Agnes, who married a king of France, and Queen Gertrude of Hungary. At the end of the row is Hedwig's niece, Saint Elizabeth of Thuringia. Beneath all these figures, at the bottom of the picture, is Hedwig's youngest sister, Mechthild, who was the abbess of a German convent.

---

1. *Der Hedwigs-Codex von 1353.* In older scholarship, Hedwig's father is frequently identified as Berthold VI rather than Berthold III. See Lyon, "Cooperation, Compromise and Conflict Avoidance," 351–372, for the misconceptions inherent in this older numbering system for the Andechs lineage.

There are various details in this illumination that suggest a loving family scene. Saint Hedwig's parents are holding hands in the center of the image. To their right, Saint Elizabeth of Thuringia is extending her hand to her own mother, Queen Gertrude of Hungary. And on the opposite side of the image, Hedwig's brother Duke Otto is clasping the arm of another of her brothers, Bishop Ekbert. Despite these features, this picture cannot be labeled a family portrait in the modern sense, because it does not depict Hedwig and her birth family at an actual moment in time. Hedwig's parents and her sister Agnes had all died before Elizabeth was born, making this impressive family gathering a historical impossibility.

The image instead constitutes a pictorial representation of a family tree. The illuminator has ignored the issue of chronology in order to show in a single illustration several prominent, but noncontemporary, members of different generations of the Andechs lineage.[2] Here, hand-holding and arm-clasping are creative ways to draw the lines between relatives on a genea-logical chart and to embed Saint Hedwig within a positive depiction of her birth family. However, they reveal nothing about the interactions among her brothers and sisters. While this image of close family bonds is therefore deceptive, its idealized vision of noble family life nonetheless merits further attention. All eight of these siblings held eminent positions in medieval Europe's elite society, whether inside or outside the German kingdom. Analyz-ing the sources for their contacts with one another therefore provides an especially vivid picture of the sibling bond's value for the German upper aristocracy—even beyond the borders of the empire.

In particular, the evidence for these Andechs brothers and sisters makes it possible to address in detail three issues that I have yet to examine at length. First, the roles played by sisters in the political life of their sibling groups. Second, the changing dynamics of sibling relationships over time—especially in the wake of political crises like the assassination of 1208, the acquisition of new lordships by the siblings, and the deaths of family members. Third, the place of the sibling group within extended kinship networks, and the fundamental differences be-tween the sibling bond and the bonds connecting more distant relatives.

The Eight Siblings as Children, ca. 1175–1195

Duke Berthold III of Merania, who is positioned at the center of the Schlackenwerther Codex illumination, belonged to the generation of the late

---

2. Hucker, "Familienbild der Meranier"; more generally, Bourdieu, *Logic of Practice*, 84.

twelfth-century aristocracy that—with the exception of the Staufens and Welfs—included few large fraternal groups. He had only one brother, a half brother, significantly younger, who joined the cathedral chapter at Bamberg at a young age.[3] Berthold also had four sisters and half sisters, but there is very little evidence connecting him to any of them.[4] When he first began to appear in sources during the 1160s and early 1170s, his father, Count Berthold II of Andechs, was already in possession of several comital lordships scattered across Franconia, Bavaria, Tyrol, and Carniola (figure 5).[5] The elder Berthold was also a frequent visitor to the court of Emperor Frederick I Barbarossa, where his success at cultivating *Königsnähe* played a crucial role in his lineage's rapid rise into the uppermost circles of the aristocracy.[6] In the year 1173,

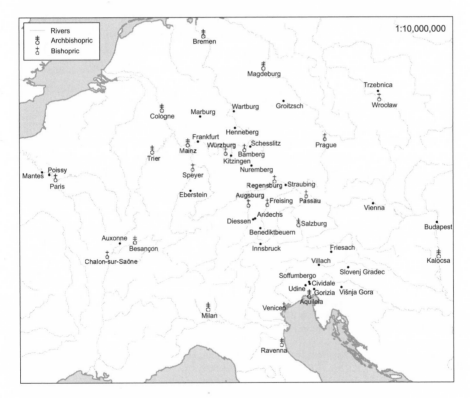

FIGURE 5.   Places of significance for the Andechs lineage, ca. 1195–1250.

3. Van Eickels, "Die Andechs-Meranier," 145.

4. For more on this point, see chapter 2.

5. *Die Traditionen des Klosters Asbach*, 42–43, no. 55; UB Enns, 1:673, no. 157, 1:739–740, no. 403.

6. The best published account of the family's rise is Schütz, "Das Geschlecht der Andechs-Meranier," 37–111.

the emperor enfeoffed him with the march of Istria on the Adriatic coast.[7] Four years later, Berthold II's younger brother, Otto, was elected bishop of Bamberg. And in 1180, Berthold III benefited from the lineage's close ties to the imperial court when he received from Barbarossa the titular duchy of Merania to the south of the Istrian peninsula.[8] Berthold II's *Königsnähe* also seems to have played a role in his choice of wives for the young Berthold III, since the imperial court is where the senior Berthold had contact with Count Dedo of Groitzsch from the Wettin lineage, who agreed to marry his daughter, Agnes, to Berthold III at some point in the early 1170s.[9]

During the same period that the Andechs lineage was accumulating prestigious lordships, this new couple began to enjoy a very different kind of familial success. Most if not all of their four sons and four daughters were born by 1185.[10] Whether accident or a more conscious form of family planning lay behind this abundance of children is impossible to determine. Regardless, the survival of eight children to adulthood makes the Andechs lineage somewhat anomalous, since in other lineages, the sibling groups that came to power in the early 1200s tended to be much smaller. If husband, wife, and children were ever together as one grand family as the image in the Schlackenwerther Codex depicts, such a gathering must have occurred during the earliest years of the new generation, not after the four brothers and four sisters had reached adulthood and acquired their own titles. However, only six of these eight siblings are named in sources written prior to their father's death in 1204, meaning there is no piece of evidence that directly connects all the members of this nuclear family during their lifetimes.[11] Further undermining the codex's representation of family unity is a series of events that unfolded in the mid-1190s. Duchess Agnes of Merania died in 1195, and

---

7. For the background to this event, see Štih, "Krain in der Zeit der Grafen von Andechs," 21.

8. For more on Bishop Otto and Berthold III becoming duke, see chapter 4. For the obscure duchy of Merania, see Herrmann, "Die Grafen von Andechs," 5–16; Aigner, "Das Herzogtum Meranien."

9. *Genealogia Wettinensis*, 229–230. For Dedo, see chapter 3; for his presence at the imperial court with Berthold II, MGH DD F I, 2:387–388, no. 475.

10. I will refer here to eight Andechs siblings, though it is certainly possible that there were additional members of this generation who died young. Borgolte ("Stiftergedenken in Kloster Dießen," 258) identifies a "*Chonradus monachus filius ducis*" in the Diessen necrologies as a possible son of Berthold III. There are also scholars who argue that the daughter whom Berthold III betrothed to a member of the Serbian elite during the Third Crusade was a fifth daughter, but it is more likely that this was simply an early marriage proposal for one of the other four. See *Historia de expeditione Friderici Imperatoris*, 31.

11. The lack of sources also makes it impossible to draw any clear conclusions about the early childhoods of these siblings. Contemporary texts do not indicate where they were educated or how much time they spent together as young children.

around the same time, Duke Berthold III arranged marriages for three of their daughters, sending all of them to royal or ducal courts outside the German kingdom to wed. Some of the richest surviving sources for these three women date from the earliest years of their marriages, before their father's death in 1204. As a result, the years around 1200 provide valuable evidence for examining when, why, and how these sisters had the opportunity to develop relationships with their siblings.

The Marriages of Three Sisters, ca. 1195–1204

The sisters Hedwig, Agnes, and Gertrude each maintained very different kinds of connections to their siblings after their marriages. Hedwig, during her half-century career as duchess of Silesia, had direct contact with only one other member of her generation according to the surviving sources—and only on one or two occasions. In 1202–1203, her husband, Duke Henry I of Silesia, drew up a charter detailing his endowment of the newly founded Cistercian convent at Trzebnica. The text reports that Hedwig's brother Ekbert, who was then bishop-elect of Bamberg, and her uncle Poppo, a member of the Bamberg cathedral chapter, were both present near Wrocław for this event.[12] Although Hedwig is not named in the document, her role as a prominent patroness of Trzebnica suggests she would have come into contact with Ekbert and Poppo on this occasion. In addition, a later hagiographic source for Hedwig, written around the year 1300, states that the Cistercian nuns who first populated Trzebnica all came from the convent of Saint Theodore in Bamberg.[13] According to the same text, the first abbess of Trzebnica had been Hedwig's teacher as a child in the Franconian convent of Kitzingen to the west of Bamberg.[14] Ekbert and Poppo may therefore have journeyed to Silesia in the company of the new nuns and abbess in order to assist in the establishment of the convent—and to reinforce the bonds connecting Trzebnica and Hedwig to the duchess's natal family.

This same hagiographic work also provides the only surviving evidence for what may have been a second meeting between Hedwig and Ekbert. In the section praising Hedwig for her austerity, the anonymous author writes,

---

12. *Schlesisches Urkundenbuch*, 1, 54–58, no. 83. Since Ekbert was not elected bishop until March of 1203, the charter could not have been drawn up at the time of the original donation. See also Schütz, "Das Geschlecht der Andechs-Meranier," 150; Appelt, "Vorarbeiten zum Schlesischen Urkundenbuch," 47–50.

13. *Vita S. Hedwige*, 5.54, p. 237. This is an edition of the *Legenda maior* included in the Schlackenwerther Codex.

14. Ibid.

"Her brother the lord Ekbert, bishop of Bamberg, whom she revered and loved—as it was fitting to love a brother (*ut decuit diligere fratrem*)—once became angry with her and admonished her" because of how frequently she fasted.[15] Although this type of story is easy to dismiss as a hagiographic topos, the explicit reference to Ekbert is noteworthy. As will be discussed further below, the bishop of Bamberg maintained more contact with his brothers and sisters than any other member of this generation of the Andechs lineage. As a result, the reference to Ekbert in this passage conforms to a much broader pattern of his sibling relationships. Regardless, after 1203, no source from Duchess Hedwig of Silesia's own lifetime suggests direct contacts between her and any of her siblings.

The sister seated next to Hedwig in the Schlackenwerther Codex illumination provides an even more striking example of someone who became isolated from her siblings following her marriage. Agnes wed King Philip II Augustus of France, whose marital misadventures are well-known.[16] In 1193, he separated from Ingeborg of Denmark the day after their wedding and immediately sought an annulment. A council comprising mainly the king's allies soon declared the marriage invalid, but Ingeborg appealed to the pope. Three years later, in 1196, while the question of the marriage's validity remained unresolved, Philip took as his new wife Duke Berthold III's daughter Agnes.[17] However, they never had their marriage officially recognized by the church. Innocent III, who became pope in 1198, insisted that Philip's separation from Ingeborg had violated canon law. The situation was still unsettled when Agnes died in 1201 soon after giving birth to her second child.

No source indicates that Agnes saw any member of her birth family after she married Philip in 1196. She spent the ensuing five years in France, never returning to the German kingdom. Her death came while she was residing at Poissy, just outside Paris, and she was buried near Mantes—far from the Andechs lineage's centers of lordship. There was seemingly no opportunity for her to interact with any of her siblings during her brief marriage. What is even more noteworthy, however, is that none of her brothers, sisters, or other blood relatives—including her father, who was still alive in 1201—made any effort to remember her in death. No extant charter drawn up by any member

---

15. Ibid., 3.22, p. 230. See also Gottschalk, *St. Hedwig*, 181.

16. Baldwin, *Government of Philip Augustus*, 82–87; Baldwin, "La vie sexuelle de Philippe Auguste"; Duby, *Knight, Lady and Priest*, 205–206.

17. Why Philip arranged this particular marriage is unclear, though the anonymous author of the *Gesta Innocentii III* describes Agnes as a woman of great beauty: *Deeds of Pope Innocent III*, 66. Philip almost certainly had not met Agnes prior to their betrothal, but perhaps her reputation preceded her.

of her birth family refers to Agnes in or after 1201.[18] Moreover, another key source for Andechs memorial strategies, a codex produced at the Augustinian house of canons at Diessen in Bavaria, is similarly silent. Sometime between the years 1204 and 1210—so within a decade of Agnes's death—one of the community's canons compiled a manuscript that included among other texts a pair of necrologies as well as copies of the most important property donations to the religious house.[19] Members of Agnes's birth family appear throughout this manuscript because the lineage's patronage had been central to the community's success. Indeed, every member of the Andechses known to have died between approximately 1100 and 1204 is included in the Diessen necrologies—except for Agnes.[20] Her mother (d. 1195) is listed, as is her paternal great-uncle Bishop Otto II of Bamberg (d. 1196) and her father (d. 1204). But her name was not entered in either necrology by the canon who wrote the manuscript.

Agnes, the first member of her generation to die, was thus forgotten by her sibling group. None of her brothers and sisters made any effort to preserve her memory, either by having her name recorded in a necrology or by making a donation to a monastic community for the sake of her soul. To understand why, the broader context of her marriage to Philip must be considered. Because of the king's difficulties with the papacy, Agnes's precise status at the French court was uncertain throughout the five years of their union. She was never crowned queen. Many people considered her to be a mere concubine.[21] And during the final months of her life, she was exiled from the royal court as Philip sought to appease Pope Innocent III. Thus, one reason why Agnes was ignored by her birth family may be that her marriage never proved to be as prestigious as Berthold III may have initially hoped. Her union with Philip was generally recognized as uncanonical, and even members of Agnes's own family may have decided that she had become involved in a scandal that was best forgotten. Since her marriage was brief and she was still very young at the time of her death, it was easy for her to disappear from her sibling group.

Both Hedwig and Agnes can be contrasted with a third sister. At some point in the late 1190s, Gertrude married Andreas, the younger son of King

---

18. See below for other Andechs siblings' efforts to memorialize dead brothers and sisters.

19. Munich, Bayerische Staatsbibliothek, Clm 1018.

20. For the most recent edition of these necrological entries, see Borgolte, "Stiftergedenken in Kloster Dießen," 255–289. Agnes is also missing from another necrology that includes several of her Andechs relatives. See Suckale-Redlefsen, "Gebetbuch."

21. Conklin, "Ingeborg of Denmark," 42–43. Pope Innocent III eventually recognized Agnes's two children by Philip as legitimate, but there is no evidence that these children had close contacts with any members of the Andechs family.

Béla III of Hungary.[22] When Béla died in 1196, his eldest son, Emeric, succeeded him as king, but Andreas soon challenged his older sibling for the throne.[23] A set of monastic annals reports that Andreas fared poorly in this conflict and was even captured by his brother in the year 1203. Then, Andreas's "wife, the daughter of Duke Berthold of Merania, was stripped of all her possessions, and [Emeric] permitted her to return to her homeland (*suam patriam*)."[24] Gertrude thus had the chance after several years of marriage to return to the German kingdom and reestablish contacts with her relatives—an opportunity that most German noblewomen who married distant lords never had. Since her father, Duke Berthold III of Merania, died in mid-1204 while she was living in exile, she may have even witnessed the transfer of power within the Andechs lineage to her brothers. With Emeric's death later in the year 1204, Andreas was freed and "recalled his wife with great honor."[25] As we will soon see, Gertrude's brief and unexpected stay in the German kingdom seems to have laid the foundation for the relationships she maintained with several of her brothers after her return to Hungary to rejoin her husband.

The evidence for these three sisters highlights several key aspects of sororal relationships more generally within the German upper aristocracy. Marriages to kings and nobles whose territories lay beyond the borders of the German kingdom tended to isolate women from their sibling groups. Agnes, who married King Philip II Augustus of France, provides an extreme example from one end of the spectrum of possible relationships. There is very little contemporary evidence from Andechs circles for her *existence*—let alone her interactions with her siblings. Hedwig, with her short-lived ties to a single brother, seems to be more typical.[26] Meanwhile, Gertrude's union offers a perspective from the opposite end of the spectrum of sisters who married. Her return to the German kingdom to live in exile with her natal family, several years after her marriage had taken place, gave her the opportunity as an adult to establish close contacts with siblings she might otherwise have never seen. Thus, while the illuminator of the Schlackenwerther Codex sought to portray Hedwig and all her siblings together as one big family,

---

22. They probably married in or around the year 1197: Hucker, "Der Königsmord von 1208," 119–120.

23. Engel, *Realm of St. Stephen*, 88–89.

24. *Annales Admuntenses*, 590.

25. Ibid. Duke Berthold III of Merania died on August 12, 1204, and King Emeric of Hungary on November 30 of the same year. If the *Annales Admuntensis* are correct in dating Gertrude's exile from Hungary to 1203, she would have spent several months in the German kingdom.

26. See chapter 2.

these sisters' lives demonstrate how unlikely such a scenario actually was for the upper aristocracy of the Staufen period. The sibling bond simply did not play as central a role in most noblewomen's lives as it did in the lives of their brothers.

Succession and Fraternal Relationships, 1203–1208

During the late 1190s and early 1200s, just as these three sisters were leaving their natal family behind to marry, three of their brothers were beginning to play an increasingly prominent role in their father's affairs. Here too, however, the image presented in the Schlackenwerther Codex is deceptive. Seated closest to Duke Berthold III of Merania in the illumination is his son Berthold, who was presumably assigned this preeminent position because he obtained the most illustrious title of any of his brothers: patriarch of Aquileia. But Berthold did not become patriarch until 1218, almost fifteen years after Berthold III died. Moreover, he was the youngest of the duke's sons, and no source written prior to his father's death makes any mention of him. Berthold's early life and career are a mystery until 1206, when Pope Innocent III describes him in a letter as the cathedral provost of Bamberg.[27] The sons seated further to their father's left in the illumination were thus the key figures in the lineage in earlier years.

One of these, Ekbert, has already been mentioned in relation to his sister Hedwig. Sources from the late 1180s and early 1190s suggest that Ekbert may have initially been intended to succeed to one of his father's secular lordships, but by 1192 at the latest, he had been placed in the cathedral chapter at Bamberg.[28] There, his great-uncle Otto was bishop and his paternal uncle, Poppo, Berthold III's half brother, already a canon.[29] Ekbert's entrance into the chapter was therefore part of the lineage's ongoing efforts to dominate this diocese in Upper Franconia. By April of 1200, when he witnessed one of King Philip of Swabia's charters, Ekbert had risen to become cathedral provost.[30] However, in the witness list to this charter, he is not included with the other ecclesiastics. Instead, he is named immediately after his father among the lay magnates, suggesting that he remained closely linked to his lineage's

---

27. See below, and van Eickels, "Die Andechs-Meranier," 146.

28. Two early sources that suggest Ekbert was still in the secular sphere at the time they were written are Ertl, "Die Geschichte Innsbrucks," 70–72, no. 3, and *Die Traditionen des Klosters Schäftlarn*, 320–322, no. 321. Ekbert first appears as a cathedral canon in Bamberg, Staatsarchiv, Bamberger Urkunden no. 391.

29. For Otto, see chapter 4. For Poppo, see below.

30. Reg. Imp. 5, vol. 1:17, no. 43.

secular power in this period—despite his church career. Three years later, when he was elected bishop of Bamberg, he was not yet the canonical age of thirty required to hold episcopal office.[31] Nevertheless, Pope Innocent III agreed to consecrate him, possibly because the pope was hoping to gain Berthold III's support in the midst of the conflict between Philip of Swabia and Otto of Brunswick for the German throne.[32] Ekbert's rapid rise from canon to cathedral provost to bishop in only eleven years was thus the direct result of his father's efforts to obtain for his son this key episcopal office. Considering how difficult it was for most secular princes to arrange for a son or brother to acquire a specific bishopric, Berthold III's success is evidence for the Andechs lineage's influence within the diocese of Bamberg.[33] During the course of Ekbert's three and a half decades as bishop, he would regularly play a central role in promoting his siblings' political and territorial interests over those of his church.

Seated at the end of the row in the Schlackenwerther Codex image—and noticeably smaller than their two brothers—are Otto and Henry, who were Berthold III's eldest sons. They had been designated to succeed to their father's secular lordships since the mid-1190s, when they first began to appear in sources alongside the duke. However, Berthold III seems not to have assigned his heirs specific lordships during his lifetime. In the small number of texts from the 1190s and early 1200s in which Otto and Henry are named, each is identified only as *filius ducis* or *dominus*.[34] Because no extant source hints at any conflict between the brothers in the years after their father died, there is no reason to believe Berthold III had remained undecided on the succession during his lifetime. In contrast to many of his contemporaries, he simply did not put his plans into effect prior to his death—perhaps because he died, on August 12, 1204, at the relatively young age of fifty or so.[35]

The earliest surviving source to provide direct evidence for the division of the lineage's secular lordships between Otto and Henry is a charter from May 1205, when King Philip of Swabia was holding court in Nuremberg.[36] Included in this document's witness list, alongside their younger brother Bishop Ekbert of Bamberg, are *"Otto Dux Meranie"* and *"Heinricus Marchio Ystrie."* These are the titles the two eldest brothers would use throughout their lives.

---

31. Ussermann, *Episcopatus Bambergensis*, 139–140, no. 155.

32. Van Eickels, "Die Andechs-Meranier," 149; Schütz, "Die Andechs-Meranier in Franken," 30.

33. See chapter 3.

34. See, for example, *Die Urkunden des Klosters Raitenhaslach*, 42, no. 44; MHDC, 1:271–273, no. 369; MHDC, 4, pt. 1:1–3, no. 1524.

35. For Berthold III's career, see Schütz, "Die Andechs-Meranier in Franken," 27–30.

36. Reg. Imp. 5, vol. 1:33, no. 111; UB Enns, 2:498–500, no. 347.

Thanks to the much better survival rate of thirteenth-century wax seals than twelfth-century ones for the German upper aristocracy, we also know that these titles appear on their earliest seals. Significantly, the only distinguishing feature between Otto's and Henry's first seals are their different titles. Both are equestrian seals, with the rider facing the same direction, and each rider is holding a banner and a shield—a design identical to their father's seal.[37] Such equestrian seals were common among the *principes imperii* more generally, and Otto and Henry were thus both depicting themselves sigillographically as members of the uppermost ranks of the aristocracy.[38]

However, the duchy of Merania and the march of Istria were not rich lordships. Neither came with abundant rights and territories along the Adriatic coast. Their prestigious titles made Otto and Henry eminent princes, but they brought little in the way of lands and followers.[39] As a result, the focal points of Otto's and Henry's lordships were the rights and territories they inherited from their father in other parts of the kingdom. The Danube River seems to have served as the main dividing line between their holdings.[40] Otto received his father's comital lordship north of the Danube near Passau as well as everything in the diocese of Bamberg and Franconia more broadly. Henry obtained all the family lands in Bavaria south of the Danube, including the county of Andechs, and the lineage's rights and territories in Tyrol and Carniola. Because of the scattered nature of the Andechs patrimony, the only region where the two brothers inherited neighboring properties was in Lower Bavaria near the confluence of the Inn and Danube Rivers. Even there, the connection between the pair was short-lived. In 1207, Duke Otto I of Merania sold his comital rights in the area to the bishop of Passau.[41]

The significant distance that separated their centers of lordship helps explain why Otto and Henry had few close contacts with one another.[42] During the years immediately after their father died, Otto spent most of his time on his Franconian properties strengthening his lordship there.[43] Henry,

---

37. For fragments of Otto's first seal, see Bamberg, Staatsarchiv, Bamberger Urkunden nos. 445, 449, and 478. For Henry's seal, see Klagenfurt, Kärntner Landesarchiv, Allgemeine Urkundenreihe A 47 and C 1188. For a photograph of Duke Berthold III's seal, see Schütz, "Die Andechs-Meranier in Franken," 22.

38. See, generally, Schöntag, "Das Reitersiegel als Rechtssymbol"; Fenske, "Adel und Rittertum," 94–100. See also Bedos-Rezak, "Art of Chivalry," 18.

39. Schütz, "Die Andechs-Meranier in Franken," 22, 26.

40. Schütz "Das Geschlecht der Andechs-Meranier," 69; Holzfurtner, *Die Grafschaft der Andechser*, 306, 389; Oefele, *Geschichte der Grafen von Andechs*, 96–97.

41. MB, 29, pt. 1:539–541, no. 591. See also Holzfurtner, *Die Grafschaft der Andechser*, 285–287.

42. For a similar point, see Spieß, *Familie und Verwandtschaft*, 276.

43. See Bamberg, Staatsarchiv, Bamberger Urkunden nos. 445, 448, and 449.

meanwhile, sought to control his diverse holdings across the southeast of the empire by traveling extensively throughout Bavaria, Tyrol, and Carniola.[44] As previous chapters have shown, most princely lineages possessed collections of rights and properties that lay in close proximity to one another, meaning that brothers who succeeded to the lineage's lordships typically had overlapping territorial interests that strengthened fraternal relationships. For two brothers who were secular lords to have such disparate centers of power and influence was therefore rare in this period.[45] This does not mean, however, that the sibling bond was of limited significance within the Andechs lineage during these years. Though the Otto-Henry bond was not a strong one in this generation, other sibling relationships were important in both of these lords' lives.

Bishop Ekbert of Bamberg's connection to his older brother Otto quickly emerged as crucial for politics and lordship in Franconia. Within the diocese of Bamberg, the transfer of power from Duke Berthold III to Otto seems to have gone virtually unnoticed—though it should not have. A half century earlier, in 1149, Berthold III's father, Berthold II, had agreed to a treaty with Bishop Eberhard of Bamberg.[46] This agreement concerned several valuable rights and properties in Upper Franconia, including castles near Bamberg whose ownership was disputed by the Andechs lineage and the cathedral church.[47] According to the treaty, the bishop agreed to enfeoff Berthold II and his eldest son and heir (Berthold III) with many of these rights and properties, but only for their lifetimes. After their deaths, everything was to revert fully to the bishopric. As a result, the Andechs lineage's position within Upper Franconia should have been severely undermined when Duke Berthold III of Merania died. But Ekbert's rapid ascent to the episcopal office in Bamberg is a clear sign that Berthold III was anxious that the terms of the treaty not be implemented. Ekbert showed his loyalty to his brother and his lineage after his father's death by doing nothing to enforce the church of Bamberg's claims to the disputed properties. His brother Otto remained in control of these lands and rights throughout his career. The sibling bond between Ekbert and Otto thus became the linchpin for the lineage's power and influence inside Upper Franconia.[48]

---

44. See MHDC, 4, pt. 1:24, no. 1573 and 31–33, nos. 1596–1598; UB Enns, 1:695–696, no. 226; *Die Traditionen des Klosters Weihenstephan*, 288–289, no. 350.

45. For some comparable cases, see chapter 5.

46. Bamberg, Staatsarchiv, Bamberger Urkunden no. 247.

47. For a detailed account of this dispute, see Schütz, "Die Andechs-Meranier in Franken," 14–19.

48. Frenken, "Hausmachtpolitik und Bischofsstuhl," 737–738.

A grand occasion eventually brought the three oldest Andechs brothers together again—three years after their 1205 meeting at the royal court in Nuremberg. On June 21, 1208, Otto married Beatrice, the heiress to the count-palatine of Burgundy and the niece of King Philip of Swabia. The wedding took place in the king's presence in the cathedral at Bamberg, with Bishop Ekbert presiding over the ceremony and Henry attending. This was an impressive moment for the three Andechs siblings, one that reinforced their lineage's prominent standing within the upper aristocracy. But the moment was short-lived. In the hours after the wedding, while King Philip of Swabia was resting in the episcopal palace in Bamberg, he was assassinated by the Wittelsbach count-palatine of Bavaria—possibly with Bishop Ekbert's and Margrave Henry's support. Precisely how this murderous plot unfolded is difficult to determine, because contemporary and near-contemporary sources offer very different versions of events. The chronicler Burchard of Ursberg, writing two decades after the murder, directly links both the bishop and the margrave to the assassination, but other authors are not as explicit in connecting the brothers with the plot.[49] Subsequent events nonetheless suggest that Ekbert and Henry were implicated in the whole affair. Even if not active coconspirators, they had failed to keep the king safe while he was under their protection.[50]

At a large gathering of German magnates in Frankfurt in November of the same year, Philip's former rival for the throne, Otto of Brunswick, formally stripped Henry of his march of Istria and his other imperial fiefs.[51] A short time later, Henry also lost his episcopal fiefs in Tyrol and saw his Bavarian lands and rights seized by the duke of Bavaria.[52] Ekbert, because he was a prelate as well as a *princeps imperii*, could not be judged as harshly at the royal court. He appealed to Pope Innocent III, who designated a pair of papal legates to investigate the question of Ekbert's involvement in Philip's assassination.[53] In the ensuing years, Ekbert was never removed from his episcopal office, but he was nevertheless unable to exercise effectively any of his duties as bishop of Bamberg.[54] Adding to the difficulties for the Andechs brothers, in early March 1209, one of Philip of Swabia's ministerials hunted down and

49. Burchard of Ursberg, *Die Chronik*, 252. Compare *Regestum Innocentii III papae*, 347–349, no. 152; Otto of St. Blasien, *Chronica*, 148–150; Arnold of Lübeck, *Chronica Slavorum*, 7.12, 283; Herman of Niederalteich, *Annales*, 385–386.

50. For a similar point, see van Eickels, "Die Andechs-Meranier," 150. Compare Hucker, "Der Königsmord von 1208," 117–120.

51. Reg. Imp. 5, vol. 1:78–80, nos. 240d, 243.

52. Schütz, "Das Geschlecht der Andechs-Meranier," 76–77.

53. Schütz, "Die Andechs-Meranier in Franken," 34–36.

54. Frenken, "Hausmachtpolitik und Bischofsstuhl," 767.

killed the count-palatine of Bavaria, who had struck the fatal blow against the king.[55] Henry fled the German kingdom within three weeks to protect his own life.[56] In or around the same time, Bishop Ekbert took flight as well.

Thus, an Andechs sibling group that had looked to be on the ascent within the imperial aristocracy only a few months earlier was suddenly in disarray. During the years of the civil war, Otto, Henry, and Ekbert were—alongside the Welf brothers—the only fraternal group consisting of three lords that was active in the nine lineages under investigation here. They were also the largest sibling group to cultivate *Königsnähe* at the court of Philip of Swabia during the decade he ruled as king. Duke Otto I of Merania's prestigious marriage to Philip's niece, the heiress to the county-palatine of Burgundy, is clear evidence for the influence that the Andechs brothers were able to exert at the Staufen court in the years immediately after their father's death. Following Philip's murder, however, the lords within this generation of the Andechs lineage were confronted with a new political reality. In response, they relied on a new set of sibling relationships to preserve their positions within the upper aristocracy.

The Andechs Siblings at the Hungarian Royal Court, 1206–1218

To understand the enduring significance of the sibling bond inside the Andechs lineage in the wake of King Philip's assassination, it is necessary to look beyond the borders of the German kingdom. Bishop Ekbert of Bamberg and Margrave Henry of Istria lost the ability to exercise their lordship in the months after June 1208, but that does not mean they were rendered politically impotent. After fleeing the empire, they worked to rebuild their standing inside the imperial elite while living in exile. To accomplish this, they sought safety and protection in a place where a different pair of Andechs siblings had risen to prominence in the preceding years: Hungary. There, their sister Queen Gertrude had established herself as an influential figure since returning from her own exile in the German kingdom in late 1204. Indeed, because of Gertrude, Ekbert had already visited the Hungarian royal court on at least one occasion. On November 29, 1206, Pope Innocent III wrote to the bishop and granted him permission to delay a planned visit to Rome. According to the letter, Ekbert had received messengers from the Hungarian court announcing that his sister Gertrude had given birth to a son. Moreover,

---

55. Otto of St. Blasien, *Chronica*, 150–152; Spindler, "Grundlegung und Aufbau," 29.

56. The timing of his flight is suggested by Joseph Freiherr von Hormayr, *Kritisch-diplomatische Beyträge*, 2:271–272, no. 117.

the messengers "asked that you [Ekbert] postpone everything else you are doing and hasten to those regions. The boy must be baptized, but before this happens, your presence is expected."[57]

Gertrude's influence at the Hungarian court also manifested itself in another way during this period. The youngest brother in her generation of the Andechs lineage, Berthold, was elected archbishop of Kalocsa in Hungary in 1205–1206. Contemporary sources leave little doubt that his sudden promotion from cathedral provost of Bamberg to archbishop was linked to his familial connections rather than his qualifications for the office. On June 7, 1206, Pope Innocent III wrote to King Andreas to express his doubts about Berthold's appropriateness for the position.[58] The pope informed the king that he had designated two German churchmen to investigate Berthold's age and erudition. Ten months later, in April 1207, Innocent III wrote to Andreas again, after he had received the findings of the German ecclesiastics. As he explains in this letter, "if it had been discovered that [Berthold's] learning was not outstanding but was at least sufficient, and that he was not of the canonical age but was at least in the neighborhood of that age, . . . we would have granted a dispensation, so great did we desire to satisfy your will."[59] But the pope then makes it clear that Berthold was much too young and much too uneducated for him to even consider bending the rules. The archbishop-elect would not be consecrated until 1211—after he had received a basic education and had turned thirty years of age as required by canon law. Nevertheless, from 1207 onward, Berthold frequently appeared in King Andreas's charters as archbishop-elect.[60] Despite the pope's refusal to consecrate him, he remained an important figure at the Hungarian royal court because of his sister Gertrude's position as queen.

Thus, when Ekbert and Henry fled to Hungary after King Philip's assassination, they joined a pair of well-entrenched siblings there and created a very different intragenerational grouping from the one that had been operating previously in the German kingdom. The sister and three brothers based at the Hungarian court after 1208 demonstrate just how quickly intragenerational relationships could develop and change as necessary. The

---

57. *Die Register Innocenz' III.*, 9:338–339, no. 185. For the possibility of additional contacts between Ekbert and the Hungarian court in these years, see Hautum, "Ekbert von Meran," 112.

58. *Die Register Innocenz' III.*, 9:141–143, no. 74.

59. *Patrologia latina*, vol. 215, cols. 1132–1134, no. 39. For this episode, see also Sweeney, "Innocent III," 32–33.

60. *Codex diplomaticus Hungariae*, 3, pt. 1:44, 47, 66, 69. At some point in this period, he briefly traveled to Vicenza in order to receive the necessary education he had been lacking. See *Patrologia latina*, vol. 215, cols. 1534–1535, no. 220.

political significance of this new sibling group is most evident in one of King Andreas II of Hungary's 1209 charters. As this document explains,

> The provost Adolf has frequently exposed his person and possessions to danger and has exerted himself faithfully in our service and in the service of our dearest wife, the queen, [on embassies] to the lord pope as well as to the emperors and various princes. [Therefore], at the insistence of the queen and of her venerable brothers, namely Archbishop Berthold of Kalocsa and the bishop of Bamberg and the margrave, whom [Adolf] has ceaselessly and faithfully served above and beyond all their other followers—and for whom he has more frequently exposed his person to the danger of death—we grant to Adolf and his sister [the following property].[61]

Although this charter is frustratingly vague about Adolf's service to the four Andechs siblings, it nevertheless suggests that the Hungarian court had emerged as the focal point of efforts to restore Henry and Ekbert to their positions in the German kingdom. A trusted figure in the service of the king and queen of Hungary was playing a key role in protecting the lineage's interests, and all these siblings were anxious to reward him for his actions. Thus, hundreds of miles away from Bamberg and other traditional centers of Andechs lordship, three brothers and a sister—including a pair accused of regicide—had forged a new set of sibling relationships that would have far-reaching significance in the coming years.

Absent from King Andreas's charter is any reference to the eldest of the four brothers, Duke Otto I of Merania. Unlike his younger siblings Ekbert and Henry, he had not been implicated in the plot to assassinate Philip of Swabia.[62] He had therefore remained in the empire, and beginning in early 1209, he attached himself closely to the court of the Welf king Otto.[63] Although the duke had not supported Otto of Brunswick in earlier years of the conflict over the royal throne, his reasons for seeking *Königsnähe* during this period are clear. With a new ruler on the throne and his brothers living in exile, his own position in the German kingdom depended on his ability to forge close ties at court. Whether he also sought to convince Otto of Brunswick to restore

---

61. The earliest surviving copy of this charter is a transsumt preserved in a 1246 charter of Andreas and Gertrude's son King Béla IV: Budapest, Magyar Országos Levéltár, DF 68752. The edition printed in *Codex diplomaticus Hungariae*, 3, pt. 1:76–78, is based on an even later transsumt and has numerous errors.

62. Schütz, "Das Geschlecht der Andechs-Meranier," 78–79.

63. *Reg. Imp.* 5, vol. 1:82, no. 252; 1:90–91, no. 287a; 1:93, nos. 294–296; 1:95, no. 300; 1:98, no. 306; 1:141, nos. 487–488.

his brothers Henry and Ekbert to their former positions is not as clear. By the early 1210s, Henry had returned to the empire but would confine himself to his alodial lands in the region of Carniola. The margrave would never again be a significant figure in the political life of the German kingdom.[64] Ekbert, meanwhile, did not reestablish his control over the diocese of Bamberg until the mid-1210s, after he and Duke Otto I of Merania had begun to support the new Staufen claimant to the throne, Frederick II.[65] Thus, for several years after 1208, Otto was the only Andechs brother exercising lordship inside the empire.

During the early 1210s, the Hungarian court was the one place where an Andechs sibling group continued to affect political developments directly. Queen Gertrude's ongoing influence there is evident in a chronicle report for the year 1210: "Because the king of the Hungarians was unable to capture a certain stronghold with his own troops, he employed—by the advice of his wife (*consilio uxoris sue*), who was German by birth—an army consisting of Germans who were staying in his land."[66] Supporting the queen at court throughout this period was her brother Berthold. In 1209, he had appeared for the first time with the title of ban (*bannus*) of Croatia. This title, which he received from the king, designated him as a governor or vice-regent and gave him judicial and military authority in the region.[67] In one of his own charters from the year 1211, he seems to exhibit even grander notions of his place in the Hungarian kingdom; the inscription reads, "Berthold by the grace of God archbishop-elect of Kalocsa [and] duke of Dalmatia and Croatia."[68] His prominent position alongside his sister is evident again in the year 1213, when he was a leading figure at Gertrude's court while Andreas was conducting a military campaign on the frontiers of the kingdom. The two siblings together managed the affairs of the realm in the king's absence.[69]

The close connection between Gertrude and Berthold was abruptly severed later in the year 1213 when the queen was assassinated by a group of conspirators from the Hungarian aristocracy. No contemporary source

---

64. On August 24, 1211, Henry drew up a charter in the town of Slovenj Gradec in modern-day Slovenia: MHDC, 1:329, no. 430. Despite the fact that he had been stripped of all his imperial fiefs, he used his old seal on this charter: Klagenfurt, Kärntner Landesarchiv, Allgemeine Urkundenreihe C 1188.

65. Despite his delayed return to Bamberg, Ekbert played a much more active role in imperial politics during the early 1210s than his brother Henry did. See Schütz, "Die Andechs-Meranier in Franken," 36–37, and van Eickels, "Die Andechs-Meranier," 150.

66. *Chronica regia Coloniensis*, 186.

67. Engel, *Realm of St. Stephen*, 92.

68. Budapest, Magyar Országos Levéltár, DF 206838. For other titles he held during his time in Hungary, see Schütz, "Das Geschlecht der Andechs-Meranier," 84.

69. Budapest, Magyar Országos Levéltár, DF 206842, DF 206846.

offers an explicit motive for her killing, but her growing influence at court and the influx of Germans she was welcoming into the kingdom were presumably factors.[70] Later authors would provide more dramatic explanations for her death. An especially vivid telling of the story can be found among the late medieval sources from the house of canons at Diessen in Bavaria:

> The wedding of [Gertrude's] daughter Saint Elizabeth and Landgrave Ludwig [IV] of Thuringia was celebrated in Hungary at the city of Buda. Patriarch Berthold of Aquileia, the brother of the queen, was present for this marriage and saw there a Hungarian countess of great beauty, whom he beset and overcame, though she was unwilling. This countess of course complained to her husband about the injury inflicted upon her, but the patriarch derided her claims against him and retired to his own lands. A short time later, the aforesaid count had a perverse suspicion that the queen had been a coconspirator in the wickedness which had befallen his wife and that she had given her consent to it. And so, at a moment suitable to the count, he paid for and gathered certain nefarious men, who during the night entered the queen's chamber and hanged her, choking her to death.[71]

There are numerous reasons to be suspicious of this version of events. Since Gertrude's daughter Elizabeth was born in 1207, she could not possibly have celebrated her wedding before her mother's death in 1213.[72] Moreover, the late medieval sources disagree about which of Gertrude's brothers was involved in this affair; some texts indicate the culprit was not Berthold but Bishop Ekbert of Bamberg.[73] Despite these inconsistencies, this legend is evidence for the enduring belief that the Andechs siblings exerted a great deal of influence at the Hungarian court in the early thirteenth century. As later writers embellished the story of Gertrude's assassination, the strong link between the queen and her brothers remained central to the event—and even became the reason why she was killed.

Notably, Ekbert was the sibling who most actively sought to memorialize Gertrude after her death. In 1216, he drew up a charter in which he finalized a grant that she had previously made to the convent of Saint Theodore in Bamberg for the preservation of her memory.[74] The next year, the bishop

70. Engel, *Realm of St. Stephen*, 91; Bak, "Queens as Scapegoats," 226–228.

71. *De fundatoribus monasterii Diessenses*, 331.

72. For more on Elizabeth, see below.

73. See, for example, John of Viktring, *Liber certarum historiarum*, 1:128, and Henry of Mügeln, *Chronicon*, 205–206.

74. Bamberg, Staatsarchiv, Bamberger Urkunden no. 475.

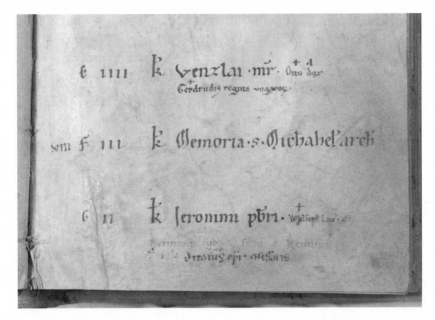

FIGURE 6.   The entry for Queen Gertrude of Hungary (*Gerdrudis regina ungarorum*) in the Bamberg cathedral necrology. Staatsbibliothek Bamberg, Msc. Lit. 161, fol. 20r. Photo Gerald Raab. Courtesy of Staatsbibliothek Bamberg.

made a gift of his own to the monastery of Saint Michaelsberg in Bamberg and requested that masses be said for himself, his father, Duke Berthold III, and his sister Gertrude.[75] Since his father had been dead for more than a decade, Gertrude's murder must have been the impetus behind this donation. One additional piece of evidence lends further credence to the argument that Ekbert was strongly affected by his sister's death. Gertrude's name is recorded in a contemporary hand in the Bamberg cathedral's necrology (figure 6).[76] The only other members of the Andechs lineage included in this necrology are the ones who were bishops of Bamberg, members of the cathedral chapter, or secular lords in Franconia. Gertrude's inclusion therefore does not fit the general pattern, an indication that her name was entered in the necrology for reasons that were unrelated to the church's traditional memorial strategies. Thus, the charter evidence and this necrological entry both suggest that Ekbert had an especially strong reaction to the death of the sister who had

75. Bamberg, Staatsarchiv, Bamberger Urkunden no. 481. There is no mention of his deceased sister Agnes in this second charter.

76. Bamberg, Staatsbibliothek, Msc. Lit. 161, fol. 20r.

sheltered him following the assassination of King Philip of Swabia.[77] Here, more than anywhere else in the sources for the Andechs lineage, it may be possible to catch a glimpse of an emotional attachment between siblings.

The Brothers and the Southeast of the Empire, 1218–1228

Ekbert's 1217 charter in memory of his sister Gertrude was witnessed by his brothers Duke Otto I of Merania and Margrave Henry of Istria. No other source indicates these two siblings had been together in the decade since the fateful day of Otto's wedding. The wide distances separating their lands and rights had continued to keep them apart. Although the bishop's charter does not include an exact date or a location, it seems likely that Otto and Henry acted as witnesses on the eve of the departure of King Andreas II of Hungary and a large army for the start of the Fifth Crusade.[78] One of the most important chroniclers for this expedition, Oliver of Paderborn, reports that both the duke of Merania and the bishop of Bamberg accompanied the king of Hungary, and Henry's presence at Ekbert's donation suggests that he may have as well.[79] Whether their fourth brother, Archbishop Berthold, joined them is unclear.[80] Regardless, Andreas's brief campaign to the Holy Land provided yet another opportunity for at least some of the Andechs brothers to work cooperatively. That Bishop Ekbert of Bamberg was a participant in this new intragenerational group of crusaders is additional evidence for the crucial role he played in shaping sibling dynamics within his lineage. This ecclesiastical lord, not one of his older brothers who held a secular lordship, stood at the center of many of the sibling group's political networks.

The crusade of late 1217 and early 1218 was the last time that the Hungarian royal court served as the center of gravity for any of the Andechs siblings. In March of 1218, Archbishop Berthold of Kalocsa was elected patriarch of Aquileia, and by October of the same year, he had begun to

---

77. Bamberg, Staatsarchiv, Bamberger Urkunden no. 543, which is dated February 8, 1230, is another charter of Bishop Ekbert of Bamberg in which he makes a grant intended, in part, to preserve his sister's memory.

78. Bamberg, Staatsarchiv, Bamberger Urkunden no. 481. The dating formula of the charter includes the phrase "in the year that there was an expedition to Jerusalem." However, because the majority of witnesses were Bamberg cathedral canons and ministerials, the charter was probably drawn up in Bamberg.

79. Oliver of Paderborn, *Historia Damiatina*, 162–163. For Henry, see Sweeney, "Hungary in the Crusades," 478–479.

80. Powell (*Anatomy of a Crusade*, 161) indicates that Berthold was present at Damietta in 1219, but this is over a year after his brothers had already returned to the German kingdom.

issue charters from his new see.[81] As a result, for the first time in more than a decade, all four brothers held positions inside the empire. However, a significant geographical gulf continued to separate the lineage's interests in the southeast of the empire from its lordships in Franconia. Two different focal points for the Andechs siblings are thus evident during the late 1210s and 1220s.

In Franconia, the bond between Bishop Ekbert of Bamberg and Duke Otto I of Merania continued to shape many of their political and territorial interests. After the bishop reestablished his position in his diocese in the years around 1215, these brothers were frequently together in and around Bamberg, working in close contact with one another to dominate regional affairs.[82] No evidence indicates either of them ever became entangled in any serious local disputes that led to violence. These siblings seem to have effectively eliminated opposition to their lordship during their years together in Upper Franconia.[83] In contrast, Duke Otto I of Merania had much more difficulty dominating the political scene in the other region where he exercised lordship, his wife's county-palatine of Burgundy. In the year 1222, Otto became embroiled in a dispute with the local prelate there, the archbishop of Besançon, because the duke had constructed a castle on a site where his predecessor as count-palatine had vowed no castle would ever be built. When Otto refused to destroy the castle or to explain his actions at the archiepiscopal court, he was excommunicated and his lands were placed under interdict.[84] The duke's initial reaction to his excommunication was to return to the shelter of his brother Ekbert's diocese of Bamberg. There, on October 20, 1223, he issued a series of five charters, in which he made lavish donations to various religious communities for the sake of his soul.[85] These charters all reference his brother Ekbert's episcopacy in the dating clause. It is tempting to speculate that the duke's excommunication arose, at least in part, from his inexperience exercising lordship in a region where the leading ecclesiastic was not a close relative.

---

81. Härtel, *I patti con il patriarcato di Aquileia*, 86–89, no. 5.

82. See, for example, Bamberg, Staatsarchiv, Bamberger Urkunden nos. 477, 480, 3220; *Urkundenbuch der Deutschordens-Commende Langeln*, 7–8, no. 7. Compare Schütz, "Die Andechs-Meranier in Franken," 37.

83. For example, it is only after Otto and Ekbert are both dead that another local power in Franconia, the monastery of Banz, complains about the castle-building activities of the Andechs lineage: Bamberg, Staatsarchiv, Bamberger Urkunden no. 599.

84. *Trente-sept documents Bourguignons*, 511–513, no. 21.

85. Bamberg, Staatsarchiv, Bamberger Urkunden nos. 513, 515–517; *Die Traditionen des Stiftes Diessen*, 120–121, no. 13.

Bishop Ekbert's influence in Franconia can be seen in his ties to the eighth member of this generation: Abbess Mechthild of Kitzingen. Brother and sister were first named together in 1215, when the bishop of Bamberg confirmed one of the Franconian convent's property agreements while Mechthild was abbess-elect.[86] In subsequent years, Ekbert may have played a role in two charters issued by King Henry (VII), in which the king granted special protection to the convent.[87] As we will soon see, Mechthild also helped Ekbert intervene in the affairs of their niece Elizabeth of Thuringia following the death of her husband. Though the sources are scant for the relationship between bishop and abbess, it is nevertheless noteworthy that Mechthild's only known ties with any of her siblings were with Ekbert, who was the focal point of so many connections within this sibling group.

The situation was much more complicated for the Andechs lineage in the southeast of the empire. When Berthold arrived in 1218 in the patriarchate—which included an extensive swath of territory to the east and northeast of Venice—he must have already been familiar with the region from his years as ban of Croatia. Nevertheless, it was apparently Andechs family politics, not Hungarian politics, that played the pivotal role in his election. In 1209, after stripping Berthold's brother Henry of the march of Istria, King Otto IV of Brunswick granted it in fief to the patriarch at the time.[88] When Berthold obtained the patriarchate in 1218, the march was therefore once more in family hands. If the Staufen king Frederick II influenced Berthold's election, as some scholars believe, he may have been signaling his willingness to forgive the Andechses for their involvement in his uncle's assassination.[89] Further evidence for this possibility emerges two years later in November of 1220, when Henry joined his brother Berthold at Frederick II's court in Italy, just north of Rome. This was Henry's first known appearance at the court of any German king or emperor since his brother Otto's fateful wedding day in 1208. While there, he acted as a witness when Frederick II confirmed Berthold's possession of the march of Istria.[90] Although Henry thus acknowledged his loss of this lordship, he nevertheless continued to title

---

86. *Regesta diplomatica necnon epistolaria*, 2:298, no. 1626.

87. *Historia diplomatica Friderici Secundi*, 3:346–347; 4, pt. 2:643.

88. Buttazzoni, "Del patriarca Volchero," 197–198. See also Reg. Imp. 5, vol. 1:83–84, no. 258a.

89. Schütz, "Das Geschlecht der Andechs-Meranier," 84; Bosl, "Europäischer Adel im 12./13. Jahrhundert," 39.

90. *Acta imperii inedita*, 1:175–176, no. 198.

himself *marchio Istrie* in subsequent years—without any apparent interference from Frederick II or his own younger brother.[91]

Berthold's position as patriarch frequently required him to be in northern Italy in the region around Udine and Cividale during the years after 1218, but he also spent long periods in other parts of the patriarchate, including Carniola and Carinthia.[92] His territorial interests therefore overlapped with those of his brother Henry, who spent much of his time on his lordships in Carniola after 1209. Berthold also came into contact with another of his brothers, Ekbert, who as bishop of Bamberg was in possession of numerous properties in southern Carinthia—including the town of Villach within the patriarchate's borders.[93] These three brothers, who had come to know each other as adults at the Hungarian royal court in 1209, therefore constituted a formidable political bloc along the southeastern frontier of the empire starting in the late 1210s.[94]

The most intriguing source for this Ekbert-Berthold-Henry sibling group during these years is unquestionably Ulrich von Liechtenstein's *Frauendienst*, written in the mid-thirteenth century. This work, the earliest first-person narrative in German literature, has long perplexed scholars, because it is unclear which elements of the work are fictional and which are based on historical events from Ulrich's own lifetime.[95] For the study of the Andechs lineage, this problem manifests itself in the text's description of a knightly tournament supposedly held at Friesach in Carinthia.[96] According to Ulrich, Duke Leopold VI of Austria arranged for a meeting of the leading lords from the southeast of the empire in order to help settle a dispute between Margrave Henry of Istria and Duke Bernhard of Carinthia. This gathering also attracted large numbers of ministerials and lesser nobles, who soon decided to organize a tournament in the field outside the town. For ten days,

---

91. See, for example, *Die Traditionen des Stiftes Diessen*, 117–118, no. 11, where on January 25, 1223, he titles himself *"Heinricvs dei gratia marchio Ystrie."* See also MHDC, 4, pt. 1:301, no. 2257, a charter of Patriarch Berthold from the year 1243, in which the deceased Henry is explicitly referred to as margrave of Istria.

92. Härtel, "Zur Herrschaftspraxis," 91–94; Schmidinger, *Patriarch und Landesherr*, 90–96. One piece of evidence for Henry's presence in northern Italy alongside the patriarch is Wiesflecker, *Die Regesten der Grafen von Görz*, 1:111, no. 410. For Berthold's career more generally, see Paschini, "Bertoldo di Merania" (1919, 1920).

93. Dopsch, *Österreichische Geschichte*, 326.

94. The only source I have found that even suggests the potential for tension between any of them is Wiesflecker, *Die Regesten der Grafen von Görz*, 1:108, no. 396.

95. Krenn, "Historische Figuren?"

96. Ulrich von Liechtenstein, *Frauendienst*, verses 177–339.

knights fought and died outside the walls of Friesach as part of the games. Eventually,

> Prince Leopold of Austria
> spoke: "It concerns me now
> that we do nothing else here
> but joust; I did not come here for that.
> A conference did I arrange for here
> and I wanted to mediate the hatred
> that the duke of Carinthia for a long time now
> has had for Margrave Henry."

> The patriarch of Aquileia
> spoke: "This here is too costly [in lives]."
> The bishop of Bamberg spoke:
> "It is truly distasteful to me
> that we should remain here in vain.
> I have asked my brother to come here,
> I mean the noble margrave
> of Istria, who is also present."[97]

These three lords' efforts to halt the violence ultimately failed, and the tournament continued for several more days. According to the text, all of this occurred in early May, and historians have speculated that the gathering—if it ever occurred—probably took place in 1224. Such a date is plausible, given what is known about the itineraries of these three Andechs brothers.[98] However, no other source refers in any way to this tournament, making it impossible to confirm the details of Ulrich's account.[99] Despite this fact, *Frauendienst* is a valuable source in one important respect. Ulrich von Liechtenstein was a prominent Styrian ministerial who knew the politics of the southeast of the empire very well.[100] As a result, even if Berthold and Ekbert never spoke the words that Ulrich attributed to them, their presence alongside Henry in this text is evidence that Ulrich considered all three Andechs brothers to have constituted an influential political bloc in regional affairs during the early years of his own career.

---

97. Ibid., verses 237–238. My translation is based partially on the modern German translation by Franz Viktor Spechtler.

98. For Henry and Ekbert, see especially BUB, 2:77–78, no. 249. For Berthold, see the narrative of his career in Paschini, "Bertoldo di Merania" (1919): 37–38.

99. The one detail that can be confirmed is the conflict between the duke of Carinthia and members of the Andechs family. See Dopsch, "Zwischen Dichtung und Politik," 88–93.

100. Freed, *Noble Bondsmen*, 249–265.

A decade after Berthold's move to the patriarchate of Aquileia brought him into closer contact with his brothers Ekbert and Henry, sibling dynamics inside this generation underwent another change. In late 1227 or early 1228, the Wittelsbach duke finally restored to Henry some of the territories in the old Andechs heartland of western Bavaria that had been stripped from him after Philip of Swabia's assassination.[101] Henry's reintegration into the Bavarian political community was complete by May 14, 1228, when he attended a grand gathering of magnates at Straubing on the Danube to celebrate the knighting of the duke's young son and heir. Also in attendance were his brothers Bishop Ekbert of Bamberg and Duke Otto I of Merania.[102] Ekbert's presence on this occasion is unsurprising. His bishopric had owned rights and properties in Bavaria since the eleventh century, and because of his long-standing connections to the duchy, he may even have played a role in negotiating the reconciliation between his brother Henry and the Bavarian duke.[103] Otto's decision to attend the Straubing festivities is more difficult to explain, however. He had not been involved in Bavarian politics since 1207, when he sold his comital lordship north of the Danube to the bishop of Passau.[104] Moreover, no evidence indicates he had seen his brother Henry at any point during the previous decade—since the two had witnessed Ekbert's 1217 donation and possibly participated in the Fifth Crusade together.

To understand Duke Otto I of Merania's appearance alongside his brother Henry, it is necessary to look ahead two months to July 18, 1228, when the margrave died. Henry had made a series of donations to religious communities in the preceding days that make it clear his death was neither sudden nor unexpected.[105] Nevertheless, he could not put all his affairs in order as he may have wished. Although the margrave had married an heiress from a Carniolan comital lineage almost a quarter century earlier, the couple had no children at the time of his death.[106] As a result, his brothers became the heirs to many

---

101. *Annales Scheftlarienses maiores*, 338; Holzfurtner, *Die Grafschaft der Andechser*, 359–360.

102. Herman of Niederalteich, *Annales*, 391.

103. Thorau, *König Heinrich (VII.)*, 178–179.

104. This twenty-year gap in Otto's involvement in Bavarian affairs has been overlooked by many historians. One reason for this is that one of Otto's charters for a Bavarian monastery—Munich, Bayerisches Hauptstaatsarchiv, Benediktbeuern Urkunden, no. 25—has been incorrectly dated to 1218–1219 by some scholars. The only legible part of the date is "m cc x" because the hole made in the parchment for one of the seals destroyed the rest of it. However, the witness list clearly fits with the witness lists of other charters of his from the period 1228–1229.

105. See, for example, Oefele, *Geschichte der Grafen von Andechs*, 241, no. 14; *Urkunden- und Regestenbuch des Herzogtums Krain*, 2:38–41, nos. 51–57.

106. An early modern necrology from the Carniolan monastery of Sittich (Stična in Slovenia) indicates that the pair had multiple children who were buried in the monastery, but no thirteenth-century source verifies this claim. See Schumi, "Nicrologia."

of his rights and properties. Viewed from this perspective, Otto's presence at Straubing may be an indication that the duke already knew the margrave's death was imminent. Throughout the spring and early summer of 1228, Otto remained in close proximity to his younger brother.[107] And on July 28, only ten days after Henry's death, the duke issued a charter for the Bavarian monastery of Benediktbeuern.[108] In it, he confirmed one of the margrave's grants from his final days. The witness list includes at least a half-dozen people who had also witnessed Henry's final bequests, meaning that Otto very quickly established ties with some of his dead brother's most loyal followers.

That Duke Otto was well prepared to succeed his brother in mid-1228 is further evidenced by his earlier decision in November of 1227 to mortgage his county-palatine of Burgundy to a French nobleman.[109] After two decades of attempting to exert his authority in the county-palatine, his position there remained a precarious one.[110] Trying to establish himself as his brother Henry's heir hundreds of miles away in Bavaria, Tyrol, and Carniola—while simultaneously continuing to push his claims to Burgundy—would have been a monumental task. The duke's decision to mortgage the county-palatine may therefore have been designed to free him temporarily from his commitments in Burgundy as he prepared for his brother's childless death. By inheriting many of Henry's lands and rights, Duke Otto I of Merania acquired territorial interests in Bavaria for the first time in two decades. He also found himself drawn into the politics of the southeast of the empire, a region he had not visited since his father was alive.[111]

Otto traveled to this unfamiliar corner of Andechs family lordship in the closing months of 1228 in order to secure his claims to his brother's properties in Carniola. There, he met his brother Berthold. On October 29, 1228, the two drew up a charter confirming the sale of several pieces of property in Carniola by the house of canons at Diessen: "We, Berthold, by the grace of God patriarch of the holy church of Aquileia, together with our brother, the illustrious Duke Otto of Merania, want everyone to know . . ."[112]

---

107. They were together at the court of King Henry (VII) in Nuremberg in June or early July. *Historia diplomatica Friderici Secundi*, 3:377–378. See also Reg. Imp. 5, vol. 2:744, no. 4106.

108. Munich, Bayerisches Hauptstaatsarchiv, Benediktbeuern Urkunden, no. 30.

109. *Cartulaire des comtes de Bourgogne*, 14–17, no. 14.

110. Compare Schütz, "Das Geschlecht der Andechs-Meranier," 83–84; Bur, "Les relations entre la Champagne et la Franche-Comté," 139; and Allemand-Gay, *Le pouvoir des comtes de Bourgogne*, 142–143.

111. MHDC, 4, pt. 1:1–3, no. 1524.

112. *Die Traditionen des Stiftes Diessen*, 122–124, no. 14. According to the same charter this sale was carried out partly "by the authority of our venerable brother, the bishop of Bamberg," who apparently was not present at the time.

Significantly, this is the earliest extant document to name these two brothers together. Whether both participated in the Fifth Crusade is only speculation. No source directly connects these siblings prior to 1228—when Berthold was approximately forty-seven years of age and Otto older still. Berthold had spent the preceding decades active in Hungary and the patriarchate of Aquileia, while Otto had been exercising lordship in Franconia and Burgundy. Hundreds of miles had thus separated these brothers for much of their adult lives, and it seems that they barely knew each other as their relationship took center stage in the sibling group's closing years.

The decade and a half separating Queen Gertrude of Hungary's death in 1213 from Margrave Henry of Istria's in 1228 was a remarkable period in the history of the Andechs lineage. A wide range of sources from these years shows members of this sibling group collaborating with one another at the imperial court and in various regions where the brothers exercised lordship. None of this evidence suggests that all the living Andechs brothers and sisters ever made common cause together in support of a uniform and static vision of their lineage's political and territorial interests. Indeed, it is impossible to argue there was even a single Andechs sibling group operating in these years. Nevertheless, the sources from this period demonstrate especially well how cooperative sibling relationships could work to the advantage of individual lords as they sought to exercise their own lordship and extend their own influence at court.

The Imperial Court and the Final Years of the Generation

A few months after his first known meeting as an adult with his brother Berthold, Duke Otto I of Merania married his daughter Agnes to Frederick II, the heir to the Babenberg duchies of Austria and Styria. Her dowry consisted of a number of her paternal uncle Henry's former lands and rights in and around Carniola.[113] After this marriage, Otto would never again take interest in this region, an indication that the union was intended to free him from exercising lordship there. Otto had only a single minor son when his brother Henry died, yet in late 1228 he controlled properties and rights extending from Burgundy to Carniola—a distance of approximately four hundred miles. Increasingly after his 1227 mortgaging of Burgundy and the 1229 marriage of his daughter Agnes, however, he was in a position to focus his attention solely on the old Andechs heartlands, a more manageable collection of territories in Franconia, Bavaria, and Tyrol running from Bamberg south to Innsbruck.

---

113. Lechner, *Die Babenberger*, 213; Štih, "Krain in der Zeit der Grafen von Andechs," 35.

The duke continued, however, to claim one piece of his brother Henry's inheritance in the southeast of the empire, and this led to the only recorded dispute between two siblings in this generation of the Andechs lineage. In his charter of July 28, 1228, written ten days after Henry's death, Otto used the title "by the grace of God duke of Merania, count-palatine of Burgundy and margrave of Istria."[114] Throughout the late 1210s and early 1220s, Henry had continued to title himself margrave of Istria, despite the fact that his brother Patriarch Berthold was the one who held the march as an imperial fief. Berthold never challenged Henry's use of the title, but when Duke Otto I of Merania attempted to assert his own claim to it as Henry's heir, the patriarch apparently objected. This can be surmised from a charter issued by Emperor Frederick II in July of 1230, two years after Henry's death. The document details a settlement between the brothers and confirms the duke's decision to abandon all his claims to the march of Istria.[115] As with many of the intragenerational disputes discussed in previous chapters, this one seems to have been the result of brothers trying to renegotiate succession and inheritance plans when something unexpected—in this case, Henry's childless death—threw a father's patrimonial divisions into disarray. Moreover, like the Welf brothers King Otto of Brunswick and Count-Palatine Henry of the Rhine, the Andechs brothers Otto and Berthold had little opportunity to forge a strong bond with one another during their early lives.[116] Prior to 1228, they lacked a close relationship that might have enabled them to settle the dispute over the march of Istria quickly and quietly between themselves.[117]

While the cession of his claim to Istria effectively ended Otto's links to the southeast of the empire, he nevertheless developed closer ties to his brother Berthold during the early 1230s. The imperial court provided an occasion to settle their dispute in July of 1230, because both were at the emperor's side for another reason: Frederick II's negotiations with Pope Gregory IX. The duke and the patriarch are named together in many of the diplomatic exchanges on the eve of the Treaty of San Germano between pope and emperor, and

---

114. Munich, Bayerisches Hauptstaatsarchiv, Benediktbeuern Urkunden, no. 30. He never used a seal that included all three of these titles.

115. There are two nineteenth-century printed editions of this charter, each one based on different earlier editions: *Historia diplomatica Friderici Secundi*, 3:205–206; *Codice diplomatico Istriano*, 2:436–437, no. 249.

116. See chapter 5.

117. For a similar observation about dispute resolutions, see Brown, *Unjust Seizure*, 138. The lack of evidence for siblings' property disputes within the German upper aristocracy contrasts sharply with the evidence for family property disputes in France. See, for example, Livingstone, *Out of Love for My Kin*, 204–233.

Otto and Berthold were two of the six German princes who swore to act as guarantors of the treaty on Frederick's behalf.[118] One year later, the Andechs siblings again gathered at the imperial court. For six months between December of 1231 and May of 1232, all three surviving brothers—Otto, Berthold, and Bishop Ekbert of Bamberg—traveled with the emperor in northeast Italy between Ravenna, Venice, and Aquileia. In April of 1232, these siblings were three of the twelve magnates who formally mediated the burgeoning conflict between Frederick and his son King Henry (VII).[119] This half-year period, when the brothers were named together in more than twenty-five imperial charters, is the longest and best-documented phase of intense fraternal interaction within this generation of the Andechs lineage. By the early 1230s, these three were some of the oldest *principes imperii,* and their extended stay south of the Alps suggests they formed an especially influential political bloc at the imperial court.[120]

In late May 1232, Otto, Berthold, and Ekbert departed from Frederick II when he ended his travels in northern Italy and turned his attention toward his Sicilian kingdom. The three brothers would never be together again. Duke Otto I of Merania died two years later on May 7, 1234, in his early sixties. Because his only son was still a minor, his brothers Ekbert and Berthold would remain the dominant figures in the lineage throughout the mid-1230s. In earlier years, these two churchmen had taken very different approaches to managing the complex interplay between family expectations and ecclesiastical office. The bishop of Bamberg had consistently supported his brothers Duke Otto and Margrave Henry—even at the expense of his own church. Berthold, in contrast, had sought to strengthen the rights of his patriarchate, and as his assertion of Aquileia's claim to the march of Istria reveals, he was even willing to challenge his brothers. This does not mean, however, that Berthold was rigidly opposed to his siblings' secular pursuits— as Bishop Otto I of Freising had been almost a century earlier.[121] The patriarch confirmed various property donations that Henry and Otto made to religious communities in the southeast of the empire, and he even made a grant of his own for the sake of Henry's soul.[122]

---

118. *Die Aktenstücke zum Frieden,* 61–63, no. 5; see also ibid., 46–47, no. 14 and 68–69, nos. 10–11. See also Stürner, *Friedrich II. Teil 2,* 184.

119. MGH Const., 2:210, no. 170. For the other imperial charters from this period that include all three brothers in the witness lists, see Reg. Imp. 5, vol. 1:380–394, nos. 1917–1980.

120. For more on this point, see chapter 7.

121. See chapter 3.

122. *Urkunden- und Regestenbuch des Herzogtums Krain,* 2:59, no. 78 and 2:60–61, no. 81; MHDC, 4, pt. 1:270–271, no. 2184.

Despite their different approaches to balancing family and office, the relationship between Ekbert and Berthold was strong during the closing years of their lives. In 1233, the patriarch issued a charter confirming that he had given the bishop permission to establish a hospital outside the walls of the Carinthian town of Villach, a Bamberg possession within the borders of the patriarchate.[123] The same year, when Ekbert was captured and briefly imprisoned during a war against the duke of Carinthia, the pope asked Berthold to intervene.[124] The brothers also remained influential figures at the court of Emperor Frederick II during this period. Their involvement in imperial politics reached its peak in 1235–1236, when they played a central role in the conflict between the emperor and Duke Frederick II of Austria. As one contemporary source explains, "The king of Bohemia devastated Austria on the order of the emperor. The duke of Bavaria and the bishop of Passau besieged the town of Linz. . . . And the patriarch of Aquileia together with the bishop of Bamberg entered Styria in a hostile manner and despoiled the churches."[125] In early 1237, they then spent several months at Vienna with the emperor as he organized the affairs of the southeast of the empire.[126]

Bishop Ekbert of Bamberg, whom one contemporary described as "a great and warlike man," died on June 5, 1237.[127] With his passing, there ceased to be an active sibling group within the Andechs lineage for the first time in four decades. During the late 1230s and 1240s, the only surviving members of this generation were Patriarch Berthold and Abbess Mechthild of Kitzingen, and no extant source suggests they ever had any contact with one another. When Berthold died in 1251 and Mechthild died three years later, this generation came to an end—eight decades after it had begun. By then, the Andechs lineage had already ceased to be politically significant. The childless death of Duke Otto I of Merania's only son in 1248 prompted various secular and ecclesiastical lords to seize the remaining Andechs lands and rights. It was a quick and quiet end for a lineage that had played such a prominent role in the politics of the Staufen period.

The rapid decline of Andechs influence during the 1240s does not diminish the importance of the generation that dominated the political scene in central Europe in the opening decades of the thirteenth century. As I

123. MHDC, 4, pt. 1:216–217, no. 2079.

124. *Epistolae saeculi XIII*, 1:442–443, no. 546.

125. *Annales S. Rudberti Salisburgenses*, 786. See also Dopsch, *Österreichische Geschichte*, 189–194; Hausmann, "Kaiser Friedrich II.," 251–256.

126. Herman of Niederalteich, *Annales*, 392. For more on the role of these brothers at the imperial court in these years, see chapter 7.

127. Ibid., 392–393.

have shown here, the rich sources for these eight brothers and sisters reveal with unusual clarity how and why some siblings collaborated effectively at the levels of regional lordship and imperial politics. The four Andechs brothers, in particular, provide an excellent case study for understanding the value of sibling relationships in this aristocratic society, because different groupings of these brothers worked together in a variety of situations over the span of four decades. The abundant evidence for these brothers also makes it possible to appreciate another dimension of the sibling bond, one that has received little attention in the modern scholarship on noble families. Specifically, the sources for the four Andechs brothers suggest that sibling relationships were more consistently cooperative and politically efficacious than any other type of kin relationship within German noble lords' extended kinship groups.

Delineating the Andechs Extended Kin Group

Since the late twentieth century, scholarship on the medieval nobility has frequently analyzed all the relationships between both close family members and more distant relatives under the single rubric of the *kin group* or *kindred*.[128] Yet in their roles as uncles, nephews, cousins, and in-laws, the four Andechs brothers interacted with their more distant relatives in a variety of ways that defy easy comparison with their sibling interactions.[129] As I have argued throughout this book, the succession and inheritance practices employed within the lineages under investigation here ensured that brothers—and sometimes sisters—would have at least some overlapping political and territorial interests. In the opening decades of the thirteenth century, all four Andechs brothers collaborated with one another for periods ranging from a few months to several years at a time as they supported each other across vast stretches of central Europe from the diocese of Bamberg, to Hungary, to the imperial court in Italy. And yet, despite this environment of sibling solidarity, each of the four brothers interacted with a different set of relatives within their extended kinship network. There was no comparable foundation for shared interests outside the sibling group, in their relationships with their more distant kinsmen and kinswomen (see figure 7).

---

128. See, for example, Althoff, *Family, Friends and Followers*, 23–64; Tanner, *Families, Friends and Allies*, 9–17; Livingstone, *Out of Love for My Kin*, 27–59.

129. Of the four sisters in this generation, Saint Hedwig is the only one whose extended kin relationships can be reconstructed in any detail. See Gottschalk, *St. Hedwig*, 180–193.

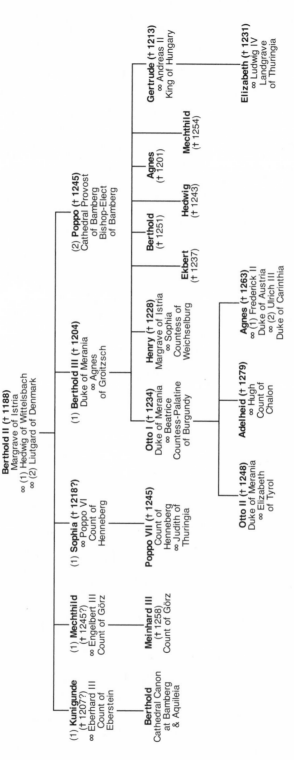

FIGURE 7. Members of the extended kin network of the Andechs brothers referenced in this chapter.

Significantly, no relative from outside their natal family developed close ties to all four of these siblings. Indeed, only two members of the Andechs lineage's extended kin group are even named in extant sources alongside all of them. The first is their paternal uncle, Poppo, a member of the cathedral chapter at Bamberg from the mid-1180s and—after his nephew Ekbert's death in 1237—bishop-elect.[130] Because of his longstanding connection to this Franconian diocese, Poppo maintained close ties to both Ekbert and Duke Otto I of Merania.[131] However, he is named together with Margrave Henry of Istria only once in an extant source; similarly, only one document suggests that Poppo and Patriarch Berthold of Aquileia had any contact with each other.[132] The second relative to appear alongside all four brothers was one of their brothers-in-law: King Andreas II of Hungary. Berthold, Ekbert, and Henry all spent time at his royal court in the early 1200s and maintained connections to him even after the assassination of their sister Gertrude.[133] Duke Otto I of Merania, in contrast, seems to have collaborated with him only once, when they briefly participated together in the Fifth Crusade.[134] Thus, the brothers did not share a common set of extended kin relationships on which they all relied. In their varying roles as uncles, cousins, and affines, each had strikingly different interactions with their distant relatives.

The four brothers' most famous niece was Saint Elizabeth of Thuringia, who appears with all of them in the Schlackenwerther Codex illumination of Saint Hedwig of Silesia's family.[135] As noted above, the youngest of the eight Andechs siblings, Abbess Mechthild of Kitzingen, is not seated next to her three sisters in this image. Instead, the illuminator placed her at the feet of her parents in order to have space beside Queen Gertrude of Hungary for a more illustrious member of the kin group: the queen's daughter, Elizabeth. That the late medieval descendants of the Andechs lineage would be anxious to call attention to Saint Elizabeth—and to place her in close proximity to the lineage's other prominent saint, Hedwig—is not surprising. Nevertheless,

---

130. Frenken, "Poppo," 170.

131. See, for example, Bamberg, Staatsarchiv, Bamberger Urkunden nos. 469, 473, 480, 481, 483, and 551; as well as *Urkundenbuch der Deutschordens-Commende Langeln*, 5–8, nos. 5–7.

132. Bamberg, Staatsarchiv, Bamberger Urkunden no. 481; Wiesflecker, *Die Regesten der Grafen von Görz*, 1:126, no. 474.

133. See above. For contacts in the years after Gertrude's assassination, see *Epistolae saeculi XIII*, 1:310–311, no. 393; Dienst, "Zum Grazer Vertrag," 35–37.

134. Oliver of Paderborn, *Historia Damiatina*, 162.

135. See figure 4. This illumination further emphasizes the extended kin network of the Andechs lineage through its placement above a second image on the manuscript page, which depicts Hedwig's wedding to the duke of Silesia.

later memorial strategies are rarely reflective of actual family relationships, and Elizabeth's appearance in this illumination is no exception.

Elizabeth died in November of 1231 after dedicating her final years to founding a hospital and caring for the poor.[136] Only three and a half years later, on May 27, 1235, Pope Gregory IX formally announced her canonization. The entire process leading to her elevation to sainthood thus occurred with remarkable speed.[137] The canonization dossier drawn up during these years includes, among other texts, a written record of testimony obtained through interviews with some of Elizabeth's former maidservants. This testimony preserves a story told by one of the women about Elizabeth and her maternal uncle Bishop Ekbert of Bamberg.[138] According to the maidservant, following the death of her husband, Landgrave Ludwig IV of Thuringia, in 1227, Elizabeth's brothers-in-law tried to seize the properties Elizabeth had been promised to support her in her widowhood.[139] These brothers-in-law drove Elizabeth and her household from the Thuringian court at the Wartburg, and for a short time, Elizabeth was essentially homeless.

Soon, however, one of her maternal aunts, Abbess Mechthild of Kitzingen, came to her aid. Mechthild brought Elizabeth and her household to Bishop Ekbert, who decided to arrange a new marriage for Elizabeth—despite the fact that she wanted to devote her remaining days to prayer and to the care of the poor and the sick. She was sent, unwillingly, to one of his castles near Bamberg while Ekbert sought another husband for her. A short time later, some of Landgrave Ludwig IV's followers passed through Bamberg on their way back to Thuringia with the body of their lord. Bishop Ekbert released Elizabeth from the castle so she could view her husband's remains. Then, when Ludwig's vassals declared that they would help her secure the properties her husband had promised to her, Ekbert relented completely and allowed her to return to Thuringia.

At times, this account of events reads more like a carefully crafted saint's life than the written record of a maidservant's oral testimony. Indeed, the story of a wicked uncle locking a saintly woman in a tower against her will sounds like a hagiographic topos. The way the story unfolds in the *Libellus* leaves no doubt that the principal reason why these events were included was

136. For a brief biography, see Schütz, "Das Geschlecht der Andechs-Meranier," 131–144.

137. Klaniczay, *Holy Rulers*, 285–286.

138. This testimony survives today in two recensions—though neither of them is the original sent to the pope in early 1235. Here, I am using the second, lengthier recension: *Der sog. Libellus*, 37–40. See also *Life and Afterlife of St. Elizabeth*, 203–204.

139. See chapter 7 for more on these Ludowing brothers.

to highlight Elizabeth's saintly virtues. The other members of her household were tearful and frightened when they learned of Bishop Ekbert's plans for Elizabeth. But Elizabeth consoled them and explained calmly, "'If my uncle hands me over to someone in marriage against my will, I will protest in spirit and in words. And if I do not have another way of escaping, I will secretly cut off my own nose, so that no one will care for me, so mutilated and deformed will I be.'"[140] Since this dramatic speech is intended to demonstrate Elizabeth's inner strength and commitment to the spiritual life, quite possibly the entire account of her imprisonment has been embellished.

Nevertheless, it is essential to recognize that the *Libellus* does not mention a generic uncle but a specific one, an indication that this account of Elizabeth's life cannot be dismissed so easily as hagiographic fabrication. Bishop Ekbert of Bamberg demonstrated throughout his career that he was willing to intervene in a range of family matters, and as a result, this story of his contacts with his niece Elizabeth must be viewed through a wider lens. Ekbert probably met the young Elizabeth in 1209 when he was residing at the Hungarian court after King Philip of Swabia's assassination. He may also have had a hand in arranging her marriage into the Ludowing lineage, since his diocese lay in close proximity to Thuringia.[141] Finally, Ekbert's unusually strong relationship with Elizabeth's mother, Gertrude, must also be taken into account.[142] Considering these factors, the general outlines of the story in the *Libellus* may be open to another interpretation—if we read between the lines of hagiographic rhetoric. Elizabeth, stripped of the properties promised her in her widowhood, was destitute when she arrived in Bamberg. Her uncle therefore attempted to arrange a marriage for her, since a new husband could provide her with some economic support. When Landgrave Ludwig's men assured the bishop that they would help her regain her rights in Thuringia, Ekbert abandoned the plan and released her rather than forcing her to marry against her will. In other words, the bishop may have been seeking to secure his niece's future, not disrupt her plans to lead a spiritual life, when he sought a husband for her.

None of Ekbert's brothers appears in a contemporary or near-contemporary source alongside Elizabeth. Berthold, during his time as archbishop of Kalocsa in the early 1200s, had frequently been in attendance at the Hungarian royal court while Elizabeth was a young girl, but there is no direct evidence connecting them during her lifetime. After her canonization,

---

140. *Der sog. Libellus*, 38–39.
141. Schütz, "Das Geschlecht der Andechs-Meranier," 131.
142. See above.

however, Patriarch Berthold became a prominent figure in promoting her rapidly expanding cult.[143] On April 30, 1251, he drew up a charter while at Slovenj Gradec in modern-day Slovenia, in which he agreed to grant all his lands and rights in the region to the church of Aquileia at the time of his death. This agreement was made "in the church of the blessed Elisabeth" in Slovenj Gradec, a church that Berthold had helped dedicate to his niece.[144] According to the necrology of the church of Aquileia, he also made a special donation to his own cathedral church so that the feast of Saint Elizabeth would be celebrated appropriately there.[145] Nevertheless, these efforts to bind himself to the sainted Elizabeth seem not to be reflective of close ties between the two during her lifetime.

Elizabeth's interactions—and lack thereof—with her uncles are comparable to these lords' contacts with their other nieces. Only one of Duke Otto I of Merania's five daughters developed close ties with any of her paternal uncles, and here too, marriage was a central issue. As noted above, the duke married his daughter Agnes to Duke Frederick II of Austria in the early 1230s and included in her dowry properties in the southeast of the empire that he had inherited after his brother Henry's death. A short time after the wedding, Duke Frederick II of Austria clashed with Emperor Frederick II, and both Bishop Ekbert and Patriarch Berthold participated in the military campaigns against the duke in 1236–1237.[146] The duke of Austria was still an outlaw in the eyes of the emperor when, on December 11, 1238, Patriarch Berthold consented to the foundation of a new convent in Carniola. His charter of that day states, "We confirm to the monastery in perpetuity all grants or donations made piously and justly. . . . [We do this] by our authority and in the name of our dear niece Duchess Agnes of Austria and of her brother Otto [II], the illustrious duke of Merania and count-palatine of Burgundy, our nephew."[147] The order in which Agnes and Duke Otto II are listed is evidence that Agnes, not her brother, was the one with important property rights in the southeast of the empire.

Agnes's status as heiress to her lineage's Carniolan properties became more significant in 1243, when Duke Frederick II of Austria repudiated her in

143. For the popularity of Elizabeth's cult and the creation of her *beata stirps*, see Klaniczay, *Holy Rulers*, 295.

144. UB Steiermark, 3:153–154, no. 88.

145. De Rubeis, *Monumenta ecclesiae Aquilejensis*, col. 720. See also cols. 682–683.

146. Dopsch, *Österreichische Geschichte*, 190–192; for Agnes's involvement in this conflict, Lechner, *Die Babenberger*, 282.

147. BUB, 2:173–177, no. 335.

order to take a new wife. Agnes immediately fought the dissolution of her marriage by appealing to the papal court.[148] However, the duke died childless only three years later, leaving Agnes in control of her valuable dowry. At this point, Patriarch Berthold of Aquileia began to show much greater interest in Agnes's affairs. During the two years between September 1246 and September 1248, uncle and niece were together on four separate occasions.[149] The location listed in all four of these documents was the castle of Soffumbergo near the Italian town of Udine. Since these are the only references to Agnes during this two-year period, Agnes may have been residing in this castle, which lay much closer to Berthold's centers of power and authority as patriarch than to the Andechses' Carniolan lands. Moreover, the four charters naming Berthold and Agnes together all involved lands and rights that belonged to Agnes's dowry, an indication that he was keeping a close eye on her portion of the family inheritance. Indeed, the patriarch even arranged a new marriage for Agnes, and in 1250, he and her second husband agreed to a division of the Andechs lands and rights in the southeast of the empire.[150]

That the Ekbert-Elizabeth and Berthold-Agnes relationships provide the only evidence for uncle-niece interactions in this generation of the Andechs lineage is unsurprising. As I have argued previously, the brother-sister bond tended not to be a strong one either, except in those cases when individual brothers and sisters had overlapping territorial interests and lived in close proximity to one another. However, these uncle-niece relationships differ from brother-sister relationships in one significant way. Neither Elizabeth nor Agnes is shown exercising agency in her dealings with Ekbert and Berthold. Both were subject to their uncles' authority in ways that find few if any parallels in Queen Gertrude of Hungary's relationships with Ekbert and Berthold. The generation gap is clearly one reason for this difference; Ekbert and Berthold were born a quarter century before Elizabeth and Agnes. But there seems to be more to these stories as well. These uncle-niece relationships were not embedded in traditions of cooperative and collaborative interactions in the same way that sibling relationships were.

The differences between Ekbert and Berthold's roles as brothers and their roles as uncles are also evident in their contacts with their nephew, Duke Otto II of Merania (d. 1248), the last secular lord in the Andechs lineage. Ekbert briefly served as Otto II's guardian before his own death in 1237, but

148. Lechner, *Die Babenberger*, 292–293.
149. BUB, 2:307–308, no. 440; 2:310–311, no. 443; 2:313–314, nos. 446–447.
150. Dopsch, *Österreichische Geschichte*, 340; *Urkunden- und Regestenbuch des Herzogtums Krain*, 2:137–140, no. 174.

there is little evidence for strong ties between them.[151] Patriarch Berthold, meanwhile, showed no interest in his nephew, whose main lordships lay in Franconia and Bavaria. The patriarch only concerned himself with the lineage's rights and properties in the southeast of the empire, in and around Carniola. As a result, as Duke Otto II struggled to maintain his position as a leading magnate during the mid-1240s, his last surviving paternal uncle, Berthold, did not support him.[152]

These examples concerning the Andechs brothers and their nieces and nephews highlight two key issues. First, these interactions tended not to be as frequent or long-lived as interactions between siblings. Margrave Henry, Bishop Ekbert, and Patriarch Berthold all had more nieces and nephews than they had siblings, but the sources for their relationships with these relatives are sparse. Henry had died in 1228 before his nephew Otto II or any of Otto II's sisters had even reached the age of majority. Similarly, Bishop Ekbert's death in 1237 occurred just as Otto II became an adult. The generation gap, in some instances, therefore limited the possibility of relationships ever developing between uncles and their nieces and nephews. Second, extended kin groups tended to be more dispersed geographically than sibling groups, thus diminishing the likelihood of intersecting territorial and political interests. Extended kin simply had fewer reasons to develop strong relationships—even if their adult lives overlapped for long periods.[153]

This second point comes into clearer focus when the relationships between the Andechs brothers and their cousins are examined. These four siblings had more than a dozen first cousins and numerous more-distant ones.[154] However, very few sources suggest close contacts between any of these Andechs brothers and any of their cousins. For example, in 1231, their first cousin Berthold of Eberstein drew up a charter that begins, "Berthold, by the grace of God provost of Aquileia and of Saint Stephen's in Bamberg."[155] This Eberstein cousin therefore seems to have been simultaneously holding offices in both Bishop Ekbert and Patriarch Berthold's cathedral chapters, yet we know nothing about how this may have worked in practice.[156] Simi-

---

151. *Die Traditionen des Stiftes Diessen,* 52–53, no. 38.
152. Schütz, "Die Andechs-Meranier in Franken," 43–48.
153. For some differing perspectives on uncles, see Livingstone, *Out of Love for My Kin,* 34–41; Gillingham, *Kingdom of Germany,* 15; Leyser, "German Aristocracy," 37.
154. Kist, "Die Nachfahren," 42–45.
155. Bamberg, Staatsarchiv, Bamberger Urkunden no. 552. See also Frenken, "Hausmachtpolitik und Bischofsstuhl," 730–731.
156. Berthold of Eberstein's only known appearance with his two cousins was in Vienna in 1237, when both Andechs brothers were supporting Emperor Frederick II in his conflict with the duke of Austria. See UB Enns, 3:55–57, no. 50.

larly, Ekbert is named only once in a charter of his distant cousins margraves John I and Otto III of Brandenburg, when in 1230 the margraves agreed to make a grant to a monastery "at the petition of our relative (*consanguinei nostri*) the lord Ekbert, bishop of Bamberg."[157] In most other cases, there is not even this much evidence for connections between cousins. And even when sources for this kinship bond do exist, the relationships can be difficult to characterize. The cooperative links between Duke Otto I of Merania and Count Poppo VII of Henneberg on the one hand, and the conflictual relationship between Patriarch Berthold of Aquileia and Count Meinhard III of Görz on the other, share few commonalities.

Duke Otto I of Merania appears in a broad range of sources with his first cousin Count Poppo VII of Henneberg (d. 1242), who exercised lordship in the region around Würzburg to the west of Bamberg.[158] Poppo witnessed one of Otto's monastic gifts in 1216/1218 and agreed to act as a trustee (*salamannus*) for the grant.[159] The duke and the count also participated in the Fifth Crusade together.[160] In subsequent years, Otto twice intervened to arrange peace agreements between Poppo and his rivals. In 1224, the duke resolved the conflict between Poppo and his wife, Judith, on the one side and Judith's half brother Landgrave Ludwig IV of Thuringia on the other.[161] Eight years later, the duke mediated a peace between the count and the bishop of Würzburg.[162] And when Otto drew up a charter for the Bavarian religious house of Diessen while residing in his Franconian castle of Scheßlitz on November 6, 1230, those present included "our brother, the venerable lord bishop of Bamberg, and the illustrious Count Poppo of Henneberg."[163]

The close relationship between Otto and Poppo shows the potential durability of the cousin bond within the German aristocracy. However, the duke of Merania did not have a similarly strong and enduring relationship with any of his other cousins from the Henneberg lineage—or from any other lineage with kinship ties to the Andechses.[164] Indeed, the foundation for

157. *Schlesisches Urkundenbuch*, 1:233–234, no. 318.

158. Wagner, "Entwurf einer Genealogie," 51–52, 60–62.

159. Bamberg, Staatsarchiv, Bamberger Urkunden no. 477. Bamberger Urkunden no. 478 also names Poppo, but this charter is probably a forgery. Another of Otto's cousins, Margrave Diepold of Vohburg, is also listed in both of these charters, but he appears much less frequently with Otto in the surviving sources than Poppo does.

160. Powell, *Anatomy of a Crusade*, 238.

161. See chapter 7.

162. MB, 37:252–255, no. 234.

163. *Die Traditionen des Stiftes Diessen*, 135–138, no. 17.

164. Count Poppo VII of Henneberg had at least five siblings: Wagner, "Entwurf einer Genealogie," 57–65.

Otto and Poppo's relationship was an unusual one. They were neighbors in Franconia, but neighbors whose territorial interests were quite divergent and therefore not competitive. The count of Henneberg's sphere of influence lay within the diocese of Würzburg, while the duke of Merania's most valuable holdings lay within the diocese of Bamberg. One factor in their ability to forge a strong relationship was therefore their separate but adjacent lordships. Not all cousins found themselves in a similar situation.

Patriarch Berthold of Aquileia had a very different relationship with another first cousin: Count Meinhard III of Görz (d. 1258). During the late 1100s, Duke Berthold III of Merania's sister Mechthild—an aunt of the four Andechs brothers—had married Count Engelbert III of Görz (Gorizia in Italy), by whom she bore a son, Meinhard.[165] In the immediate wake of this union, there were few if any contacts between lords from the Andechs and Görz lineages.[166] Then, beginning in 1218, Patriarch Berthold began to have regular contact with members of the Görz lineage, because they held the advocacy for the church of Aquileia. Moreover, one of the main centers of the counts' lordship lay along the modern Italian-Slovenian border just east of his diocesan seat.[167] Although Berthold and Meinhard often worked together peacefully as churchman and advocate, they also inherited from their predecessors a variety of long-standing conflicts over competing claims to rights and properties within the patriarchate.[168]

On November 27, 1234, Berthold and Meinhard III settled a dispute over tolls and other economic interests along key trade routes through the mountains and valleys in the region. The charter drawn up on this occasion is noteworthy, because Meinhard is referred to as "our dear cousin and vassal" (*dilectum nepotem et fidelem nostrum*).[169] This document, sealed by both men but explicitly drawn up in Berthold's name, labels Meinhard as *nepos noster* a total of eleven times, while identifying him as *Comes Meinhardus* only once. The text clearly emphasizes the blood connection between the pair rather than their relationship as prelate and church advocate, yet this blood connection had obviously not been able to overcome the tensions inherent in the traditional relationship between the patriarchs and the counts of Görz. Throughout the 1230s and 1240s, Berthold is named in more sources with

---

165. Štih, *Studien zur Geschichte*, 162.

166. One exception is a gathering of regional magnates during the year 1202: see MHDC, 4, pt. 1:1–3, no. 1524.

167. For the counts' holdings, see Štih, *Studien zur Geschichte*, 11–39.

168. Härtel, "Vom nicht zustandegekommenen Frieden," 545–546.

169. Vienna, Österreichisches Staatsarchiv, AUR 1234.XI.27 (printed edition: MHDC, 4, pt. 1:222–223, no. 2094).

Count Meinhard III than with any other relative, yet there is no indication that the cousin bond between them shaped their interactions. Indeed, in 1250, one of Patriarch Berthold's charters even makes explicit reference to a new war (*werra*) he was waging against Meinhard.[170] Thus, it was first and foremost the count's position as advocate for the church of Aquileia that defined their conflictual relationship.[171]

The bond between Berthold and Meinhard clearly contrasts with the bond between Duke Otto I of Merania and Count Poppo VII of Henneberg. In the case of Otto and Poppo, the principal reason why these two lords developed a close relationship seems to have been their kinship bond. Their two natal families otherwise had few overlapping interests that may explain their frequent interactions with one another. The relationship between Berthold and Meinhard, on the other hand, is evidence that the connection between cousins could not necessarily bind together lords whose competing lordships were more likely to generate tensions than close cooperation. Thus, cousins could occasionally develop strong relationships, but this occurred much less frequently with cousins than siblings, because members of different lineages inevitably had different interests and foci.

Affines, relatives by marriage, add a final layer of complexity to the Andechs brothers' extended kinship group. Duke Otto I of Merania and Margrave Henry of Istria both wed heiresses and remained married to these women for more than twenty years. However, neither of their wives brought to the marriage a large family with extensive political networks. This was the natural price one paid for marrying an heiress, who was by definition a noblewoman with few if any close male relatives.

At some point during the opening decade of the thirteenth century, Henry married Sophia, the only child of the Carniolan nobleman Count Albert of Weichselburg (Višnja Gora in Slovenia). This marriage eventually brought the margrave new lands and rights in Carniola, but in the early years of the union, its main benefit was to bind Henry more closely to the count of Weichselburg.[172] Their first known appearance together is preserved in a document from 1202, while Henry's father, Duke Berthold III of Merania, was still alive.[173] During subsequent years, the count and the margrave continued to collaborate with one another.[174] Albert even witnessed

---

170. *Urkunden- und Regestenbuch des Herzogtums Krain*, 2:137, no. 174.

171. See various entries in Wiesflecker, *Die Regesten der Grafen von Görz*, 1:119–146.

172. Štih, *Studien zur Geschichte*, 125–126, 136–137; Hauptmann, "Krain," 394–397.

173. MHDC, 4, pt. 1:1–3, no. 1524.

174. Ibid., 4, pt. 1:31–32, no. 1596. See also ibid., 4, pt. 1:32–33, no. 1597.

one of Henry's charters from the year 1209, an indication that the count was standing by his son-in-law in the wake of King Philip's assassination.[175] After Albert died in late 1209 or 1210, however, Henry promptly lost this familial connection—almost two decades before his own death.

Duke Otto I of Merania's marriage on June 21, 1208, to Beatrice, the heiress to the county-palatine of Burgundy, created a more complicated set of affinal relationships. The union had presumably been intended to strengthen the bond between Beatrice's paternal uncle, King Philip of Swabia, and the members of the Andechs lineage.[176] Philip's assassination on the day of the wedding quickly ended this possibility, however, and Beatrice brought with her into the marriage few other active familial connections.[177] Beatrice provided the duke of Merania with valuable lands and rights attached to a prestigious lordship, but she could not integrate him into a dense family group offering him new social and political relationships. Otto's career as count-palatine of Burgundy therefore faced significant challenges from the beginning. The Andechs familial circles had no links to this distant region along the empire's border with the kingdom of France, and Beatrice had no comparable family group in Burgundy awaiting his arrival.

Despite these challenges, Duke Otto I made a determined effort throughout the 1210s and early 1220s to exert his authority over the county-palatine and to exercise lordship there.[178] But his efforts to establish himself in this region were hampered by Count Stephen II of Auxonne (d. 1242), a distant cousin of Beatrice. Stephen claimed on the basis of direct male descent that he was the rightful claimant to the county-palatine of Burgundy.[179] As a local nobleman whose ancestors had exercised lordship in the region throughout the twelfth century, the count held a stronger position inside the county-palatine than the duke of Merania—an outsider—during the 1210s and 1220s. Conflict between Otto and Stephen seems to have erupted almost immediately after the duke's marriage to Beatrice, prompting the archbishop of Besançon and other local lords to intervene and arrange a

---

175. Unfortunately, this charter survives only in a seventeenth-century copy: see UB Steiermark, 2:155–156, no. 100.

176. Schütz, "Die Andechs-Meranier in Franken," 31.

177. For Beatrice's father, the Staufen count-palatine Otto of Burgundy, see chapter 5. Since Emperor Frederick II was Beatrice's cousin, this marriage also created a kinship bond between Duke Otto I and this future ruler. In 1208, however, Frederick II was only thirteen years of age and had yet to travel to the German kingdom from Sicily.

178. For this lordship, see Allemand-Gay, *Le pouvoir des comtes de Bourgogne*, 49–54.

179. Mariotte, *Le comté de Bourgogne*, 73–85.

peace between the pair in October of 1211.[180] During subsequent years, the two continued to pursue competing interests in Burgundy that led to occasional disputes.[181]

Lacking strong political networks and mired in a conflict with a rival claimant, Duke Otto I of Merania devised a new plan for his Burgundian lordship once he and his wife, Beatrice, began to have children. In 1222, he agreed to marry one of his daughters to Stephen's grandson, the son of Count John of Chalon, within ten years.[182] Four years later, in 1226, he made an agreement with Count Theobald IV of Champagne to marry his only son and heir, Otto II, to Theobald's daughter once the boy reached the age of fourteen.[183] The delayed dates for both of these marriages indicate that the duke of Merania was moving very quickly after the births of his daughter and son to use them to strengthen his position in Burgundy. Determined to create an effective familial network in the region, he found spouses for these children long before they were the canonical age for marriage. Although his daughter Alice eventually wed Stephen's grandson, this union failed to put an end to the conflict between Duke Otto I and the family of the count of Auxonne.[184] Meanwhile, the planned marriage for the young Otto II never took place. Thus, for the Andechs brothers Henry and Otto, affinal bonds never formed the basis for strong and enduring kin relationships—or for new, politically efficacious family bonds. In this respect, the affinal relationships of these two Andechs brothers conform to the more general pattern seen here. Most distant relatives played lesser roles in these lords' lives than their siblings played.

Admittedly, this has been only a brief survey of some of the four Andechs brothers' extended kin relationships, and the kinship groups surrounding other lineages would unquestionably offer different perspectives. Nevertheless, this case study is valuable precisely because of the diversity it reveals. Throughout this book, I have argued that generational change and

---

180. *Trente-sept documents Bourguignons,* 498–501, no. 11.

181. Allemand-Gay, *Le pouvoir des comtes de Bourgogne,* 142–143. The most serious conflict between the pair dates from the mid-1220s: *Cartulaire des comtes de Bourgogne,* 13–14, no. 13.

182. The marriage contract is summarized in Chifflet, *Lettre touchant Beatrix,* 74, no. 35. The original charter is catalogued as Besançon, Archives Departementales du Doubs, Trésor des Chartes B 400, but it is missing.

183. Otto's charter is *Layettes du Trésor des Chartes,* 2:64–66, no. 1738. Theobald's charter is Besançon, Archives Departementales du Doubs, Trésor des Chartes B 21 and is edited in *Cartulaire des comtes de Bourgogne,* 10–12, no. 11.

184. Allemand-Gay, *Le pouvoir des comtes de Bourgogne,* 144–145; *Cartulaire des comtes de Bourgogne,* 20–21, no. 18.

geography were two crucial factors shaping sibling interactions. Relationships between brothers and sisters varied from generation to generation and lineage to lineage as a result of the differing sizes of sibling groups and the distances separating brothers and sisters. However, the effect of these factors on family dynamics becomes even more pronounced when the focus shifts from siblings to wider kinship groups. Generalizing about the types of bonds that developed between extended kin is impossible, because different family members experienced these bonds in such dramatically different ways. Aunts and uncles, nieces and nephews, cousins and in-laws could all play important roles in German nobles' lives as each one built around himself his own network of close relatives and extended kin. Still, no other set of relatives within the extended kin group was as consistent a feature of princely politics and lordship as the sibling group. The relationships between brothers and sisters thus emerge from the sources as distinctive within this society.

The last surviving document to suggest a close connection between any of the eight Andechs brothers and sisters analyzed here dates from 1247. Ten years after Bishop Ekbert of Bamberg's death, Abbess Mechthild of Kitzingen made a donation so that candles would be kept burning at his tomb.[185] It is a fitting final glimpse at the relationships shaping this generation, for Ekbert had been at the center of many of the sibling groups that had formed in earlier years. He was, moreover, the only member of this generation to have maintained ties with three of his four sisters. The bishop's career thus provides a wide array of evidence for the ways in which the sibling bond could shape a magnate's political and territorial strategies. In addition, Ekbert's own donations for his sister Gertrude's soul—as well as Mechthild's donation for his—suggest that there may have been an emotional dimension to his sibling relationships, one that is only occasionally visible in the extant sources. Despite these hints of emotional attachment, however, the loving scene depicted in the Schlackenwerther Codex is a deceptive image of the lineage. At no time were all those family members gathered together as adults in a grand display of Andechs power and influence.

Nevertheless, from Bamberg to Budapest and from Friesach to Ravenna, different sets of Andechs brothers and sisters collaborated with one another throughout the early decades of the thirteenth century. The political efficacy of their sibling relationships is manifest in a broad range of sources that show the members of this generation working together to promote and protect

---

185. Bamberg, Staatsarchiv, Bamberger Urkunden no. 645.

each other's interests. There is no one moment that captures the complex dynamics operating within this generation. Instead, the strength of these relationships can be appreciated only by reconstructing the entire arc of these siblings' lives together from birth to death. Viewed from this perspective, the bonds between brothers and sisters appear to have been uniquely suited to maintaining and expanding the Andechs lineage's position in the German kingdom—and in central Europe more widely. Indeed, at a time when other German princely lineages were decreasing in size, it is striking that the lineage led by eight siblings was the one to experience the most dramatic rise into the uppermost reaches of the pan-European aristocracy.[186] As will become clear in the next chapter, even in the wake of King Philip of Swabia's assassination in 1208, none of the other lineages under investigation here was able to exert such far-reaching influence within the empire or beyond its borders.

---

186. See also Schneidmüller, "Die Andechs-Meranier."

❦ CHAPTER 7

The Uncertain Future of Lineages
Siblings during the Reign of Frederick II

King Philip of Swabia's assassination in 1208 ended the generation of Emperor Frederick I Barbarossa's children. At the time of Barbarossa's death in 1190, his five adult sons had been well positioned to play prominent roles in imperial politics; eighteen years later, however, all of them were dead. Only a single male heir survived in the next generation: Emperor Henry VI's son, Frederick II, the future emperor, who was a boy of thirteen living in Sicily. Meanwhile, the Welf claimant to the German throne, Otto of Brunswick, saw the wheel of fortune turn briefly in his favor. On the brink of defeat in early 1208, he soon had his kingship recognized by Philip's former supporters. His older brother, Count-Palatine Henry of the Rhine, with whom he had quarreled, returned to his side. And in October of 1209, Pope Innocent III even crowned him emperor in Rome.[1] However, Otto did not maintain his dominant position in the German kingdom and the empire for very long. Because of his attempts to press imperial claims in Italy, he quickly lost the support of Pope Innocent III and many of the *principes imperii*.[2] As a result, as early as 1211, a faction of secular and ecclesiastical princes began plotting the royal election of Frederick II.[3]

---

1. Hucker, *Kaiser Otto IV*, 110–116.
2. Schneidmüller, *Die Welfen*, 255–260.
3. Stürner, *Friedrich II. Teil 1*, 130–131.

One year later, Frederick traveled from Sicily to the German kingdom, where on December 9, 1212, he was crowned king at Mainz.

Between 1212 and 1215, members of the Andechs, Babenberg, Ludowing, Wettin, Wittelsbach, and Zähringen lineages all witnessed royal charters while attending Frederick II's court. However, the only sibling group active within any of these lineages during this period was the four Andechs brothers.[4] Other lineages had only single lords involved in imperial politics in this period. At Speyer in December of 1212, for example, the witnesses to one royal charter included Duke Berthold V of Zähringen, an only son; Duke Ludwig I of Bavaria, also an only son; and Landgrave Herman of Thuringia, whose three brothers were already dead.[5] Two months later on February 14, 1213, Duke Leopold VI of Austria was present at Frederick II's court; his only brother had died a decade and a half earlier in 1198.[6] Similarly, when Margrave Dietrich of Meissen and Lower Lusatia witnessed one of Frederick's charters for the first time in June of 1214, he was the only surviving male of his generation.[7] If King Frederick II—an only child—is included in this list, then six of the seven foremost lineages with ties to the Staufen royal court in this period were led by lords who had no brothers during the mid-1210s.

Significantly, none of these magnates had sons who were old enough to appear in witness lists alongside them in these years. As a result, with the exception of Duke Otto I of Merania and Bishop Ekbert of Bamberg, the *principes imperii* attending Frederick II's court in the opening years of his reign were not enmeshed in political networks based on close family relationships. The contrast between the beginning of Frederick II's kingship and the beginning of his grandfather Frederick Barbarossa's reign sixty years earlier is therefore striking. Whereas Frederick I was surrounded by a series of strong father-son and sibling groups operating inside the upper aristocracy during the 1150s, Frederick II and his court knew only one comparable family bloc in the early years, that of the Andechses. Under Barbarossa, the 1160s and 1170s saw the political role of fraternal relationships expand as the Andechs, Ascanian, Babenberg, Ludowing, Wettin, Wittelsbach, and Zähringen lineages all had generations with multiple brothers rise to prominence. The later decades of Frederick II's reign, on the other hand, were not character-

---

4. Otto and Ekbert first appeared together at Frederick's court on July 29, 1215: MGH DD F II, 2:290–292, no. 316.

5. Ibid., 2:22–24, no. 181.

6. Ibid., 2:36–38, no. 187.

7. Ibid., 2:129–131, no. 230.

ized by a significant increase in the number of sibling groups active within the upper aristocracy.

Instead, throughout Frederick II's time as king and emperor, most princely lineages experienced a decrease in size—and, in several cases, extinction in the male line. When Duke Berthold V of Zähringen died in 1218, his only son was already dead. The line of the dukes of Zähringen thus came to an abrupt end. This is the first of the nine lineages investigated here to exit the stage of German history, but it would not be the last to do so during the first half of the thirteenth century. At the time of Duke Leopold VI of Austria's death in 1230, he had only one surviving son, Duke Frederick II of Austria, whose childless death in 1246 ended the Babenberg lineage. The last surviving male of the Ludowing lineage of the landgraves of Thuringia died in 1247. And Duke Otto II of Merania, the last secular prince in the Andechs lineage, died childless in 1248. Only the Ascanians, Welfs, Wettins, and Wittelsbachs would still be prominent lineages in the upper aristocracy in the year 1300.

Even in the princely lineages that did survive the Staufen period, the early decades of the thirteenth century were a period of contraction. The three Welf brothers—Count-Palatine Henry of the Rhine, Emperor Otto IV, and Duke William of Lüneburg—were survived by only a single male heir: William's son, Otto, known as Otto the Child, who was (ironically) the only adult male of the Welf lineage after Count-Palatine Henry died in 1227. Duke Ludwig I of Bavaria (d. 1231), the only son of Duke Otto I of Bavaria, had only one child of his own: Duke Otto II (d. 1253). As a result, throughout the first half of the thirteenth century, a father and a son—neither of whom had any brothers—led the Wittelsbachs. In the Wettin lineage, meanwhile, three of the five branches that had originated with the sons of Margrave Conrad of Wettin (d. 1157) were extinct in the male line by 1220. When Emperor Frederick II crossed the Alps in 1235 to enter the German kingdom for the first time in fifteen years, Margrave Henry of Meissen and Lower Lusatia (d. 1288) and his second cousin Count Dietrich I of Brehna (d. 1266/1267) were the only adult male lords in the lineage. The Ascanians did have three fraternal groups active in three different branches of the lineage during the 1220s and 1230s, but none included more than two brothers. The days of Albert the Bear working together with his seven adult sons along the frontiers of Saxony were long since past.[8]

Contemporaries were well aware of the changes taking place inside the German aristocracy in the first half of the thirteenth century. A midcentury

---

8. See chapters 3 and 4.

scribe at the monastery of Niederalteich provided a list of more than three dozen Bavarian lords whose rights and properties had passed to the Wittelsbach dukes of Bavaria during the early 1200s, because these lords had died without heirs.[9] This was clearly a period of lineage extinction and decline on a much larger scale than just the nine lineages examined here.[10] Indeed, the aristocracy of the later Staufen period seems to have been entering a transitional phase comparable to the one that reshaped the aristocracy a century earlier during the Investiture Controversy.[11] In the decades around 1250, as some leading lineages faded from the political scene, others took advantage of the power vacuum by seizing their princely lordships and rising higher within the ranks of the upper aristocracy.[12]

Although there were significantly fewer siblings active within the princely elite in Frederick II's reign than in earlier years, the groups of brothers and sisters that do appear in the sources from this period reinforce key themes in this book. As we saw in the previous chapter, the Andechs sibling group of these years offers some of the best evidence we have for the political efficacy of sibling solidarity. In other lineages, the sibling relationships that developed in the first half of the thirteenth century further nuance our understanding of how brothers and sisters could impact one another's territorial and political interests. The changing character of secular lordship and imperial politics during Frederick II's reign forced siblings to interact with each other under new conditions. Nevertheless, collaboration and cooperation remained the foundation for most sibling relationships. Conflict, when it did erupt, was the product of uncertain succession and inheritance scenarios, much like in previous generations. Meanwhile, at the imperial court, the absence of large, influential sibling groups led Emperor Frederick II to rely on other types of relationships to exert his authority and to build consensus among the *principes imperii*.

A New Succession Strategy: Joint Lordship

By the closing decades of the Staufen period, some princely lineages had experienced multiple generations in which secular lords had failed to acquire new lordships for younger sons. In many cases, small inheritances—at least by the standards of the upper aristocracy—had been passed down from

---

9. *Genealogia Ottonis II.*, 377–378.
10. Freed, *Counts of Falkenstein*, 63–67.
11. See chapter 1.
12. For more on this point, see below.

father to son to grandson without the family accumulating any new rights and properties to augment the patrimony. As a result, branches of some of these lineages reached a point in the thirteenth century when the inheritance was simply insufficient to divide reasonably, even if a lord had only two sons who needed to be allocated shares. In a few cases, magnates responded to this situation by employing a form of succession that had not been used during any of the earlier generations of these nine upper aristocratic lineages: joint lordship, whereby two brothers acted as co-lords and shared all power and authority. More than any other inheritance and succession strategy in use within the German kingdom, joint lordship depended on the strength and durability of fraternal relationships to function effectively.

The practice of having two or more brothers share control of the patrimony was not unique to the German kingdom of the thirteenth century.[13] Moreover, joint lordship was widely dispersed geographically in medieval Europe. Georges Duby found evidence of this form of succession in some eleventh-century sources from the Mâconnais region of France, and Theodore Evergates identifies it as a commonplace practice in the county of Champagne during the central Middle Ages.[14] Despite this evidence for the existence of joint lordships across different periods and regions, little research has been conducted into the question of how it shaped the relationships between brothers who were co-lords.[15] Fortunately, examples from the upper aristocracy of the Staufen period provide an opportunity to analyze this issue in detail.

One of the earliest instances of joint lordship in the lineages investigated here appears within a branch of the Wettins. For almost fifteen years following the death of their father in 1221, the brothers Otto II and Dietrich I exercised joint lordship over the county of Brehna. As the great-grandsons of Conrad of Wettin, these siblings were the descendants of an illustrious magnate from the early years of the Staufen period—yet the sources suggest they themselves exerted minimal influence inside the German kingdom. Because their father and grandfather had both failed to acquire any new lordships

---

13. Leyser, "German Aristocracy," 38; Rödel, "Die Burg als Gemeinschaft," 109. An interesting case from the early twelfth century is that of the two brothers Gottfried and Otto, who were counts of Cappenberg before they both joined a community of Premonstratensians: Arnold, *Power and Property*, 163.

14. Duby, "Lineage, Nobility and Knighthood," 69–74; Evergates, *Aristocracy in the County of Champagne*, 120–121. See also Barthélemy, *La société dans le comté de Vendôme*, 528–530; for another region of Europe, see Fügedi, *Elefánthy*, 26.

15. Spieß (*Familie und Verwandtschaft*, 203–204) also observes that there has been very little research conducted on the topic of joint lordship.

FIGURE 8. The joint seal of Counts Otto II and Dietrich I of Brehna on a charter from the year 1226. Brandenburgisches Landeshauptarchiv (BLHA), Potsdam, Rep. 10B Dobrilugk U 9. Courtesy of Brandenburgisches Landeshauptarchiv.

through marriage, *Königsnähe*, or some other means, the two brothers had only one small comital lordship to which they could succeed.[16]

Two extant charters confirming monastic grants, one from 1226 and the other from 1231, provide glimpses into the arrangement between Otto and Dietrich. Although the bodies of the texts provide few interesting details about the brothers, the inscriptions are significant; one reads "Otto and Dietrich, by the grace of God counts of Brehna" (*Otto et Theodericus dei gratia comites de Bren*), while the other is identical except for reversing the order of their names.[17] These two inscriptions may therefore suggest equal standing between the Brehna brothers. Moreover, these comital brothers shared a single seal with an inscription that reads "Seal of Otto and Dietrich counts of Brehna." Strikingly, this seal employs one of the Wettin lineage's traditional sigillographic images; it shows only a single knight holding a shield in one hand and a banner in the other (figure 8).[18] This is an extraordinary piece of evidence for how strongly linked brothers could be in their joint lordship.[19] Indeed, since this is the only seal Otto and Dietrich are known to have used while they were both alive, it suggests that the two brothers wanted themselves to be represented as inseparable co-lords of their county.

Unfortunately, the few surviving sources for these Brehna siblings do not offer sufficient evidence to analyze their interactions in more detail. However, the margraves John I (d. 1266) and Otto III (d. 1267) of Brandenburg provide a better-documented case of brothers exercising joint lordship. Great-grandsons of Albert the Bear, these brothers shared control of their

---

16. For the county of Brehna, see Pätzold, *Die frühen Wettiner*, 127–128. Under the year 1223, the *Chronicon Montis Sereni* (208) identifies only Otto, without Dietrich, as the advocate for the monastery on the Lauterberg. This may suggest the brothers divided some of their rights, but it seems more likely—given the early date—that Dietrich was still a minor.

17. CDS 1 A, 3:264–265, no. 375 and 3:315, no. 452. Interestingly, in two other charters that survive only as later copies they are "*Otto dei gracia et Theodericus frater eius comites de Brenen.*" See CDS 1 A, 3:232, no. 326 and 3:293, no. 417. For the unusualness of this switching of the order of names in charter inscriptions, compare the case of the Ludowings Henry IV Raspe and Conrad below.

18. Potsdam, Brandenburgisches Landeshauptarchiv, Rep. 10B Zisterzienserkloster Dobrilugk U9. See also Posse, *Die Siegel der Wettiner*, vol. 1, table X.

19. Other examples of joint seals from the early thirteenth century include those of Counts Dietrich and Henry of Honstein (Wolfenbüttel, Niedersächsisches Landesarchiv, Staatsarchiv, StA WO 25 Urk 67) and Counts Ulrich and Eberhard of Württemberg (Stuttgart, Landesarchiv Baden-Württemberg, Hauptstaatsarchiv, B 457 U 586). However, neither of these seals includes the figure of a person. Dukes John and Albert of Saxony also used a joint seal on a 1261 charter, but their seal has two standing knights with a shield between them rather than a single knight: Dresden, Sächsisches Staatsarchiv, Hauptstaatsarchiv, 10001, Ältere Urkunden, no. 609. For joint seals more generally, see Ewald, *Siegelkunde*, 104–105.

march for more than a quarter century.[20] When their father died in 1220, both were young children. By 1225, John had reached the age of major- ity, and from then on, both brothers ceased to be under the authority of a guardian.[21] Still, Otto's precise position vis-à-vis his older brother during the late 1220s is difficult to know. While the inscription of one of their charters from September 27, 1228, identifies the siblings as "John and Otto, by the grace of God margraves of Brandenburg" (*Johannes et Otto dei gratia mar- chiones Brandenburgenses*), another of their charters from seven months later describes the two as "John, by the grace of God margrave of Brandenburg, and his brother Otto" (*Johannes dei gratia marchio Brandenburgensis et Otto frater eius*).[22] Otto's lack of a title in the latter document, as well as in other charters from this period, suggests he was not yet acting as a formal co-lord alongside his older brother. Nevertheless, the two were consistently listed together in sources from the late 1220s, with Otto playing a role in these documents that was largely indistinguishable from that of John.[23]

Even after they were knighted together on May 11, 1231, Otto's position in the lineage apparently remained somewhat undefined.[24] In December of 1231, Emperor Frederick II drew up a charter concerning the brothers' claims to the march; according to the document,

> our dear prince John, margrave of Brandenburg, begged our imperial dig- nity that we deign, out of the grace of our highness, to concede and confirm the march of Brandenburg—with every honor and all its appurtenances, along with the other imperial fiefs that his father, Albert, the former mar- grave of Brandenburg, held from our hand . . . —together with the duchy of Pomerania to the same John and to his brother, Otto, if John should happen to die first, and to the heirs of each of them. Moreover, consider- ing the devotion and faith of the aforesaid former margrave, their father, Albert, . . . how he devotedly served us and the empire as long as he lived, we hope to receive even more loving service from the same brothers John and Otto, who are, as it were, the successors to his paternal faithfulness.[25]

The language of this imperial charter is decidedly vague about Otto's role. While it clearly states that Otto would receive the march only if his brother died,

---

20. The relationship between the brothers changed in 1258, as I will discuss below.

21. *Chronica principum Saxoniae*, 478.

22. *Codex diplomaticus Brandenburgensis*, 1, vol. 16:399, no. 9 and 1, vol. 5:33–34, no. 27.

23. *Regesten der Markgrafen von Brandenburg*, 2:126–130, nos. 586–598.

24. For their knighting, see *Chronica principum Saxoniae*, 478.

25. *Historia diplomatica Friderici Secundi*, 4, pt. 1:270–271. For this charter, see also Goez, *Der Leihezwang*, 99–100.

it also indicates that the emperor expected Otto to serve him faithfully in the same manner as his older brother—and their father. Thus, while Frederick II did not grant Otto equal legal standing with John, the emperor did recognize a potentially influential political position for him alongside his older brother.

Regardless of the imperial court's perspective, Otto was unquestionably acting as co-margrave inside the march of Brandenburg by the mid-1230s. Prior to 1233, John had been the only one to seal the brothers' charters. But in that year, there is a reference to both brothers sealing a document, and an extant charter dated July 13, 1235, still has their two seals attached.[26] Although they did not use a joint seal like the Brehna brothers, they were clearly exercising joint lordship. From the mid-1230s onward, John and Otto are consistently named in the sources as *marchiones Brandenburgensis*—with no apparent distinction in their status. Besides Otto acquiring a seal and using the title *marchio* more regularly, however, little else seems to have changed in the siblings' relationship in the years after 1233. The two had already been collaborating regularly since they were young men, and this pattern persisted. Between 1225 and 1250, John and Otto are listed together in sources from the march of Brandenburg on more than thirty-five occasions—as compared to only three times when one appears without the other inside the borders of the lordship.[27] During that same quarter century, there are only five calendar years during which no source places them together. Occasionally, one would travel without the other to Emperor Frederick II's court or to the court of his son King Henry (VII), but such trips were infrequent. Neither brother seems to have been interested in cultivating *Königsnähe*.[28] Since both John and Otto were married by the mid-1230s, the most common reason for their occasional separations from one another seems to have been their having to attend to their wives' territorial holdings.[29] On the whole, however, these periods of separation were rare in the decades before 1250.

---

26. *Regesten der Markgrafen von Brandenburg,* 2:134, no. 612 and 2:138, no. 629. The 1235 charter is Magdeburg, Landeshauptarchiv Sachsen-Anhalt, Rep. U21b Kloster Neuendorf no. 4. I have been unable to locate any charters on which John's and Otto's seals are sufficiently well preserved to enable any kind of close analysis. The best I have found is Magdeburg, Landeshauptarchiv Sachsen-Anhalt, Rep. U21 IV Domstift Stendal no. 36. On this charter, each seal has the image of a standing knight with an eagle visible on both the shield and the banner that each knight is holding. Unfortunately, almost none of the lettering is visible on either seal.

27. Fey, *Reise und Herrschaft*, 55. What is striking is that the brothers seem to have held virtually no property separately. This may be the result of the aforementioned 1196 charter, in which their father and uncle converted all their alodial lands and rights into fiefs held from the archbishops of Magdeburg (see chapter 5).

28. For more on this point, see below.

29. See, for example, *Regesten der Markgrafen von Brandenburg*, 2:139–140, no. 634.

While the charter evidence demonstrates that these brothers had close contacts with one another, the narrative sources from the region depict most vividly how their joint lordship functioned in practice. Throughout their careers, John and Otto became embroiled in conflicts with their neighbors. Otto was even briefly imprisoned by the bishop of Halberstadt in the late 1230s, and after his release, the situation remained tense. Within a short time, the margraves were once more at war with the bishop and their other rivals. The *Gesta archiepiscoporum Magdeburgensium* describes subsequent events:

> In the year of the Lord 1240, the margraves of Brandenburg were lacking any outside support and were resisting [the margrave of] Meissen around Köpenick and Mittenwalde with the men of their own land. At that time, Archbishop [Willibrand of Magdeburg] allied with Bishop [Meinhard] of Halberstadt and invaded the march of Brandenburg with a strong army, encamping beyond the Biese River. Margrave John, recognizing what was happening, left his brother behind to confront [the margrave of] Meissen and traveled quickly, riding day and night with the few men he had been able to take. Having collected a band of people armed with clubs and bows, and with only a few knights, he began the battle. With the Lord bestowing victory [on him], some were drowned in the Biese, others were killed, and still others led into captivity. Among them, the bishop of Halberstadt was captured, and the archbishop, wounded, barely escaped to the castle of Calbe. . . . [Later,] the archbishop, with the margrave of Meissen giving the aid of his own forces, collected an army and burned the village of Wolmirstedt. Proceeding from there, when he realized that the margrave [of Meissen] had fallen ill and was staying in his own land, lest it seem that he was doing nothing, he constructed the castle of Rogätz and from there made the whole moorland into a desert. And not content with these things, while Margrave John was occupied with unremitting attacks against [the margrave of] Meissen in Neumark, he [the archbishop] sent his ministerials with a strong army against the Havelland. These men, crossing a bridge at Plaue, devastated the land by fire and plundering. Because of this, Margrave Otto rushed against them with the few men he had been able to take. He attacked them, fought them, and turned them to flight, capturing many.[30]

---

30. *Gesta archiepiscoporum Magdeburgensium*, 422. See also Schultze, *Die Mark Brandenburg*, 1:145–147, for the dates of these events.

The brothers appear here as allies working together with impressive efficiency to fend off attacks on their march from two different directions. Their common cause in defense of their lands is thus a powerful example of some of the potential advantages of joint lordship. Because they were both margraves of Brandenburg, both were heavily invested in the preservation of their rights and properties within the lordship. Indeed, their fraternal bond proved to be significantly more effective as the basis for military cooperation than the bonds of friendship and alliance connecting their rivals. The late thirteenth-century *Chronicle of the Princes of Saxony*, in its description of the brothers, therefore offers an appropriate summary of their careers: "After they had reached the age of majority, with one deferring to the other, they lived together harmoniously as was fitting for brothers (*concorditer ut fratres decuit convixerunt*); and on account of this harmony, they trampled their enemies underfoot, exalted their friends, increased their lands and revenues, and expanded their fame, glory, and power."[31]

Joint lordship never became a common form of succession within the upper aristocracy of the German kingdom. In some parts of the realm, noblemen consciously avoided the practice.[32] Nevertheless, the few cases of joint lordship that date to the later Staufen period highlight the essential role played by the sibling bond in princely lineages' succession plans. That multiple sons should succeed to their father's patrimony was such a well-established principle within these lineages that the sharing of a single lordship by two brothers was deemed to be a reasonable option by some princes. This form of succession could be effective, because the promotion of internal stability was so critical to the success of aristocratic lineages throughout the twelfth and thirteenth centuries. German lords clearly understood that fraternal disputes, perhaps more than any other type of dispute, had the potential to destroy lordships and to invite external threats to the patrimony. As a result, regardless of whether these brothers enjoyed each other's company, many of them willingly worked together as co-lords to safeguard their standing within the upper aristocracy.

Siblings' Responses to Unstable Succession Arrangements: Two Cases from the Ludowing Lineage

The emergence of joint lordship as a viable form of succession highlights the adaptability of sibling relationships during the later Staufen period.

---

31. *Chronica principum Saxoniae*, 478.

32. In Austria, for example, King Rudolf I of Habsburg was forced to alter his own succession plans in 1283 after the local nobility refused to support his efforts to introduce joint lordship into their duchy. See MGH Const., 3:328–330, no. 344.

Throughout the century since most of the lineages under investigation here had been founded, three or four generations had successfully utilized the custom of partible inheritance to provide multiple siblings with independent lordships and a voice in imperial politics. By the early 1200s, this custom had led to extraordinary variation in the nature of the rights and properties held by members of these nine lineages. As a result, it becomes increasingly difficult to generalize about succession and inheritance practices over the course of Emperor Frederick II's reign. Nevertheless, sibling relationships remained a central component of most patrimonial plans—even when lords chose not to employ a strategy as extreme as joint lordship. During the thirteenth century, siblings repeatedly found themselves having to adapt to new succession circumstances and new political conditions that had few if any parallels in earlier generations of their lineages.

The extant sources for two pairs of siblings from the Ludowing lineage provide especially vivid evidence for the types of intragenerational relationships that could develop in this period of unstable and fluctuating family situations. In particular, this rich source material illuminates two issues for which it is difficult to find detailed information during the Staufen period: brother-sister conflict and unanticipated fraternal succession. The central figure for both these sets of sibling relationships was Landgrave Ludwig IV of Thuringia, the husband of Saint Elizabeth of Thuringia.[33] When Ludwig's father, Landgrave Herman of Thuringia, died in 1217, he was the eldest surviving male heir. During his earliest years as landgrave, Ludwig IV and his half sister Judith clashed violently as a result of the uncertain succession in the wake of her husband's death. Later, Ludwig departed on crusade, never to return to the German kingdom. When he died in 1227, he left behind a minor son and two younger brothers, whose relationship in the late 1220s and early 1230s was largely defined by the uncertain succession created by Ludwig IV's death.

Judith, Landgrave Herman's daughter by his first wife, married Margrave Dietrich of Meissen during the mid-1190s.[34] A quarter century later, in 1221, Dietrich died while their only surviving son was still a young child. The widowed Judith, in the immediate wake of her husband's death, began to work closely with her half brother Landgrave Ludwig IV of Thuringia, who was quite possibly a decade younger than she was.[35] The interactions

---

33. For Elizabeth, see chapter 6.
34. For the background to this marriage, see *Chronicon Montis Sereni*, 165–166, 177.
35. For Herman's two marriages, see Weller, *Die Heiratspolitik des deutschen Hochadels*, 610–615.

between these siblings are described most extensively in the *Cronica Rein-hardsbrunnensis*, a fourteenth-century text compiled on the basis of a series of lost, earlier historical sources from Thuringia.[36] Most of the account of Landgrave Ludwig IV's career—including everything concerning his relationship with his sister Judith—was written by one of his own chaplains.[37] Although Ludwig is therefore painted in a positive light throughout this section of the chronicle, several extant charters make it possible to construct a more nuanced view of his interactions with Judith.

Shortly before Margrave Dietrich of Meissen died on February 1, 1221, he designated his brother-in-law Ludwig IV as his son's guardian in the event of his death. As a result, soon after Dietrich died, the landgrave of Thuringia received a messenger informing him of the margrave's death. According to the *Cronica Reinhardsbrunnensis*, "When [Ludwig] heard this news, he was deeply saddened and set out quickly on his way in order to console his sister (*ad consolandum sororem suam*)."[38] Whether the landgrave was genuinely concerned for Judith after her husband died is impossible to know, but there are reasons to be skeptical. The chronicler explains that Ludwig, on arriving in the march of Meissen, secured from the nobles and ministerials a promise to choose him as the next margrave if his young nephew should die without heirs.[39] For the landgrave, therefore, Dietrich's death was an opportunity to expand his own influence and the reach of his lordship.[40] The speed and efficiency with which Ludwig entrenched himself in the march of Meissen in this period is evident in a charter drawn up only six weeks after Dietrich died. In it, "Judith by the grace of God margravine of Meissen and Lower Lusatia, her son, Henry, by the grace of God margrave of Meissen and Lower Lusatia, and Ludwig landgrave of Thuringia and count-palatine of Saxony" made a joint donation for the salvation of Dietrich's soul. The document, which survives in two copies, is noteworthy, because both Judith and Ludwig affixed their seals to it.[41] This is the earliest case I have found, among the nine lineages examined here, of a lay sister's and brother's seals hanging from the same charter (figure 9).

---

36. *Cronica Reinhardsbrunnensis*, 596–600.

37. Tebruck, *Die Reinhardsbrunner Geschichtsschreibung*, 16–19.

38. *Cronica Reinhardsbrunnensis*, 596.

39. Ibid., 597.

40. Patze, *Die Entstehung der Landesherrschaft*, 1:263–264.

41. Dresden, Sächsisches Staatsarchiv, Hauptstaatsarchiv, 10001, Ältere Urkunden, no. 236 (printed edition: CDS 1 A, 3:210–211, no. 289). For women's seals more generally, see Bedos-Rezak, "Women, Seals and Power."

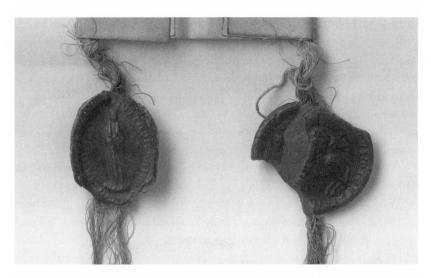

FIGURE 9.   The seals of Margravine Judith of Meissen (left) and her half brother Landgrave Ludwig IV of Thuringia (right) on a charter from the year 1221. Sächsisches Staatsarchiv, Hauptstaatsarchiv Dresden, 10001 Ältere Urkunden no. 236. Courtesy of Sächsisches Staatsarchiv.

The *Cronica Reinhardsbrunnensis* reports that Landgrave Ludwig's initial visit to Meissen ended with his leaving Judith and her son "in the good tranquillity of peace" while he turned his attention to affairs in his own lands. Thereafter, "the landgrave frequently entered the march of Meissen to visit and console his sister and her son."[42] Once again, however, the chronicler indicates that Ludwig was doing much more than just attending to Judith and Henry's needs on these trips. He soon took charge of administering justice within the march.[43] According to a letter that Emperor Frederick II probably wrote in March of 1222, Ludwig and Judith were also illicitly attempting during this period to usurp some of the bishop of Meissen's rights inside his own diocese.[44] The landgrave was thus playing an active role alongside his sister in protecting and expanding the siblings' power and authority in the march.

The relationship between Ludwig and Judith soon frayed, however, because of the landgrave's increasingly self-interested actions vis-à-vis Judith's young son. On one of his trips to the march of Meissen, he secured promises

---

42. *Cronica Reinhardsbrunnensis*, 597.
43. Ibid.
44. CDS 2, 1:89–90, no. 96.

from several churches that they would enfeoff him with his nephew's fiefs if the boy died without heirs.[45] Ludwig was slowly gaining more and more control in the region, and by mid-1222, Judith was no longer a significant figure within her son's lordships. When the landgrave and his nephew held court at Delitzsch in Lower Lusatia on June 6 of that year, his half sister was not even present.[46] There was little she could do to challenge Ludwig's growing influence, however, because he had brought a large military contingent with him on this occasion. As the *Cronica Reinhardsbrunnensis* then explains, "And so, from that day forward, hatred (*odium*) arose between them, such that his sister strove to limit his right of guardianship [over her son]."[47]

The conflict between the two siblings intensified the subsequent year when Judith quickly and unexpectedly arranged a marriage with a Franconian nobleman, Count Poppo VII of Henneberg.[48] Although no source offers an explicit motive for Judith's decision to remarry, she may well have been seeking to create a new alliance in order to offset Ludwig's position in her son's lands. This move proved ineffective, however, for the landgrave soon invaded the march of Meissen with a large army. Throughout the spring of 1223, he systematically captured the main strongholds in the region and even celebrated Easter in the key town of Dresden.[49] Peace between the siblings was established only the next year, when Duke Otto I of Merania intervened in the dispute.[50] A charter drawn up in Judith's name on February 20, 1226, provides the only evidence to suggest that the two were once more cooperating with one another during this period. According to the text, Judith's son, Henry, made a property donation to a monastery "by the counsel of our dear brother (*dilecti fratris nostri*) Landgrave Ludwig of Thuringia."[51] Soon thereafter, Ludwig departed on crusade, never to return.

The relationship between Judith and her half brother provides some of the richest surviving evidence from the Staufen period for a noblewoman's sibling interactions. Although the version of events in the *Cronica Reinhardsbrunnensis* was originally written at the court of Landgrave Ludwig, it is nowhere contradicted by extant charters, suggesting that the chronicle provides a reasonable perspective on the pair's relationship. Two points, in particular,

---

45. *Cronica Reinhardsbrunnensis*, 597.
46. CDS 2, 1:88–89, no. 95.
47. *Cronica Reinhardsbrunnensis*, 598. See also Elpers, "*Während sie die Markgrafschaft leitete*," 165–166.
48. For Poppo, see chapter 6, and Wagner, "Entwurf einer Genealogie," 60–61.
49. *Cronica Reinhardsbrunnensis*, 598–599.
50. Ibid., 600. See chapter 6.
51. CDS 1 A, 3:249, no. 351.

are worth emphasizing about their interactions with one another. First, Judith and Ludwig's relationship conforms to a broader trend I have noted in earlier chapters.[52] Their interactions were made possible by the fact that Judith married a lord from a neighboring lordship rather than being sent by her father to marry a nobleman in a distant corner of the German kingdom—or beyond. The march of Meissen's close proximity was central to Landgrave Ludwig's ability to maintain a strong interest in his sister and nephew's affairs while simultaneously exercising effective lordship in Thuringia. As with so many other noblewomen, Judith's contacts with her sibling were thus shaped by the geographical scope of her father's marriage plans for his children.

Second, these two half siblings found themselves in a situation that would have been unimaginable for two brothers and was, moreover, decidedly uncommon for brother-sister pairs as well. Ludwig became involved in affairs in Meissen and Lower Lusatia only because Judith's husband, Margrave Dietrich, was unwilling to permit Judith to raise their young son without a male lord's support. A maternal uncle was not the only family member who could act as guardian for a young heir, however, and various other close relatives often fulfilled this role within noble families during the Staufen period.[53] A brother becoming involved in the guardianship of his sister's child was therefore unusual within the lineages investigated here. Initially, Dietrich's decision to designate Ludwig IV as his heir's guardian seemed to be a good one, for Ludwig and Judith cooperated effectively with one another in 1221 and early 1222. But as the landgrave's ambitions grew, Judith was forced to choose between protecting her young son's interests and assisting her half brother in his efforts to expand his own lordship. Thus, much like the disputes between secular brothers analyzed in earlier chapters, conflict erupted in this case because of the shifting nature of the relationship between this brother and sister once succession and inheritance plans changed unexpectedly. Judith's widowhood and young son altered the sibling dynamic in this generation in ways that neither Judith nor Ludwig could have anticipated, helping to trigger the dispute between them.

Only on very rare occasions do the surviving sources show women, in their roles as sisters, shaping political and territorial interests alongside the other members of their generation as dramatically as Judith. Moreover, it is

---

52. See especially chapters 2 and 6.

53. Duke Ludwig I of Bavaria's paternal uncles acted as his guardians in the mid-1180s (see chapter 4), and a paternal first cousin was guardian for the young Margraves John I and Otto III of Brandenburg.

difficult to argue that most noblewomen belonged to sibling *groups* during the Staufen period. While they frequently developed a close relationship with *one* of their siblings, they tended not to interact with multiple members of their generation—as was so often the case with their brothers. Judith is a case in point. After Landgrave Ludwig IV of Thuringia died on crusade in 1227, his two younger brothers became the most prominent male members of the Ludowing lineage. Judith did not develop close relationships with either of these siblings, however. Instead, it was the interactions between the two brothers that would define the next decade of the lineage's history.

Prior to Ludwig's death in 1227, his wife, Elizabeth, had provided her husband with a son and heir.[54] However, this boy was only five years of age when his father died. As a result, during the late 1220s, Ludwig's younger sibling Henry IV Raspe (d. 1247), who was approximately twenty-five years old at the time of his brother's death, began to exercise authority over the lineage's lordships. Another brother, Conrad (d. 1240), also became increasingly involved in regional and imperial affairs during the same period.[55] Indeed, Ludwig's death had a profound effect on both Henry Raspe and Conrad, because their older sibling had been in possession of all the lineage's lordships. During the late 1210s and early 1220s, Ludwig had employed the title "land-grave of Thuringia and count-palatine of Saxony" while also controlling the lineage's lands and rights in Hesse to the west of Thuringia.[56] This consolidation of power in the hands of the oldest surviving son was, of course, unusual given the German aristocracy's tradition of partible inheritance. In earlier generations of the Ludowing lineage, younger brothers had routinely played prominent roles alongside the eldest. Beginning with the children of Count Ludwig "the Leaper" of Thuringia (d. 1123), three consecutive generations of the Ludowings had included younger brothers named Henry Raspe who had possessed the lineage's rights and properties in Hesse. This succession strategy had not led to the emergence of separate branches within the lineage, however, because none of these Henry Raspes had married.[57]

---

54. *Cronica Reinhardsbrunnensis*, 597.

55. For a more detailed account of the Ludowing family in these years, see Werner, "Reichsfürst zwischen Mainz und Meißen."

56. See, for example, Gotha, Thüringisches Staatsarchiv, QQ I d 18, and the attached seal (printed edition: CDS 1 A, 3:218–219, no. 305).

57. For the Ludowing marriages, see Weller, *Die Heiratspolitik des deutschen Hochadels*, 576–626. In all three generations, the lordship in Hesse had reverted to the eldest son, who had outlived his younger brother in each instance. See Patze, *Die Entstehung der Landesherrschaft*, 1:507.

This pattern changed only when Herman—the father of Ludwig IV, Henry IV Raspe, and Conrad—acquired all the lineage's lordships during the 1180s and early 1190s.[58] After Herman's death in 1217, Ludwig IV succeeded to everything, perhaps because his two younger brothers were still minors at the time. Even as they grew older, however, Ludwig IV continued to maintain control of the entire patrimony, and neither Henry IV Raspe nor Conrad is identified with a noble title in any documents from the late 1210s and early 1220s.[59] Henry Raspe is first labeled *comes* in one of his older brother's charters issued in the year 1227, and the timing of his appearance with this title suggests that Landgrave Ludwig IV was permitting him to exercise lordship in Ludowing lands only because of his own impending departure on crusade.[60]

Sources from the period immediately after Ludwig's departure and subsequent death suggest that Henry IV Raspe was not content with being a mere placeholder. He is never identified in a contemporary document as guardian to his young nephew, Ludwig IV's son. Instead, he was clearly operating as landgrave and count-palatine in his own right, and everyone from Ludowing ministerials to the pope and emperor quickly recognized him as Ludwig's successor.[61] Moreover, Henry appears to have wed very soon after Ludwig's death. His own marriage, combined with his efforts to strip Ludwig IV's wife, Elizabeth, of the properties set aside to support her in her widowhood, indicate that he was anxious to eliminate any claims to the patrimony that his older brother's spouse and son possessed.[62] Henry IV Raspe's actions in the wake of Ludwig IV's death were not designed to consolidate power only in his own hands, however, for his younger brother, Conrad, also began to appear much more consistently in the surviving sources after 1227.

While it is impossible to determine what role Conrad was originally intended to play within this generation of the Ludowing lineage, there is no reason to think Ludwig IV planned to give him a significant portion of the patrimony.[63] Although partible inheritance was the norm for the German

58. See chapters 4 and 5.

59. See, for example, CDS 1 A, 3:188–189, no. 257 and 3:243–244, no. 344. See also Werner, "Reichsfürst zwischen Mainz und Meißen," 128–129.

60. CDS 1 A, 3:275–276, no. 393.

61. Werner, "Reichsfürst zwischen Mainz und Meißen," 141. The inscription of a charter dated May 16, 1228, reads, "Henry, by the grace of God landgrave of Thuringia and count-palatine of Saxony": CDS 1 A, 3:289–290, no. 412.

62. For more on this incident, see chapter 6.

63. Werner, "Reichsfürst zwischen Mainz und Meißen," 128–129.

aristocracy, Ludwig IV seems to have been reluctant to involve his younger brothers in his lordship. As a result, when Ludwig died, Conrad's situation improved greatly. On four occasions in 1228, he gave his consent as "*frater noster*" to Henry Raspe's property arrangements, whereas in the preceding decade, he had consented to only eight of Ludwig IV's more than thirty charters.[64] One year later, in 1229, the two surviving brothers were listed for the first time in an inscription as coactors—"Henry, by the grace of God landgrave of Thuringia and count-palatine of Saxony, and his brother Conrad"—with both siblings also affixing their seals to this document.[65] The text of the charter confirms a property arrangement between "our ministerial (*ministerialis noster*) Dietrich" and the monastery of Reinhardsbrunn, language that suggests the siblings were functioning as co-lords over at least some members of the Ludowing ministerialage. Conrad thus emerged from relative obscurity soon after Ludwig IV's death to become a prominent figure in the new sibling dynamic that was shaping this lineage's political and territorial interests.

Understanding the precise nature of this sibling dynamic is difficult, however, because the extant sources from the early 1230s fail to provide a clear picture of the brothers' succession arrangement. Consider, for example, a pair of charters from the year 1231 that record a property donation to the Teutonic order.[66] These two documents are virtually identical; they are written in the same hand, record the same donation, include the same witness list, and are both dated to the first day of November. There is one significant difference, however, found in the inscriptions: one names only Henry IV Raspe, while the other adds "and his brother C[onrad]." The second of these documents also includes Conrad's seal alongside Henry's. The charters themselves offer no explanation for why two versions of the same property donation were recorded—or preserved. One reason may be that both charters were deemed necessary, presumably by members of the Teutonic order, because there was no consensus on whether Conrad had any legitimate claims to the piece of property being granted.[67] In subsequent years, the situation did not

---

64. CDS 1 A, 3:288–290, nos. 411–412 and 3:290–292, nos. 414–415.

65. Gotha, Thüringisches Staatsarchiv, QQ I g 48 (printed edition: CDS 1 A, 3:296–297, no. 424). See also Werner, "Reichsfürst zwischen Mainz und Meißen," 145–147.

66. Marburg, Hessisches Staatsarchiv, Urk. A II Deutsch Orden 1231 (printed editions: CDS 1 A, 3:311–313, nos. 447–448).

67. Compare White, *Custom, Kinship, and Gifts*, 34–37. One other possible explanation is that the charters record two separate grants of property in the same place, but this seems less likely since the scribe makes no effort to distinguish between the properties in the two charters.

become any clearer. Indeed, a survey of the titles with which Conrad appears in charters written during the early 1230s further highlights the complexity of the patrimonial division the brothers deployed following Ludwig's death. Conrad's charter inscriptions include "by the grace of God landgrave of Thuringia";[68] "by the grace of God junior landgrave of Thuringia";[69] "count-palatine of Saxony";[70] and in a 1234 charter drawn up in the names of both brothers, "Henry, by the grace of God landgrave of Thuringia, [and] Conrad count-palatine of Saxony, brothers."[71] At the very least, this suggests a great deal of confusion among the scribes of the region regarding Conrad's position vis-à-vis his older brother.[72]

The sigillographic evidence from these years offers evidence that clarifies some of this confusion. Conrad employed two different seal matrices in the years 1233–1234.[73] Since many noblemen employed the same seal matrix for decades, Conrad's utilization of two during the same period is noteworthy.[74] One of these seals, a traditional equestrian seal, is almost identical to the seal that Henry IV Raspe used during this period—with two important exceptions. The inscription on Conrad's reads, "Seal of Conrad, landgrave of Thuringia and count-palatine of Saxony,"[75] while the inscription on Henry's reads, "Henry by the grace of God landgrave of Thuringia and count-palatine of Saxony" (figure 10).[76] Thus, Henry's name is in the nominative case, whereas Conrad's is in the genitive, and Conrad's seal lacks the phrase *dei gratia*. These differences are significant, because they indicate that Conrad recognized his older brother as the true holder of the offices of landgrave and count-palatine, while he simply enjoyed use of the titles.[77]

---

68. CDS 1 A, 3:315–316, no. 453.

69. Ibid., 3:338–339, no. 484.

70. Ibid., 3:341–342, no. 491.

71. Ibid., 3:367, no. 523. See also ibid., 3:307, no. 441; 3:309, no. 444; 3:314, no. 451.

72. Most charters issued by members of the Ludowing family in this period were written by scribes from local monastic communities. There is very little evidence for a Ludowing family chancery: Patze, *Die Entstehung der Landesherrschaft*, 1:533.

73. Posse, *Die Siegel der Wettiner*, vol. 1, table XIII, identifies four different seal matrices for Conrad. The first two of these date from 1229 and 1231, but careful analysis is impossible as a result of their poor condition in surviving copies.

74. Werner, "Reichsfürst zwischen Mainz und Meißen," 151, n. 109.

75. Wolfenbüttel, Niedersächsisches Landesarchiv, Staatsarchiv, StA WO 25 Urk 111 (printed edition: CDS 1 A, 3:367, no. 523).

76. The inscription is well preserved on Marburg, Hessisches Staatsarchiv, Urk. A II Deutsch Orden 1231.

77. Schöntag, "Amts-, Standesbezeichnungen und Titel," 161. See also Bedos-Rezak, "Art of Chivalry," 13–14.

FIGURE 10. The equestrian seals of Landgrave Henry IV Raspe (left) and his brother Conrad of Thuringia (right) on a charter from the year 1234. Niedersächsisches Landesarchiv (NLA), Staatsarchiv Wolfenbüttel, StA WO 25 Urk 111. Courtesy of Niedersächsisches Landesarchiv.

The second of Conrad's seals complicates this picture somewhat (figure 11). Conrad is depicted seated, holding a banner in his right hand and a shield in his left; the lineage's heraldic symbol, a lion rampant, is visible on both banner and shield. The inscription is the same as on his other seal.[78] This seal survives on one of Conrad's charters from 1233, and it also hangs from a 1234 charter drawn up in the names of both Henry and Conrad.[79] On this latter document, Conrad actually made a double-sided imprint in the wax, using both this seal type and his more traditional equestrian seal. Because seals depicting seated figures were not typically used by secular nobles in the German kingdom during the Staufen period, Conrad's simultaneous employment of this second seal is difficult to explain.[80] In the wake of Landgrave Ludwig IV's death, Conrad suddenly found himself playing a much more prominent role than he ever expected to have prior to 1227, and he owed this expanded power and authority to his brother Henry Raspe more than anyone else. At the very least, therefore, this seal may have been his way of reveling in his newfound status as an eminent lord—while also acknowledging, through the muted language of the inscription, that his brother Henry Raspe was the one who gave him this opportunity.

---

78. Wolfenbüttel, Niedersächsisches Landesarchiv, Staatsarchiv, StA WO 25 Urk 108.

79. Ibid., StA WO 25 Urk 111.

80. Kahsnitz, "Konrad I." For some of the broader interpretational challenges of seals such as these, see Bedos-Rezak, *When Ego Was Imago,* 152–156.

FIGURE 11.   The second seal used by Conrad of Thuringia in the years 1233–1234. Niedersächsisches Landesarchiv (NLA), Staatsarchiv Wolfenbüttel, StA WO 25 Urk 108. Courtesy of Niedersächsisches Landesarchiv.

The language of the charters and the sigillographic evidence do not permit definitive conclusions about the nature of the succession arrangement
between Henry IV Raspe and Conrad.[81] Regardless, a range of extant sources

81. Werner, "Reichsfürst zwischen Mainz und Meißen," 148. The situation with these brothers is comparable to that of the three Wittelsbach brothers active in the mid-twelfth century. See
chapter 3.

indicates that they created for themselves two separate spheres of influence, a tactic that led to a very successful partnership between them. Increasingly in the years from 1231 onward, Henry IV Raspe focused on the lineage's Thuringian heartlands, while Conrad began to exercise lordship over the Ludowings' rights and properties in Hesse. Conrad's own charters from this period typically concern the lineage's interests in this region to the west of Thuringia, and several also attest to his frequent presence there.[82] In addition, various sources indicate that he fought a fierce war with the archbishop of Mainz over lordly prerogatives in the region. For example, an entry in the *Cronica Reinhardsbrunnensis* reports that Conrad besieged and captured the archbishop's most important Hessian town, Fritzlar, in the year 1232.[83] All of this source material would seem to indicate that shortly after Ludwig's death and Henry Raspe's succession, Conrad started to fulfill the traditional role of a younger brother within the Ludowing lineage. By exercising lordship in Hesse and never marrying, his career matches the profile of younger sons in preceding generations.[84]

Conrad's influential position alongside Henry IV Raspe was not limited to Hesse during the early 1230s. Papal and imperial documents from these years are especially valuable for their depiction of him as a lord who was playing an increasingly active role in affairs beyond the borders of his lineage's lordships. The canonization process for his sister-in-law Elizabeth, who had died in 1231, seems to have been the trigger for his acquiring a higher profile outside regions of Ludowing power.[85] During the summer months of 1234, Conrad was the only German magnate to travel south of the Alps to Rieti, where Emperor Frederick II and Pope Gregory IX were holding court together during one of their brief periods of reconciliation. While there, he secured a series of privileges from both pope and emperor for the hospital in Marburg that Elizabeth had founded and that both Henry Raspe and Conrad had helped endow. A bull of Gregory IX dated July 1, 1234, makes clear the active role the younger brother was playing as a negotiator in this period: "Conrad requested from us, with the great earnestness of his prayers, that we give assent to his desires and those of his brother and compassionately deign

---

82. See, for example, CDS 1 A, 3:307, no. 441; 3:309, no. 444; 3:315–316, no. 453.

83. *Cronica Reinhardsbrunnensis*, 614. For a more detailed account of this conflict, see Werner, "Reichsfürst zwischen Mainz und Meißen," 162–167.

84. Werner, "Reichsfürst zwischen Mainz und Meißen," 152–153, discusses some of the evidence that suggests Conrad may have intended to marry, though he never did. Curiously, Conrad never appears with the traditional title of *comes* for Hesse. For the title, see Patze, *Die Entstehung der Landesherrschaft*, 1:507–510.

85. Schütz, "Das Geschlecht der Andechs-Meranier," 141.

to confer the hospital on [the Teutonic order]."[86] As Conrad's journey to Italy thus shows, this youngest brother had risen from obscurity to the highest circles of European politics in only a few short years.

Conrad's first foray into papal and imperial affairs would not be his last. Only a few months after his trip to Italy, in November of 1234, he joined the Teutonic order and quickly emerged as an important player in the order's political maneuverings with the emperor and the papacy. His decision to become a Teutonic knight also had a profound effect on his relationship with Henry IV Raspe, a point to which I will return below. During the years between Ludwig IV's death in 1227 and Conrad's joining the order in 1234, the evidence indicates that the two brothers Henry Raspe and Conrad quickly formed a strong partnership that enabled them to expand Ludowing power in Hesse and Thuringia. An unforeseen event, in the form of Ludwig IV's unexpected death, was essential for uniting these two brothers and forging a strong bond between them.

This case of fraternal succession therefore demonstrates how quickly and effectively some siblings could activate their relationships to confront potential crises. Moreover, Henry IV Raspe and Conrad's response to an unexpected change in the succession offers a clear contrast to the response of their older brother, Ludwig IV, and half sister, Judith. Conflict was not inevitable when patrimonial arrangements were thrown into doubt. Some siblings sought—and found—compromise in moments of intrafamilial flux. Henry IV Raspe and Conrad also show, as several other fraternal pairs have, that brothers could work together surprisingly well without clearly defining the precise terms of the succession and inheritance divisions between them. Throughout the Staufen period, the sibling bond proved to be sufficiently malleable and adaptable that most brothers could navigate successfully a wide range of difficult, potentially combustible situations.

Illegitimate Siblings

As the co-margraves of Brandenburg and the four Ludowing siblings demonstrate, sibling relationships during the opening decades of the thirteenth century were frequently shaped by different family circumstances than the relationships in earlier generations of these nine lineages. Unexpected changes to succession and inheritance plans were undoubtedly an important factor

---

86. CDS 1 A, 3:347–348, no. 500. See also ibid., 3:355–356, no. 510; and more generally, Werner, "Reichsfürst zwischen Mainz und Meißen," 170–174.

in this. However, it is also clear that the declining size of lineages, combined with a shrinking pool of resources, forced some nobles to relate to their siblings in new ways. Before considering how these changes affected imperial politics under Emperor Frederick II, another type of sibling relationship must be addressed briefly, because it provides additional evidence for the flexibility of sibling relationships during this period of contracting princely lineages.

As noted in previous chapters, males of the upper aristocracy who embarked on ecclesiastical careers were rare throughout the second half of the Staufen period. The generations active in these decades continued to include multiple sons who became secular lords, but the overwhelming majority of these noblemen had no brothers who entered the church. Among the lineages under investigation here, only two included secular princes who sought ecclesiastical offices for any of their male children.[87] The brothers Bishop Ekbert of Bamberg and Patriarch Berthold of Aquileia from the Andechs lineage have already been discussed.[88] The Wettin lineage, meanwhile, included three members who acquired prominent positions as ecclesiastics in the years between 1200 and 1250. However, all three were illegitimate.

Illegitimate brothers—and to an even greater extent, illegitimate sisters—are difficult to locate in the surviving sources from the German kingdom of the Staufen period. Whether this shortage of evidence for bastards is a product of inadequate source material, a bias against illegitimacy, or an actual absence of illegitimate children within noble society is difficult to determine.[89] On the one hand, since we do know of a few bastard children born to members of the upper aristocracy, it seems likely that there were others about whom we do not know. If their fathers did not formally recognize them, most probably vanished into obscurity.[90] On the other hand, given the religious reform movements at work during the early twelfth century, it is also possible that the church hierarchy's efforts to strengthen the bond of marriage had met with some success by the Staufen period, leading to low rates of illegitimate births within the upper aristocracy.[91] But all of this

---

87. In two additional families, the Welfs and the Ascanians, it is the generation that comes to power after the death of Emperor Frederick II that includes multiple brothers who obtained prominent offices in the church. See below.

88. See chapter 6.

89. Bulst, "Illegitime Kinder"; Schmugge, *Kirche, Kinder, Karrieren*, 21–22.

90. For the source difficulties surrounding one illegitimate child, see Jordan, "Heinrich der Löwe," 140–143. Compare also Freed, *Counts of Falkenstein*, 51–52; Spieß, *Familie und Verwandtschaft*, 381–389.

91. Sprandel ("Die Diskriminierung," 491) contends that the German nobility was more influenced than the French nobility was by the church in the high and late Middle Ages. See also Brundage, *Law, Sex, and Christian Society*, 297–313.

is mere speculation. Regardless of the reason, very few bastard children can be identified—or analyzed in terms of their relationships with any of their siblings of legitimate birth.

Bishop Dietrich of Naumburg (1243–1272) is a notable exception.[92] This prelate, born to an unidentified mother, was the illegitimate son of Margrave Dietrich of Meissen (d. 1221), whose legitimate wife, Judith of Thuringia, has been discussed above. Dietrich was therefore the half brother of Judith's son, Margrave Henry of Meissen (d. 1288), who became a central figure in Dietrich's life during his years as bishop. At the time of Dietrich's initial episcopal election, only one faction within the cathedral chapter of Naumburg supported him, while other canons favored another candidate. However, Dietrich's half brother Margrave Henry strongly backed his claim and intervened to ensure that Dietrich obtained the office.[93] Because illegitimate birth was an impediment to obtaining episcopal office according to canon law, he needed a special dispensation from the pope before he could be consecrated.[94]

Nevertheless, by the time Pope Innocent IV issued a dispensation on July 21, 1243, for the illegitimate Dietrich to be consecrated, he was already acting as bishop, at least in his brother's view.[95] A month earlier, he had appeared as a witness to one of Margrave Henry's charters—as "bishop of Naumburg."[96] Following him in the witness list is Henry, the cathedral provost of Meissen, a second illegitimate brother of the margrave. The naming of these two bastard siblings as witnesses to one of their legitimate brother's agreements is the earliest piece of evidence for this unusual sibling group. All three appear together again six months later, in December of 1143, when "our brother Dietrich, bishop-elect of Naumburg, and our brother Henry, cathedral provost of Meissen," acted as witnesses a second time for Margrave Henry.[97] In two additional charters drawn up in their brother's name, both dated to May of 1252, they were again included in the witness lists.[98]

92. Bishop Dietrich of Merseburg (1201–1215) is also a well-documented illegitimate bishop, but his only brother died a quarter century before his election. Rogge ("Wettiner als Bischöfe," 1071–1072) mistakenly identifies Margrave Conrad II of Lower Lusatia (d. 1210) as this Bishop Dietrich's half brother, but this margrave was actually a cousin.

93. Rogge, "Wettiner als Bischöfe," 1075–1076; Lutz, *Heinrich der Erlauchte*, 190–192.

94. Landau, "Das Weihehindernis der Illegitimität"; Schmugge, *Kirche, Kinder, Karrieren*, 33–40.

95. *Urkundenbuch des Hochstifts Naumburg*, 214–215, nos. 189–190.

96. CDS 2, 15:7, no. 6.

97. Ibid., 15:8–9, no. 8. The title "bishop-elect" here suggests that the question of the legitimacy of Dietrich's prelacy was not yet answered.

98. *Urkundenbuch des Hochstifts Naumburg*, 277–279, nos. 257–258. For Cathedral Provost Henry, see also CDS 2, 1:115, no. 125 and 1:119, no. 131.

The references to the bishop of Naumburg in these charters are noteworthy, for no other prelate from the lineages examined here appears with such frequency as a witness to a lay brother's property agreements. The opposite situation—secular lords witnessing the charters of their siblings who were bishops—is much more commonplace. And yet Margrave Henry of Meissen is not named as a witness in any of his illegitimate half brother Dietrich's extant charters. This suggests that the margrave and the bishop had a very different relationship than other secular-ecclesiastical sibling pairs. Dietrich's holding of a relatively minor bishopric may explain this, but his illegitimacy also apparently placed him in a subordinate position vis-à-vis Henry. This lack of equal status—atypical for legitimate brothers—may help explain why the bishop of Naumburg eventually clashed with Margrave Henry.[99] Tensions are first evident in 1247, when the pope warned Henry against despoiling the church of Naumburg, and during the 1250s, the conflict intensified further as Dietrich sought support from several of his brother's rivals in the region.[100] Finally, on April 25, 1259, the bishop was forced to make peace and to acknowledge that his church was under the margrave's protection; in Dietrich's charter from that day, there is no mention of his blood relationship with Margrave Henry.[101] The bishop would never again be a significant figure in his half brother's political and territorial interests, an indication that the sibling bond between them had been permanently damaged.

Too few examples exist from the upper aristocracy of illegitimate brothers interacting with their legitimate siblings to determine whether Bishop Dietrich of Naumburg's experience was typical. However, comparing Dietrich's relationship with his half brother Margrave Henry of Meissen to the fraternal relationships of other bishops reveals distinct differences. None of the bishops of legitimate birth analyzed here was as ineffective politically—and as powerless within his sibling group—as the illegitimate bishop of Naumburg. Other prelates frequently supported their secular brothers, but there is little evidence to suggest that secular lords were in a position to dominate their ecclesiastical brothers. Dietrich, however, was never able to establish an independent position for himself, and it seems reasonable to conclude that his illegitimacy played a role in his weakness. Although he was identified in one of the margrave of Meissen's charters as *frater*—with no indication he was a bastard—Dietrich was not Henry's legitimate brother, and their relationship seems to reflect this inequality.

99. Rogge, "Wettiner als Bischöfe," 1078–1083.
100. *Urkundenbuch des Hochstifts Naumburg*, 238–239, no. 213.
101. Ibid., 337–338, no. 306.

In broader terms, the relationship between Henry and Dietrich is also noteworthy because, as mentioned above, the entire Wettin lineage had declined significantly in size by the early decades of the thirteenth century. Margrave Henry of Meissen and Lower Lusatia was his father's only legitimate child, and by the early 1240s, only one other legitimate great-grandson of Conrad of Wettin (d. 1157) survived in the direct line of male descent. Henry's decision to throw his weight behind Dietrich's episcopal election may well be a reflection of this shortage of other close male relatives on whom the margrave could rely for political support. Perhaps an illegitimate brother became a significant participant in his sibling group's political and territorial strategies only when his legitimate brothers needed him to bolster a shrinking kin group. This may explain why so little evidence survives for illegitimate siblings during the baby-boom generation of the early Staufen period. Of course, the silence of the sources permits no clear conclusions. It is nevertheless striking that the years of Emperor Frederick II's reign witnessed a variety of sibling relationships that have no obvious equivalents among the sibling relationships in earlier generations of the lineages investigated here.

Frederick II and Otto the Child: Imperial Politics in the Absence of Strong Sibling Groups

During the years when many of the sibling groups discussed in this chapter were operating, Emperor Frederick II was largely absent from the German kingdom. In the period between 1220 and 1250, he spent almost all his time south of the Alps. His only extended stays in the German kingdom occurred during the years 1235–1237, and this brief period was therefore a critical one for framing the relationship between the last Staufen emperor and the leading members of the German aristocracy. Indeed, fifty-five years and two generations after Emperor Frederick I stripped Henry the Lion of his duchies, the political landscape had been so completely transformed that their descendants, Frederick II and Otto the Child, could end the hostility between their lineages and forge a new alliance. This event provides a final opportunity to consider some of the ways that sibling dynamics within the German upper aristocracy influenced the course of imperial politics during the Staufen period.

The act of reconciliation between Frederick II and Otto the Child unfolded in 1235 when the emperor crossed the Alps from Italy and entered the German kingdom for the first time in fifteen years. Holding court at Mainz in August of that year, he sought to reassert his authority in the German kingdom by proclaiming a public peace in the imperial lands north of the

Alps.[102] As part of his efforts to stabilize the political situation in the realm, Frederick II also drew up a charter at Mainz for Otto the Child, the only grandson of Henry the Lion in the male line. According to this text,

> although we had planned for a long time to effect the closer binding of our dear relative (*dilectum consanguineum nostrum*) Otto of Lüneburg to the faith of the empire and to our devotion, neither a suitable time nor place presented itself. For this reason, it was appropriate to pursue this plan, which we had conceived for him, when the opportunity came to pass because of our happy arrival in Germany. We announced a general meeting of the court at Mainz for the reformation of the state of the whole land, and the said Otto—who was summoned to that same court—came. There, while we were presiding, with our princes assisting us, and we were setting everything in order concerning the reformation of the state of the land, the famed Otto of Lüneburg came before us on bended knees. Setting aside all the hatred and rancor that had been able to exist between our forefathers (*proavos nostros*), he placed himself totally in our hands.[103]

Otto gave the emperor all his alodial castles and properties, those lands and rights that had remained in the possession of the Welf lineage after Henry the Lion's fall. Frederick II promptly returned everything to Otto as imperial fiefs and also enfeoffed him with Henry the Lion's old principal residence, the town of Brunswick. Acting with the consent of the princes, the emperor then created out of these properties a new duchy, thus elevating Otto into the ranks of the *principes imperii*.[104] Although Frederick II's actions in 1235 have not generated as much scholarly debate as his grandfather's actions in 1180, the creation of the duchy of Brunswick-Lüneburg is nevertheless another key moment in the long history of the complex relationship between imperial and princely forms of authority.[105]

One of the principal reasons why Frederick II journeyed to the German kingdom in 1235 was the rebellion of his eldest son, Henry (VII), who had been crowned king in 1220.[106] Henry had been a minor at the time and

---

102. Weiler, "Reasserting Power," 258–260; Abulafia, *Frederick II*, 239–244.
103. MGH Const., 2:263–265, no. 197.
104. Boshof, "Die Entstehung des Herzogtums," 269–274.
105. Schneidmüller, *Die Welfen*, 280; Arnold, *Medieval Germany*, 190; Barraclough, *Origins of Modern Germany*, 235.
106. Weiler, "Reasserting Power," 242–245; Abulafia, *Frederick II*, 235–239.

did not attain the age of majority until 1227. Thereafter, he and his father increasingly came into conflict over the nature of his royal authority. King Henry (VII) sought to rule the German kingdom in his own right, but by the early 1230s, Emperor Frederick II had come to view his son as an imperial official with no independent authority. Refusing to accept his father's tight control, Henry (VII) rebelled in the autumn of 1234 with the support of a small group of German bishops and ministerials. A short time later, the king also allied with some of Frederick II's enemies in Italy, a move that finally forced his father's hand. The emperor had little choice but to quash his son's rebellion with a display of force.[107]

After arriving in the German kingdom in April of 1235, Frederick II spent the ensuing months rapidly putting an end to Henry (VII)'s uprising. As he traveled across the kingdom, many of the *principes imperii* flocked to his court to show their loyalty to the emperor. At a grand gathering in July at Worms, Henry (VII) submitted to his father, and the emperor also celebrated his own wedding with Isabella, the sister of King Henry III of England. In August, Frederick II held court at Mainz, where he proclaimed a public peace (*Reichslandfrieden*) and created the duchy of Brunswick-Lüneburg for the Welf Otto the Child. He also participated in the translation of Saint Elizabeth of Thuringia's relics in May 1236 at Marburg. The emperor was thus at the height of his authority and influence north of the Alps during this period.[108]

The emperor's own conception of his imperial authority, as it is possible to reconstruct on the basis of the surviving sources of the years 1235–1236, recognized the essential role of the *principes imperii* in the maintenance of order and stability.[109] During this visit to the German kingdom, Frederick II was attempting neither to undermine the princes' power nor to strengthen centralized government in the realm. Instead, he was anxious to bind the magnates more tightly to him—as he did with Otto the Child—by emphasizing their status as his vassals.[110] The *principes imperii* were free to exercise lordship in their own territories as they saw fit, but because they were imperial vassals, they were also responsible for maintaining the integrity of the empire as a whole. In the language of the time, the emperor was the head

107. Weiler, *Kingship, Rebellion*, 3–10; Stürner, *Friedrich II. Teil 2*, 275–285, 296–301.
108. Weiler, "Reasserting Power," 268–269.
109. Arnold, "Emperor Frederick II," 250–252.
110. Boshof, "Reichsfürstenstand und Reichsreform," 65–66.

of the body politic, and the magnates were the shoulders and limbs. It was therefore impossible for the emperor to act without the princes—or for the princes to function without the emperor.[111] Consensual lordship remained the foundation for imperial authority, much as it had been throughout the earlier decades of the Staufen period.[112] Emperor Frederick II's efforts to connect the *principes imperii* more closely to him by emphasizing the lord-vassal relationship were thus an attempt to strengthen his position vis-à-vis the magnates—without undermining completely the basis for political life inside the German kingdom.

How was Frederick II, after a fifteen-year absence, able to have such political success inside the German kingdom in 1235–1236? The analysis of sibling relationships certainly cannot provide a definitive answer to this question, but it offers a useful framework for comparing this period to other key moments in the political history of the Staufen period. The first point to emphasize is that within the nine lineages examined here, there were only five pairs of brothers active in imperial politics in 1235.[113] These included Bishop Ekbert of Bamberg and Patriarch Berthold of Aquileia from the Andechs lineage; Landgrave Henry IV Raspe of Thuringia and his younger brother, Conrad, from the Ludowing lineage; Margraves John I and Otto III of Brandenburg from the Ascanian lineage; Count Henry I of Anhalt and Duke Albert I of Saxony from a second branch of the Ascanian lineage; and Counts Albert and Herman II of Orlamünde from still a third branch of the Ascanian lineage.[114]

Even this brief list is deceptive, however. In September of 1234, the emperor expressed his desire to have either Patriarch Berthold of Aquileia or Bishop Ekbert of Bamberg serve as one of the arbiters for Otto the Child's planned reconciliation.[115] But Berthold did not join Frederick II on his journey north of the Alps and was not directly involved in the affairs of the German kingdom in 1235–1236, since his patriarchate lay far from the traditional centers of German political life.[116] As a result, Ekbert was the only member of the Andechs lineage to be a regular visitor to the imperial

111. Ibid., 63–64.

112. Schneidmüller, "Konsensuale Herrschaft," 76–81.

113. I do not include in this number the Staufen half brothers Henry (VII) and Conrad, the sons of Emperor Frederick II, since only Henry (VII) had obtained the age of majority by 1235.

114. For more details about these various fraternal pairs, see chapters 5 and 6 and the earlier sections of this chapter.

115. MGH Const., 2:227–228, no. 186. See also Boshof, "Die Entstehung des Herzogtums," 269–270.

116. See chapter 6. Ekbert and Berthold do not appear together at the imperial court at any time between May of 1232 and January of 1237.

court during the emperor's stay in the kingdom. Another fraternal pair also had only one member actively involved in German politics during the years 1235–1236. Count Albert of Orlamünde had disappeared even more thoroughly than Patriarch Berthold from German politics by 1235. He remained in the north, focused on the lordships he had received from the Danish king.[117] His brother, Count Herman II of Orlamünde, was a frequent visitor to the court during Frederick II's stay in the German kingdom, but these siblings did not constitute a fraternal group with any political influence in this period.[118]

The political efficacy of fraternal relationships during these years was complicated further by the fact that Conrad of Thuringia, the younger brother of Landgrave Henry IV Raspe, had joined the Teutonic order in 1234. At the time of Frederick II's arrival in the German kingdom, Conrad was at the papal court finalizing the canonization of his sister-in-law Elizabeth.[119] After Conrad returned to the German realm, both he and Henry IV Raspe attended the imperial court in Mainz in August of 1235. While there, Conrad witnessed one of his brother's charters.[120] Thereafter, however, his political and territorial interests ceased to overlap with those of his older sibling as frequently as they had during the early 1230s. Conrad initially worked to promote Saint Elizabeth's cult and later played an increasingly prominent role in the political maneuverings of the Teutonic order. His relationship with his older brother did not intensify again until the opening months of 1240, during Conrad's brief time as master of the Teutonic order prior to his death on July 24 of the same year.[121] As a result, the Ludowing brothers are another fraternal pair that was not acting together as a strong family bloc during the years when the emperor was seeking to reassert his authority north of the Alps.[122]

When Frederick II issued the charter that formally elevated the Welf Otto the Child into the ranks of the *principes imperii* in August of 1235, only two pairs of magnate brothers were named in the lengthy witness list: Margraves John I and Otto III of Brandenburg and Count Henry I of Anhalt and Duke Albert I of Saxony.[123] Fraternal groups within the upper aristocracy, which had played such an essential role in the collapse of Henry the Lion's power

117. See chapter 5.
118. Reitzenstein, *Regesten der Grafen von Orlamuende*, 68–84.
119. Caemmerer, "Konrad, Landgraf von Thüringen," 44–45.
120. Ibid., 47; *Regesta diplomatica necnon epistolaria*, 3:100, no. 552.
121. *Regesta diplomatica necnon epistolaria*, 3:149–154, nos. 879–904.
122. Caemmerer, "Konrad, Landgraf von Thüringen," 48–57.
123. MGH Const., 2:263–265, no. 197.

and authority in the years around 1180, were virtually nonexistent when Henry's grandson Otto the Child was enfeoffed with the newly created duchy of Brunswick-Lüneburg. The small sizes of upper aristocratic lineages in and around the year 1235 mean that the majority of magnates active in this period lacked the fraternal bonds that were so frequently the basis for political cooperation—and political success—during earlier years. Other types of relationships thus became more important for princes looking to surround themselves with close allies.

Viewed from this perspective, the agreement between Emperor Frederick II and Otto the Child comes into clearer focus. Frederick II first demonstrated his willingness to reconcile with Otto in late 1234—as he was losing the political support of his closest adult relative, his rebellious eldest son King Henry (VII). Meanwhile, Otto the Child and his wife did not yet have any sons who had reached the age of majority. The distantly related Frederick and Otto, who were both only children, therefore had compelling reasons for ending the hostility between their lineages and forging a new alliance. In a period when sibling groups were lacking throughout the upper aristocracy, the emperor and the duke had the opportunity to fill the void with a new political relationship. Binding themselves to each other as German ruler and *princeps imperii*, lord and vassal, was an effective strategy in 1235, when both needed to look outside their own immediate families for allies.

Because Emperor Frederick II departed the German kingdom for Italy in 1237 and never returned to his lands north of the Alps, his reconciliation with Otto the Child did not lead to a close relationship in the ensuing years. Nevertheless, throughout the 1240s, the duke of Brunswick-Lüneburg remained loyal to the Staufen emperor. Unlike some of the other *principes imperii*—including, most notably, Landgrave Henry IV Raspe of Thuringia—Otto refused to cast his support behind the papacy in the violent clash between pope and emperor during Frederick's final years.[124] In 1246, and again in 1247, when small groups of German princes elected new kings in opposition to Frederick II and his son Conrad, Otto the Child remained true to the emperor.[125] The events of 1235 therefore succeeded in creating a new political bond between Frederick and Otto, one that survived the turbulent decade of the 1240s. In a period when strong sibling groups were absent from the imperial court, these two distant cousins turned to each other to stabilize their authority and their lineages.

124. Schneidmüller, *Die Welfen*, 284–285.
125. Wolf, *Die Entstehung des Kurfürstenkollegs*, 42.

Shifting Family Dynamics at the End of the Staufen Period

Staufen royal authority had already collapsed inside the German kingdom by the time of Emperor Frederick II's death in Italy in the year 1250. Frederick II's son Conrad IV (d. 1254), who had been elected king in 1237, was never able to effectively establish his own position within the realm either before or after his father died. Meanwhile, beginning in 1246 with the royal election of Landgrave Henry IV Raspe of Thuringia, the German princes selected a series of non-Staufen candidates for the throne. Although some scholars have labeled this period from Frederick II's death to Rudolf of Habsburg's election in 1273 an "interregnum," this term is misleading.[126] Kings reigned throughout this period—indeed, frequently more than one at the same time—but none of them was able to exert strong authority over the whole realm.[127]

In the midst of all of this political upheaval, a pair of princely brothers acting as co-lords made a decision that would have far-reaching consequences for the German upper aristocracy. On November 29, 1253, Duke Otto II of Bavaria died and was succeeded by his two sons, Ludwig and Henry, who began to exercise joint lordship over the duchy.[128] According to the annalist Herman of Niederalteich, two years later, in 1255, "around Easter, Dukes Ludwig and Henry of Bavaria divided between themselves their principalities. The name of duke, with [Lower] Bavaria, fell to Henry as his share . . . [and] Upper Bavaria with the county-palatine of the Rhine fell to Ludwig as his share."[129] The Wittelsbach brothers thus split the duchy of Bavaria into two pieces and began to exercise lordship independently over their own sections. In this, the brothers acted without the permission of any king or emperor, making this an unprecedented decision by the pair.[130] That such a prestigious duchy and imperial fief was treated like a piece of family property highlights the rapid decline of German royal power and authority in the wake of Emperor Frederick II's death.[131]

Only three years after the division of Bavaria, Margraves John I and Otto III of Brandenburg made the decision to split their own imperial fief, the march

126. Barraclough, *Origins of Modern Germany*, 240; Haverkamp, *Medieval Germany*, 263.

127. Weiler, "Image and Reality."

128. This case of joint lordship is complicated by the fact that Duke Otto II was also count-palatine of the Rhine. Rather than giving one lordship to one son and the other to the second son, however, he arranged for both to exercise joint lordship over Bavaria. See Spindler, "Grundlegung und Aufbau," 69–70.

129. Herman of Niederalteich, *Annales*, 397. See also Heimann, *Hausordnung und Staatsbildung*, 29–31; Moeglin, "La discorde," 279–280.

130. Krieger, *Die Lehnshoheit*, 74–77; Holzfurtner, *Die Wittelsbacher*, 43–44; more generally, Spieß, *Familie und Verwandtschaft*, 201–202.

131. See chapter 1 for more on this point.

of Brandenburg.[132] Leading magnates in other lineages soon pursued the same course of action. The Welf duchy of Brunswick-Lüneburg, created in 1235, was divided for the first time only three decades later in 1267, and the first division of the Ascanian duchy of Saxony occurred in 1295.[133] Prior to the mid-thirteenth century, only the emperor had been able to split an imperial fief—as evidenced by the 1156 creation of the duchy of Austria and the 1180 division of the duchy of Saxony.[134] This is one reason why joint lordship had emerged as such an effective strategy for satisfying younger sons' claims to the patrimony during the later Staufen period. After 1255, the new trend toward dividing imperial fiefs, and viewing them as family property, meant that multiple heirs could receive independent princely lordships, even if their father held only one imperial fief. As a result, noble succession underwent profound changes. By the early fifteenth century, the Wittelsbachs had split Bavaria into four parts, and they were not the only lineage to divide their princely lordships on multiple occasions in this period.[135] Fragmented duchies and marches thus became a commonplace feature of the late medieval German landscape.

The driving force behind this fragmentation was another generational shift within the German upper aristocracy. In the lineages under investigation here, very few sibling groups were politically active during the closing years of the reign of Emperor Frederick II. The Andechses, Babenbergs, and Ludowings all became extinct in the male line during the later 1240s, and the leading magnates in other lineages had few if any brothers. This contraction within the upper aristocracy was short-lived, however. The generation that rose to prominence in the 1250s and 1260s bore a striking resemblance to the generation that had burst onto the political scene a century earlier under Frederick Barbarossa. Nine of Duke Otto the Child of Brunswick's children survived to adulthood, and his four sons included two secular magnates and two bishops. Margrave John I of Brandenburg was outlived by seven sons, two of whom became ecclesiastical princes. John's brother, Margrave Otto III, was survived by four sons. Meanwhile, in another branch of the Ascanian lineage, five sons outlived Count Henry I of Anhalt. And in the Wettin lineage, Margrave Henry of Meissen and Lower Lusatia (d. 1288) divided his lordships among his three sons. These large fraternal groups ensured that the imperial princes of the later 1200s would experience a decidedly different family dynamic than their fathers and grandfathers had during the preceding decades of the thirteenth century.

---

132. Schultze, *Die Mark Brandenburg*, 1:168–171.
133. Krieger, *Die Lehnshoheit*, 76; Schneidmüller, *Die Welfen*, 284.
134. See chapters 3 and 4.
135. For the Wettin lineage, for example, see Rogge, *Herrschaftsweitergabe*.

As patrimonial divisions became increasingly complicated after 1250, the volume of written records needed to arrange a lineage's succession plans rapidly grew. Indeed, the middle decades of the thirteenth century were the critical period for the transition from an oral to a written culture of managing succession and inheritance. The proliferation inside the German kingdom of several kinds of family documents—especially marriage contracts, testaments, and treaties between relatives—suggests that family relationships were beginning to be regulated in new ways.[136] Most significantly for this study, written agreements between brothers reminding them of the obligations they owed to one another and of the friendship they ought to share with each other multiplied after 1250.[137] New succession practices, new types of documents, and new legalese in the sources all indicate that German aristocratic society's perception of the sibling bond was changing during the late thirteenth and early fourteenth centuries. For all these reasons, the end of the Staufen period is a fitting moment with which to close this book.

The opening decades of the thirteenth century witnessed the continuation of a trend that had begun a century earlier, with the founders of the nine lineages under investigation here. The fluctuating sizes of sibling groups, together with the custom of partible inheritance, combined to generate strikingly different sibling dynamics from lineage to lineage and generation to generation. The variability—and adaptability—of sibling relationships is most apparent during the reign of Emperor Frederick II, when shrinking lineages and limited resources forced siblings to confront together the uncertain future of their families and lordships. For the German kingdom as a whole, shifting sibling dynamics over time also meant that brothers—and to a lesser extent sisters— exerted different degrees of influence over the realm's political life at different moments during the Staufen period. At no time under Emperor Frederick II did large sibling blocs, with the exception of the Andechses, affect the course of political events as dramatically as sibling groups had done during the 1170s and early 1180s. And yet, despite the significant variations in sibling groups across lineages and generations, siblings tended to maintain close and cooperative relationships that were rarely, if ever, fractured by conflict. Even in the midst of the uncertainty and instability of the closing decades of the Staufen period, collaboration remained a centerpiece of sibling relationships.

---

136. Spieß, *Familie und Verwandtschaft*, 21–22; Rogge, *Herrschaftsweitergabe*, 12–15; Nolte, *Familie, Hof und Herrschaft*, 20–22.

137. Spieß, *Familie und Verwandtschaft*, 276–277; more generally, Müller, *Besiegelte Freundschaft*, 57–59, 281.

Conclusion

In the Western tradition, the first person in human history to have a brother was also the first person to commit fratricide: "Cain said to Abel his brother, 'Let us go out to the field.' And when they were in the field, Cain rose up against his brother Abel, and killed him. Then the Lord said to Cain, 'Where is Abel your brother?' He said, 'I do not know; am I my brother's keeper?'" (Gen. 4:8–9). When Romulus later killed his brother, Remus, at the founding of Rome, the sibling bond became even more closely associated with violence. Augustine of Hippo, for example, saw in both fratricides proof of the inherent divisiveness of the earthly city, since—even between brothers—anger, envious hatred, and the selfish lust for glory are commonplace.[1] He was not alone in holding such views. In subsequent centuries, the story of Cain and Abel, and to a lesser extent that of Romulus and Remus as well, continued to serve a broad range of moralizing purposes for medieval authors expounding on the evils of man.[2]

Fratricide was not something confined solely to the pages of theological texts by the central Middle Ages. In 1082, Count Berenguer Ramon II of Barcelona murdered his own brother in order to gain control of their father's

---

1. Augustine, *De civitate dei*, 15.5, 457–458.
2. Voyer, "Image de l'exclusion." More generally, Davidoff, *Thicker than Water*, 35–36.

patrimony.[3] Three-quarters of a century later, in 1155, King Inge of Norway orchestrated an attack against one of his brothers, Sigurd, that ended in the latter's violent death.[4] Additional examples of fratricide can be found in other parts of western Europe during this period as well.[5] Even if fraternal conflict did not culminate in murder, some rivalrous brothers could be bitter enemies. King Sancho II of Castile (1065–1072) imprisoned one of his brothers and sent the other into exile—before dying by an assassin's hand while besieging one of his sister's castles.[6] King Henry I of England captured his older brother Duke Robert of Normandy in battle in 1106 and kept him in custody in England for the remaining twenty-eight years of his life.[7] And Duke Bolesław III of Poland blinded his older brother, Zbigniew, in 1112 after years of tension between the two.[8]

These cases of fratricide and fraternal conflict help highlight the distinctiveness of sibling relationships within the German upper aristocracy of the Staufen period. No member of the nine aristocratic lineages under investigation here committed fratricide, and the few cases of fraternal conflict that can be gleaned from the sources are the exceptions that prove the rule of cooperative bonds. Sibling solidarity was the norm for the German magnates of the twelfth and thirteenth centuries, and brothers and sisters frequently developed politically efficacious relationships that lasted for years or decades. To understand fully why cooperation was more commonplace than conflict within this elite would require a much broader survey of medieval sibling relationships than scholars have up to now attempted. Detailed case studies of siblings belonging to noble lineages from other regions of Europe would provide a clearer picture of the specific constellation of political, territorial, and familial circumstances that led German princely brothers and sisters to relate to one another in the ways they did. Similarly, analyzing siblings from the lesser nobility of the German kingdom would make it easier to determine how these nine upper aristocratic lineages conform—or do not conform—to broader patterns.

Nevertheless, the brothers and sisters who have been the focus of this book do permit several conclusions. Indeed, the generations of the upper aristocracy that exercised lordship during the Staufen period provide a remarkably coherent narrative arc for the history of sibling relationships. Nine lords

3. Taylor, "Inheritance of Power," 141–142.
4. Bagge, *Viking Stronghold*, 42–43.
5. See, for example, Beitscher, "'As the Twig Is Bent,'" 190.
6. *Latin Chronicle of the Kings of Castile*, 3–4.
7. Aird, *Robert Curthose*, 247–252.
8. *Gesta principum Polonorum*, 270–275; Bisson, *Crisis of the Twelfth Century*, 185–189.

who rose to prominence during the late eleventh and early twelfth centuries took advantage of the turmoil of the Investiture Controversy to accumulate lands and rights while simultaneously founding new noble lineages. Their numerous children—or, in some cases, grandchildren—were able to enjoy the fruits of these founders' labors. The generation active during the reign of Emperor Frederick I Barbarossa consisted of a series of sibling groups that operated as cohesive political blocs at both the regional level and the imperial court. Subsequent generations that reached adulthood in the late 1100s and early 1200s tended not to include such an abundance of brothers and sisters, but sibling relationships nevertheless remained a significant feature of family politics during this period. Only in the final years of the Staufen period, as some lineages died out in the male line and others teetered on the brink of extinction, did the sibling bond fade somewhat from the political scene—though only for a decade or two, before a new generation made up of several prominent fraternal groups came of age after 1250.

From the large generations of the mid-twelfth century to the smaller sibling groups active during the closing decades of Emperor Frederick II's reign, brothers and sisters of the German upper aristocracy consistently sought to minimize conflict and foster cooperative bonds. Siblings in the nine lineages under investigation here founded and patronized monastic houses together, acted as ambassadors and peace negotiators for one another, helped each other acquire fiefs and imperial privileges, and fought together on military campaigns both north and south of the Alps. In contrast, the relationships that these nobles developed with their extended kin were much more diverse. The pattern of close, efficacious bonds evident within sibling groups cannot be repeated with other, more distant relatives. Within these nine lineages, the relationships between brothers and sisters possessed distinctive qualities that simply did not manifest themselves as frequently within extended kin groups.

Two factors are critical to understanding why collaboration was the basis for so many sibling relationships during the Staufen period. First, German nobles accepted partible inheritance as the norm. There was no tradition of primogeniture to which eldest sons and brothers could turn in an effort to consolidate the patrimony in their own hands. To the contrary, eldest sons and brothers frequently sought to protect and promote their younger siblings' territorial interests, so that those brothers could be effective allies at the regional level and at the imperial court. Thus, the goal of both fathers and brothers was to have multiple members of a generation belong to the ranks of the *principes imperii*. Because everyone in the upper aristocracy recognized partible inheritance as standard practice, distributing lordships among multiple siblings in this way did not lead to violent jealousy or conflict. Instead, in the vast majority of cases, it promoted cooperation.

Second, the fluctuating size of generations during the Staufen period limited cases of shrinking patrimonies being divided among too many siblings. Lineages consistently avoided the potential for conflicts to arise as a result of sibling groups having insufficient resources to maintain their standing within the upper aristocracy. Admittedly, I am unaware of any extant sources that could be used to argue that the noblemen and noblewomen under investigation here practiced birth control to limit the number of legitimate children they had. Nevertheless, it is difficult to imagine that the widespread decline in the size of fraternal groups during the late twelfth and early thirteenth centuries happened by chance. Members of the baby-boom generation that came of age in the 1140s and 1150s—at a time when these nine lineages had abundant resources—seem to have been reluctant to have numerous sons of their own. This trend appears to have continued until the mid-thirteenth century, when the extinction of several lineages created new opportunities for lords to acquire new lordships for their children. It is therefore tempting to speculate that German nobles sought to regulate family size based on the patrimonial resources that would be available to the next generation. Such a strategy would have promoted sibling solidarity by ensuring that there were not too many brothers and sisters trying to survive off a patrimony that was too small.

Examining how and why siblings cooperated with one another within the German upper aristocracy of the Staufen period shines a light on a variety of issues—including succession, inheritance, generational size, and intrafamilial conflict and rivalry—that have long interested family historians. Careful analysis of the relationships between brothers and sisters reveals numerous problems with the way these issues were framed by the old "Schmid-Duby thesis" of the medieval noble lineage. The sibling bond therefore offers scholars the opportunity to understand the family's significance for noble society from a new perspective, one that is independent from twentieth-century debates about the *Sippe*, the *Geschlecht*, and other family structures. Most significantly for this book, analyzing sibling relationships has made it possible to offer a new narrative of German political history during the twelfth and thirteenth centuries.

From the fall of Henry the Lion, to the civil war of the early 1200s, to the crises that followed the collapse of the Staufen dynasty, the political efficacy of the sibling bond frequently impacted the course of imperial politics. While the relationships between brothers and sisters cannot, by themselves, explain all the key political events that occurred in the German duchies or at the imperial court, they can help us understand with greater clarity how kingship and lordship worked in practice during the twelfth and thirteenth centuries. Because the Staufen rulers relied on consultation with the *principes imperii* to govern the kingdom and the empire effectively, consensual lordship was a cornerstone of politics in this period. As a result, sibling groups had the potential to form powerful political blocs, with multiple brothers—and occasionally sisters—exerting their influence simultaneously at the regional level and the imperial court. The varying size and composition of aristocratic sibling groups thus shaped and reshaped the composition of the German kingdom's political community throughout the Staufen period. From decade to decade, political dynamics changed as sibling dynamics changed.

Two letters, written by a sister to her brother, provide the appropriate final words on the sibling bond during the Staufen period. The Hungarian princess Sophia was betrothed to Henry, the eldest son of King Conrad III, in the year 1139.[9] Soon thereafter, Sophia left Hungary for the German kingdom to learn the German language and German court culture in advance of her wedding. After her father died in 1141, however, the relationship between his successor—Sophia's brother Géza II—and King Conrad III soured.[10] As a result, the planned marriage was abandoned, while Sophia was still residing in the German realm.[11]

The young princess's plight in the ensuing months can be reconstructed with the help of a collection of letters preserved in a twelfth-century manuscript written at the double monastery of Admont.[12] One of the letters, written by Sophia and addressed to her brother Géza II, opens, "To her lord and brother G[éza], most powerful king of the Hungarian people, that exile and pilgrim sister of his [Sophia] [sends] the most sweet affection with the service of siblinghood (*cum servicio germanitatis*). So long as I am pondering the glory of the magnificence of your realm [and] so long as I am considering the excellence of your name, most loving brother (*frater amantissime*), the good fortune of your own affairs is in a certain way like a sweet consolation from the countless miseries that I have endured up until now."[13] Sophia goes

---

9. Roitner, "Die ungarische Königstochter Sophia," 185.

10. Engel, *Realm of St. Stephen*, 50–51; Weller, *Die Heiratspolitik des deutschen Hochadels*, 46–52.

11. The most detailed twelfth-century account of subsequent events is provided by Herbord of Michelsberg in *De vita et operibus beati Ottonis*, 1.38, 322–331. For another account of these events, see *Gesta archiepiscoporum Salisburgensium*, 44, chap. 19.

12. I would like to thank Hill Museum & Manuscript Library for providing me with images of the manuscript folios containing the letters (Klagenfurt, Universitätsbibliothek, Perg.-Hs. 7, f. 2b–5a). A printed edition of the letters can be found in Jaksch, "Zur Lebensgeschichte Sophia's," 372–379.

13. Jaksch, "Zur Lebensgeschichte Sophia's," 374–375, no. 6.

on to complain bitterly about her situation, explaining how she was being treated "as the basest of handmaids" by the German king—and how she now understands "how lamentable the Babylonian captivity is." She then continues, "I humbly seek the counsel of your piety, asking that for the hope of eternal reward you not spurn the petition of my desolate condition. I truly pray and desire with your fraternal assistance (*fraterno tui auxilio*) to flee, naked anyhow and despoiled, from the shipwreck of this world to the haven of a monastery and a quiet life." She names Admont as the convent she would like to enter, and in her efforts to convince Géza of her plan, reminds him that Admont "is bordering on your kingdom." She closes by offering an additional incentive: "If I obtain my wish . . . and accomplish this as quickly as possible, I will pray to the Lord without intermission no less for you than for me."

According to other letters in the collection, Géza did not immediately accede to his sister's request.[14] Within a year, however, Sophia had joined the community at Admont. Soon thereafter, she wrote again to her brother, thanking him profusely for the riches he had sent to her, apparently to be used as her entrance gift to the convent.[15] The speed with which she embraced the spiritual life is evident in the salutation of this second letter addressed to her brother: "To her most glorious lord and brother [Géza], most victorious king of the Huns, [Sophia], formerly his sister (*quondam germana*), now his servant and the servant of Christ."[16] The shift in language from the first letter—when Sophia so strongly emphasized the obligations and emotional attachments created by the sibling bond—to the second letter is striking. From a biological perspective, it is of course impossible to cease to be a sister while one's siblings are still alive.[17] The phrase *quondam germana* may therefore indicate that Sophia and her fellow nuns were using the letter to present an idealized vision of how one was supposed to enter a convent, leaving one's natal family behind in the process.[18]

Regardless, what makes *quondam germana* so striking in this letter is how out of place it is in noble society's reflections on the sibling bond. It is a piece of rhetoric that, while evocative, finds few echoes in other sources—or in the ways that most siblings related to one another in the twelfth- and

14. Ibid., 375–376, no. 7; 377, no. 9.
15. Ibid., 372, no. 1.
16. Ibid.
17. For other discussions of this point, see Lubich, *Verwandtsein*, 5–7; Pradelle, "Un exemple de liens adelphiques," 68.
18. For the Admont nuns' knowledge of the form and rhetoric of letter writing, see Beach, "Voices from a Distant Land," 37.

thirteenth-century German kingdom. Most noblewomen who entered convents during the Staufen period made no effort to end contacts with their brothers and sisters. Moreover, very few members of the German lineages under investigation here, whether they resided in the secular or the ecclesiastical sphere, showed any interest in severing ties with their siblings. Some, for reasons of geography, had limited contacts with the other members of their generation, but conscious efforts to dissolve the bonds between brothers and sisters were rare. The phrase *servicium germanitatis* that appears in Sophia's initial letter to her brother is more reflective of the distinctive set of expectations connected to sibling relationships during the Staufen period. The most fitting phrase, however, is another one that Sophia uses in this first letter to Géza, as she is begging him to help her enter Admont: "*Ea propter, frater, quasi ad turrem fortitudinis confugio ad te*" (Therefore, brother, I flee to you as if to a tower of strength).

APPENDIX

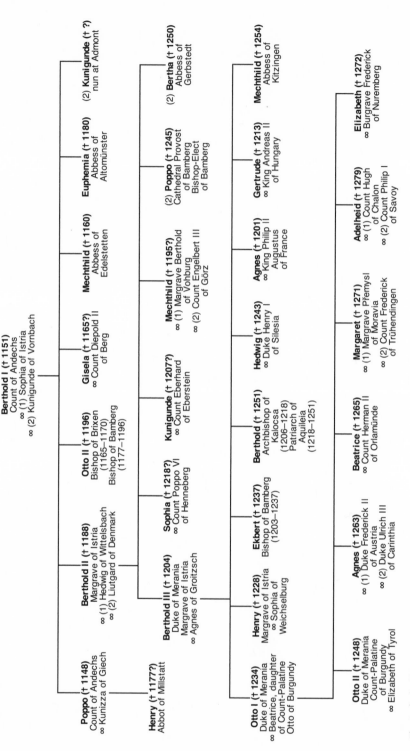

Berthold I († 1151)
Count of Andechs
∞ (1) Sophia of Istria
∞ (2) Kunigunde of Vornbach

Poppo († 1148)
Count of Andechs
∞ Kunizza of Giech

Henry († 1177?)
Abbot of Millstatt

Berthold II († 1188)
Margrave of Istria
∞ (1) Hedwig of Wittelsbach
∞ (2) Liutgard of Denmark

Otto II († 1196)
Bishop of Brixen
(1165–1170)
Bishop of Bamberg
(1177–1196)

Gisela († 1165?)
∞ Count Diepold II
of Berg

Mechthild († 1160)
Abbess of
Edelstetten

Euphemia († 1180)
Abbess of
Altomünster

(2) **Kunigunde** († ?)
nun at Admont

Berthold III († 1204)
Duke of Merania
Margrave of Istria
∞ Agnes of Groitzsch

Sophia († 1218?)
∞ Count Poppo VI
of Henneberg

Kunigunde († 1207?)
∞ Count Eberhard
of Eberstein

Mechthild († 1195?)
∞ (1) Margrave Berthold
of Vohburg
∞ (2) Count Engelbert III
of Görz

(2) **Poppo** († 1245)
Cathedral Provost
of Bamberg
Bishop-Elect
of Bamberg

(2) **Bertha** († 1250)
Abbess of
Gerbstedt

Otto I († 1234)
Duke of Merania
Count-Palatine
of Burgundy
∞ Beatrice, daughter
of Count-Palatine
Otto of Burgundy

Henry († 1228)
Margrave of Istria
∞ Sophia of
Weichselburg

Ekbert († 1237)
Bishop of Bamberg
(1203–1237)

Berthold († 1251)
Archbishop of
Kalocsa
(1206–1218)
Patriarch of
Aquileia
(1218–1251)

Hedwig († 1243)
∞ Duke Henry I
of Silesia

Agnes († 1201)
∞ King Philip II
Augustus
of France

Gertrude († 1213)
∞ King Andreas II
of Hungary

Mechthild († 1254)
Abbess of Kitzingen

Otto II († 1248)
Duke of Merania
Count-Palatine
of Burgundy
∞ Elizabeth of Tyrol

Agnes († 1263)
∞ (1) Duke Frederick II
of Austria
∞ (2) Duke Ulrich III
of Carinthia

Beatrice († 1265)
∞ Count Herman II
of Orlamünde

Margaret († 1271)
∞ (1) Margrave Přemysl
of Moravia
∞ (2) Count Frederick
of Trühendingen

Adelheid († 1279)
∞ (1) Count Hugh
of Chalon
∞ (2) Count Philip I
of Savoy

Elizabeth († 1272)
∞ Burgrave Frederick
of Nuremberg

The Andechs Lineage

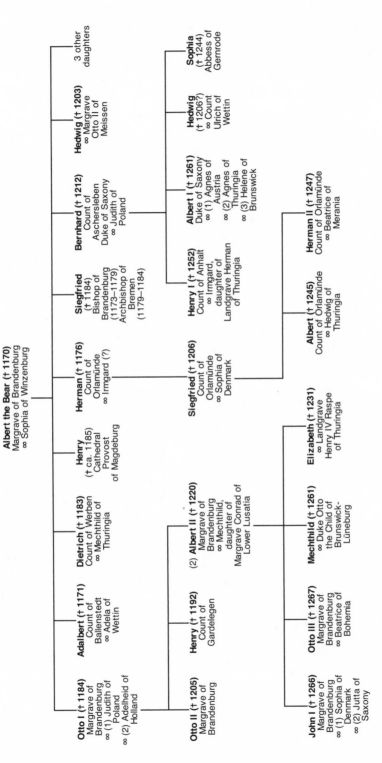

The Ascanian Lineage

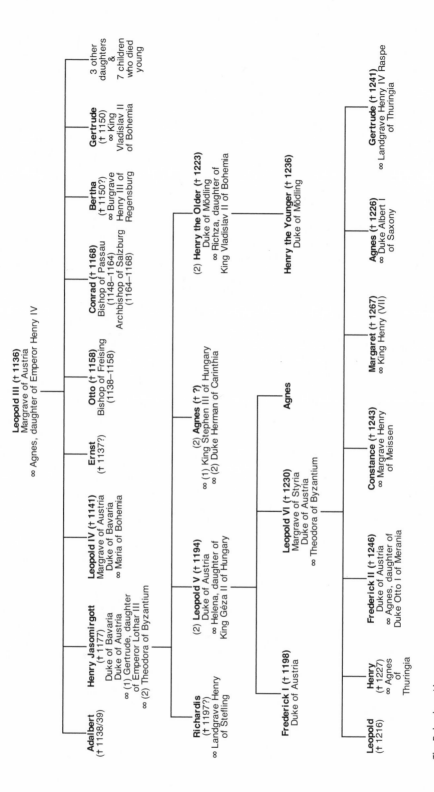

Leopold III († 1136)
Margrave of Austria
∞ Agnes, daughter of Emperor Henry IV

Adalbert
(† 1138/39)

Henry Jasomirgott
(† 1177)
Duke of Bavaria
Duke of Austria
∞ (1) Gertrude, daughter
of Emperor Lothar III
∞ (2) Theodora of Byzantium

Leopold IV († 1141)
Margrave of Austria
Duke of Bavaria
∞ Maria of Bohemia

Ernst
(† 1137?)

Otto († 1158)
Bishop of Freising
(1138–1158)

Conrad († 1168)
Bishop of Passau
(1148–1164)
Archbishop of Salzburg
(1164–1168)

Bertha
(† 1150?)
∞ Burgrave
Henry III of
Regensburg

Gertrude († 1150)
∞ King
Vladislav II
of Bohemia

3 other
daughters
&
7 children
who died
young

Richardis
(† 1197?)
∞ Landgrave Henry
of Stefling

(2) Leopold V († 1194)
Duke of Austria
∞ Helena, daughter of
King Géza II of Hungary

Agnes († ?)
∞ (1) King Stephen III of Hungary
∞ (2) Duke Herman of Carinthia

(2) Henry the Older († 1223)
Duke of Mödling
∞ Richza, daughter of
King Vladislav II of Bohemia

Frederick I († 1198)
Duke of Austria

Leopold VI († 1230)
Margrave of Styria
Duke of Austria
∞ Theodora of Byzantium

Agnes

Henry the Younger († 1236)
Duke of Mödling

Henry
(† 1227)
∞ Agnes
of
Thuringia

Frederick II († 1246)
Duke of Austria
∞ Agnes, daughter of
Duke Otto I of Merania

Constance († 1243)
∞ Margrave Henry
of Meissen

Margaret († 1267)
∞ King Henry (VII)

Agnes († 1226)
∞ Duke Albert I
of Saxony

Gertrude († 1241)
∞ Landgrave Henry IV Raspe
of Thuringia

Leopold
(† 1216)

The Babenberg Lineage

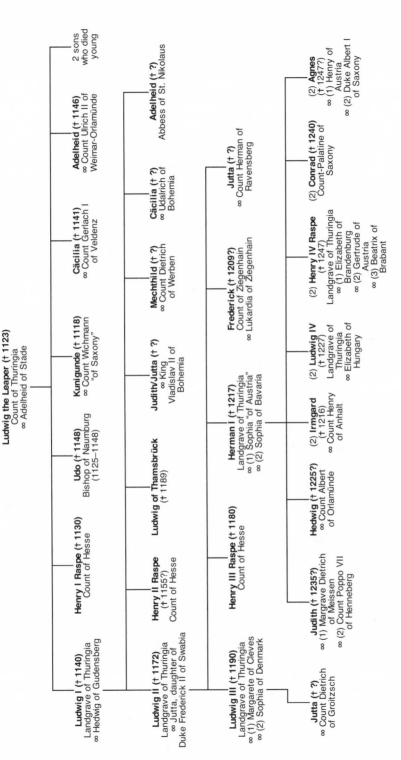

Ludwig the Leaper († 1123)
Count of Thuringia
∞ Adelheid of Stade

2 sons who died young

Adelheid († 1146)
∞ Count Ulrich II of Weimar-Orlamünde

Cäcilia († 1141)
∞ Count Gerlach I of Veldenz

Kunigunde († 1118)
∞ Count Wichmann "of Saxony"

Udo († 1148)
Bishop of Naumburg (1125–1148)

Henry I Raspe († 1130)
Count of Hesse

Ludwig I († 1140)
Landgrave of Thuringia
∞ Hedwig of Gudensberg

Adelheid († ?)
Abbess of St. Nikolaus

Cäcilia († ?)
∞ Udalrich of Bohemia

Mechthild († ?)
∞ Count Dietrich of Werben

Judith/Jutta († ?)
∞ King Vladislav II of Bohemia

Ludwig of Thamsbrück († 1189)

Henry II Raspe († 1155?)
Count of Hesse

Ludwig II († 1172)
Landgrave of Thuringia
∞ Jutta, daughter of Duke Frederick II of Swabia

Jutta († ?)
∞ Count Herman of Ravensberg

Frederick († 1209?)
Count of Ziegenhain
∞ Lukardia of Ziegenhain

Herman I († 1217)
Landgrave of Thuringia
∞ (1) Sophia "of Austria"
∞ (2) Sophia of Bavaria

Henry III Raspe († 1180)
Count of Hesse

Ludwig III († 1190)
Landgrave of Thuringia
∞ (1) Margarete of Cleves
∞ (2) Sophia of Denmark

(2) Agnes († 1247?)
∞ (1) Henry of Austria
∞ (2) Duke Albert I of Saxony

(2) Conrad († 1240)
Count-Palatine of Saxony

(2) Henry IV Raspe († 1247)
Landgrave of Thuringia
∞ (1) Elizabeth of Brandenburg
∞ (2) Gertrude of Austria
∞ (3) Beatrix of Brabant

(2) Ludwig IV († 1227)
Landgrave of Thuringia
∞ Elizabeth of Hungary

(2) Irmgard († 1216)
∞ Count Henry of Anhalt

Hedwig († 1225?)
∞ Count Albert of Orlamünde

Judith († 1235?)
∞ (1) Margrave Dietrich of Meissen
∞ (2) Count Poppo VII of Henneberg

Jutta († ?)
∞ Count Dietrich of Groitzsch

The Ludowing Lineage

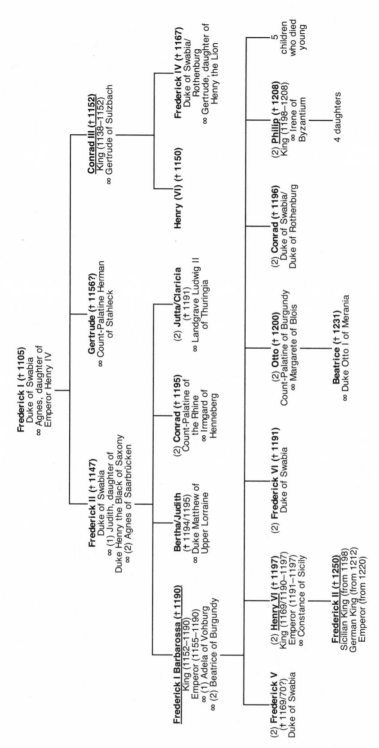

The Staufen Lineage

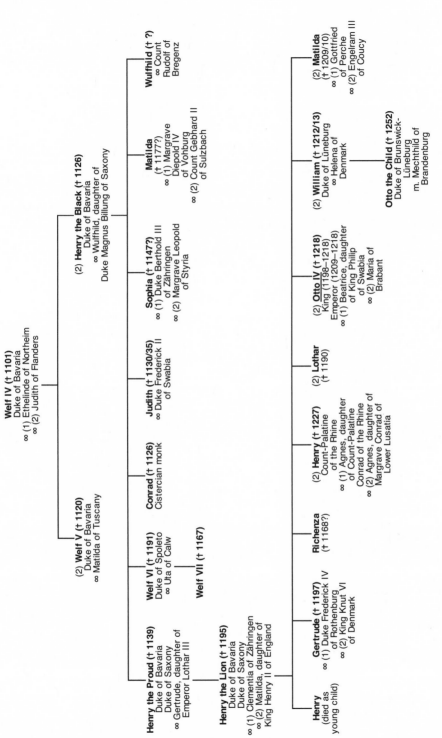

Welf IV († 1101)
Duke of Bavaria
∞ (1) Ethelinde of Northeim
∞ (2) Judith of Flanders

(2) Welf V († 1120)
Duke of Bavaria
∞ Matilda of Tuscany

(2) Henry the Black († 1126)
Duke of Bavaria
∞ Wulfhild, daughter of
Duke Magnus Billung of Saxony

Henry the Proud († 1139)
Duke of Bavaria
Duke of Saxony
∞ Gertrude, daughter of
Emperor Lothar III

Welf VI († 1191)
Duke of Spoleto
∞ Uta of Calw

Conrad († 1126)
Cistercian monk

Judith († 1130/35)
∞ Duke Frederick II
of Swabia

Sophia († 1147?)
∞ (1) Duke Berthold III
of Zähringen
∞ (2) Margrave Leopold
of Styria

Matilda
(† 1177?)
∞ (1) Margrave
Diepold IV
of Vohburg
∞ (2) Count Gebhard II
of Sulzbach

Wulfhild († ?)
∞ Count
Rudolf of
Bregenz

Welf VII († 1167)

Henry the Lion († 1195)
Duke of Bavaria
Duke of Saxony
∞ (1) Clementia of Zähringen
∞ (2) Matilda, daughter of
King Henry II of England

Henry
(died as
young child)

Gertrude († 1197)
∞ (1) Duke Frederick IV
of Rothenburg
∞ (2) King Knut VI
of Denmark

Richenza
(† 1168?)

(2) Henry († 1227)
Count-Palatine
of the Rhine
∞ (1) Agnes, daughter
of Count-Palatine
Conrad of the Rhine
∞ (2) Agnes, daughter of
Margrave Conrad of
Lower Lusatia

(2) Lothar
(† 1190)

(2) Otto IV († 1218)
King (1198–1218)
Emperor (1209–1218)
∞ (1) Beatrice, daughter
of King Philip
of Swabia
∞ (2) Maria of
Brabant

(2) William († 1212/13)
Duke of Lüneburg
∞ Helena of
Denmark

Matilda
(† 1209/10)
∞ (1) Gottfried
of Perche
∞ (2) Engelram III
of Coucy

Otto the Child († 1252)
Duke of Brunswick-
Lüneburg
m. Mechthild of
Brandenburg

The Welf Lineage

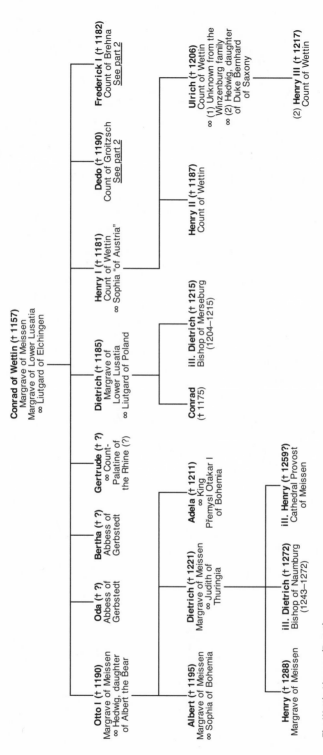

The Wettin Lineage (Part 1)

Conrad of Wettin († 1157)
Margrave of Meissen
Margrave of Lower Lusatia
∞ Liutgard of Eichingen

Otto I († 1190)
Margrave of Meissen
∞ Hedwig, daughter
of Albert the Bear

Oda († ?)
Abbess of
Gerbstedt

Bertha († ?)
Abbess of
Gerbstedt

Gertrude († ?)
∞ Count-
Palatine of
the Rhine (?)

Dietrich († 1185)
Margrave of
Lower Lusatia
∞ Liutgard of Poland

Henry I († 1181)
Count of Wettin
∞ Sophia "of Austria"

Dedo († 1190)
Count of Groitzsch
See part 2

Frederick I († 1182)
Margrave of Meissen
See part 2

Albert († 1195)
Margrave of Meissen
∞ Sophia of Bohemia

Dietrich († 1221)
Margrave of Meissen
∞ Judith of
Thuringia

Adela († 1211)
∞ King
Přemysl Otakar I
of Bohemia

Conrad
(† 1175)

ill. Dietrich († 1215)
Bishop of Merseburg
(1204–1215)

Henry II († 1187)
Count of Wettin

Ulrich († 1206)
Count of Wettin
∞ (1) Unknown from the
Winzenburg family
∞ (2) Hedwig, daughter
of Duke Bernhard
of Saxony

Henry († 1288)
Margrave of Meissen

ill. Dietrich († 1272)
Bishop of Naumburg
(1243–1272)

ill. Henry († 1259?)
Cathedral Provost
of Meissen

(2) Henry III († 1217)
Count of Wettin

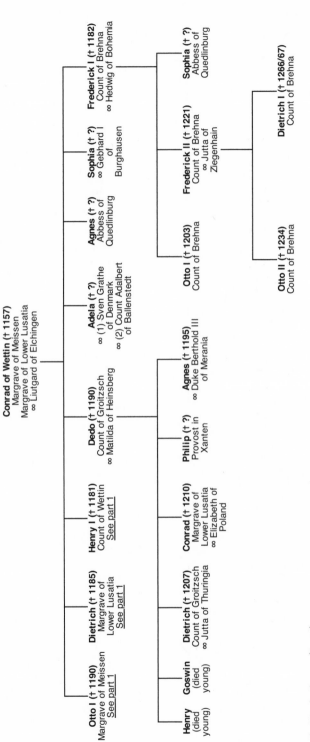

The Wettin Lineage (Part 2)

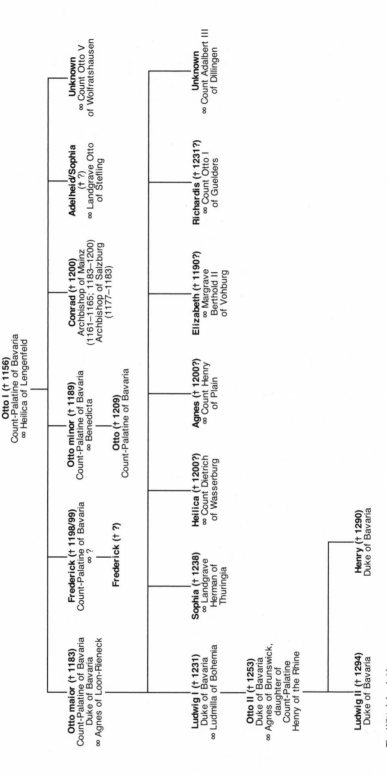

Otto I († 1156)
Count-Palatine of Bavaria
∞ Heilica of Lengenfeld

Otto maior († 1183)
Count-Palatine of Bavaria
Duke of Bavaria
∞ Agnes of Loon-Rieneck

Frederick († 1198/99)
Count-Palatine of Bavaria
∞ ?

Otto minor († 1189)
Count-Palatine of Bavaria
∞ Benedicta

Conrad († 1200)
Archbishop of Mainz
(1161–1165; 1183–1200)
Archbishop of Salzburg
(1177–1183)

Adelheid/Sophia
(† ?)
∞ Landgrave Otto
of Stefling

Unknown
∞ Count Otto V
of Wolfratshausen

Frederick († ?)

Otto († 1209)
Count-Palatine of Bavaria

Sophia († 1238)
∞ Landgrave
Herman of
Thuringia

Heilica († 1200?)
∞ Count Dietrich
of Wasserburg

Agnes († 1200?)
∞ Count Henry
of Plain

Elizabeth († 1190?)
∞ Margrave
Berthold II
of Vohburg

Richardis († 1231?)
∞ Count Otto I
of Guelders

Unknown
∞ Count Adalbert III
of Dillingen

Ludwig I († 1231)
Duke of Bavaria
∞ Ludmilla of Bohemia

Otto II († 1253)
Duke of Bavaria
∞ Agnes of Brunswick,
daughter of
Count-Palatine
Henry of the Rhine

Henry († 1290)
Duke of Bavaria

Ludwig II († 1294)
Duke of Bavaria

The Wittelsbach Lineage

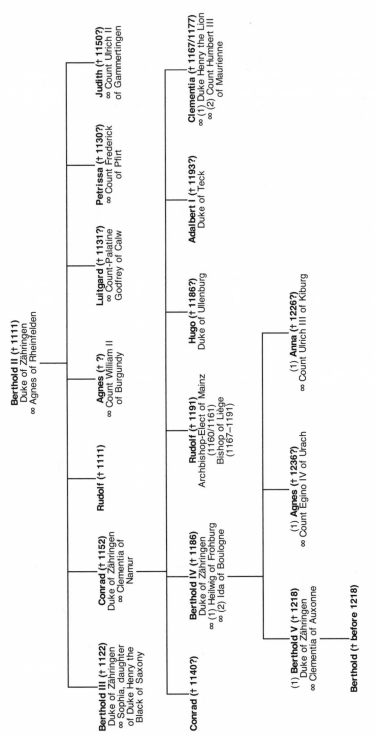

The Zähringen Lineage

❧ Works Cited

Archival Sources

Bamberg, Staatsarchiv
  Bamberger Urkunden nos. 247, 391, 445, 448, 449, 469, 473, 475, 477, 478, 480, 481, 483, 513, 515, 516, 517, 543, 551, 552, 599, 645, 3220
Bamberg, Staatsbibliothek
  Msc. Lit. 161
Besançon, Archives Departementales du Doubs
  Trésor des Chartes B 21, B400
Budapest, Magyar Országos Levéltár
  DF 68752, 206838, 206842, 206846
Dresden, Sächsisches Staatsarchiv, Hauptstaatsarchiv
  10001 Ältere Urkunden nos. 236, 609
Gotha, Thüringisches Staatsarchiv
  QQ I d 18, 20a, 21
  QQ I g 48
Klagenfurt, Kärntner Landesarchiv
  Allgemeine Urkundenreihe A 47, C 1188
Magdeburg, Landeshauptarchiv Sachsen-Anhalt
  Rep. U 1 XVIII no. 4b
  Rep. U 21 IV Domstift Stendal nos. 2, 8, 15, 16, 36
  Rep. U21b Kloster Neuendorf no. 4
Marburg, Hessisches Staatsarchiv
  Urk. A II Deutsch Orden 1231
  Urk. A II Kl. Lippoldsberg 1198
Munich, Bayerische Staatsbibliothek
  Clm 1018
Munich, Bayerisches Hauptstaatsarchiv
  Benediktbeuern Urkunden, nos. 25, 30
Potsdam, Brandenburgisches Landeshauptarchiv
  Rep. 10B Zisterzienserkloster Dobrilugk U9
Stuttgart, Landesarchiv Baden-Württemberg, Hauptstaatsarchiv
  B 457 U 586
Vienna, Österreichisches Staatsarchiv
  AUR 1234.XI.27
Wolfenbüttel, Niedersächsisches Landesarchiv, Staatsarchiv
  StA WO 17 Urk 12
  StA WO 25 Urk 27, 67, 108, 111

Published Primary Sources

Acta imperii inedita saeculi XIII. Edited by Eduard Winkelmann. Vol. 1. Innsbruck, 1880.

Annales Admuntenses. Edited by Wilhelm Wattenbach. In MGH SS 9:569–600. Hanover: Hahn, 1851.

Annales Austriae: Continuatio Claustroneoburgensis I. Edited by Wilhelm Wattenbach. In MGH SS 9:607–613. Hanover: Hahn, 1851.

Annales Marbacenses. Edited by Franz-Josef Schmale. In *Die Chronik Ottos von St. Blasien und die Marbacher Annalen,* 159–253. Darmstadt: Wissenschaftliche Buchgesellschaft, 1998.

Annales monasterii de Wintonia. Edited by Henry Richards Luard. In *Rerum Britannicarum medii aevi scriptores* 36, part 2:3–125. London: Longman, 1865.

Annales Palidenses. Edited by Georg H. Pertz. In MGH SS 16:48–98. Hanover: Hahn, 1859.

Annales Pegavienses. Edited by Georg H. Pertz. In MGH SS 16:232–270. Hanover: Hahn, 1859.

Annales Ratisbonenses. Edited by Wilhelm Wattenbach. In MGH SS 17:577–590. Hanover: Hahn, 1861.

Annales Reicherspergenses. Edited by Wilhelm Wattenbach. In MGH SS 17:439–476. Hanover: Hahn, 1861.

Annales Scheftlarienses maiores. Edited by Philipp Jaffé. In MGH SS 17:335–343. Hanover: Hahn, 1861.

Annales S. Rudberti Salisburgenses. Edited by Wilhelm Wattenbach. In MGH SS 9:758–810. Hanover: Hahn, 1851.

Annales Stadenses. Edited by Johann M. Lappenberg. In MGH SS 16:271–379. Hanover: Hahn, 1859.

Annalista Saxo. Edited by Georg Waitz. In MGH SS 6:542–777. Hanover: Hahn, 1844.

Arnold of Lübeck. *Chronica Slavorum.* Edited by Georg H. Pertz. In MGH SSrG 14. Hanover: Hahn, 1868.

Augustine. *De civitate dei.* Edited by Bernhard Dombart and Alphons Kalb. In *Corpus christianorum, series latina* 48. Turnhout: Brepols, 1955.

Baumann, F. L. von. "Das Benediktbeurer Traditionsbuch." *Archivalische Zeitschrift, Neue Folge* 20 (1914): 1–82.

Böhmer, J. F. *Regesta Imperii.* Part 4. Vol. 3, *Die Regesten des Kaiserreiches unter Heinrich VI. 1165 (1190)–1197.* Revised by Gerhard Baaken. Cologne: Böhlau Verlag, 1972.

———. *Regesta Imperii.* Part 5, *Die Regesten des Kaiserreiches unter Philipp, Otto IV, Friedrich II, Heinrich (VII), Conrad IV, Heinrich Raspe, Wilhelm und Richard (1198–1272).* 3 vols. Revised by Julius Ficker and Eduard Winkelmann. Innsbruck, 1881–1901.

Braunshweigische Reimchronik von Gandersheim. Edited by Ludwig Weiland. In MGH, *Deutsche Chroniken* 2:430–574. Hanover: Hahn, 1877.

Burchard of Ursberg. *Die Chronik des Propstes Burchard von Ursberg.* Edited by Matthias Becher. In *Quellen zur Geschichte der Welfen und die Chronik Burchards von Ursberg,* 100–311. Darmstadt: Wissenschaftliche Buchgesellschaft, 2007.

Cartulaire des comtes de Bourgogne (1166–1321). Edited by J. Gauthier, J. de Sainte-Agathe, and R. de Lurion. Vol. 8 of *Mémoires et documents inédits pour servir a l'histoire de la Franche-Comté*. Besançon, 1908.

Chronica principum Saxoniae. Edited by Oswald Holder-Egger. In MGH SS 25:468–480. Hanover: Hahn, 1880.

Chronica regia Coloniensis. Edited by Georg Waitz. In MGH SSrG 18. Hanover: Hahn, 1880.

Chronicon Montis Sereni. Edited by Ernst Ehrenfeuchter. In MGH SS 23:130–226. Hanover: Hahn, 1874.

Chronicon Ottenburanum. Edited by Ludwig Weiland. In MGH SS 23:609–630. Hanover: Hahn, 1874.

Codex diplomaticus Anhaltinus. Edited by Otto von Heinemann. 6 vols. Dessau, 1867–1883.

Codex diplomaticus Austriaco-Frisingensis. Edited by Joseph von Zahn. Part 2, vol. 31 of *Fontes rerum Austriacarum*. Vienna: Hof- und Staatsdruckerei, 1870.

Codex diplomaticus Brandenburgensis. Part 1. Edited by Adolph Friedrich Riedel. 25 vols. Berlin: G. Reimer, 1838–1863.

Codex diplomaticus et epistolarius regni Bohemiae. Vol. 2. Edited by Gustavus Friedrich. Prague, 1912.

Codex diplomaticus Hungariae ecclesiasticus ac civilis. Vol. 3, part 1. Edited by Georg Fejér. Buda, 1829.

Codex diplomaticus Saxoniae regiae. Part 1. Series A, *Urkunden der Markgrafen von Meissen und Landgrafen von Thüringen, 948–1234*. 3 vols. Edited by Otto Posse and Hubert Ermisch. Leipzig: Giesecke & Devrient, 1882–1898.

Codex diplomaticus Saxoniae regiae. Part 2. 18 vols. Edited by Otto Posse and Hubert Ermisch. Leipzig: Giesecke & Devrient, 1864–1902.

Codex Falkensteinensis: Die Rechtsaufzeichnungen der Grafen von Falkenstein. Edited by Elisabeth Noichl. In QE NF 29. Munich: C. H. Beck, 1978.

Codice diplomatico Istriano. Vol. 2. Edited by Pietro Kandler. Trieste, 1862.

Conrad of Scheyern. *Chronicon*. Edited by Philipp Jaffé. In MGH SS 17:615–628. Hanover: Hahn, 1861.

Constitutiones et acta publica imperatorem et regum. MGH Const., vols. 1–3. Edited by Ludwig Weiland and Jakob Schwalm. Hanover: Hahn, 1893–1906.

Cosmas of Prague. *The Chronicle of the Czechs*. Translated by Lisa Wolverton. Washington, DC: Catholic University of America Press, 2009.

Cronica Reinhardsbrunnensis. Edited by Oswald Holder-Egger. In MGH SS 30, part 1:490–656. Hanover: Hahn, 1896.

Cronica S. Petri Erfordensis moderna. Edited by Oswald Holder-Egger. In MGH SSrG 42:117–369. Hanover: Hahn, 1899.

Das Baumgartenberger Formelbuch. Edited by Hermann Baerwald. Part 2, vol. 25 of *Fontes Rerum Austriacarum*. Vienna: Hof- und Staatsdruckerei, 1866.

De fundatoribus monasterii Diessenses. Edited by Philipp Jaffé. In MGH SS 17:328–331. Hanover: Hahn, 1861.

The Deeds of Pope Innocent III by an Anonymous Author. Translated by James M. Powell. Washington, DC: Catholic University of America Press, 2004.

Der Hedwigs-Codex von 1353: Sammlung Ludwig. 2 vols. Edited by Wolfgang Braunfels. Berlin: Gebr. Mann Verlag, 1972.

Der sog. Libellus de dictis quatuor ancillarum s. Elisabeth confectus. Edited by Albert Huyskens. Kempten: Kösel, 1911.

Die Admonter Briefsammlung. Edited by Günther Hödl and Peter Classen. In MGH, *Die Briefe der deutschen Kaiserzeit* 6. Munich: MGH, 1983.

Die Aktenstücke zum Frieden von S. Germano 1230. Edited by Karl Hampe. In MGH, *Epistolae selectae* 4. Berlin: Weidmann, 1926.

Die Regesten der Bischöfe von Passau. Vol. 1. Edited by Egon Boshof. Munich: C. H. Beck, 1992.

Die Register Innocenz' III. Vol. 9. Edited by Andrea Sommerlechner. Vienna: Verlag der österreichischen Akademie der Wissenschaften, 2004.

Die Reinhardsbrunner Briefsammlung. Edited by Friedel Peeck. In MGH, *Epistolae selectae* 5. Weimar: Hermann Böhlaus Nachfolger, 1952.

Die Tegernseer Briefsammlung des 12. Jahrhunderts. Edited by Helmut Plechl. In MGH, *Die Briefe der deutschen Kaiserzeit* 8. Hanover: Hahn, 2002.

Die Traditionen des Hochstifts Freising. Vol. 2. Edited by Theodor Bitterauf. In QE NF 5. Munich, 1909. Reprint, Aalen: Scientia Verlag, 1967.

Die Traditionen des Klosters Schäftlarn, 760–1305. Edited by Alois Weissthanner. In QE NF 10:1. Munich: C. H. Beck, 1953.

Die Traditionen des Klosters Scheyern. Edited by Michael Stephan. In QE NF 36:1. Munich: C. H. Beck, 1986.

Die Traditionen des Klosters Weihenstephan. Edited by Bodo Uhl. In QE NF 27:1. Munich: C. H. Beck, 1972.

Die Traditionen und das älteste Urbar des Klosters St. Ulrich und Afra in Augsburg. Edited by Robert Müntefering. In QE NF 35. Munich: C. H. Beck, 1986.

Die Traditionen und Urkunden des Stiftes Diessen 1114–1362. Edited by Waldemar Schlögl. In QE NF 22:1. Munich: C. H. Beck, 1967.

Die Traditionen, Urkunden und Urbare des Klosters Asbach. Edited by Johann Geier. In QE NF 23. Munich: C. H. Beck, 1969.

Die Traditionen, Urkunden und Urbare des Klosters Neustift bei Freising. Edited by Hermann-Joseph Busley. In QE NF 19. Munich: C. H. Beck, 1961.

Die Traditionsbücher des Hochstifts Brixen vom zehnten bis in das vierzehnte Jahrhundert. Edited by Oswald Redlich. Vol. 1 of *Acta Tirolensia.* Innsbruck, 1886. Reprint, Aalen: Scientia Verlag, 1973.

Die Urkunden des Klosters Indersdorf. Vol. 1. Edited by Friedrich Hector Grafen Hundt. In *Oberbayerisches Archiv für vaterländische Geschichte* 24 (1863): 1–400.

Die Urkunden des Klosters Raitenhaslach 1034–1350. Edited by Edgar Krausen. In QE NF 17:1. Munich: C. H. Beck, 1959.

Die Urkunden Heinrichs des Löwen, Herzogs von Sachsen und Bayern. Edited by Karl Jordan. In MGH, *Laienfürsten- und Dynastenurkunden der Kaiserzeit* 1. Leipzig: Karl W. Hiersemann, 1941.

Die Urkunden Friedrichs I. Edited by Heinrich Appelt. MGH, *Die Urkunden der deutschen Könige und Kaiser* 10. 5 vols. Hanover: Hahn, 1975–1990.

Die Urkunden Friedrichs II. Edited by Walter Koch. MGH, *Die Urkunden der deutschen Könige und Kaiser* 14. 3 vols. Hanover: Hahn, 2002–2010.

Die Urkunden Konrads III. und seines Sohnes Heinrich. Edited by Friedrich Hausmann. MGH, *Die Urkunden der deutschen Könige und Kaiser* 9. Vienna: Hermann Böhlaus Nachf., 1969.

Die Urkunden Lothars III. und der Kaiserin Richenza. Edited by Emil von Ottenthal and Hans Hirsch. MGH, *Die Urkunden der deutschen Könige und Kaiser* 8. Berlin: Weidmann, 1927.

Die Urkunden und Urbare des Klosters Schäftlarn. Edited by Alois Weissthanner. In QE NF 10:2. Munich: C. H. Beck, 1957.

Eike von Repgow. *Sachsenspiegel: Lehnrecht.* Edited by Karl August Eckhardt. In MGH, *Fontes iuris Germanici antiqui, nova series* 1, pt. 2. Hanover: Hahn, 1956.

Engelhard of Langheim. *Vita Mechtildis.* Edited by Gottfried Henschen. In *Acta sanctorum*, May 7, 436–449. Paris: Victor Palmé, 1866.

Epistolae saeculi XIII e regestis pontificum Romanorum selectae. Vol. 1. Edited by Karl Rodenburg. MGH. Berlin: Weidmann, 1883.

Fundatio et notae monasterii Ensdorfensis. Edited by Oswald Holder-Egger. In MGH SS 15, part 2:1079–1084. Hanover: Hahn, 1888.

Genealogia Ottonis II. ducis Bavariae et Agnetis Ducissae. Edited by Philipp Jaffé. In MGH SS 17:376–378. Hanover: Hahn, 1861.

Genealogia Wettinensis. Edited by Ernst Ehrenfeuchter. In MGH SS 23:226–230. Hanover: Hahn, 1874.

Gesta archiepiscoporum Magdeburgensium. Edited by Wilhelm Schum. In MGH SS 14:361–486. Hanover: Hahn, 1883.

Gesta archiepiscoporum Salisburgensium. Edited by Wilhelm Wattenbach. In MGH SS 11:1–103. Hanover: Hahn, 1854.

Gesta principum Polonorum: The Deeds of the Princes of the Poles. Translated by Paul W. Knoll and Frank Schaer. Budapest: Central European University Press, 2003.

Gilbert of Mons. *Chronicle of Hainaut.* Translated by Laura Napran. Woodbridge: Boydell, 2005.

——. *La chronique de Gislebert de Mons.* Edited by Léon Vanderkindere. Brussels: Kiessling, 1904.

Henry of Mügeln. *Chronicon.* Edited by Eugenius Travnik. In *Scriptores rerum Hungaricarum: Tempore ducum regumque stirpis Arpadianae gestarum* 2:87–223. Budapest, 1938.

Herbord of Michelsberg. *De vita et operibus beati Ottonis Babenbergensis episcopi.* Edited by Lorenz Weinrich. In *Vitae sanctorum episcoporum Adalberti Pragensis et Ottonis Babenbergensis historiam Germanicam et Slavicam illustrantes*, 272–493. Darmstadt: Wissenschaftliche Buchgesellschaft, 2005.

Herman of Niederalteich. *Annales.* Edited by Philipp Jaffé. In MGH SS 17:381–407. Hanover: Hahn, 1861.

Hildegard of Bingen. *Epistolarium.* Edited by L. Van Acker. In *Corpus christianorum, continuatio mediaevalis* 91. Turnhout: Brepols, 1991–2001.

Historia de expeditione Friderici Imperatoris (Der sogennante Ansbert). Edited by Anton Chroust. In MGH SSrG, NS 5:1–115. Berlin: Weidmann, 1928.

Historia diplomatica Friderici Secundi. Edited by Jean-Louis-Alphonse Huillard-Bréholles. 7 vols. Paris: Henri Plon, 1852–1861.

Historia ducum Veneticorum. Edited by Henry Simonsfeld. In MGH SS 14:72–88. Hanover: Hahn, 1883.

Historia Welforum cum continuatione Steingademensi. Edited by Matthias Becher. In *Quellen zur Geschichte der Welfen und die Chronik Burchards von Ursberg*, 34–91. Darmstadt: Wissenschaftliche Buchgesellschaft, 2007.

I patti con il patriarcato di Aquileia 880–1255. Edited by Reinhard Härtel. Vol. 12 of *Pacta Veneta*. Rome: Viella, 2005.

John of Viktring. *Liber certarum historiarum*. Edited by Fedor Schneider. In MGH SSrG 36, part 1. Hanover: Hahn, 1909.

Lambert of Ardres. *The History of the Counts of Guines and Lords of Ardres*. Translated by Leah Shopkow. Philadelphia: University of Pennsylvania Press, 2001.

Lampert of Hersfeld. *Annales*. Edited by Oswald Holder-Egger. In MGH SSrG 38:1–304. Hanover: Hahn, 1894.

The Latin Chronicle of the Kings of Castile. Translated by Joseph F. O'Callaghan. Tempe: Arizona Center for Medieval and Renaissance Studies, 2002.

Layettes du Trésor des Chartes. Vol. 2. Edited by Alexandre Teulet. Paris: Henri Plon, 1866.

The Life and Afterlife of St. Elizabeth of Hungary: Testimony from Her Canonization Hearings. Translated by Kenneth Baxter Wolf. Oxford: Oxford University Press, 2011.

Mainzer Urkundenbuch. Edited by Peter Acht. Vol. 2, parts 1–2. Darmstadt: Selbstverlag der hessischen historischen Kommission Darmstadt, 1968 and 1971.

Monumenta Boica, 60 vols. Munich, 1763–1916.

Monumenta historica ducatus Carinthiae. Edited by August von Jaksch and Hermann Wiessner. 11 vols. Klagenfurt, 1896–1972.

Oliver of Paderborn. *Historia Damiatina*. In *Die Schriften des Kölner Domscholasters, späteren Bischofs von Paderborn und Kardinalbischofs von S. Sabina Oliverus*, edited by Hermann Hoogeweg, 159–282. Tübingen, 1894.

Origines Guelficae. Vol. 3. Edited by G. W. Leibniz, C. L. Scheidt, J. G. Eccard, J. G. Gruber, and J. H. Jung. Hanover, 1752.

Otto of Freising. *Chronica; sive, Historia de duabus civitatibus*. Edited by Adolf Hofmeister. In MGH SSrG 45. Hanover: Hahn, 1912.

Otto of Freising, and Rahewin. *Gesta Friderici I. Imperatoris*. Edited by Georg Waitz and Bernhard von Simson. In MGH SSrG 46. Hanover: Hahn, 1912.

Otto of St. Blasien. *Chronica*. Edited by Franz-Josef Schmale. In *Die Chronik Ottos von St. Blasien und Die Marbacher Annalen*, 15–157. Darmstadt: Wissenschaftliche Buchgesellschaft, 1998.

Patrologia latina. Vol. 215. Edited by J. P. Migne. Paris: Garnier, 1855.

Posse, Otto. *Die Siegel der Wettiner bis 1324 und der Landgrafen von Thüringen bis 1247*. 2 vols. Leipzig: Giesecke & Devrient, 1888.

Regesta archiepiscopatus Magdeburgensis. Vol. 1. Edited by George Adalbert von Mülverstedt. Magdeburg: E. Baensch, 1876.

Regesta diplomatica necnon epistolaria historiae Thuringiae. Edited by Otto Dobenecker. 4 vols. Jena: Gustav Fischer, 1896–1939.

Regesten der Markgrafen von Brandenburg aus Askanischem Hause. Vol. 2. Edited by Hermann Krabbo. Leipzig: Duncker & Humblot, 1911.

Regestum Innocentii III papae super negotio Romani imperii. Edited by Friedrich Kempf. Vol. 12 of *Miscellanea historiae pontificiae*. Rome: Pontificia Università Gregoriana, 1947.

Roger of Howden. *Chronica*. Edited by William Stubbs. In *Rerum Britannicarum medii aevi scriptores* 51. London: Longman, 1868–1871.

Salzburger Urkundenbuch. Vol. 2. Edited by Willibald Hauthaler and Franz Martin. Salzburg: Gesellschaft für Salzburger Landeskunde, 1916.

Schlesisches Urkundenbuch. Vol. 1. Edited by Heinrich Appelt. Cologne: Hermann Böhlaus Nachf., 1963.

Schoolmeesters, Émile. *Les regesta de Raoul de Zaehringen, Prince-Évêque de Liége 1167–1191.* Liége: L. Grandmont-Donders, 1881.

Schumi, Franz. "Nicrologia." *Archiv für Heimatkunde* 1 (1883): 190–191.

Thuringia sacra; sive, Historia monasteriorum quae olim in Thuringia floruerunt. Edited by Heinrich Friedrich Otto and Johann Martin Schamel. Frankfurt: Ex officina Weidmanniana, 1737.

Trente-sept documents Bourguignons, de 1201 à 1248. In *Mémoires et documents inédits pour servir a l'histoire de la Franche-Comté,* 3:485–535. Besançon, 1844.

Ulrich von Liechtenstein. *Frauendienst.* Edited by Franz Viktor Spechtler. Göppingen: Kümmerle Verlag, 1987.

——. *Frauendienst: Aus dem Mittelhochdeutschen ins Neuhochdeutsche übertragen.* Translated by Franz Viktor Spechtler. Klagenfurt: Wieser Verlag, 2000.

Urkundenbuch der Deutschordens-Commende Langeln und der Klöster Himmelpforten und Waterler in der Grafschaft Wernigerode. Edited by Eduard Jacobs. Vol. 15 of *Geschichtsquellen der Provinz Sachsen.* Halle: Otto Hendel, 1882.

Urkundenbuch des Herzogthums Steiermark. Edited by Joseph von Zahn and Gerhard Pferschy. 4 vols. Graz: Verlag des Historischen Vereins für Steiermark, 1875–1975.

Urkundenbuch des Hochstifts Naumburg, Teil 2 (1207–1304). Edited by Hans K. Schulze. Cologne: Böhlau Verlag, 2000.

Urkundenbuch des Landes ob der Enns. Edited by Verwaltungs-Ausschuss des Museum Francisco-Carolinum zu Linz. 11 vols. Vienna, 1852–1956.

Urkundenbuch zur Geschichte der Babenberger in Österreich. Edited by Heinrich Fichtenau, Erich Zöllner, Oskar Frh. von Mitis, Heide Dienst, and Christian Lackner. 4 vols. Vienna: Adolf Holzhausens Nachfolger and Oldenbourg, 1950–1997.

Urkunden- und Regestenbuch des Herzogtums Krain. Edited by Franz Schumi. 2 vols. Ljubljana, 1882–1887.

Ussermann, Aemilian. *Episcopatus Bambergensis sub s. sede apostolica chronologice ac diplomatice illustratus.* St. Blasien, 1802.

Vita S. Hedwige. Edited by Joseph Van Hecke. In *Acta sanctorum,* October 8, 224–265. Paris: Victor Palmé, 1866.

Weissthanner, Alois. "Regesten des Freisinger Bischofs Otto I. (1138–1158)." *Analecta sacri ordinis Cisterciensis* 14 (1958): 151–222.

Wiesflecker, Hermann. *Die Regesten der Grafen von Görz und Tirol, Pfalzgrafen in Kärnten.* Vol. 1. Innsbruck: Universitätsverlag Wagner, 1949.

Secondary Sources

Abulafia, David. *Frederick II: A Medieval Emperor.* London: Allen Lane, 1988.

Aigner, Toni. "Das Herzogtum Meranien: Geschichte, Bedeutung, Lokalisierung." In *Die Andechs-Meranier: Beiträge zur Geschichte Europas im Hochmittelalter,* edited by Andreja Eržen and Toni Aigner, 39–54. Kamnik: Kulturverein Kamnik, 2001.

Aird, William M. *Robert Curthose: Duke of Normandy, c. 1050–1134.* Woodbridge: Boydell, 2008.

Airlie, Stuart. "The Aristocracy." In *The New Cambridge Medieval History*, vol. 2, edited by Rosamond McKitterick, 431–450. Cambridge: Cambridge University Press, 1995.

Alexandre-Bidon, Danièle, and Didier Lett. *Children in the Middle Ages: Fifth-Fifteenth Centuries.* Translated by Jody Gladding. Notre Dame, IN: University of Notre Dame Press, 1999.

Allemand-Gay, Marie Thérèse. *Le pouvoir des comtes de Bourgogne au XIIIe siècle.* Cahiers d'Études Comtoises. Vol. 36. Paris: Les Belles Lettres, 1988.

Althoff, Gerd. "Die Historiographie bewältigt: Der Sturz Heinrichs des Löwen in der Darstellung Arnolds von Lübeck." In *Die Welfen und ihr Braunschweiger Hof im hohen Mittelalter*, edited by Bernd Schneidmüller, 163–182. Wiesbaden: Harrassowitz Verlag, 1995.

——. *Die Macht der Rituale: Symbolik und Herrschaft im Mittelalter.* Darmstadt: Primus Verlag, 2003.

——. *Die Ottonen: Königsherrschaft ohne Staat.* 2nd ed. Stuttgart: Verlag W. Kohlhammer, 2005.

——. "Die Zähringer: Herzöge ohne Herzogtum." In *Die Zähringer: Schweizer Vorträge und neue Forschungen*, edited by Karl Schmid, 81–94. Vol. 3 of Veröffentlichungen zur Zähringer-Ausstellung. Sigmaringen: Jan Thorbecke Verlag, 1990.

——. *Family, Friends and Followers: Political and Social Bonds in Early Medieval Europe.* Translated by Christopher Carroll. Cambridge: Cambridge University Press, 2004.

——. "Friedrich von Rothenburg: Überlegungen zu einem übergangenen Königssohn." In *Festschrift für Eduard Hlawitschka zum 65. Geburtstag*, edited by Karl Rudolf Schnith and Roland Pauler, 307–316. Kallmünz Opf.: Verlag Michael Lassleben, 1993.

——. "Konfliktverhalten und Rechtsbewußtsein: Die Welfen in der Mitte des 12. Jahrhunderts." *Frühmittelalterliche Studien* 26 (1992): 331–352.

——. *Spielregeln der Politik im Mittelalter: Kommunikation in Frieden und Fehde.* Darmstadt: Primus Verlag, 1997.

Appelt, Heinrich. *Privilegium minus: Das staufische Kaisertum und die Babenberger in Österreich.* 2nd ed. Vienna: Hermann Böhlaus Nachf., 1976.

——. "Vorarbeiten zum Schlesischen Urkundenbuch: Die Echtheit der Trebnitzer Gründungsurkunden (1203/18)." *Zeitschrift des Vereins für Geschichte Schlesiens* 71 (1937): 1–56.

Arnold, Benjamin. "Emperor Frederick II (1194–1250) and the Political Particularism of the German Princes." *Journal of Medieval History* 26 (2000): 239–252.

——. *Medieval Germany, 500–1300: A Political Interpretation.* Toronto: University of Toronto Press, 1997.

——. *Power and Property in Medieval Germany: Economic and Social Change c. 900–1300.* Oxford: Oxford University Press, 2004.

——. *Princes and Territories in Medieval Germany.* Cambridge: Cambridge University Press, 1991.

———. "The Western Empire, 1125–1197." In *The New Cambridge Medieval History*, vol. 4, part 2, edited by David Luscombe and Jonathan Riley-Smith, 384–421. Cambridge: Cambridge University Press, 2004.

Assing, Helmut. "Der Aufstieg der Ludowinger in Thüringen." In *Brandenburg, Anhalt und Thüringen im Mittelalter: Askanier und Ludowinger beim Aufbau fürstlicher Territorialherrschaften*, edited by Tilo Köhn, Lutz Partenheimer, and Uwe Zietmann, 241–294. Cologne: Böhlau Verlag, 1997.

Assmann, Erwin. "Friedrich Barbarossas Kinder." *Deutsches Archiv für Erforschung des Mittelalters* 33 (1977): 435–472.

Auge, Oliver. *Handlungsspielräume fürstlicher Politik im Mittelalter: Der südliche Ostseeraum von der Mitte des 12. Jahrhunderts bis in die frühe Reformationszeit*. Ostfildern: Jan Thorbecke Verlag, 2009.

Aurell, Martin. "Rompre la concorde familiale: Typologie, imaginaire, questionnements." In *La parenté déchirée: Les luttes intrafamiliales au Moyen Âge*, edited by Martin Aurell, 9–59. Turnhout: Brepols, 2010.

Baaken, Katrin. "Welf IV., der 'geborene Italiener' als Erbe des Welfenhauses." In Bauer and Becher, *Welf IV.*, 199–225.

Bachrach, Bernard S. "Henry II and the Angevin Tradition of Family Hostility." *Albion* 16 (1984): 111–130.

Bachrach, David S. "Exercise of Royal Power in Early Medieval Europe: The Case of Otto the Great." *Early Medieval Europe* 17 (2009): 389–419.

Bagge, Sverre. *From Viking Stronghold to Christian Kingdom: State Formation in Norway, c. 900–1350*. Copenhagen: Museum Tusculanum Press, 2010.

Bak, János M. "Queens as Scapegoats in Medieval Hungary." In *Queens and Queenship in Medieval Europe*, edited by Anne J. Duggan, 223–233. Woodbridge: Boydell, 1997.

Baldwin, John W. *The Government of Philip Augustus: Foundations of French Royal Power in the Middle Ages*. Berkeley: University of California Press, 1986.

———. "La vie sexuelle de Philippe Auguste." In *Mariage et sexualité au Moyen Âge: Accord ou crise?* edited by Michel Rouche, 217–229. Paris: Presses de l'Université de Paris-Sorbonne, 2000.

Barraclough, Geoffrey. *The Origins of Modern Germany*. New York: Capricorn Books, 1963.

Barrow, Julia. "Cathedrals, Provosts and Prebends: A Comparison of Twelfth-Century German and English Practice." *Journal of Ecclesiastical History* 37 (1986): 536–564.

———. "Education and the Recruitment of Cathedral Canons in England and Germany 1100–1225." *Viator* 20 (1989): 117–138.

Barthélemy, Dominique. *La société dans le comté de Vendôme de l'an mil au XIVe siècle*. Paris: Fayard, 1993.

Bartlett, Robert. *England under the Norman and Angevin Kings 1075–1225*. Oxford: Clarendon Press, 2000.

———. *The Making of Europe: Conquest, Colonization, and Cultural Change, 950–1350*. Princeton, NJ: Princeton University Press, 1993.

Bastress-Dukehart, Erica. "Sibling Conflict within Early Modern German Noble Families." *Journal of Family History* 33 (2008): 61–80.

Bauer, Dieter R., and Matthias Becher, eds. *Welf IV.: Schlüsselfigur einer Wendezeit; Regionale und europäische Perspektiven.* Munich: C. H. Beck, 2004.

Beach, Alison I. "Voices from a Distant Land: Fragments of a Twelfth-Century Nuns' Letter Collection." *Speculum* 77 (2002): 34–54.

Bedos-Rezak, Brigitte. "The Social Implications of the Art of Chivalry: The Sigillographic Evidence (France 1050–1250)." In *Form and Order in Medieval France: Studies in Social and Quantitative Sigillography*, 6:1–31. Aldershot: Variorum, 1993.

——. *When Ego Was Imago: Signs of Identity in the Middle Ages.* Leiden: Brill, 2011.

——. "Women, Seals and Power in Medieval France, 1150–1350." In *Form and Order in Medieval France: Studies in Social and Quantitative Sigillography*, 9:61–82. Aldershot: Variorum, 1993.

Beitscher, Jane K. "'As the Twig Is Bent . . .': Children and Their Parents in an Aristocratic Society." *Journal of Medieval History* 2 (1976): 181–192.

Bellow, Adam. *In Praise of Nepotism: A Natural History.* New York: Doubleday, 2003.

Berwinkel, Holger. *Verwüsten und Belagern: Friedrich Barbarossas Krieg gegen Mailand (1158–1162).* Tübingen: Niemeyer, 2007.

Beumann, Helmut. "Der altmärkische Bistumsplan Heinrichs von Gardelegen." *Historisches Jahrbuch* 58 (1938): 108–119.

Biereye, Wilhelm. "Die Urkunden des Grafen Albrecht von Orlamünde und Holstein." *Zeitschrift der Gesellschaft für Schleswig-Holsteinische Geschichte* 57 (1928): 1–152.

Bisson, Thomas N. *The Crisis of the Twelfth Century: Power, Lordship, and the Origins of European Government.* Princeton, NJ: Princeton University Press, 2009.

Bitschnau, Martin. "Gries-Morit." In *Tiroler Burgenbuch*, vol. 8, edited by Oswald Trapp and Magdalena Hörmann-Weingartner, 207–256. Bozen: Verlagsanstalt Athesia, 1989.

Blamires, Alcuin. "'Sisterhood,' the Poor Relation of 'Brotherhood' in Medieval Writings? *Ipomadon* as Case-Study." In Cassagnes-Brouquet and Yvernault, *Frères et soeurs,* 211–220.

Borgolte, Michael. *Sozialgeschichte des Mittelalters: Eine Forschungsbilanz nach der deutschen Einheit.* Munich: R. Oldenbourg Verlag, 1996.

——. "Stiftergedenken in Kloster Dießen: Ein Beitrag zur Kritik bayerischer Traditionsbücher." *Frühmittelalterliche Studien* 24 (1990): 235–289.

Boshof, Egon. "Die Entstehung des Herzogtums Braunschweig-Lüneburg." In *Heinrich der Löwe*, edited by Wolf-Dieter Mohrmann, 249–274. Göttingen: Vandenhoeck & Ruprecht, 1980.

——. "Reichsfürstenstand und Reichsreform in der Politik Friedrichs II." *Blätter für deutsche Landesgeschichte* 122 (1986): 41–66.

Bosl, Karl. "Europäischer Adel im 12./13. Jahrhundert: Die internationalen Verflechtungen des bayerischen Hochadelsgeschlechtes der Andechs-Meranier." *Zeitschrift für bayerische Landesgeschichte* 30 (1967): 20–52.

Bouchard, Constance B. *Sword, Miter, and Cloister: Nobility and the Church in Burgundy, 980–1198.* Ithaca, NY: Cornell University Press, 1987.

——. *"Those of My Blood": Constructing Noble Families in Medieval Francia.* Philadelphia: University of Pennsylvania Press, 2001.

Bourdieu, Pierre. *The Logic of Practice.* Translated by Richard Nice. Stanford, CA: Stanford University Press, 1990.

Bray, Alan. *The Friend.* Chicago: University of Chicago Press, 2003.

Brinken, Bernd. *Die Politik Konrads von Staufen in der Tradition der Rheinischen Pfalz-grafschaft.* Bonn: Ludwig Röhrscheid Verlag, 1974.

Brown, Warren C. *Unjust Seizure: Conflict, Interest, and Authority in an Early Medieval Society.* Ithaca, NY: Cornell University Press, 2001.

Brown, Warren C., and Piotr Górecki. "What Conflict Means: The Making of Medieval Conflict Studies in the United States, 1970–2000." In *Conflict in Medieval Europe: Changing Perspectives on Society and Culture,* edited by Warren C. Brown and Piotr Górecki, 1–35. Aldershot: Ashgate, 2003.

Brundage, James A. *Law, Sex, and Christian Society in Medieval Europe.* Chicago: University of Chicago Press, 1987.

Brunner, Karl. *Österreichische Geschichte 907–1156: Herzogtümer und Marken vom Un-garnsturm bis ins 12. Jahrhundert.* 2nd ed. Vienna: Ueberreuter, 2003.

Brunner, Otto. *Land and Lordship: Structures of Governance in Medieval Austria.* Translated by Howard Kaminsky and James van Horn Melton. Philadelphia: University of Pennsylvania Press, 1992.

Brüsch, Tania. *Die Brunonen, ihre Grafschaften und die sächsische Geschichte: Herrschaftsbil-dung und Adelsbewußtsein im 11. Jahrhundert.* Husum: Matthiesen Verlag, 2000.

Buc, Philippe. *The Dangers of Ritual: Between Early Medieval Texts and Social Scientific Theory.* Princeton, NJ: Princeton University Press, 2001.

——. *"Principes gentium dominantur eorum:* Princely Power between Legitimacy and Illegitimacy in Twelfth-Century Exegesis." In *Cultures of Power: Lordship, Status, and Process in Twelfth-Century Europe,* edited by Thomas N. Bisson, 310–331. Philadelphia: University of Pennsylvania Press, 1995.

Bulst, Neithard. "Illegitime Kinder—viele oder wenige? Quantitative Aspekte der Illegitimität im spätmittelalterlichen Europa." In *Illegitimität im Spätmittelalter,* edited by Ludwig Schmugge, 21–39. Munich: R. Oldenbourg Verlag, 1994.

Bumke, Joachim. *Courtly Culture: Literature and Society in the High Middle Ages.* Translated by Thomas Dunlap. Berkeley: University of California Press, 1991.

Bur, Michel. "Les relations entre la Champagne et la Franche-Comté (Xe–XIIIe siècles)." *Mémoires de la Société pour l'Histoire du Droit et des Institutions des anciens pays bourguignons, comtois et romands* 38 (1981): 131–141.

Burkhardt, Stefan. *Mit Stab und Schwert: Bilder, Träger und Funktionen erzbischöflicher Herrschaft zur Zeit Kaiser Friedrichs Barbarossas; Die Erzbistümer Köln und Mainz im Vergleich.* Ostfildern: Jan Thorbecke Verlag, 2008.

Buttazzoni, Carlo. "Del patriarca Volchero e della agitazioni politiche a' suoi tempi, a. 1204–1218: Con 13 documenti annotati." *Archeografo Triestino,* n.s. 2 (1871): 157–220.

Büttner, Heinrich. "Allerheiligen in Schaffhausen und die Erschließung des Schwarz-waldes im 12. Jahrhundert." In *Schwaben und Schweiz im frühen und hohen Mittelalter: Gesammelte Aufsätze von Heinrich Büttner,* edited by Hans Patze, 191–207. Sigmaringen: Jan Thorbecke Verlag, 1972.

——. "Zähringerpolitik im Trierer Raum während der zweiten Hälfte des 12. Jahr-hunderts." *Rheinische Vierteljahrsblätter* 33 (1969): 47–59.

Caemmerer, Erich. "Konrad, Landgraf von Thüringen, Hochmeister des deutschen Ordens († 1240)." *Zeitschrift des Vereins für Thüringische Geschichte und Altertumskunde* 28 (1910/1911): 43–80.

Carsten, Janet. "Cultures of Relatedness." Introduction to *Cultures of Relatedness: New Approaches to the Study of Kinship*, edited by Janet Carsten, 1–36. Cambridge: Cambridge University Press, 2000.

Cassagnes-Brouquet, Sophie, and Martine Yvernault, eds. *Frères et soeurs: Les liens adelphiques dans l'Occident antique et médiéval*. Turnhout: Brepols, 2007.

Chifflet, Pierre-François. *Lettre touchant Beatrix comtesse de Chalon, laquelle declare quel fut son Mary, quels ses enfans, ses ancestres, & ses armes*. Dijon, 1656.

Chittolini, Giorgio. "The 'Private,' the 'Public,' the State." *Journal of Modern History* 67, supp. (1995): S34–S61.

Cicirelli, Victor G. "Sibling Relationships in Cross-Cultural Perspective." *Journal of Marriage and the Family* 56 (1994): 7–20.

Conklin, George. "Ingeborg of Denmark, Queen of France, 1193–1223." In *Queens and Queenship in Medieval Europe*, edited by Anne J. Duggan, 39–52. Woodbridge: Boydell, 1997.

Constable, Giles. *Letters and Letter-Collections*. Typologie des sources du Moyen Âge occidental 17. Turnhout: Brepols, 1976.

———. *The Reformation of the Twelfth Century*. Cambridge: Cambridge University Press, 1996.

Costambeys, Marios, Matthew Innes, and Simon MacLean. *The Carolingian World*. Cambridge: Cambridge University Press, 2011.

Crouch, David. *The Beaumont Twins: The Roots and Branches of Power in the Twelfth Century*. Cambridge: Cambridge University Press, 1986.

———. *The Birth of Nobility: Constructing Aristocracy in England and France 900–1300*. Harlow: Pearson/Longman, 2005.

Crouch, David, and Claire de Trafford. "The Forgotten Family in Twelfth-Century England." *Haskins Society Journal* 13 (1999): 41–63.

Csendes, Peter. "Die Doppelwahl von 1198 und ihre europäischen Dimensionen." In *Staufer und Welfen: Zwei rivalisierende Dynastien im Hochmittelalter*, edited by Werner Hechberger and Florian Schuller, 156–171. Regensburg: Verlag Friedrich Pustet, 2009.

———. *Heinrich VI*. Darmstadt: Wissenschaftliche Buchgesellschaft, 1993.

———. *Philipp von Schwaben: Ein Staufer im Kampf um die Macht*. Darmstadt: Wissenschaftliche Buchgesellschaft, 2003.

Davidoff, Leonore. "Kinship as a Categorical Concept: A Case Study of Nineteenth Century English Siblings." *Journal of Social History* 39 (2005): 411–428.

———. *Thicker than Water: Siblings and Their Relations 1780–1920*. Oxford: Oxford University Press, 2012.

d'Avray, David. *Medieval Marriage: Symbolism and Society*. Oxford: Oxford University Press, 2005.

Dendorfer, Jürgen. *Adelige Gruppenbildung und Königsherrschaft: Die Grafen von Sulzbach und ihr Beziehungsgeflecht im 12. Jahrhundert*. Munich: Kommission für bayerische Landesgeschichte, 2004.

——. "Roncaglia: Der Beginn eines lehnrechtlichen Umbaus des Reiches?" In *Stau-fisches Kaisertum im 12. Jahrhundert: Konzepte—Netzwerke—Politische Praxis*, edited by Stefan Burkhardt, Thomas Metz, Bernd Schneidmüller, and Stefan Weinfurter, 111–132. Regensburg: Schnell & Steiner, 2010.

de Rubeis, Bernardo Maria, ed. *Monumenta ecclesiae Aquilejensis*. Strassburg, 1740.

Deuer, Wilhelm. "Abt Heinrich aus dem Geschlecht der Grafen von Andechs-Giech (1166–nach 1177) und seine Bedeutung für das Kloster Millstatt." In *Studien zur Geschichte von Millstatt und Kärnten: Vorträge der Millstätter Symposien 1981–1995*, edited by Franz Nikolasch, 319–340. Klagenfurt: Verlag des Ge-schichtsvereins für Kärnten, 1997.

Dienst, Heide. "Werden und Entwicklung der babenbergischen Mark." In *Österreich im Hochmittelalter (907 bis 1246)*, edited by Kommission für die Geschichte Österreichs, 63–102. Vienna: Verlag der österreichischen Akademie der Wis-senschaften, 1991.

——. "Zum Grazer Vertrag von 1225 zwischen Herzog Leopold VI. von Österreich und Steier und König Andreas II. von Ungarn." *Mitteilungen des Instituts für österreichische Geschichtsforschung* 90 (1982): 1–48.

Dilcher, Gerhard. "An den Ursprüngen der Normbildung—Verwandtschaft und Bruderschaft als Modelle gewillkürter Rechtsformen." In *Verwandtschaft, Freundschaft, Bruderschaft: Soziale Lebens- und Kommunikationsformen im Mittel-alter*, edited by Gerhard Krieger, 37–55. Berlin: Akademie Verlag, 2009.

Dopsch, Heinz. "Die Wittelsbacher und das Erzstift Salzburg." In Glaser, *Wittelsbach und Bayern,* vol. 1, part 1, *Die Zeit der frühen Herzöge: Von Otto I. zu Ludwig dem Bayern*, 268–284.

——. *Österreichische Geschichte 1122–1278: Die Länder und das Reich*. 2nd ed. Vienna: Verlag Carl Ueberreuter, 1999.

——"Salzburg im Hochmittelalter: 1. Die Äussere Entwicklung." In *Geschichte Salz-burgs*, vol. 1, edited by Heinz Dopsch, 229–336. Salzburg: Universitätsverlag Anton Pustet, 1981.

——. "Zwischen Dichtung und Politik: Herkunft und Umfeld Ulrichs von Liech-tenstein." In *Ich, Ulrich von Liechtenstein: Literatur und Politik im Mittelalter*, edited by Franz Viktor Spechtler and Barbara Maier, 49–104. Klagenfurt: Wieser Verlag, 1999.

Drell, Joanna H. *Kinship and Conquest: Family Strategies in the Principality of Salerno during the Norman Period, 1077–1194*. Ithaca, NY: Cornell University Press, 2002.

Duby, Georges. *The Knight, the Lady and the Priest: The Making of Modern Marriage in Medieval France*. Translated by Barbara Bray. New York: Pantheon Books, 1983.

——. "Lineage, Nobility and Knighthood: The Mâconnais in the Twelfth Century; A Revision." Translated by Cynthia Postan. In *The Chivalrous Society*, 59–80. Berkeley: University of California Press, 1977.

——. *Medieval Marriage: Two Models from Twelfth-Century France*. Translated by Elborg Forster. Baltimore: Johns Hopkins University Press, 1978.

——. "Northwestern France: The 'Youth' in Twelfth-Century Aristocratic Society." Translated by Frederic L. Cheyette. In *Lordship and Community in Medieval*

Europe: Selected Readings, edited by Frederic L. Cheyette, 198–209. New York: Holt, Rinehart, and Winston, 1968.

Duggan, Lawrence G. *Bishop and Chapter: The Governance of the Bishopric of Speyer to 1552*. New Brunswick, NJ: Rutgers University Press, 1978.

Dungern, Otto Freiherr von. "Constitutional Reorganisation and Reform under the Hohenstaufen." Translated by Geoffrey Barraclough. In *Mediaeval Germany 911–1250: Essays by German Historians*, 2:203–233. Oxford: Basil Blackwell, 1938.

———, ed. *Genealogisches Handbuch zur bairisch-österreichischen Geschichte*. Graz: Verlag Leuschner & Lubensky, 1931.

Eberl, Immo. "Die Grafen von Berg, ihr Herrschaftsbereich und dessen adelige Familien." *Ulm und Oberschwaben* 44 (1982): 29–171.

Ehlers, Joachim. "Deutsche Scholaren in Frankreich während des 12. Jahrhunderts." In *Schulen und Studium im sozialen Wandel des hohen und späten Mittelalters*, edited by Johannes Fried, 97–120. Sigmaringen: Jan Thorbecke Verlag, 1986.

———. *Heinrich der Löwe: Eine Biographie*. Munich: Siedler, 2008.

———. "Heinrich der Löwe und der sächsische Episkopat." In *Ausgewählte Aufsätze: Joachim Ehlers*, edited by Martin Kintzinger and Bernd Schneidmüller, 451–488. Berlin: Duncker & Humblot, 1996.

Elliott, Dyan. *Spiritual Marriage: Sexual Abstinence in Medieval Wedlock*. Princeton, NJ: Princeton University Press, 1993.

Elpers, Bettina. *"Während sie die Markgrafschaft leitete, erzog sie ihren kleinen Sohn*: Mütterliche Regentschaften als Phänomen adeliger Herrschaftspraxis." In *Fürstin und Fürst: Familienbeziehungen und Handlungsmöglichkeiten von hochadeligen Frauen im Mittelalter*, edited by Jörg Rogge, 153–166. Ostfildern: Jan Thorbecke Verlag, 2004.

Engel, Pál. *The Realm of St. Stephen: A History of Medieval Hungary, 895–1526*. Translated by Tamás Pálosfalvi. London: I. B. Tauris, 2001.

Engels, Odilo. "Beiträge zur Geschichte der Staufer im 12. Jahrhundert (I)." In *Stauferstudien: Beiträge zur Geschichte der Staufer im 12. Jahrhundert*, edited by Erich Meuthen and Stefan Weinfurter, 32–115. Sigmaringen: Jan Thorbecke Verlag, 1996.

———. *Die Staufer*. 8th ed. Stuttgart: Kohlhammer, 2005.

Ertl, Thomas. "Die Geschichte Innsbrucks von 1180 bis 1239, dargestellt anhand der überlieferten Urkunden." *Tiroler Heimat* 61 (1997): 35–75.

Evergates, Theodore. *The Aristocracy in the County of Champagne, 1100–1300*. Philadelphia: University of Pennsylvania Press, 2007.

———. "The Feudal Imaginary of Georges Duby." *Journal of Medieval and Early Modern Studies* 27 (1997): 641–660.

Ewald, Wilhelm. *Siegelkunde*. Munich: R. Oldenbourg, 1914.

Feldmann, Karin. "Herzog Welf VI. und sein Sohn: Das Ende des süddeutschen Welfenhauses." PhD diss., University of Tübingen, 1971.

Fenske, Lutz. *Adelsopposition und kirchliche Reformbewegung im östlichen Sachsen*. Göttingen: Vandenhoeck and Ruprecht, 1977.

———. "Adel und Rittertum im Spiegel früher heraldischer Formen und deren Entwicklung." In *Das ritterliche Turnier im Mittelalter*, edited by Josef Fleckenstein, 75–160. Göttingen: Vandenhoeck and Ruprecht, 1985.

Fey, Hans-Joachim. *Reise und Herrschaft der Markgrafen von Brandenburg (1134–1319)*. Cologne: Böhlau Verlag, 1981.

Fichtenau, Heinrich. *Living in the Tenth Century: Mentalities and Social Orders*. Translated by Patrick J. Geary. Chicago: University of Chicago Press, 1991.

Ficker, Julius. *Vom Reichsfuerstenstande: Forschungen zur Geschichte der Reichsverfassung zunächst im XII. und XIII. Jahrhunderte*. Vol. 1. Innsbruck: Wagner, 1861.

Flohrschütz, Günther. "Machtgrundlagen und Herrschaftspolitik der ersten Pfalzgrafen aus dem Haus Wittelsbach." In Glaser, *Wittelsbach und Bayern,* vol. 1, part 1, *Die Zeit der frühen Herzöge: Von Otto I. zu Ludwig dem Bayern*, 42–110.

Fox, Robin. *Kinship and Marriage: An Anthropological Perspective*. Cambridge: Cambridge University Press, 1983.

Freed, John B. *The Counts of Falkenstein: Noble Self-Consciousness in Twelfth-Century Germany*. Philadelphia: American Philosophical Society, 1984.

———. "The Creation of the *Codex Falkensteinensis* (1166): Self-Representation and Reality." In *Representations of Power in Medieval Germany 800–1500*, edited by Björn Weiler and Simon MacLean, 189–210. Turnhout: Brepols, 2006.

———. "Medieval German Social History: Generalizations and Particularism." *Central European History* 25 (1992): 1–26.

———. *Noble Bondsmen: Ministerial Marriages in the Archdiocese of Salzburg, 1100–1343*. Ithaca, NY: Cornell University Press, 1995.

Frenken, Ansgar. "Hausmachtpolitik und Bischofsstuhl: Die Andechs-Meranier als oberfränkische Territorialherren und Bischöfe von Bamberg." *Zeitschrift für bayerische Landesgeschichte* 63 (2000): 711–786.

———. "Poppo, Dompropst und *Electus Bambergensis*: Ein unterschätzter Protagonist Andechser Hausmachtpolitik in Franken." *Bericht des historischen Vereins Bamberg* 137 (2001): 169–184.

Freytag, Hans-Joachim. "Der Nordosten des Reiches nach dem Sturz Heinrichs des Löwen." *Deutsches Archiv für Erforschung des Mittelalters* 25 (1969): 471–530.

Fried, Pankraz. "Die Herkunft der Wittelsbacher." In Glaser, *Wittelsbach und Bayern,* vol. 1, part 1, *Die Zeit der frühen Herzöge: Von Otto I. zu Ludwig dem Bayern*, 29–41.

Fügedi, Erik. *The Elefánthy: The Hungarian Nobleman and His Kindred*. Translated by Csaba Farkas. Budapest: CEU Press, 1998.

Fuhrmann, Horst. *Germany in the High Middle Ages c. 1050–1200*. Translated by Timothy Reuter. Cambridge: Cambridge University Press, 1986.

Gall, Franz. "Die 'Herzoge' von Mödling." *Archiv für österreichische Geschichte* 120 (1953): 3–44.

Garnier, Claudia. *Die Kultur der Bitte: Herrschaft und Kommunikation im mittelalterlichen Reich*. Darmstadt: Wissenschaftliche Buchgesellschaft, 2008.

Genzinger, Franz. "Grafschaft und Vogtei der Wittelsbacher vor 1180." In Glaser, *Wittelsbach und Bayern,* vol. 1, part 1, *Die Zeit der frühen Herzöge: Von Otto I. zu Ludwig dem Bayern*, 111–125.

Georgi, Wolfgang. "Wichmann, Christian, Philipp und Konrad: Die 'Friedensmacher' von Venedig?" In *Stauferreich im Wandel: Ordnungsvorstellungen und Politik in der Zeit Friedrichs Barbarossas*, edited by Stefan Weinfurter, 41–84. Stuttgart: Jan Thorbecke Verlag, 2002.

Gillingham, John B. *The Kingdom of Germany in the High Middle Ages (900–1200).* London: The Historical Association, 1971.

Glaser, Hubert, ed. *Wittelsbach und Bayern.* Vol. 1, parts 1–2, *Die Zeit der frühen Herzöge: Von Otto I. zu Ludwig dem Bayern.* Munich: Hirmer Verlag and R. Piper & Co. Verlag, 1980.

Glover, Lorri. *All Our Relations: Blood Ties and Emotional Bonds among the Early South Carolina Gentry.* Baltimore: Johns Hopkins University Press, 2000.

Goetz, Hans-Werner. *Das Geschichtsbild Ottos von Freising: Ein Beitrag zur historischen Vorstellungswelt und zur Geschichte des 12. Jahrhunderts.* Cologne: Böhlau Verlag, 1984.

Goez, Werner. *Der Leihezwang: Eine Untersuchung zur Geschichte des deutschen Lehnrechtes.* Tübingen: J. C. B. Mohr (Paul Siebeck), 1962.

Gold, Penny Schine. *The Lady and the Virgin: Image, Attitude, and Experience in Twelfth-Century France.* Chicago: University of Chicago Press, 1985.

Goldberg, Eric J. *Struggle for Empire: Kingship and Conflict under Louis the German, 817–876.* Ithaca, NY: Cornell University Press, 2006.

Göldel, Caroline. *Servitium Regis und Tafelgüterverzeichnis: Untersuchungen zur Wirtschafts- und Verfassungsgeschichte des deutschen Königtums im 12. Jahrhundert.* Sigmaringen: Jan Thorbecke Verlag, 1997.

Goody, Jack. *The Development of the Family and Marriage in Europe.* Cambridge: Cambridge University Press, 1983.

Görich, Knut. "'. . . damit die Ehre unseres Onkels nicht gemindert werde . . .': Verfahren und Ausgleich im Streit um das Herzogtum Bayern 1152–1156." In *Die Geburt Österreichs: 850 Jahre Privilegium minus,* edited by Peter Schmid and Heinrich Wanderwitz, 23–35. Regensburg: Schnell & Steiner, 2007.

——. *Friedrich Barbarossa: Eine Biographie.* Munich: C. H. Beck, 2011.

——. "Jäger des Löwen oder Getriebener der Fürsten? Friedrich Barbarossa und die Entmachtung Heinrichs des Löwen." In *Staufer und Welfen: Zwei rivalisierende Dynastien im Hochmittelalter,* edited by Werner Hechberger and Florian Schuller, 98–117. Regensburg: Verlag Friedrich Pustet, 2009.

——. "Versuch zur Rettung von Kontingenz; oder, Über Schwierigkeiten beim Schreiben einer Biographie Friedrich Barbarossas." *Frühmittelalterliche Studien* 43 (2009): 179–197.

Gottschalk, Joseph. *St. Hedwig: Herzogin von Schlesien.* Cologne: Böhlau Verlag, 1964.

Griffiths, Fiona J. "Siblings and the Sexes within the Medieval Religious Life." *Church History* 77 (2008): 26–53.

Gropper, Gerald. *Die Doppelwahlen von 1198 und 1257 im Spiegel der Historiographie.* Neuried: Ars et unitas, 2003.

Groß, Reiner. *Die Wettiner.* Stuttgart: Verlag W. Kohlhammer, 2007.

Grundmann, Herbert. *Der Cappenberger Barbarossakopf und die Anfänge des Stiftes Cappenberg.* Cologne: Böhlau Verlag, 1959.

Guerreau-Jalabert, Anita, Régine Le Jan, and Joseph Morsel. "De l'histoire de la famille à l'anthropologie de la parenté." In *Les tendances actuelles de l'histoire du Moyen Âge en France et en Allemagne,* edited by Jean-Claude Schmitt and Otto Gerhard Oexle, 433–446. Paris: Publications de la Sorbonne, 2002.

Hajdu, Robert. "Family and Feudal Ties in Poitou, 1100–1300." *Journal of Interdisciplinary History* 8 (1977): 117–139.

Härtel, Reinhard. "Vom nicht zustandegekommenen, gebrochenen und miß-brauchten Frieden." In *Träger und Instrumentarien des Friedens im hohen und späten Mittelalter*, edited by Johannes Fried, 525–559. Sigmaringen: Jan Thorbecke Verlag, 1996.

———. "Zur Herrschaftspraxis des Patriarchen Berthold von Aquileia." In *Kärntner Landesgeschichte und Archivwissenschaft: Festschrift für Alfred Ogris zum 60. Geburtstag*, edited by Wilhelm Wadl, 91–103. Klagenfurt: Verlag des Geschichtsvereines für Kärnten, 2001.

Hauck, Karl. "Haus- und sippengebundene Literatur mittelalterlicher Adelsgeschlechter, von Adelssatiren des 11. und 12. Jahrhunderts her erläutert." In *Geschichtsdenken und Geschichtsbild im Mittelalter*, edited by Walther Lammers, 165–199. Darmstadt: Wissenschaftliche Buchgesellschaft, 1965.

Hauptmann, Ludmil. "Krain." In *Erläuterungen zum historischen Atlas der österreichischen Alpenländer*, vol. 1, part 4, 309–483. Vienna: Verlag von Adolf Holzhausens Nachfolger, 1929.

Hauser, Sigrid. *Staufische Lehnspolitik am Ende des 12. Jahrhunderts 1180–1197*. Frankfurt: Peter Lang, 1998.

Hausmann, Friedrich. "Kaiser Friedrich II. und Österreich." In *Probleme um Friedrich II.*, edited by Josef Fleckenstein, 225–308. Sigmaringen: Jan Thorbecke Verlag, 1974.

Hautum, Ernst. "Ekbert von Meran, Bischof von Bamberg: 1203–1237." PhD diss., University of Erlangen, 1924.

Haverkamp, Alfred. *Medieval Germany, 1056–1273*. Translated by Helga Braun and Richard Mortimer. 2nd ed. Oxford: Oxford University Press, 1988.

Hechberger, Werner. *Adel im fränkisch-deutschen Mittelalter: Zur Anatomie eines Forschungsproblems*. Ostfildern: Jan Thorbecke Verlag, 2005.

———. "Konrad III.: Königliche Politik und 'staufische Familieninteressen'?" In *Grafen, Herzöge, Könige: Der Aufstieg der frühen Staufer und das Reich (1079–1152)*, edited by Hubertus Seibert and Jürgen Dendorfer, 323–340. Ostfildern: Jan Thorbecke Verlag, 2005.

———. *Staufer und Welfen 1125–1190: Zur Verwendung von Theorien in der Geschichtswissenschaft*. Cologne: Böhlau Verlag, 1996.

Heimann, Heinz-Dieter. *Hausordnung und Staatsbildung: Innerdynastische Konflikte als Wirkungsfaktoren der Herrschaftsverfestigung bei den wittelsbachischen Rheinpfalzgrafen und den Herzögen von Bayern*. Paderborn: Ferdinand Schöningh, 1993.

Heinemann, Lothar von. *Heinrich von Braunschweig, Pfalzgraf bei Rhein*. Gotha: Friedrich Andreas Perthes, 1882.

Heinemeyer, Karl. "Der Prozeß Heinrichs des Löwen." *Blätter für deutsche Landesgeschichte* 117 (1981): 1–60.

Herlihy, David. "Land, Family and Women in Continental Europe, 701–1200." *Traditio* 18 (1962): 89–120.

———. "The Making of the Medieval Family: Symmetry, Structure, Sentiment." In *Women, Family and Society in Medieval Europe: Historical Essays, 1978–1991*, edited by Anthony Molho, 135–153. Providence: Berghahn Books, 1995.

Herrmann, Erwin. "Die Grafen von Andechs und der ducatus Meraniae." *Archiv für Geschichte von Oberfranken* 55 (1975): 5–35.

———. "Zur Stadtentwicklung in Nordbayern." *Archiv für Geschichte von Oberfranken* 53 (1973): 31–78.

Heuermann, Hans. *Die Hausmachtpolitik der Staufer von Herzog Friedrich I. bis König Konrad III. (1079–1152).* Borna-Leipzig: Robert Noske, 1939.

Heyck, Eduard. *Geschichte der Herzoge von Zähringen.* Freiburg im Breisgau: J. C. B. Mohr, 1891.

Hillen, Christian. *Curia Regis: Untersuchungen zur Hofstruktur Heinrichs (VII.) 1220–1235 nach den Zeugen seiner Urkunden.* Frankfurt: Peter Lang, 1999.

Hlawitschka, Eduard. *Untersuchungen zu den Thronwechseln der ersten Hälfte des 11. Jahrhunderts und zur Adelsgeschichte Süddeutschlands.* Sigmaringen: Jan Thorbecke Verlag, 1987.

Holt, J. C. "Feudal Society and the Family in Early Medieval England: III. Patronage and Politics." *Transactions of the Royal Historical Society, Fifth Series* 34 (1984): 1–25.

———. "Politics and Property in Early Medieval England." *Past and Present* 57 (1972): 3–52.

Holzfurtner, Ludwig. *Die Grafschaft der Andechser: Comitatus und Grafschaft in Bayern, 1000–1180.* Historischer Atlas von Bayern, Teil Altbayern, series 2, vol. 4. Munich: Kommission für bayerische Landesgeschichte, 1994.

———. *Die Wittelsbacher: Staat und Dynastie in acht Jahrhunderten.* Stuttgart: Verlag W. Kohlhammer, 2005.

Hormayr, Joseph Freiherr von. *Kritisch-diplomatische Beyträge zur Geschichte Tirols im Mittelalter.* Vol. 2. Vienna, 1804.

Hotchin, Julie. "Women's Reading and Monastic Reform in Twelfth-Century Germany: The Library of the Nuns of Lippoldsberg." In *Manuscripts and Monastic Culture: Reform and Renewal in Twelfth-Century Germany,* edited by Alison I. Beach, 139–189. Turnhout: Brepols, 2007.

Howard, Matthew. "'We are broderen': Fraternal Bonds and Familial Loyalty within the Fifteenth-Century Romance of *Generydes.*" In *Love, Marriage, and Family Ties in the Later Middle Ages,* edited by Isabel Davis, Miriam Müller, and Sarah Rees Jones, 129–142. Turnhout: Brepols, 2003.

Howe, John. "The Nobility's Reform of the Medieval Church." *American Historical Review* 93 (1988): 317–339.

Hucker, Bernd Ulrich. "Der Königsmord von 1208: Privatrache oder Staatsstreich?" In *Die Andechs-Meranier in Franken: Europäisches Fürstentum im Mittelalter,* 111–128. Mainz: Verlag Philipp von Zabern, 1998.

———. "Familienbild der Meranier im Codex der hl. Hedwig." In *Die Andechs-Meranier in Franken: Europäisches Fürstentum im Mittelalter,* 266. Mainz: Verlag Philipp von Zabern, 1998.

———. *Kaiser Otto IV.* Hanover: Hahn, 1990.

Huffman, Joseph P. *The Social Politics of Medieval Diplomacy: Anglo-German Relations (1066–1307).* Ann Arbor: University of Michigan Press, 2000.

Hye, Franz-Heinz. "Die Grafen von Andechs und Tirol." In *Historische Beziehungen zwischen Schwaben und Tirol von der Römerzeit bis zur Gegenwart,* edited by Wolfram Baer and Pankraz Fried, 47–53. Augsburg: Rosenheimer Verlagshaus, 1989.

Jaksch, August von. "Zur Lebensgeschichte Sophia's, der Tochter König Bela's II. von Ungarn." *Mitteilungen des Instituts für österreichische Geschichtsforschung* II. Ergänzungsband (1888): 361–379.

Johns, Susan M. *Noblewomen, Aristocracy and Power in the Twelfth-Century Anglo-Norman Realm.* Manchester: Manchester University Press, 2003.

Johnson, Christopher H., and David Warren Sabean, eds. *Sibling Relations and the Transformations of European Kinship, 1300–1900.* New York: Berghahn, 2011.

Jordan, Karl. "Heinrich der Löwe und seine Familie." *Archiv für Diplomatik* 27 (1981): 111–144.

———. *Henry the Lion: A Biography.* Translated by P. S. Falla. Oxford: Clarendon Press, 1986.

Jussen, Bernhard. "Famille et parenté: Comparaison des recherches françaises et allemandes." In *Les tendances actuelles de l'histoire du Moyen Âge en France et en Allemagne,* edited by Jean-Claude Schmitt and Otto Gerhard Oexle, 447–460. Paris: Sorbonne, 2002.

———. "Perspektiven der Verwandtschaftsforschung fünfundzwanzig Jahre nach Jack Goodys *Entwicklung von Ehe und Familie in Europa.*" In *Die Familie in der Gesellschaft des Mittelalters,* edited by Karl-Heinz Spieß, 275–324. Ostfildern: Jan Thorbecke Verlag, 2009.

Kahsnitz, Rainer. "Konrad I., Landgraf von Thüringen, als Regent in Hessen (1231–1234)." In *Die Zeit der Staufer: Geschichte—Kunst—Kultur,* edited by Reiner Haussherr, 1:51–52. Stuttgart: Württembergisches Landesmuseum, 1977.

———. "Siegel des Pfalzgrafen Friedrich." In Glaser, *Wittelsbach und Bayern,* vol. 1, part 2, *Die Zeit der frühen Herzöge: Von Otto I. zu Ludwig dem Bayern,* 38–39.

Kannowski, Bernd. "The Impact of Lineage and Family Connections on Succession in Medieval Germany's Elective Kingdom." In *Making and Breaking the Rules: Succession in Medieval Europe, c. 1000–c. 1600,* edited by Frédérique Lachaud and Michael Penman, 13–22. Turnhout: Brepols, 2008.

Keller, Hagen. "Die Zähringer und die Entwicklung Freiburgs zur Stadt." In *Die Zähringer: Eine Tradition und ihre Erforschung,* edited by Karl Schmid, 17–29. Vol. 1 of Veröffentlichungen zur Zähringer-Ausstellung. Sigmaringen: Jan Thorbecke Verlag, 1986.

———. *Zwischen regionaler Begrenzung und universalem Horizont: Deutschland im Imperium der Salier und Staufer 1024 bis 1250.* Frankfurt am Main: Propyläen Verlag, 1990.

Kienast, Walther. *Der Herzogstitel in Frankreich und Deutschland (9. bis 12. Jahrhundert).* Munich: R. Oldenbourg Verlag, 1968.

Kirchner-Feyerabend, Cornelia. *Otto von Freising als Diözesan- und Reichsbischof.* Frankfurt am Main: Peter Lang, 1990.

Kist, Johannes. "Die Nachfahren des Grafen Berthold I. von Andechs." *Jahrbuch für fränkische Landesforschung* 27 (1967): 41–240.

Klaniczay, Gábor. *Holy Rulers and Blessed Princesses: Dynastic Cults in Medieval Central Europe.* Translated by Éva Pálmai. Cambridge: Cambridge University Press, 2002.

Klebel, Ernst. "Die Grafen von Görz als Landesherren in Oberkärnten." *Carinthia I* 125 (1935): 59–82, 218–246.

Kleinjung, Christine. "Geistliche Töchter—abgeschoben oder unterstützt? Überlegungen zum Verhältnis hochadeliger Nonnen zu ihren Familien im 13. und 14. Jahrhundert." In *Fürstin und Fürst: Familienbeziehungen und Handlungsmöglichkeiten von hochadeligen Frauen im Mittelalter*, edited by Jörg Rogge, 21–44. Ostfildern: Jan Thorbecke Verlag, 2004.

Kosto, Adam J. *Making Agreements in Medieval Catalonia: Power, Order, and the Written Word, 1000–1200*. Cambridge: Cambridge University Press, 2001.

Krabbo, Hermann. "Die Markgrafen Otto I., Otto II. und Albrecht II. von Brandenburg." *Forschungen zur Brandenburgischen und Preußischen Geschichte* 24 (1911): 323–370.

Kraus, Andreas. "Das Herzogtum der Wittelsbacher: Die Grundlegung des Landes Bayern." In Glaser, *Wittelsbach und Bayern*, vol. 1, part 1, *Die Zeit der frühen Herzöge: Von Otto I. zu Ludwig dem Bayern*, 165–200.

——. "Heinrich der Löwe und Bayern." In *Heinrich der Löwe*, edited by Wolf-Dieter Mohrmann, 151–214. Göttingen: Vandenhoeck & Ruprecht, 1980.

Krenn, Gerald. "Historische Figuren und/oder Helden der Dichtung? Untersuchungen zu den Personen im Roman 'Frauendienst.'" In *Ich, Ulrich von Liechtenstein: Literatur und Politik im Mittelalter*, edited by Franz Viktor Spechtler and Barbara Maier, 105–132. Klagenfurt: Wieser Verlag, 1999.

Krieb, Steffen. *Vermitteln und Versöhnen: Konfliktregelung im deutschen Thronstreit 1198–1208*. Cologne: Böhlau Verlag, 2000.

Krieger, Karl-Friedrich. *Die Lehnshoheit der deutschen Könige im Spätmittelalter (ca. 1200–1437)*. Aalen: Scientia Verlag, 1979.

Lamke, Florian. "Die frühen Markgrafen von Baden, die Hessonen und die Zähringer: Konstellationen südwestdeutscher Adelsfamilien in der Zeit des Investiturstreits." *Zeitschrift für die Geschichte des Oberrheins* 154 (2006): 21–42.

Lammers, Walther. *Geschichte Schleswig-Holsteins: Das Hochmittelalter bis zur Schlacht von Bornhöved*. Vol. 4, part 1. Neumünster: Karl Wachholtz Verlag, 1981.

Lamprecht, Karl. *Deutsche Geschichte*. 3rd ed. Vol. 3. Freiburg im Breisgau: Hermann Heyfelder, 1906.

Landau, Peter. "Das Weihehindernis der Illegitimität in der Geschichte des kanonischen Rechts." In *Illegitimität im Spätmittelalter*, edited by Ludwig Schmugge, 41–53. Munich: R. Oldenbourg Verlag, 1994.

Lansing, Carol. *The Florentine Magnates: Lineage and Faction in a Medieval Commune*. Princeton, NJ: Princeton University Press, 1991.

Laudage, Johannes. *Friedrich Barbarossa (1152–1190): Eine Biografie*. Regensburg: Verlag Friedrich Pustet, 2009.

——. *Otto der Grosse (912–973): Eine Biographie*. Regensburg: Verlag Friedrich Pustet, 2001.

Le Jan, Régine. *Famille et pouvoir dans le monde Franc (VIIe–Xe siècle): Essai d'anthropologie sociale*. Paris: Publications de la Sorbonne, 1995.

Lechner, Karl. *Die Babenberger: Markgrafen und Herzoge von Österreich 976–1246*. 6th ed. Vienna: Böhlau Verlag, 1996.

Lett, Didier. "Brothers and Sisters: New Perspectives on Medieval Family History." In *Hoping for Continuity: Childhood, Education and Death in Antiquity and the Middle Ages*, edited by Katariina Mustakallio, Jussi Hanska, Hanna-Leena

Sainio, and Ville Vuolanto, 13–23. Rome: Institutum Romanum Finlandiae, 2005.

Lewis, Andrew W. "Anticipatory Association of the Heir in Early Capetian France." *American Historical Review* 83 (1978): 906–927.

Leyser, Karl J. "Frederick Barbarossa and the Hohenstaufen Polity." *Viator* 19 (1988): 153–176.

——. "Frederick Barbarossa, Henry II and the Hand of St. James." *English Historical Review* 90 (1975): 481–506.

——. "The German Aristocracy from the Ninth to the Early Twelfth Century: A Historical and Cultural Sketch." *Past and Present* 41 (1968): 25–53.

——. "Ottonian Government." *English Historical Review* 96 (1981): 721–753.

——. *Rule and Conflict in an Early Medieval Society: Ottonian Saxony.* Bloomington: Indiana University Press, 1979.

Lindner, Michael. "Friedrich Barbarossa, Heinrich der Löwe und die ostsächsischen Fürsten auf dem Merseburger Pfingsthoftag des Jahres 1152." *Zeitschrift für Geschichtswissenschaft* 43 (1995): 197–209.

Livingstone, Amy. "Aristocratic Women in the Chartrain." In *Aristocratic Women in Medieval France*, edited by Theodore Evergates, 44–73. Philadelphia: University of Pennsylvania Press, 1999.

——. *Out of Love for My Kin: Aristocratic Family Life in the Lands of the Loire, 1000–1200.* Ithaca, NY: Cornell University Press, 2010.

Lubich, Gerhard. *Auf dem Weg zur "Güldenen Freiheit": Herrschaft und Raum in der Francia orientalis von der Karolinger- zur Stauferzeit.* Husum: Matthiesen Verlag, 1996.

——. "Beobachtungen zur Wahl Konrads III. und ihrem Umfeld." *Historisches Jahrbuch* 117 (1997): 311–339.

——. *Verwandtsein: Lesarten einer politisch-sozialen Beziehung im Frühmittelalter (6.–11. Jahrhundert).* Cologne: Böhlau Verlag, 2008.

Lutz, Wolf Rudolf. *Heinrich der Erlauchte (1218–1288), Markgraf von Meißen und der Ostmark (1221–1288), Landgraf von Thüringen und Pfalzgraf von Sachsen (1247–1263).* Erlangen: Palm & Enke, 1977.

Lynch, Joseph H. *The Medieval Church: A Brief History.* London: Longman, 1992.

Lyon, Jonathan R. "Cooperation, Compromise and Conflict Avoidance: Family Relationships in the House of Andechs, ca. 1100–1204." PhD diss., University of Notre Dame, 2004.

——. "Fathers and Sons: Preparing Noble Youths to Be Lords in Twelfth-Century Germany." *Journal of Medieval History* 34 (2008): 291–310.

——. "The Withdrawal of Aged Noblemen into Monastic Communities: Interpreting the Sources from Twelfth-Century Germany." In *Old Age in the Middle Ages and the Renaissance: Interdisciplinary Approaches to a Neglected Topic*, edited by Albrecht Classen, 143–169. Berlin: Walter de Gruyter, 2007.

Macé, Laurent. "Les frères au sein du lignage: La logique du lien adelphique chez les seigneurs de Montpellier (XIIe siècle)." In Cassagnes-Brouquet and Yvernault, *Frères et soeurs,* 127–136.

Marcus, Paul. *Herzog Bernhard von Anhalt (um 1140 bis 1212) und die frühen Askanier in Sachsen und im Reich.* Frankfurt: Peter Lang, 1993.

Mariotte, Jean-Yves. *Le comté de Bourgogne sous les Hohenstaufen 1156–1208*. Cahiers d'Études Comtoises. Vol. 4. Paris: Les Belles Lettres, 1963.

Martindale, Jane. "Succession and Politics in the Romance-Speaking World, c. 1000–1140." In *England and Her Neighbours, 1066–1453: Essays in Honour of Pierre Chaplais*, edited by M. Jones and M. Vale, 19–41. London: Hambledon Press, 1989.

Mayer, Hans Eberhard. "Gleichnamige Geschwister im Mittelalter." *Archiv für Kulturgeschichte* 89 (2007): 1–17.

Meier, Rudolf. *Die Domkapitel zu Goslar und Halberstadt in ihrer persönlichen Zusammensetzung im Mittelalter*. Göttingen: Vandenhoeck & Ruprecht, 1967.

Milanich, Nara. "Whither Family History? A Road Map from Latin America." *American Historical Review* 112 (2007): 439–458.

Miller, Naomi J., and Naomi Yavneh. "Thicker than Water: Evaluating Sibling Relations in the Early Modern Period." Introduction to *Sibling Relations and Gender in the Early Modern World: Sisters, Brothers and Others*, edited by Naomi J. Miller and Naomi Yavneh, 1–14. Aldershot: Ashgate, 2006.

Mitteis, Heinrich. *Der Staat des hohen Mittelalters: Grundlinien einer vergleichenden Verfassungsgeschichte des Lehnszeitalters*. 2nd ed. Weimar: Hermann Böhlaus Nachfolger, 1944.

Mitterauer, Michael. "Mittelalter." In *Geschichte der Familie*, edited by Andreas Gestrich, Jens-Uwe Krause, and Michael Mitterauer, 160–363. Stuttgart: Alfred Kröner Verlag, 2003.

——. *Sozialgeschichte der Familie: Kulturvergleich und Entwicklungsperspektiven*. Vienna: Braumüller, 2009.

Moeglin, Jean-Marie. "La discorde dans les familles princières de l'Empire: Essai sur sa portée politique." In *La parenté déchirée: Les luttes intrafamiliales au Moyen Âge*, edited by Martin Aurell, 279–291. Turnhout: Brepols, 2010.

Moore, R. I. *The First European Revolution, c. 970–1215*. Oxford: Blackwell, 2000.

Moraw, Peter. "Fürstentum, Königtum und 'Reichsreform' im deutschen Spätmittelalter." *Blätter für deutsche Landesgeschichte* 122 (1986): 117–136.

——. "Über Typologie, Chronologie und Geographie der Stiftskirche im deutschen Mittelalter." In *Untersuchungen zu Kloster und Stift*, edited by Max-Planck-Institut für Geschichte, 9–37. Göttingen: Vandenhoeck & Ruprecht, 1980.

Morsel, Joseph. *L'aristocratie médiévale: La domination sociale en Occident (Ve–XVe siècle)*. Paris: Armand Colin, 2004.

Mortimer, Richard. "Knights and Knighthood in Germany in the Central Middle Ages." In *The Ideals and Practice of Medieval Knighthood*, edited by Christopher Harper-Bill and Ruth Harvey, 86–103. Woodbridge: Boydell, 1986.

Müller, Mario. *Besiegelte Freundschaft: Die brandenburgischen Erbeinungen und Erbverbrüderungen im späten Mittelalter*. Göttingen: V & R Unipress, 2010.

Müssel, Karl. "Bischof Otto II. von Bamberg: Ein Lebensbild zum Gedenken an seinen Todestag vor 800 Jahren." *Archiv für Geschichte von Oberfranken* 76 (1996): 7–42.

Neel, Carol L. "The Historical Work of Burchard of Ursberg, III: The Historian and His Sources." *Analecta Praemonstratensia* 59 (1983): 19–42.

Niederkorn, Jan Paul. "Konrad III. als Gegenkönig in Italien." *Deutsches Archiv für Erforschung des Mittelalters* 49 (1993): 589–600.

Nolte, Cordula. *Familie, Hof und Herrschaft: Das verwandtschaftliche Beziehungs- und Kommunikationsnetz der Reichsfürsten am Beispiel der Markgrafen von Brandenburg-Ansbach (1440–1530).* Ostfildern: Jan Thorbecke Verlag, 2005.

Nye, Robert A. "Kinship, Male Bonds, and Masculinity in Comparative Perspective." *American Historical Review* 105 (2000): 1656–1666.

Oefele, Edmund Freiherr von. *Geschichte der Grafen von Andechs.* Innsbruck: Wagner, 1877.

Oehring, Siglinde. *Erzbischof Konrad I. von Mainz im Spiegel seiner Urkunden und Briefe (1161–1200).* Darmstadt: Hessische Historische Kommission Darmstadt / Historische Kommission für Hessen, 1973.

Oexle, Otto Gerhard. "Soziale Gruppen in der Ständegesellschaft: Lebensformen des Mittelalters und ihre historischen Wirkungen." In *Die Repräsentation der Gruppen: Text—Bilder—Objekte,* edited by Otto Gerhard Oexle and Andrea von Hülsen-Esch, 9–44. Göttingen: Vandenhoeck & Ruprecht, 1998.

Opll, Ferdinand. *Friedrich Barbarossa.* Darmstadt: Wissenschaftliche Buchgesellschaft, 1990.

Oschema, Klaus. "Blood-Brothers: A Ritual of Friendship and the Construction of the Imagined Barbarian in the Middle Ages." *Journal of Medieval History* 32 (2006): 275–301.

Panzer, Stephan. "Die Chronik Arnolds von Lübeck: Darstellungsabsicht und Adressaten." In *Die Chronik Arnolds von Lübeck: Neue Wege zu ihrem Verständnis,* edited by Stephan Freund and Bernd Schütte, 45–71. Frankfurt am Main: Peter Lang, 2008.

Parisse, Michel. "Les ducs et le duché de Lorraine au XIIe siècle 1048–1206." *Blätter für deutsche Landesgeschichte* 111 (1975): 86–102.

Parlow, Ulrich. *Die Zähringer: Kommentierte Quellendokumentation zu einem südwestdeutschen Herzogsgeschlecht des hohen Mittelalters.* Stuttgart: W. Kohlhammer Verlag, 1999.

Partenheimer, Lutz. *Albrecht der Bär: Gründer der Mark Brandenburg und des Fürstentums Anhalt.* Cologne: Böhlau Verlag, 2001.

Paschini, Pio. "Bertoldo di Merania patriarca d'Aquileia (1218–1251)." *Memorie storiche forogiuliesi* 15 (1919): 1–53.

———. "Bertoldo di Merania patriarca d'Aquileia (1218–1251)." *Memorie storiche forogiuliesi* 16 (1920): 1–94.

Patze, Hans. *Die Entstehung der Landesherrschaft in Thüringen.* Vol. 1. Cologne: Böhlau Verlag, 1962.

Pätzold, Stefan. *Die frühen Wettiner: Adelsfamilie und Hausüberlieferung bis 1221.* Cologne: Böhlau Verlag, 1997.

Patzold, Steffen. "Konflikte im Stauferreich nördlich der Alpen: Methodische Überlegungen zur Messbarkeit eines Wandels der Konfliktführung im 12. Jahrhundert." In *Verwandlungen des Stauferreichs: Drei Innovationsregionen im mittelalterlichen Europa,* edited by Bernd Schneidmüller, Stefan Weinfurter, and Alfried Wieczorek, 144–178. Darmstadt: Wissenschaftliche Buchgesellschaft, 2010.

———. "Konsens und Konkurrenz: Überlegungen zu einem aktuellen Forschungskonzept der Mediävistik." *Frühmittelalterliche Studien* 41 (2007): 75–103.

Paulus, Christof. *Das Pfalzgrafenamt in Bayern im Frühen und Hohen Mittelalter.* Munich: Kommission für bayerische Landesgeschichte, 2007.

——. "Zwischen König, Herzog und Bruder: Pfalzgraf Friedrich II. von Wittelsbach." In *München, Bayern und das Reich im 12. und 13. Jahrhundert: Lokale Befunde und überregionale Perspektiven*, edited by Hubertus Seibert and Alois Schmid, 249–282. Munich: C. H. Beck, 2008.

Petke, Wolfgang. *Kanzlei, Kapelle und königliche Kurie unter Lothar III. (1125–1137).* Cologne: Böhlau Verlag, 1985.

Pflefka, Sven. *Das Bistum Bamberg, Franken und das Reich in der Stauferzeit: Der Bamberger Bischof im Elitengefüge des Reiches 1138–1245.* Volkach: Gesellschaft für fränkische Geschichte e. V., 2005.

Pischke, Gudrun. *Die Landesteilungen der Welfen im Mittelalter.* Hildesheim: Verlag August Lax, 1987.

Plassmann, Alheydis. *Die Struktur des Hofes unter Friedrich I. Barbarossa nach den deutschen Zeugen seiner Urkunden.* Hanover: Hahn, 1998.

Pollock, Linda A. "Rethinking Patriarchy and the Family in Seventeenth-Century England." *Journal of Family History* 23 (1998): 3–27.

Powell, James M. *Anatomy of a Crusade, 1213–1221.* Philadelphia: University of Pennsylvania Press, 1986.

Pradelle, Laurence. "Un exemple de liens adelphiques à Rome au dernier siècle de la République: Marcus Tullius et son frère Quintus à la lumière de la *Correspondance* de Cicéron." In Cassagnes-Brouquet and Yvernault, *Frères et soeurs*, 59–71.

Raccagni, Gianluca. *The Lombard League, 1167–1225.* Oxford: British Academy/Oxford University Press, 2010.

Rady, Martyn. "The Filial Quarter and Female Inheritance in Medieval Hungarian Law." In . . . *The Man of Many Devices, Who Wandered Full Many Ways . . .: Festschrift in Honor of János M. Bak,* edited by Balázs Nagy and Marcell Sebök, 422–431. Budapest: CEU Press, 1999.

Ramu, G. N. *Brothers and Sisters in India: A Study of Urban Adult Siblings.* Toronto: University of Toronto Press, 2006.

Reinhard, Wolfgang. "Nepotismus: Der Funktionswandel einer papstgeschichtlichen Konstanten." *Zeitschrift für Kirchengeschichte* 86 (1975): 145–185.

Reitzenstein, C. Chl. Freiherr von. *Regesten der Grafen von Orlamuende aus Babenberger und Ascanischem Stamm.* Bayreuth, 1871.

Reuter, Timothy. *Germany in the Early Middle Ages, c. 800–1056.* London: Longman, 1991.

——. "The 'Imperial Church System' of the Ottonian and Salian Rulers: A Reconsideration." In *Medieval Polities and Modern Mentalities*, edited by Janet L. Nelson, 325–354. Cambridge: Cambridge University Press, 2006.

——. "The Medieval German *Sonderweg*? The Empire and Its Rulers in the High Middle Ages." In *Medieval Polities and Modern Mentalities*, edited by Janet L. Nelson, 388–412. Cambridge: Cambridge University Press, 2006.

——. "The Medieval Nobility in Twentieth-Century Historiography." In *Companion to Historiography*, edited by Michael Bentley, 177–202. London: Routledge, 1997.

——. "Nobles and Others: The Social and Cultural Expression of Power Relations in the Middle Ages." In *Medieval Polities and Modern Mentalities*, edited by Janet L. Nelson, 111–126. Cambridge: Cambridge University Press, 2006.

Reynolds, Susan. *Fiefs and Vassals: The Medieval Evidence Reinterpreted.* Oxford: Oxford University Press, 1994.

———. *Kingdoms and Communities in Western Europe, 900–1300.* Oxford: Clarendon, 1984.

Robinson, I. S. *Henry IV of Germany, 1056–1106.* Cambridge: Cambridge University Press, 1999.

Rödel, Volker. "Die Burg als Gemeinschaft: Burgmannen und Ganerben." In *Zur Sozial- und Kulturgeschichte der mittelalterlichen Burg: Archäologie und Geschichte,* edited by Lukas Clemens and Sigrid Schmitt, 109–139. Trier: Kliomedia, 2009.

Rogge, Jörg. *Die Wettiner: Aufstieg einer Dynastie im Mittelalter.* Ostfildern: Jan Thorbecke Verlag, 2005.

———. *Herrschaftsweitergabe, Konfliktregelung und Familienorganisation im fürstlichen Hochadel: Das Beispiel der Wettiner von der Mitte des 13. bis zum Beginn des 16. Jahrhunderts.* Stuttgart: Anton Hiersemann, 2002.

———. "Nur verkaufte Töchter? Überlegungen zu Aufgaben, Quellen, Methoden und Perspektiven einer Sozial- und Kulturgeschichte hochadeliger Frauen und Fürstinnen im deutschen Reich während des späten Mittelalters und am Beginn der Neuzeit." In *Principes: Dynastien und Höfe im späten Mittelalter,* edited by Cordula Nolte, Karl-Heinz Spieß, and Ralf-Gunnar Werlich, 235–276. Stuttgart: Jan Thorbecke Verlag, 2002.

———. "Wettiner als Bischöfe in Münster, Merseburg und Naumburg im hohen Mittelalter." *Zeitschrift für Geschichtswissenschaft* 46 (1998): 1061–1086.

Roitner, Ingrid. "Die ungarische Königstochter Sophia in Admont." *Zeitschrift des historischen Vereines für Steiermark* 95 (2004): 183–197.

Rösener, Werner. "Adel und Burg im Mittelalter: Fragen zum Verhältnis von Adel und Burg aus kulturhistorischer Sicht." *Zeitschrift für die Geschichte des Oberrheins* 150 (2002): 91–111.

Rosenwein, Barbara H. *To Be the Neighbor of Saint Peter: The Social Meaning of Cluny's Property, 909–1049.* Ithaca, NY: Cornell University Press, 1989.

Ruppel, Sophie. *Verbündete Rivalen: Geschwisterbeziehungen im Hochadel des 17. Jahrhunderts.* Cologne: Böhlau Verlag, 2006.

Schieffer, Rudolf. "Das Lehnswesen in den deutschen Königsurkunden von Lothar III. bis Friedrich I." In *Das Lehnswesen im Hochmittelalter: Forschungskonstrukte—Quellenbefunde—Deutungsrelevanz,* edited by Jürgen Dendorfer and Roman Deutinger, 79–90. Ostfildren: Jan Thorbecke Verlag, 2010.

Schlick, Jutta. *König, Fürsten und Reich (1056–1159): Herrschaftsverständnis im Wandel.* Stuttgart: Jan Thorbecke Verlag, 2001.

Schlütter-Schindler, Gabriele. "Herzog Otto I. von Wittelsbach: Erste Ergebnisse der Bearbeitung der bayerischen Herzogsregesten." In *Bayern vom Stamm zum Staat: Festschrift für Andreas Kraus zum 80. Geburtstag,* edited by Konrad Ackermann, Alois Schmid, and Wilhelm Volkert, 87–100. Munich: Verlag C. H. Beck, 2002.

———. "Wittelsbacherinnen: Die weltlichen unverheirateten und die geistlichen Töchter im 13. und 14. Jahrhundert." *Zeitschrift für bayerische Landesgeschichte* 65 (2002): 371–408.

Schmid, Karl. "Zur Problematik von Familie, Sippe und Geschlecht, Haus und Dynastie beim mittelalterlichen Adel: Vorfragen zum Thema 'Adel und Herrschaft im Mittelalter.'" *Zeitschrift für die Geschichte des Oberrheins* 105 (1957): 1–62.

Schmidinger, Heinrich. *Patriarch und Landesherr: Die weltliche Herrschaft der Patriarchen von Aquileja bis zum Ende der Staufer.* Graz: Verlag Hermann Böhlaus Nachfolger, 1954.

Schmugge, Ludwig. *Kirche, Kinder, Karrieren: Päpstliche Dispense von der unehelichen Geburt im Spätmittelalter.* Zürich: Artemis & Winkler, 1995.

Schneidmüller, Bernd. "Die Andechs-Meranier: Rang und Erinnerung im hohen Mittelalter." In *Die Andechs-Meranier: Europäisches Fürstentum im Hochmittelalter,* 55–68. Mainz: Verlag Philipp von Zabern, 1998.

——. *Die Welfen: Herrschaft und Erinnerung (819–1252).* Stuttgart: Verlag W. Kohlhammer, 2000.

——. "Konsensuale Herrschaft: Ein Essay über Formen und Konzepte politischer Ordnung im Mittelalter." In *Reich, Regionen und Europa in Mittelalter und Neuzeit: Festschrift für Peter Moraw,* edited by Paul-Joachim Heinig, Sigrid Jahns, Hans-Joachim Schmidt, Rainer Christoph Schwinges, and Sabine Wefers, 53–87. Berlin: Duncker & Humblot, 2000.

——. "Welf IV. 1101–2001: Kreationen fürstlicher Zukunft." In Bauer and Becher, *Welf IV.,* 1–29.

Schöntag, Wilfried. "Amts-, Standesbezeichnungen und Titel in Siegellegenden im 12. und 13. Jahrhundert." *Zeitschrift für die Geschichte des Oberrheins* 147 (1999): 145–169.

——. "Das Reitersiegel als Rechtssymbol und Darstellung ritterlichen Selbstverständnisses: Fahnenlanze, Banner und Schwert auf Reitersiegeln des 12. und 13. Jahrhunderts vor allem südwestdeutscher Adelsfamilien." In *Bild und Geschichte: Studien zur politischen Ikonographie,* edited by Konrad Krimm and Herwig John, 79–124. Sigmaringen: Jan Thorbecke Verlag, 1997.

Schulte, Aloys. *Der Adel und die deutsche Kirche im Mittelalter: Studien zur Sozial-, Rechts- und Kirchengeschichte.* 3rd ed. Darmstadt: Hermann Gentner, 1958.

Schultze, Johannes. *Die Mark Brandenburg.* Vol. 1. Berlin: Duncker & Humblot, 1961.

Schütz, Alois. "Das Geschlecht der Andechs-Meranier im europäischen Hochmittelalter." In *Herzöge und Heilige: Das Geschlecht der Andechs-Meranier im europäischen Hochmittelalter,* edited by Josef Kirmeier and Evamaria Brockhoff, 21–185. Munich: Haus der bayerischen Geschichte, 1993.

——. "Die Andechs-Meranier in Franken und ihre Rolle in der europäischen Politik des Mittelalters." In *Die Andechs-Meranier in Franken: Europäisches Fürstentum im Mittelalter,* 3–54. Mainz: Verlag Philipp von Zabern, 1998.

Schwarzmaier, Hansmartin. "Konrad von Rothenburg, Herzog von Schwaben: Ein biographischer Versuch." *Württembergisch Franken* 86 (2002): 13–36.

——. "*Pater imperatoris*: Herzog Friedrich II. von Schwaben, der gescheiterte König." In *Mediaevalia Augiensia: Forschungen zur Geschichte des Mittelalters,* edited by Jürgen Petersohn, 247–284. Stuttgart: Jan Thorbecke Verlag, 2001.

Schwineköper, Berent. "Heinrich der Löwe und das östliche Herzogtum Sachsen." In *Heinrich der Löwe,* edited by Wolf-Dieter Mohrmann, 127–150. Göttingen: Vandenhoeck & Ruprecht, 1980.

Scior, Volker. "Zwischen *terra nostra* und *terra sancta*: Arnold von Lübeck als Geschichtsschreiber." In *Die Chronik Arnolds von Lübeck: Neue Wege zu ihrem Verständnis,* edited by Stephan Freund and Bernd Schütte, 149–174. Frankfurt am Main: Peter Lang, 2008.

Searle, Eleanor. *Predatory Kinship and the Creation of Norman Power, 840–1066*. Berkeley: University of California Press, 1988.

Seibert, Hubertus. "Die entstehende 'territoriale Ordnung' am Beispiel Bayerns (1115–1198)." In *Stauferreich im Wandel: Ordnungsvorstellungen und Politik in der Zeit Friedrich Barbarossas*, edited by Stefan Weinfurter, 253–287. Stuttgart: Jan Thorbecke Verlag, 2002.

——. "Vom königlichen dux zum Herzog von Bayern: Welf IV. und der Südosten des Reiches." In Bauer and Becher, *Welf IV.*, 226–260.

Seidel, Kerstin. *Freunde und Verwandte: Soziale Beziehungen in einer spätmittelalterlichen Stadt*. Frankfurt: Campus Verlag, 2009.

Seitz, Reinhard W. "Zur Person der Gisela, 'Gräfin von Schwabegg,' Stifterin des Frauenklosters Edelstetten." *Archivalische Zeitschrift, Neue Folge* 80 (1997): 360–373.

Seltmann, Ingeborg. *Heinrich VI.: Herrschaftspraxis und Umgebung*. Erlangen: Verlag Palm & Enke, 1983.

Shahar, Shulamith. *Childhood in the Middle Ages*. Translated by Chaya Galai. London: Routledge, 1990.

Southern, R. W. *Western Society and the Church in the Middle Ages*. New York: Penguin, 1970.

Spieß, Karl-Heinz. *Familie und Verwandtschaft im deutschen Hochadel des Spätmittelalters: 13. bis Anfang des 16. Jahrhunderts*. Stuttgart: Franz Steiner Verlag, 1993.

——. "Lordship, Kinship, and Inheritance among the German High Nobility in the Middle Ages and Early Modern Period." In *Kinship in Europe: Approaches to Long-Term Development (1300–1900)*, edited by David Warren Sabean, Simon Teuscher, and Jon Mathieu, 57–75. New York: Berghahn Books, 2007.

Spindler, Max. "Grundlegung und Aufbau 1180–1314." In *Handbuch der bayerischen Geschichte*, vol. 2, edited by Max Spindler, 5–137. 2nd ed. Munich: C. H. Beck, 1966.

Sprandel, Rolf. "Die Diskriminierung der unehelichen Kinder im Mittelalter." In *Zur Sozialgeschichte der Kindheit*, edited by Jochen Martin and August Nitzschke, 487–502. Freiburg: Verlag Karl Alber, 1986.

Štih, Peter. "Krain in der Zeit der Grafen von Andechs." In *Die Andechs-Meranier: Beiträge zur Geschichte Europas im Hochmittelalter*, edited by Andreja Eržen and Toni Aigner, 11–37. Kamnik: Kulturverein Kamnik, 2001.

——. *Studien zur Geschichte der Grafen von Görz: Die Ministerialen und Milites der Grafen von Görz in Istrien und Krain*. Vienna: R. Oldenbourg Verlag, 1996.

Stöckel, Jan-Peter. "Die Weigerung Heinrichs des Löwen zu Chiavenna (1176): Ein Beitrag zum Heerfahrtswesen der frühen Stauferzeit." *Zeitschrift für Geschichtswissenschaft* 42 (1994): 869–882.

——. "Reichsbischöfe und Reichsheerfahrt unter Friedrich I. Barbarossa." In *Kaiser Friedrich Barbarossa: Landesausbau—Aspekte seiner Politik—Wirkung*, edited by Evamaria Engel and Bernhard Töpfer, 63–79. Weimar: Verlag Hermann Böhlaus Nachfolger, 1994.

Strayer, Joseph R. *On the Medieval Origins of the Modern State*. Princeton, NJ: Princeton University Press, 1970.

Struve, Tilman. "Die Rolle des römischen Rechts in der kaiserlichen Theorie vor Roncaglia." In *Gli inizi del diritto pubblico / Die Anfänge des öffentlichen Rechts*, edited by Gerhard Dilcher and Diego Quaglioni, 71–97. Bologna and Berlin: Società editrice il Mulino/Duncker & Humblot, 2007.

Stürner, Wolfgang. *Friedrich II. Teil 1: Die Königsherrschaft in Sizilien und Deutschland 1194–1220.* Darmstadt: Wissenschaftliche Buchgesellschaft, 1992.

——. *Friedrich II. Teil 2: Der Kaiser 1220–1250.* Darmstadt: Wissenschaftliche Buchgesellschaft, 2000.

Suckale-Redlefsen, Gude. "Gebetbuch." In *Die Andechs-Meranier in Franken: Europäisches Fürstentum im Mittelalter*, 373–374. Mainz: Verlag Philipp von Zabern, 1998.

Sweeney, James Ross. "Hungary in the Crusades, 1169–1218." *International History Review* 3 (1981): 467–481.

——. "Innocent III, Canon Law, and Papal Judges Delegate in Hungary." In *Popes, Teachers, and Canon Law in the Middle Ages*, edited by James Ross Sweeney and Stanley Chodorow, 26–52. Ithaca, NY: Cornell University Press, 1989.

Tanner, Heather J. *Families, Friends and Allies: Boulogne and Politics in Northern France and England, c. 879–1160.* Leiden: Brill, 2004.

Taylor, Nathaniel L. "Inheritance of Power in the House of Guifred the Hairy: Contemporary Perspectives on the Formation of a Dynasty." In *The Experience of Power in Medieval Europe, 950–1350*, edited by Robert F. Berkhofer III, Alan Cooper, and Adam J. Kosto, 129–151. Aldershot: Ashgate, 2005.

Tebruck, Stefan. *Die Reinhardsbrunner Geschichtsschreibung im Hochmittelalter: Klösterliche Traditionsbildung zwischen Fürstenhof, Kirche und Reich.* Frankfurt: Peter Lang, 2001.

Tellenbach, Gerd. "From the Carolingian Imperial Nobility to the German Estate of Imperial Princes." Translated by Timothy Reuter. In *The Medieval Nobility: Studies on the Ruling Classes of France and Germany from the Sixth to the Twelfth Century*, edited by Timothy Reuter, 203–242. Amsterdam: North-Holland, 1979.

Thompson, James Westfall. *Feudal Germany.* Chicago: University of Chicago Press, 1928.

Thomson, Rodney. "The Place of Germany in the Twelfth-Century Renaissance." In *Manuscripts and Monastic Culture: Reform and Renewal in Twelfth-Century Germany*, edited by Alison I. Beach, 19–42. Turnhout: Brepols, 2007.

Thorau, Peter. *König Heinrich (VII.), das Reich und die Territorien.* Berlin: Duncker & Humblot, 1998.

Töpfer, Bernhard. "Kaiser Friedrich Barbarossa—Grundlinien seiner Politik." In *Kaiser Friedrich Barbarossa: Landesausbau—Aspekte seiner Politik—Wirkung*, edited by Evamaria Engel and Bernhard Töpfer, 9–30. Weimar: Verlag Hermann Böhlaus Nachfolger, 1994.

Turner, Ralph V. *Men Raised from the Dust: Administrative Service and Upward Mobility in Angevin England.* Philadelphia: University of Pennsylvania Press, 1988.

Tyroller, Franz. *Genealogie des altbayerischen Adels im Hochmittelalter.* Göttingen: Heinz Reise Verlag, 1962.

van Eickels, Klaus. "Der Bruder als Freund und Gefährte: *Fraternitas* als Konzept personaler Bindung im Mittelalter." In *Die Familie in der Gesellschaft des Mittelalters*, edited by Karl-Heinz Spieß, 195–222. Ostfildern: Jan Thorbecke Verlag, 2009.

——. "Die Andechs-Meranier und das Bistum Bamberg." In *Die Andechs-Meranier in Franken: Europäisches Fürstentum im Mittelalter*, 145–156. Mainz: Verlag Philipp von Zabern, 1998.

van Eickels, Klaus, and Holger Kunde. "Die Herrschaft Friedburg in Oberösterreich als Bamberger Aussenbesitz: Ein neuentdecktes Urbar aus dem 14. Jahrhundert." *Bericht des historischen Vereins Bamberg* 133 (1997): 199–260.

Van Engen, John. *Sisters and Brothers of the Common Life: The Devotio Moderna and the World of the Later Middle Ages*. Philadelphia: University of Pennsylvania Press, 2008.

van Houts, Elisabeth. "Gender and Authority of Oral Witnesses in Europe (800–1300)." *Transactions of the Royal Historical Society, Sixth Series* 9 (1999): 201–220.

Venarde, Bruce L. *Women's Monasticism and Medieval Society: Nunneries in France and England, 890–1215*. Ithaca, NY: Cornell University Press, 1997.

Vogtherr, Thomas. "Wiprecht von Groitzsch: Bemerkungen zur Figur des sozialen Aufsteigers im hohen Mittelalter." In *Figuren und Strukturen: Historische Essays für Hartmut Zwahr zum 65. Geburtstag*, edited by Manfred Hettling, Uwe Schirmer, and Susanne Schötz, 157–169. Munich: K. G. Saur, 2002.

Vowinckel, Gerhard. *Verwandtschaft, Freundschaft und die Gesellschaft der Fremden: Grundlagen menschlichen Zusammenlebens*. Darmstadt: Wissenschaftliche Buchgesellschaft, 1995.

Voyer, Cécile. "Image de l'exclusion et de la transgression: Caïn, frère maudit." In *La parenté déchirée: Les luttes intrafamiliales au Moyen Âge*, edited by Martin Aurell, 379–400. Turnhout: Brepols, 2010.

Wagner, Heinrich. "Entwurf einer Genealogie der Grafen von Henneberg." *Jahrbuch des Hennebergisch-Fränkischen Geschichtsvereins* 11 (1996): 33–152.

Watts, John. *The Making of Polities: Europe, 1300–1500*. Cambridge: Cambridge University Press, 2009.

Weiler, Björn. "Image and Reality in Richard of Cornwall's German Career." *English Historical Review* 113 (1998): 1111–1142.

——. *Kingship, Rebellion and Political Culture: England and Germany, c. 1215–c. 1250*. Basingstoke: Palgrave Macmillan, 2007.

——. "Reasserting Power: Frederick II in Germany (1235–1236)." In *Representations of Power in Medieval Germany 800–1500*, edited by Björn Weiler and Simon MacLean, 241–271. Turnhout: Brepols, 2006.

——. "Suitability and Right: Imperial Succession and the Norms of Politics in Early Staufen Germany." In *Making and Breaking the Rules: Succession in Medieval Europe, c. 1000–c. 1600*, edited by Frédérique Lachaud and Michael Penman, 71–86. Turnhout: Brepols, 2008.

Weinfurter, Stefan. "Der Mut des Herzogs Friedrich I. von Schwaben: Wertewandel und Ordnungskonzepte im Investiturstreit." In *Friedrich I. (1079–1105): Der erste staufische Herzog von Schwaben*, edited by Gesellschaft für staufische Geschichte e. V., 66–77. Göppingen, 2007.

——. "Die kirchliche Ordnung in der Kirchenprovinz Salzburg und im Bistum Augsburg 1046–1215." In *Handbuch der bayerischen Kirchengeschichte*, vol. 1, edited by Walter Brandmüller, 271–328. St. Ottilien: EOS Verlag, 1998.

——. "Erzbischof Philipp von Köln und der Sturz Heinrichs des Löwen." In *Köln: Stadt und Bistum in Kirche und Reich des Mittelalters*, edited by Hanna Vollrath and Stefan Weinfurter, 455–481. Cologne: Böhlau Verlag, 1993.

——. *The Salian Century: Main Currents in an Age of Transition*. Translated by Barbara M. Bowlus. Philadelphia: University of Pennsylvania Press, 1999.

——. "Venedig 1177: Wende der Barbarossa-Zeit? Zur Einführung." In *Stauferreich im Wandel: Ordnungsvorstellungen und Politik in der Zeit Friedrich Barbarossas*, edited by Stefan Weinfurter, 9–25. Stuttgart: Jan Thorbecke Verlag, 2002.

Weinhold, Karl. *Die deutschen Frauen in dem Mittelalter*. Vol. 1. 2nd ed. Vienna: Carl Gerold's Sohn, 1882.

Weissensteiner, Johann. "Tegernsee, die Bayern und Österreich: Studien zu Tegernseer Geschichtsquellen und der bayerischen Stammessage." *Archiv für österreichische Geschichte* 133 (1983): 1–309.

Weller, Tobias. "Auf dem Weg zum 'staufischen Haus': Zu Abstammung, Verwandtschaft und Konnubium der frühen Staufer." In *Grafen, Herzöge, Könige: Der Aufstieg der frühen Staufer und das Reich (1079–1152)*, edited by Hubertus Seibert and Jürgen Dendorfer, 41–63. Ostfildern: Jan Thorbecke Verlag, 2005.

——. *Die Heiratspolitik des deutschen Hochadels im 12. Jahrhundert*. Cologne: Böhlau Verlag, 2004.

Werner, Matthias. "Reichsfürst zwischen Mainz und Meißen: Heinrich Raspe als Landgraf von Thüringen und Herr von Hessen (1227–1247)." In *Heinrich Raspe: Landgraf von Thüringen und römischer König (1227–1247); Fürsten, König und Reich in spätstaufischer Zeit*, edited by Matthias Werner, 125–271. Frankfurt: Peter Lang, 2003.

White, Stephen D. *Custom, Kinship, and Gifts to Saints: The Laudatio Parentum in Western France, 1050–1150*. Chapel Hill: University of North Carolina Press, 1988.

Wiethaus, Ulrike. "In Search of Medieval Women's Friendships: Hildegard of Bingen's Letters to Her Female Contemporaries." In *Maps of Flesh and Light: The Religious Experience of Medieval Women Mystics*, edited by Ulrike Wiethaus, 93–111. Syracuse: Syracuse University Press, 1993.

Willoweit, Dietmar. "Fürst und Fürstentum in Quellen der Stauferzeit." *Rheinische Vierteljahrsblätter* 63 (1999): 7–25.

Wolf, Armin. *Die Entstehung des Kurfürstenkollegs 1198–1298: Zur 700-jährigen Wiederkehr der ersten Vereinigung der sieben Kurfürsten*. Idstein: Schulz-Kirchner Verlag, 2000.

——. "Königswähler und königliche Tochterstämme." In *Königliche Tochterstämme, Königswähler und Kurfürsten*, edited by Armin Wolf, 1–77. Frankfurt: Vittorio Klostermann, 2002.

Wolfram, Herwig. *Conrad II, 990–1039: Emperor of Three Kingdoms*. Translated by Denise A. Kaiser. University Park: Pennsylvania State University Press, 2006.

Wolter, Heinz. "Der Mainzer Hoftag von 1184 als politisches Fest." In *Feste und Feiern im Mittelalter*, edited by Detlef Altenburg, Jörg Jarnut, and Hans-Hugo Steinhoff, 193–199. Sigmaringen: Jan Thorbecke Verlag, 1991.

Woltmann, Friedrich. *Pfalzgraf Otto von Burgund*. Halle: Buchdruckerei Hohmann, 1913.

Wolverton, Lisa. *Hastening toward Prague: Power and Society in the Medieval Czech Lands*. Philadelphia: University of Pennsylvania Press, 2001.

Zečević, Nada. "Brotherly Love and Brotherly Service: On the Relationship between Carlo and Leonardo Tocco." In *Love, Marriage, and Family Ties in the Later Middle Ages*, edited by Isabel Davis, Miriam Müller, and Sarah Rees Jones, 143–156. Turnhout: Brepols, 2003.

Zettler, Alfons. "Zähringerburgen: Versuch einer landesgeschichtlichen und burgenkundlichen Beschreibung der wichtigsten Monumente in Deutschland und in der Schweiz." In *Die Zähringer: Schweizer Vorträge und neue Forschungen*, edited by Karl Schmid, 95–176. Vol. 3 of Veröffentlichungen zur Zähringer-Ausstellung. Sigmaringen: Jan Thorbecke Verlag, 1990.

Ziegler, Wolfram. *König Konrad III. (1138–1152): Hof, Urkunden und Politik*. Vienna: Böhlau Verlag, 2008.

Zotz, Thomas. "Der südwestdeutsche Adel und seine Opposition gegen Heinrich IV." In Bauer and Becher, *Welf IV.*, 339–359.

———. "Dux de Zaringen—dux Zaringiae: Zum zeitgenössischen Verständnis eines neuen Herzogtums im 12. Jahrhundert." *Zeitschrift für die Geschichte des Oberrheins* 139 (1991): 1–44.

Zunker, Diana. "Familie, Herrschaft, Reich: Die Herforder Äbtissin Gertrud II. von der Lippe." In *Fürstin und Fürst: Familienbeziehungen und Handlungsmöglichkeiten von hochadeligen Frauen im Mittelalter*, edited by Jörg Rogge, 167–186. Ostfildern: Jan Thorbecke Verlag, 2004.

Zurstraßen, Annette. *Die Passauer Bischöfe des 12. Jahrhunderts: Studien zu ihrer Klosterpolitik und zur Administration des Bistums*. Passau: Richard Rothe, 1989.

INDEX

Adalbert (son of Leopold III), 37–38, 38n19
Adalbert of Ballenstedt, Count, 35, 44, 107
Adalbert of Teck, Duke, 74
Adela (wife of Přemysl Otakar), 146–48
Adelheid (sister of Ludwig II of Thuringia), 58
Adolf III of Holstein, Count, 110
Agnes (daughter of Henry Jasomirgott), 51
Agnes (wife of Frederick I of Swabia and Leopold III of Austria), 30, 80, 81, 93, 95
Agnes (wife of Henry of the Rhine), 138–39
Agnes of Groitzsch (wife of Berthold III of Merania), 151–52, 154
Agnes of Merania (wife of Frederick II of Austria), 177, 186–87
Agnes of Merania (wife of King Philip II Augustus of France), 151–52, 155–58, 156n17, 157n21, 169n75
Agnes of Rheinfelden (wife of Berthold II of Zähringen), 36
Albert I of Saxony, Duke, 202n19, 226, 227
Albert II of Brandenburg, Margrave, 126–27, 146, 203
Albert of Meissen, Margrave, 67, 127–28
Albert of Orlamünde, Count, 123, 145, 226, 227
Albert of Weichselburg, Count, 191–92
Albert the Bear, Margrave: children of, 31, 35, 44, 46, 99, 106–10, 121, 123, 135, 198; death of, 31, 35, 106; and election of Conrad III, 96; as founder of Ascanian lineage, 18, 96, 241; and Frederick I Barbarossa, 99; genealogical chart, 241; inheritance of, 29n54; rise to prominence of, 21–22; rivalry between Henry the Lion and, 106, 107; rivalry between Wiprecht of Groitzsch and, 30; succession plan by, 35, 106, 121
Alexander III, Pope, 66, 73–74, 86, 102, 103, 111, 113
Alfonso VIII, King of Castile, 129

Alice (daughter of Otto I of Merania), 193
Andechs lineage: and assassination of King Philip of Swabia, 148, 163–64, 170, 172, 192; brothers in, and the Southeast of the Empire from 1218–1228, 170–77; childhood of siblings in, from 1175–1195, 152–55; churchmen in, 47, 77–80, 114–15, 159–60, 165, 167, 170–73, 179; decline in size of fraternal groups in, from 1180–1210, 136; decline of, 180, 234; extended kin group of, in thirteenth century, 181–94; extinction of, 122, 198, 230, 234; and fall of Henry the Lion, 114–15, 118; final years of siblings in, after 1228, 177–81; founder of, 18, 96, 240; and Frederick I Barbarossa, 77–79, 114–15, 153–54, 197; and Frederick II, 172, 177–80, 197, 199, 226–27, 231; genealogical chart of, 240; at Hungarian royal court from 1206–1218, 164–70; and *Königsnähe* (proximity to the king), 114, 118, 153–54, 166; map of places of significance to, 153; marriages of three sisters in, from 1195–1204, 155–59; pictorial depiction of family of Berthold III, 151–52, 159, 183; *principes imperii* in, 97, 118, 163, 179; regions associated with, 14, 153–54; religious women in, 150–52; rights and properties of, 78–80; sibling bonds in, during early thirteenth century, 148–95; succession and fraternal relationships from 1203–1208, 159–64; succession plan by Berthold I, 36; women in, 52. *See also members of the lineage*
Andreas II, King of Hungary, 157–58, 158n22, 165–67, 170, 183
Arnold of Lübeck, 109–10, 116, 117, 143–44, 147
Ascanian lineage: churchmen in, 41, 41n36, 44, 46, 107–10, 220n87; creation of new lordships in, from 1180–1220, 125–27; decline of, 126–27, 145, 198, 234; in early fourteenth century, 198; and fall of

Otto of Cappenberg, Count, 43
Otto the Child of Brunswick, Duke, 198,
  223–28, 230
Ottonian period, 19, 23, 44, 59n112

partible inheritance, 4, 8, 32, 34–41, 51, 59,
  122–23, 207, 212–14, 231, 234–35
Peter of Blois, 45
Philip (son of Dedo of Groitzsch), 44–45,
  45n49
Philip, Archbishop of Cologne, 103, 104
Philip II Augustus, King of France,
  141n105, 156–57, 156n17, 158
Philip of Swabia, King: assassination of,
  135, 137, 144, 145, 148, 150, 163–64,
  165, 170, 172, 175, 185, 192, 195, 196;
  charters of, 146, 159; church career of, 47,
  130, 133; conflict between King Otto IV
  and, for imperial crown, 136, 137, 141,
  142, 143, 145–49; dates of rulership
  of, 13; election of, as king, 47, 134–35,
  145; fraternal relationships of, 129–37;
  and Frederick II, 135n72; Henry of the
  Rhine's support of, 137, 141, 143–44;
  and Italian expedition of Henry VI,
  133–34; Otto's support for, 135n74; in
  Staufen lineage, 13; titles and properties
  of, 134
popes. *See specific popes*
Poppo, Cathedral Provost and Bishop-Elect
  of Bamberg, 47, 155, 159, 183
Poppo VII of Henneberg, Count, 189–91,
  189n159, 210
Přemysl Otakar, King of Bohemia, 146–48
primogeniture, 4, 8, 32, 33, 234
princely lineages. *See* lineages; sibling
  bonds; *and specific lineages*
principes imperii (imperial princes): in Andechs lineage, 97, 118, 163, 179; in Ascanian lineage, 97, 110, 118; and Conrad
  of the Rhine, 100–101; description of,
  11–13, 234–36; equestrian seals for, 161;
  and founders of lineages, 26; and fraternal succession, 40; and Frederick I Barbarossa, 104, 105, 130; and Frederick II,
  197, 199, 225–28; and knighting of
  Frederick I Barbarossa's sons, 129; in
  Ludowing lineage, 117, 118; and Otto IV
  of Brunswick, 196; in Staufen lineage,
  134–35; in Welf lineage, 139, 143; in
  Wettin lineage, 97, 118; in Wittelsbach
  lineage, 97, 118; in Zähringen lineage, 97
Privilegium minus, 101

Rahewin, 71, 83, 85
Raitenbuch, provost of, 54–55
religious women, 56–59, 56n97, 59n112,
  150–52, 183–86, 237–38. *See also specific
  women*
Richard I, King of England, 138–42
Robert of Normandy, Duke, 233
Roger II, King of Sicily, 129
Roger of Howden, 141–42
Romulus and Remus, 232
Rudolf, Archbishop-Elect of Mainz and
  Bishop of Liège, 74–77, 80, 102
Rudolf of Habsburg, 206n32, 229
Rudolf of Rheinfelden, 27, 30n59

Sachsenspiegel, 25
Salian period, 9, 11, 19–20, 23, 24, 30, 44,
  80, 91
Sancho II, King of Castile, 233
Schlackenwerther Codex, 150–52, 154,
  155n13, 156, 158–60, 183
Schmid, Karl, 16–18, 17n4, 235
Schmid-Duby thesis, 17n4, 235
seals, 69, 161, 201, 202, 202n19, 204, 208,
  209, 214–17
sibling bonds: and brother-sister conflict, 207–12; and church careers,
  41–49, 53, 56–60, 72–87; and civil war
  (1198–1208), 145–49; conclusions on,
  233–36; of Conrad III, 91–97; and creation of new lordships from 1180–1220,
  124–28; decline in size of fraternal
  groups from 1180–1210, 120–23, 122n5,
  136, 145–46, 149, 235; at end of Staufen
  period, 196–231, 229–31, 234; examples
  of significance of, 88; and fall of Henry
  the Lion, 103–19, 121; fraternal groups
  operating inside family of Henry VI,
  131–36; fraternal pairs in 1235, 226–28;
  and fratricide, 232–33; among Frederick I
  Barbarossa's sons, 128–36; and generational size for composition of medieval
  political communities, 4; and German
  history and politics, 9–12, 234, 235–36;
  among Henry the Lion's sons, 136–45;
  historicizing of, 4–7; and illegitimate
  siblings, 219–23, 221n92; and joint lordship, 1–5, 199–206, 229, 230; of married
  women, 53–56; origins of twelfth-
  century princely lineages in German
  kingdom, 16–32; and partible inheritance, 4, 8, 32, 34–41, 51, 59, 122–23,
  207, 212, 213–14, 231, 234–35; politics